D0966111

CRUEL CREEDS, VIRTUOUS VIOLENCE

CRUEL CREEDS, VIRTUOUS VIOLENCE

Religious Violence across Culture
and History

JACK DAVID ELLER

Prometheus Books

59 John Glenn Drive
Amherst, New York 14228-2119

Published 2010 by Prometheus Books

Cover design by Nicole Sommer-Lecht
Cover image: *Guillaume of Clemont Defends Ptolemais*, by Dominique L. Papety (1815–1849)

Inquiries should be addressed to
Prometheus Books
59 John Glenn Drive
Amherst, New York 14228–2119
VOICE: 716–691–0133
FAX: 716–691–0137
WWW.PROMETHEUSBOOKS.COM

14 13 12 11 10   5 4 3 2 1

Library of Congress Cataloging-in-Publication Data

Eller, Jack David, 1959–
    Cruel creeds, virtuous violence : religious violence across culture and history / by Jack David Eller.
        p. cm.
    Includes bibliographical references and index.
    ISBN 978–1–61614–218–6 (hardcover : alk paper)
    1. Violence. 2. Violence—Religious aspects. 3. Anthropology of religion. I. Title.

GN495.2.E55 2010
306.609—dc22

2010022136

Printed in the United States of America on acid-free paper

CONTENTS

INTRODUCTION

The world is awash in books on religion and violence, but then the world is awash in religious violence. Why do we need another book on the subject?

The answer is that, while many of the previous books have made important contributions to our understanding of this essential phenomenon, none has quite finished the job. There are two main reasons for this. The first is the attitude that the authors tend to take toward religion as a possible source of violence. As McTernan has observed, "They either exaggerate religion's role, denouncing it as the root cause of all conflict, or they deny that 'real' religion could be responsible in any way for indiscriminate violence."[1] That is, some give the impression that religion is guilty of all violence in the world, and others give the impression that religion is innocent of all violence in the world. James Haught is one of the former, who, as an avowed atheist, delights in illustrating the evils that religion has done. As he writes in *Holy Horrors*, "A grim pattern is visible in history: When religion is the ruling force in a society, it produces horror. The stronger the supernatural beliefs, the worse the inhumanity. A culture dominated by intense faith invariably is cruel to people who don't share the faith—and sometimes to many who do."[2]

An example of the latter is Charles Kimball, who attempts to draw a line between "authentic" religion and "corrupted" religion. At the core of "all authentic, healthy, life-sustaining religions, one always finds this clear requirement," he writes: to love and care for each other. When the behavior of believers "is violent and destructive, when it causes suffering among their neighbors, you can be sure the religion has been corrupted and reform is desperately needed. When religion becomes evil, these corruptions are always present."[3] Although, as we will see, Kimball's analysis of "warning signs" of violent religion is useful, it will not do to assert that "real" religion lacks or suppresses violence while "false" religion exhibits or promotes it. That does not even represent the beliefs of the members of the religion, who are usually pretty sure that theirs is the true religion and that everyone else is deluded.

The study of religious violence does not need detractors or cheerleaders for religion. Both suffer from the same lack of perspective. Perhaps Lloyd Steffen comes closest to the right attitude when he suggests that religion is powerful and dangerous, and that it is dangerous for the very reasons that it is powerful.[4] However, even he continues to advance the notion of "good" versus "demonic" religion. But religion is neither a purely good thing nor a purely bad thing, neither a peaceful thing nor a violent thing. Like all human institutions, it is an ambiguous and contradictory thing. It is, in the end, a human thing—as flawed and paradoxical as we humans are.

The second reason why earlier attempts to account for religious violence have fallen short is that they have lacked the scope and breadth for a thorough vision of it. For instance, the kinds of violence that they consider are highly incomplete. Understandably, many efforts since 2001 have focused on terrorism and "holy war"—truly stark manifestations of religious violence, but hardly the only ones. Nor, of course, is all terrorism derived from religion. In fact, not all violence is derived from religion, and virtually every form of religious violence has its nonreligious or secular counterpart (there is, after all, secular war too). So, first, there are many more variations of religious violence to consider than terrorism and war. Even more, I will argue and demonstrate that discussions of religious violence have lacked a meaningful notion of violence at all, and we cannot understand religious violence in particular unless we understand violence in general.

Another aspect of the inadequacy of conventional discussions of religious violence is the range of religions that are commonly treated. Naturally, the familiar "Western" or Abrahamic religions get the most attention, that is, Christianity, Judaism, and Islam. And equally naturally, Islam has recently gotten more than its share of attention. This often turns into a comparison of which religions are more prone to violence than others and to a condemnation of "what is wrong with Islam." There are compelling reasons why these religions should get disproportionate treatment by American and Western scholars. There are also compelling reasons why this treatment is insufficient. There simply *are* other religions in the world, and a comprehensive view of religious violence demands a comprehensive view of religion. We know too much to assume that we can generalize from a few—even a few extremely important and personal— examples. Not all religions make the same claims about violence or about anything else, and not all are situated in the same historical and cultural contexts. In fact, our approach to religions and violence should be not only cross-cultural but also transhistorical; otherwise, we can be left with the sense that religious violence is somehow a new modern phenomenon, which it most assuredly is not. In the end, such a parochial approach to religion fails to grasp what religion is in the first place, again presuming that all religions are moralistic, eschatological monotheisms, which they most assuredly are not. Different religions are capable of, and commanding of, different degrees and kinds of violence, and this is what we must explain.

So the present book takes a different approach. The first thing we must do is not assume that we already understand the nature of violence or the nature of religion. Then, we must not limit ourselves to the familiar religions nor to the familiar violence. We will go beyond Christianity, Judaism, and Islam, and beyond war and terrorism. Finally, we will go beyond the typical cases of religious war and religious terrorism to examine the other, and frankly earlier and more pervasive, forms of religious violence. Along the way, we will neither demonize nor lionize religion.

Accordingly, the present book falls into three parts. In the first part, consisting of chapters 1 and 2, we will consider anew the phenomena of violence and of religion, which are too often taken for granted. We will take a more problematic and constructivist view of violence, even suggesting a model to account for the emergence and expansion of violence. As we will learn, there are very few individuals and virtually no societies that are opposed to violence in every imaginable form and circumstance. There is always "justifiable" or "legitimate" violence, if only self-defense, and this fact gets routinely overlooked. Chapter 2 will provide a similar analysis of religion, showing how diverse religious beliefs have been, how religions offer explanations and legitimations for all sorts of behavior (violence included), and how religion particularly effectively satisfies the model of violence.

The second part of the book, chapters 3 through 8, explores specific manifestations of religious violence in cross-cultural depth. These manifestations include sacrifice, self-destructive behavior, persecution, ethnoreligious conflict, war, and homicide and abuse. Each chapter furnishes a wide variety of examples from Christianity, Judaism, and Islam, as well as from Eastern religions, ancient religions, and "traditional" or tribal religions. The examples presented are not intended to be exhaustive, and could hardly be so if they were intended, but are rather illustrative of the kinds of religious violence that have been documented by historians, anthropologists, and comparative religionists.

The third part of the book contains only one chapter (chapter 9). Here we return to think about the relationship between religion and nonviolence. Not all religious traditions are violent, and some have made great achievements in the promotion of nonviolence. Most studies of religious violence do not discuss nonviolence, and most studies of religious nonviolence do not discuss violence, but the two projects are incomplete without each other.

Ultimately, religion can produce violence, and it can produce nonviolence. And nonreligion can produce violence, and it can produce nonviolence. The correct conclusion is neither "religion equals violence" nor "religion equals nonviolence." Instead, the correct conclusion will be that certain human social, cultural, and psychological arrangements produce violence and others do not; and religion sometimes fulfills the conditions for violence and sometimes the conditions for nonviolence. The solution to the problem of violence, then, is not "better religion," and certainly not "more religion," but also not exactly "less religion." It is rather the particular identities, institutions, interests, and ideologies (beliefs or doctrines) that make violence more or less likely and more or less extreme. We will not be offering a utopian outlook for the future—that we can eradicate all violence from human life—since there are biological, psychological, and social reasons why this is improbable to impossible. We will, however, hopefully emerge with a better understanding of who we are and why violence appears in us in its religious as well as nonreligious guises. What we do with this revelation is up to us.

CHAPTER 1

UNDERSTANDING VIOLENCE

There are few things in life that people claim to understand better and to deplore more than violence. They are wrong on both counts. Violence is dramatically more complex than we recognize or perhaps want to recognize: we want to believe that bad people do violence to good people for no particular reason other than the perpetrators' badness. But this cannot be true, as we will soon see. First of all, any of us can, and many of us will, commit some kind of violence during our lives, and we may do so with the noblest of intentions and the clearest of consciences. We may go to war for our country or fight to defend our family or property. This raises another point, that we do not in actuality condemn all forms of violence. Some we censure, some we commit ambivalently, and some we openly celebrate.

It is a neglected but essential fact that we cannot appreciate the relationship between religion and violence unless we grasp the nature and meaning of the two partners in this relationship. Yet our understanding of both religion and violence are inadequate. Further, we usually consider too few offspring of their troubled marriage: when we think of "religious violence," we tend to think only of holy war and (especially since September 11, 2001) religious terrorism. However, those are not the only types of religious violence or violence in general, nor are those types exclusively religious: there is also secular war and secular terrorism. So we have two projects at the outset of our study: to explore the nature of violence and to explore the nature of religion. These projects will take us to places we may not have been before and may not really want to go.

WHAT IS VIOLENCE?

Discussions and debates commence with definitions, or at least they should. What do we mean by *violence*? Again, that may seem perfectly obvious to us. It is not. Notice, for instance, that the language of violence consists of many related and overlapping but nonsynonymous terms, such as *aggression, hostility, competition*, and *conflict*. Scholars and laypeople often use these terms interchangeably, and interchangeably with *violence*, but they are not all synonyms. To start, competition need not necessarily be violent or aggressive; we speak regularly of "healthy competition," and we expect competitors like athletes to refrain from real hostility and to shake hands after the contest. Even conflict is not always violent or at least not always equally violent; there are degrees, from mild or perhaps peaceful conflict—such as a conflict of interests or of opinions—to deadly conflict.

Violence need not even be directly interpersonal, that is, a clear case of one person hitting another person. What has been called *structural violence* refers to less direct, more pervasive, and sometimes even unintentional or at least "invisible" harm (up to and including real and serious physical harm) caused by the very arrangements and institutions of society. Paul Farmer takes the concept of structural violence to be

> "sinful" social structures characterized by poverty and steep grades of social inequality, including racism and gender inequality. Structural violence is violence exerted systematically—that is, indirectly—by everyone who belongs to a certain social order: hence the discomfort these ideas provoke in a moral economy still geared to pinning praise or blame on individual actors. In short, the concept of structural violence is intended to inform the study of the social machinery of oppression.[1]

David Riches, who has studied violence extensively, makes a further distinction between violence and aggression. Examining how both specialists and the general public use the terms, he concludes that *aggression* "connotes antagonistic behavior which, even when consciously performed, is nonvolitional (and probably irrational), the immediate impulse for which lies in uncontrollable forces within the human body that are barely at all subject to reason or sense." Put another way, he sees popular and theoretical notions of aggression as referring to "an inner *tendency* (by implication, both unrelenting and ubiquitous)"—a kind of drive or instinct—separate from "the act of harm itself."[2] Violence, on the other hand, he finds to be less a name for a kind of act than a judgment, a label that people put on certain instances of acts:

> "Violence" has strong pejorative connotations. Through it, the unacceptability and illegitimacy of harming behavior is conveyed. "Violence," in this usage, clearly connotes a double distance from the harm-giving moment: not only is it invoked as *commentary* on the act, the perspective on this act is unequivocally twisted—from performer to observer. For their part, perpetrators—distancing themselves from the act—are reluctant to concede that what they have done is violence: *their* representation of what happened will be that it was self-defense, unavoidable force, freedom-fighting, social control, and so on.[3]

In response, we might insist that violence is behavior that harms someone. As an "objective" account, that is probably necessarily true. But there are many variables and nuances that make the application of such a simple definition more difficult:

- How great does the harm have to be? Are a slap and a murder both violence?
- How intentional does the harm have to be? Are accidental and purposeful injury both violence?
- How physical does the harm have to be? Are emotional abuse, verbal abuse, and physical abuse all violence?
- How undeserved does the harm have to be? Are self-defensive and offensive acts both violence? In fact, is some violence justified and justifiable—or even "justice" itself?
- How unwanted does the harm have to be? Are masochistic or self-inflicted and other-directed injuries both violence?
- How human does the victim or the perpetrator have to be? Is a tiger killing a human, or is a human killing a tiger, violence? Is bacteria killing a human, or is a human killing bacteria, violence?

This is why Riches concludes, "The question, 'what qualifies as "violence"?' in fact has no absolute answer."[4] Fortunately, there is probably no need to settle on a single definition or criterion of violence. The main point is to raise the issues: it is an imposing task—and perhaps an impossible task—to determine which behaviors are "really" violence. The determination is in the end a human evaluation: by *violence* we tend to mean "harm that we do not approve of."

There is no escaping the fact that the world is a violent place. I do not mean merely the human or social world, although it is eminently violent. But the natural world itself shows its violence; it is, as the saying goes, red in tooth and claw. At the same time, it also shows its cooperation and peace. There are cases in nonhuman animals of individuals helping each other, caring for each other, even risking injury and death for each other. There are cases of two different species interacting symbiotically for the benefit of both, when one could easily kill and eat the other. But there is no denying that organic life depends on organic death—that life eats life—and that nonliving forces (tornados, earthquakes, and tsunamis) can bring destruction. We sometimes speak of a "violent storm," but we mean that metaphorically, since I assume that nobody thinks the storm has violent passions or intentions.

Violence is ubiquitous. It is also relative. If there is such a thing as "justifiable homicide" or "just war," then violence is relative: some violence is good (according to certain people, from a certain perspective). The victim of a justifiable homicide is every bit as dead as the victim of an unjustifiable one, and a just war can be even more lethal and brutal than an unjustified one. There is no one-to-one correspondence between the scale and the acceptability of violence: a small incident can be unjustified and a large incident can be justified.

So the real issue appears to be not the damage that is inflicted by the behavior but the *legitimacy* of the behavior that caused the damage. Granted, the harm may be out of all proportion to the cause for it, but then that is precisely what earns it the verdict of illegitimacy. But all except the most total pacifists allow for the possibility and the reality of legitimate and justified violence; "make my day" laws (which allow a person to use deadly force against intruders in his or her home) are one example, and they prove our point particularly well since such laws did not exist until recently. That is, the same behavior that was illegitimate and illegal a short time ago (killing an intruder) is now in some places legitimate and legal. Of course, we can only use "appropriate force" and only in particular ways (no shooting in the back), but that simply further demonstrates that some kinds of force, even deadly force, are not just tolerable but actually rule governed, and others are not—and we decide which.

In other words, violence is only a *problem* when it crosses a certain line, when it goes beyond the bounds of "acceptable violence." And since we humans determine, based on our values and beliefs, what is acceptable violence, these bounds differ for different societies and historical periods and for different groups and individuals within a society or period. The Semai, a peaceful tribal people in

Malaysia, believed that all violence was completely unacceptable and that even bothering somebody with excessive demands was an unbearable disturbance of the peace (see chapter 9).[5] The Yanomamo, on the other hand, have been described as "fierce," placing a high value on aggression, teaching it to their children, and practicing it on each other—men hitting women, pounding each other in various kinds of "duels," and raiding each other's villages.[6] The ancient Spartans tossed weak or deformed male babies off of cliffs and raised the rest to be skilled and disciplined warriors, and the medieval Japanese developed a warrior ethos, known as *bushido*, that glorified death as the vocation of the warrior or samurai—and not so much the death of the enemy as the death of the self. The *Hagakure*, an eighteenth-century treatise on the warrior code, urged the samurai to become "as one already dead," to meditate daily "on inevitable death" and on all the ways in which that death might come: "And every day without fail one should consider himself as dead."[7] Beyond that, he was taught to take his own life willingly at the order of or merely for the honor of his master. Thus even suicide was normal and noble. Presumably, the Japanese samurai would not have called war or suicide "violence"—or at least if he had, he would not have meant it in a derogatory way.

The conclusion must be that violence is not only varied but variably valued. Simply being "violent" is not automatically a problem and cause for concern and condemnation—or not by the perpetrating party, at any rate. Conceivably, a Yanomamo villager did not enjoy being raided, but he would have understood and accepted the place of raiding in his culture. Conceivably, a Japanese warrior did not enjoy being killed, but he would have understood and accepted his appointed role in life, as long as he could die in battle and in honor. So even the "victim's" point of view, which we tend to privilege in thinking about violence, is not always consistent and negative about the value of violence.

Finally, notice that we have not invoked religion so far to explain these types of violence. Arguably religious—particularly Confucian and Buddhist—concepts entered into the *bushido* code, such as the transitory nature of life and beauty and the importance of duty to one's superior. Presumably the Yanomamo had some spiritual or supernatural reason for their violence. But religion is not a necessary or sufficient component in violence. People can be violent or nonviolent with religion and without it. Most important of all, *every single form of religious violence—from war to terrorism to persecution to martyrdom and self-injury to crime and abuse—has its nonreligious correlate.* There are nonreligious wars, nonreligious terrorists, nonreligious martyrs, nonreligious violent crimes, and so on. In other words, religion is hardly single-handedly responsible for violence in the human condition.

WHAT MAKES VIOLENCE POSSIBLE— AND LIKELY?

Another assertion that many people make is that violence is perpetrated by violent people, even "bad" or "evil" people: simply put, good people do good, and bad people do bad. Violence, in this view, is possible and likely when bad and violent individuals are allowed to express their badness and violence. Psychologist Roy Baumeister dubs this the "myth of pure evil," which begins from the premise that violence *is* evil and goes on to claim that

- evil involves the intentional infliction of harm;
- evil is motivated primarily by internal or "personality" factors, especially the pleasure of doing harm;
- the victim is always innocent and good;
- the evil one is the Other, the enemy, the outsider, even the "monster";
- evil represents the very antithesis of order, peace, and stability; and
- evil-doers "lose control" over their violent emotions, especially rage and anger.[8]

This position is a myth precisely because it does not stand up to the facts. As much as we would like to think that only bad, crazy, and mean people commit violence, and that violence is fundamentally a matter of individual traits ("personality")—and therefore that *we* would be incapable of it while *they* are incapable of restraining it—all the evidence indicates that *we* and *they* are not so different after all. Psychologists and social scientists have arrived at similar conclusions: violence is mostly *learned and situational*. Unless the Semai and the Yanomamo/ Spartans/Japanese are innately different, the source of their differences lies elsewhere than in "human nature." Philip Zimbardo, one of the leading psychological researchers on violence, conducted a famous experiment or simulation in which he assigned some participants to be "prison guards" and others to be "prisoners" and set them to play their parts in a mock prison. In the so-called Stanford Prison Experiment, participants so quickly and completely fell into their roles that the level of violence and abuse necessitated shutting down the simulation early—and this despite the fact that the subjects were randomly assigned their roles and given no specific instructions on how to behave.[9] His interpretation was that people's behavior is shaped at least as much by the situations they occupy as by their "personality"—that we all know the expectations of specific circumstances and roles and act accordingly when we are in those circumstances and roles. I do not act like a prison guard most of the time, but if I were put in the position of a prison guard, I would. Thus, if we find ourselves in violent conditions, we act violently, even if it is not in our "nature."

Another even more renowned experiment illustrated the same point to a startling degree. Stanley Milgram, perplexed by the violence committed during World War II, wondered if "normal people" could be led to perpetrate extreme violence. In his "authority experiments," ordinary citizens were placed in a role of administering painful electrical shocks to other subjects as part of a "learning experiment." Of course, there was no learning experiment, and there were no other subjects. The only subjects of the experiment were the "teachers" who could not see but could hear their (nonexistent) victims. With each wrong response the teachers were told to deliver a shock and turn up the voltage. To everyone's surprise—and to the overt emotional distress of some of the shockers—a full two-thirds of them gave what they believed to be fatal jolts to their victims.[10] But why would good people do such a bad thing?

Milgram's assessment was that the shockers were surrendering themselves to authority, specifically the authority of the experimenter, the official-looking person in the white lab coat who stood over the perpetrators and gave them such instructions as "Please continue" or "The experiment requires that you continue." Without the presence and pressure of the authority figure, people would have stopped and did stop sooner (for instance, the shockers were less obedient if the authority was not there in person but rather communicating over the telephone). However, with the authority figure giving the orders and taking the responsibility, people seemed to override their own critical and empathetic responses.

Based on such experiments as well as naturalistic observations, Zimbardo arrived at a set of conditions that contribute to the incidence of violence. They include:

- an ideology or set of justifying beliefs for the actions, which is presented by the authority;

- dehumanization of the victims, that is, referring to them as "animals" or "insects" or "dirt";
- diffusion of responsibility, such that the actual perpetrator is not directly or ultimately responsible for the actions or the consequences of the actions;
- gradual escalation of the violence;
- gradual shift from "just" to "unjust" behavior;
- verbal distortions that obscure the real nature of the behavior, for example, calling harm "discipline" or "purification";
- providing no means of escape from the situation—what we might call a "totalized" or "absolute" situation;
- deindividuation, which involves methods to remove or submerge the individuality of the actors, such as hoods and masks, uniforms, and group pressures; and
- above all else, blind obedience to authority.[11]

Baumeister, who has surveyed the field of human cruelty and violence, has similarly identified four root causes of aggression: instrumental gain, sadism/pleasure, egoism (especially threatened or fragile egoism), and idealism.[12]

From these analyses, it should be apparent that violence is not at all irrational but is very explainable and, to a large extent, controllable. If we create the circumstances in which Zimbardo's or Baumeister's conditions are met, then we would only expect violence to flow from them. If, instead, we minimize these conditions—which is not impossible to do—then we could expect at least a reduction if not an elimination of violence, whatever its original source. One such source is religion. The ultimate question for us is, how and why does religion provide these conditions, not uniquely but particularly effectively?

A MODEL OF EXPANDING VIOLENCE

If we have seen anything so far, it is that violence is not a simple phenomenon but a complex and multidimensional one. In fact, we can specify six independent but related contributing dimensions or levels, allowing us to propose a model of the expanding scope and scale of violence. This model is religion independent, that is, it does not make religion a specific factor in violence. Instead, it applies to any source of violence, religion included. To the extent that religion—or anything else—activates these various areas, it will be prone to more violence and more extensive, intensive, and acceptable violence.

The six dimensions or mechanisms of violence are:

1. Instinct or the individual
2. Integration into groups
3. Identity
4. Institutions
5. Interests
6. Ideology

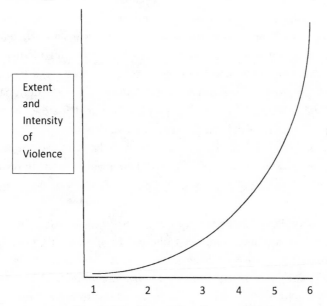

Fig. 1. The Expanding Scope of Violence

Instinct or the Individual

Humans are beings capable of committing violence. If we were not, we would not have human violence. Part of our potential for destructiveness and aggression comes from uniquely human features, and another part comes from our general characteristics as natural creatures. Just as religion is hardly the only source of human violence, so humans are not the only agents of violence in the world.

Much natural as well as social violence takes place at the individual level. When one gazelle or lion fights with another—or when one lion hunts one gazelle—individual or instinctual aggression is occurring. When one human fights with another human, this is also individual violence (although it may be and usually will be set in a context of other factors and dimensions—that is, when one soldier fights another, it is not merely individual violence). Living beings have the capacity for aggression or what is referred by ethologists (animal behaviorists) as *agonistic behavior*.

Some beings appear to be inherently more or less agonistic than others. Hamsters are not very aggressive, but grizzly bears are. Some situations or causes appear to inspire more aggression than others: feeding and mating can be reasons for protracted and deadly violence (in the case of feeding, both to the prey and to the competing predators). It would be no surprise then that carnivorous species and species that compete for mates would exhibit particular violence. At the same time, this violence is usually constrained by other instinctual forces, referred to as *inhibiting mechanisms*. For instance, when two dogs fight, they seldom fight to the death. At some point in the contest, when the dominance of one has been established, the loser will display a behavior that stops the winner from pressing his victory; the behavior may involve exposing the belly of the loser, which could result in a fatal slash but does not. The behavior signals that the fight is finished. (One consequence of this phenomenon is that unrestrained violence might be the result of a *lack* of instincts, specifically violence-inhibiting instincts.)

As in most species, males are particularly prone to aggressive behavior, and natural selection explanations have been offered. In species that have "dominance," such that one male will have more opportunity (and maybe all the opportunity) to mate, male sexual competition is a life-and-death matter; those who do not breed will be dead to the gene pool anyhow, so there is little to lose in fighting near to or to death. Also, those who win fights and mate tend to be stronger, passing that advantage to their offspring. And since most males may never mate anyhow, they constitute a genetic surplus that can be expended in defense and other agonistic activities.

Primates also compete and display. In the most humanlike, such as the chimpanzee, these displays can involve screaming, chest pounding, chasing, shaking or throwing of branches or stones, and more serious interactions that lead to physical harm. Ordinary chimps (as opposed to bonobos, a more peaceful breed) have even been known to kill babies, sometimes when the young are the spawn of competing males and sometimes for no apparent reason at all. Inhibiting mechanisms stop them sometimes, but at other times, unlike the vast majority of species, their violence continues on until serious injury or death occurs. They seem to have lost some of their instinctual inhibition against violence.

Humans are known to scream, pound their chests (symbolically or literally), chase, throw things at, and hit each other as well, and exposing one's weakness to one's attacker is not often the best way to end the attack. Humans seem to have lost even more of those inhibiting instincts, and we use culture to fill in the gaps. However, the role of instincts in human life—human violence or any-thing else—is controversial. Sigmund Freud, for instance, claimed in one ver-sion of his psychoanalytic theory that humans possess two opposing instinctual drives, one toward love and one toward hate. Or to put it better, one drive (*eros*, the life instinct) motivated humans toward more inclusive and integrating rela-tionships, with other people as well as between the various parts of the mind or self. In his theory, everything takes psychic energy, including mental operations and social relationships, and the life instinct invests energy in binding mental and social elements together. Confronting this unifying force is a death instinct (*thanatos*) that wants not so much to kill and destroy as to dis-integrate and return to a lower energy state. It is the force that pushes people apart or even unbinds the elements of the mind. Particularly after the horrors of World War I suggested that there were darker things going on in the human psyche than mere nationalism and economic interest, Freud theorized that, like all innate drives, the death instinct could not be denied or repressed. In fact, the more we tried to unite people into one peaceable human family, the fewer outlets the instinct would have, and therefore the more intense and destructive its release would be—whether aimed at others as war or at the self as mental illness.

Whether or not we want to follow Freud in his instinctual theorizing, it is no doubt true that humans have a destructive side as well as a constructive one; we have violent potential as well as nonviolent potential. He was correct at least in recognizing that humans are complex, ambiguous, and not entirely rational creatures.

Another possible factor in the violence of individuals is frustration, as psy-chologists like Miller and Dollard as well as Allport have pointed out. When a creature is faced with a frustration, such as a barrier between itself and a desired object (say, food or a mate) or a constraint on its movement (say, a chain or trap on its leg), the creature will often resort to force and aggression to eradicate that barrier or constraint. Certainly, the obstacle could be another member of the individual's own species or a member of a different "kind" or group within that species. All that is necessary is for the individual to encounter the frustration of its practical wishes (i.e., it does not entail a specific and separate "violent wish") in order for aggression to flare, as a hopefully effective response to the situation.

What this first dimension demonstrates is that individuals (and not only human individuals) can be and regularly are violent and that this violence is not unnatural nor entirely maladaptive. Humans are not exclusively violent, but neither are we exclusively nonviolent. We are both; we are paradoxical and contradictory. Any theory or intervention that does not recognize the natural capacity of humans to both help and harm misses the point and is doomed to fail.

Integration into Groups

Humans—and many other beings—are violent as individuals; they have hostility in their "nature." However, in aggregates, this violence is more common and more extreme. Everyone who has studied group or crowd behavior for the past century or more has commented that groups seem to have a mind of their own that is, ironically, more mindless than the individual. As the philosopher Nietzsche famously wrote in *Beyond Good and Evil*, "Madness is something rare in individuals—but in groups, parties, peoples, ages, it is the rule." Some observers like Howard Bloom have gone so far as to suggest that groups constitute a kind of "superorganism" with its own life and nature and characteristics.[13] Whether or not we care to go that far, it is certainly clear that integration into groups either brings out something new or adds something new to the individuals who compose the groups.

One of the first scholars to take social groups seriously as a topic of study was Gustav Le Bon, whose 1896 book *The Crowd: A Study of the Popular Mind* paints a disquieting picture of human mass behavior. In the fourth chapter of his book, which is ominously titled "A Religious Shape Assumed by All the Convictions of Crowds," he writes:

> We have shown that crowds do not reason, that they accept or reject ideas as a whole, that they tolerate neither discussion nor contradiction, and that the suggestions brought to bear on them invade the entire field of their understanding and tend at once to transform themselves into acts. We have shown that crowds suitably influenced are ready to sacrifice themselves for the ideal with which they have been inspired. We have also seen that they only entertain violent and extreme sentiments.[14]

He notes that, whether the group behavior is founded on politics, economics, race, or faith, the form of mentality and behavior that emanates from it can be expressed "by giving it the name of a religious sentiment."

This sentiment has very simple characteristics, such as worship of a being supposed superior,

> fear of the power with which the being is credited, blind submission to its commands, inability to discuss its dogmas, the desire to spread them, and a tendency to consider as enemies all by whom they are not accepted. Whether such a sentiment apply to an invisible God, to a wooden or stone idol, to a hero or to a political conception, provided that it presents the preceding character- istics, its essence always remains religious. The supernatural and miraculous are found to be present to the same extent. Crowds unconsciously accord a mysterious power to the political formula or the victorious leader that for the moment arouses their enthusiasm.[15]

Finally he discovers the ready resort to "intolerance and fanaticism" in the mobi- lized group, which

> are inevitably displayed by those who believe themselves in possession of the secret of earthly or eternal happiness. These two characteristics are to be found in all men grouped together when they are inspired by a conviction of any kind. . . . The convictions of crowds assume those characteristics of blind sub- mission, fierce intolerance, and the need of violent propaganda which are inherent in the religious sentiment.[16]

He concludes that all outbreaks or movements of mass violence "are phe- nomena of an identical kind, brought about by crowds animated by those reli- gious sentiments which necessarily lead those imbued with them to pitilessly extirpate by fire and sword whoever is opposed to the establishment of the new faith. The methods of the Inquisition are those of all whose convictions are gen- uine and sturdy."[17]

Subsequent researchers, from Freud to Eric Hoffer to Elias Canetti, have built on Le Bon's work, and the evidence is there for all to see. We will return to Eric Hoffer's work on mass movements below, because he has much to say about doctrines and ideologies. However, he also makes some comments that are relevant at this point. One is the need for "unifying agents" to keep groups cohe- sive and active, such as hatred, imitation, persuasion and coercion, leadership, action, and suspicion—most of them quite negative. Of these, he thinks that hatred "is the most accessible and comprehensive of all. . . . Mass movements can rise and spread without belief in a god, but never without belief in a devil."[18] That is, a mobilized group or movement needs an enemy, a "them," to fuel its organization and motivation. Even worse, he sees a certain organizational advantage to doing harm to the opposition: "To wrong those we hate is to add fuel to our hatred. . . . The most effective way to silence our guilty conscience is to convince ourselves and others that those we have sinned against are indeed depraved creatures, deserving every punishment, even extermination."[19] In the end, "It is probably as true that violence breeds fanaticism as that fanaticism begets violence. It is often impossible to tell which came first."[20]

Another important aspect of group dynamics, one that contributes to violence as we saw earlier, is the deindividuation that can occur only within the group. As Hoffer states:

> When we renounce the self and become part of a compact whole, we not only renounce personal advantage but are also rid of personal responsibility. There is no telling to what extremes of cruelty and ruthlessness a man will go when he is freed from the fears, hesitations, doubts, and the vague stirrings of decency that go with individual judgment. When we lose our individual independence in the corporateness of a mass movement, we find a new freedom—freedom to hate, bully, lie, torture, murder, and betray without shame and remorse.[21]

An additional and critical component of group behavior that is absent in individual behavior is the role of leadership. This has even been called by others the "leadership principle" or, more sinisterly, the *Führer Prinzip* after the Nazi experience. And Hoffer alarms us with the qualities of an effective movement leader, which are not the positive traits that we might hope for:

> Exceptional intelligence, noble character, and originality seem neither indispensable nor perhaps desirable. The main requirements seem to be: audacity and a joy in defiance; an iron will; a fanatical conviction that he is in possession of the one and only truth; faith in his destiny and luck; a capacity for passionate hatred; contempt for the present; a cunning estimate of human nature; a delight in symbols (spectacles and ceremonials); unbounded brazenness which finds expression in a disregard of consistency and fairness; a recognition that the innermost craving of a following is for communion and that there can

never be too much of it; a capacity for winning and holding the utmost loyalty of able lieutenants.[22]

Surveying the decades of experience and research, Baumeister has distilled what he calls the "group effect," which exhibits several of the features of violent potential. Components of the group effect include diffusion of responsibility, deindividuation, a division of violent labor (such that no one person performs, or even comprehends, the full scale and sequence of violence), and separation of the decision maker from the hands-on perpetrator. All this seems true, but it does not yet answer the questions of why humans are so prone to aggregate in the first place and why human aggregates take on such distinct and dangerous qualities.

Other lines of research have suggested that there is what I have come to call a "will to differentiate" in humans as well as in related nonhuman species. Experiments by Henri Tajfel show precisely this. Tajfel assigned subjects to groups with insignificant names like "red" and "blue" and gave them tasks to perform. Individuals were provided with the results of their team members as well as of the opposing team. However, as in the Milgram study above, there were no groups or teams; each individual was alone and was being fed bogus information. The heart of the experiment came afterward, when subjects were asked to evaluate the performance of their own and the other team and to indicate their attitude toward both. People consistently rated their own (imaginary) team higher in performance on the tasks and expressed a preference for theirs over the other—even though they had never met or interacted with any actual humans from either (since there were none). Tajfel's conclusion was that the mere *perception* of membership in a group or category may be enough to initiate group attachment and group judgment. He called his resulting theory "social identification theory" and described the process of social identification as occurring in three steps. First, social categories exist—reds and blues, blacks and whites, Christians and non-Christians, Americans and "terrorists," and so on. As a sheer consequence of these categories and one's place in them, people come to identify with their category, to think of themselves as "us" as opposed to "them"—"a red" versus "a blue." Finally, members use their identification for social comparison; they judge themselves by the standard of their group, seeking to minimize differences between themselves and their group—and, at least in some cases, to maximize differences between themselves and the other group.[23]

Allied work by other social scientists like Gordon Allport supports this interpretation. In his influential 1979 book, *The Nature of Prejudice*, Allport also relates negative attitudes, stereotypes, and behavior to group dynamics and to the process of categorization into groups in the first place. In fact, he defines prejudice at the outset as a group phenomenon, "an avertive or hostile attitude toward a person who belongs to a group, simply because he belongs to that group and is therefore presumed to have the objective qualities ascribed to the group."[24] Interestingly, in accord with Tajfel, this attitude may not be based on any actual experience with the other group; in fact, prejudice is probably easier to maintain and stronger in intensity *if there is no experience* of the other group.

Allport comments on this apparently universal human tendency, "Everywhere on earth we find a condition of separateness among groups." Even worse, "Once this separation exists . . . the ground is laid for all sorts of psychological elaborations. . . . And, perhaps most important of all, the separateness may lead to genuine conflicts . . . as well as to many imaginary conflicts."[25] An equally universal, and equally problematic, tendency is attributing the (alleged) characteristics of the categories to the members of the categories. Categories, he asserts, are quick and handy guides for everyday life; we cannot process every isolated experience or bit of information on its own, so we generalize. However, our categories tend to "assimilate" as much as they can, to bring as much of experience within their domain as possible. Even more, all the items (including human beings) in the same category tend to get "saturated" with the same empirical and emotional qualities, that is, we think they are alike and we feel alike about them. Finally, these categories may be more or less rational, depending on how much actual information they are based on.[26] And one of the really discouraging aspects is that our categories tend to be resistant to change, even self-repairing. He calls this procedure "re-fencing," in which "contrary evidence is not admitted and allowed to modify the generalization; rather it is perfunctorily acknowledged but excluded."[27]

Of course, this whole us/them division and even opposition between groups of the same species is not at all a uniquely human matter. Competition and conflict between groups of the same species, known as *intergroup agonistic behavior* or *intraspecies agonistic* behavior (IAB), has been observed in dozens of species. Johan van der Dennen, in a review of the available data, finds that there are sixty-four creatures that are known to practice IAB, including dolphins, wolves, hyenas, and lions, as well as ants.[28] Ants have been seen conducting virtual "wars" against neighboring colonies, lasting for hours or days and resulting in numerous deaths. Konrad Lorenz in his pioneering study of aggression found multiple types of fish, as well as rats, that will attack nonmembers of their own groups; he even suggested the term *pseudospeciation* for the dramatic creation of divisions within a species.[29] However, of the IAB species, fifty-four have been found among primates, the category that includes humans. Chimps in particular, as mentioned above, have been observed to systematically hunt down and kill off other groups—even when the two groups had only recently split apart. In other words, the enemies were former and recent friends and relatives. Van der Dennen goes so far as to ascribe humanlike qualities, such as ethnocentrism and xenophobia, to these primate groups. And if nonhuman beings can be so exclusivist and hostile, it is easy to understand how humans, with their categories and beliefs and histories, could be still more so.

Identity

Groups can be and typically are more violent than lone individuals, even when the groups are essentially fictional and imaginary. Clearly, we should not underestimate the power of human imagination in liking friends and disliking foes. And even an imaginary group can have an identity of sorts, and the flimsiest of identities—say, "red" in Tajfel's studies—appears to have its consequences. And if Benedict Anderson, a scholar on nationalism, is correct, then many if not most identities are imagined in a sense: sharing "American" identity, for instance, does not require that a person know, like, and interact with every member of the American group. That would be impossible. So large-scale aggregates and identities are what Anderson called "imagined communities"—but they are apparently no less effective and motivational for being so.[30]

Human groups probably always have at least minimal identity qualities. Even a crowd rioting in the streets after a sports championship may have a basic sense of being fans of the same team, although they do not know each other at all. In fact, the very designation "Yankees fan" or "Red Sox fan" can contribute mightily to a person's self-identity as well as to their health (in other words, walking into the wrong bar or badmouthing the wrong opposing fan may get you beaten up). This is even truer in the context of international soccer, where fans or crews from different cities or countries may engage in and actively seek confrontation with their counterparts. The fact that teams are associated with cities, and even more so with countries, may be a key element of this identification and violence.

Membership in a group or category crosses into *identification* with that group or category when it has four components: a name, a history, some salient symbols, and at least some interpersonal interaction. The name of the collectivity—whether it is "American," "Christian," "white," "baby boomer," or what have you—serves as a sort of banner or slogan; the very existence of the name makes the collectivity more real and more identifiable. One can now say, "I am an X," where X changes from an adjective to a concrete entity. It creates a self-consciousness of group membership—and of group fate: "We X's are in this together."

Social scientists refer to a group in which an individual is a member as his or her *in-group*; a group that one does not belong to is an *out-group*. However, more significant still is one's *reference group*, the group to which one looks for standards of thought, behavior, and values and for identification. In most cases, of course, one's in-group will be one's reference group, although not invariably. And the presence of an out-group may pose problems—conceptual and practical—for individuals, especially if they identify strongly with their in-group. The out-group at least differs from them, sometimes disagrees with them, and may actually interfere with them in some manner, causing "conflicts of interest" (as we will discuss below).

A group history can be a powerful cognitive and motivational factor. The history is what the collectivity has "gone through" over time, its achievements and its failures. In general (but not universally by any means), groups with a longer history have a greater authority, an extra layer of authenticity. They also have a collective memory, of success as well as of suffering. A history necessarily refers to a past, but it tends to point to a future: it may shape who the members are today and set a course of action for tomorrow—for instance, to right the wrong that was done in the past, to avenge a loss or humiliation. In other words, what is important is not so much that the group has a history as that it has a *destiny*, its imagined or ideal collective future.

Symbols are the meaningful public manifestations of the collectivity, its history, and its identity; they are where memory and identity are deposited and displayed. Its name may be one of its most salient symbols. Other symbols can include flags, songs, key objects, places, designs, clothing styles, and so on. A group can appropriate almost any part of its culture or history for symbolic elaboration and deployment—its language, its religion, major battles (victories and defeats work equally well), customs, and anything else. The more symbols a group has, and the more meaning is conveyed by them, the greater the identity-making and identity-carrying capacity.

Finally, the more actual personal interaction, ideally face-to-face interaction, the stronger the bonds of community and identity may be. As we have seen, humans can identify measurably even when face-to-face interaction is missing or impossible; the very mental impression of groupness, of category membership, works powerfully on us. And we will never interact with all the co-members of larger and more dispersed aggregates. But the ones whom we do interact with tend to have the strongest pull on us. In a certain sense, local identities are the most compelling ones, and group leaders in particular may take pains to have members interact and bond.

At the same time, "local" is flexible and relative, and identity can be transferred from the very most local and intimate level to more distant and abstract levels without any loss of strength—in fact, with some intensification. Most Americans do not feel as strongly about their neighborhood or their city as about their country; nobody would give his life for his homeowner's association. The very malleability of group identity and attachment is one of its most remarkable—and useable—features. And researchers on attachment have found that the intensity and duration of the attachment has little to do with the rewards derived from it. We seem to want and need to attach by nature, and an attachment can form and flourish in the absence of any real benefits from it or even in the presence of real disadvantages (which is one reason why punishment and persecution often do not weaken convictions but strengthen them).

It should be clear that the first and most local collectivity that meets the requirements of identity formation is the family. It is the locus of most of the individual's early experiences and interactions; it gives him or her a name, a set of related individuals, and basic habits, skills, and values. Because family is such a prominent factor and force in humans, other higher-level groups and categories tend to incorporate its relations and idioms, portraying themselves as families writ large. This can take the form of literal appropriation of kinship terminology, as in the Founding Fathers of the United States or the African American practice of referring to all co-members as "brother" or "sister." Races, ethnic groups, classes, nations, and potentially any kind of higher-order collectivity can adopt kinship forms and portray themselves as a kind of hyperfamily.

We expect, and generally see, that aggression and violence within this core collectivity is minimized or at least discouraged in most cultures. (The United States is an odd exception: Richard Gelles and Murray Straus maintain that if you are an American, "you are more likely to be physically assaulted, beaten, and killed in your own home at the hands of a loved one than anyplace else, or by anyone else in our society.")[31] The Semai, the nonviolent society we met above, consider all residents of their own village to be kinfolk, who are trusted and well treated. However, people from other villages, and especially people from other societies, are called *mai* and are not trusted. Even among the more violent Yanomamo, where fighting can occur within the village and kin group, special hostility is reserved for other villages and tribes. Accordingly, Marc Howard Ross, in a survey of ninety societies, found that violence was much more acceptable and frequent outside the local group than within it:

- No societies valued internal violence, and sixty-one (71 percent) disapproved of it.
- Twelve societies (15.6 percent) valued external violence, and only twenty-seven (35 percent) disapproved.
- Four societies (4.4 percent) experienced "endemic" local conflict, and twenty (22 percent) experienced "high" local conflict.
- Twenty-five societies (28 percent) experienced "endemic" external or intercommunity conflict, and twenty-three (26 percent) experienced "high" external conflict.[32]

Again, *local* and *remote* or *intracommunity* and *intercommunity* are relative terms. The question for us is how far a group's sense of "groupness," of shared identity, extends beyond the most local rank and how many people it includes.

There is general agreement that violence is more likely and more severe against an out-group than the in-group. (One important outcome of this trend is that *former* members of the in-group—apostates, deserters, and traitors—are particularly targets of disapproval and retribution.) In an admittedly imperfect way, the further "out" the out-group is, the greater the potential for, and approval of, violence against it. We might imagine this trajectory as a series of concentric circles, each ring a dimension of identity away from one's own. The innermost circle is the immediate family or household. The next circle out is the neighborhood. The third is the city or region. The fourth could be any intermediate level of identity—a class or caste, an ethnic group or race, an occupation, and so on. The fifth is the nation or the state. The sixth is the species, all humanity. A seventh, and hypothetically the highest, would be all life. Violence between neighborhoods is more normal and acceptable than within a neighborhood. Violence between nations and states is more normal and acceptable than within a nation (notice our different attitudes toward war and civil war). And violence against other species is more normal and acceptable than violence against "fellow" humans.

This is certainly a mnemonic model, not a highly precise predictor of actual aggression. Many other factors mitigate its simple structure. For example, the values of a society may encourage or at least allow internal violence. The society may also be internally differentiated and complex so that even at the community or neighborhood level, a "them" exists toward which violence is tolerable (the Deep South of the United States, with its history of lynching of blacks, would be one such case). In other words, there can be an "internal them," a "them among us," which challenges any simple model.

Finally, the presence or absence of cross-cutting ties is an important variable in this picture. No society is entirely internally homogeneous; rather, there are always multiple and contradictory terms of identity. Any one person may be an American, a New Yorker, a black, a male, and a Yankees fan simultaneously. These various identities link him to some other humans and distance him from others. While this might be complicated and rife for trouble, anthropologists have found that such competing and cross-cutting identities and allegiances can actually reduce or limit violence, since people cannot split off into simple binary "us-versus-them" pairs. In other words, our identities are multifaceted, which is a good thing, since we are bound by one category to some people and by other categories to other people. This is messy but also functional. As Max Gluckman, one of the first to report this phenomenon, wrote, cross-cutting identities and loyalties make for groups that can "quarrel in terms of their customary allegiances, but are restrained from violence through other conflicting allegiances which are also enjoined on them by custom." As he concluded, "these conflicting loyalties and divisions of allegiance tend to inhibit the development of open quarrelling, and . . . the greater the division in one area of society, the greater is likely to be the cohesion in a wider range of relationships—provided that there is a general need for peace, and the recognition of a moral order in which this peace can flourish."[33]

Institutions

Groups and their beliefs, practices, and values—and the moral order to which Gluckman alluded—do not and cannot exist in the abstract. They must be embodied and preserved in real, enduring, and organized institutions that constitute the ongoing social arrangements within which people live and act. An institution is a long-lasting or permanent standardized set of beliefs, behaviors, and values, usually expressed in sets of roles and the relationships between these roles. For example, marriage is an institution: it is composed of certain "parts to play" (i.e., "husband" and "wife"), certain rules and expectations for each player, sometimes certain explicit legal requirements, and certain relationships between this institution and others in the society. In one regard, a society is the sum and nexus of its various institutions, which fall into such broad classes as economic, kinship, political, and religious. These institutions give society and the human interactions that compose it their structure; they provide the "playing field" on or within which we act, given a limited and defined set of possible and normal "moves."

Which institutions exist in a society and how they are organized signifi-cantly shapes the character of life in that society, including but hardly confined to violence. For instance, if a society's marriage institution defines highly asym-metrical relations between husbands and wives and sanctions hostility or even violence as a pattern of married life, then domestic or spousal violence is much more likely than if these elements are absent. Likewise, if the institution of par-enthood contains ideas such as the lack of rights of minors or the parental "own-ership" of children, or if it endorses physical punishment as a child-rearing tech-nique, then child-directed violence will be more likely, which in turn may spawn more general social violence. In fact, in the context of such institutional arrangements as these, spousal violence or child-directed violence would not necessarily be regarded as "violence" at all, and certainly not as "unacceptable violence" or as a "social problem," but rather as "discipline" or "tough love."

Many, and perhaps the most intimate, institutions focus on the family, including the practice of dowry (the payment of wealth by a woman's family to her prospective husband or his family), which has definite consequences for the har-mony or harm between the sexes and inside the home (see chapters 4 and 8). How-ever, those intimate and family relations are set within much wider and more per-vasive social institutions of gender, economics, politics, and religion. Patriarchy is one such overarching institution or constellation of institutions, including patri-lineal kin-group membership (that is, kin systems in which children belong to their father's "line") and patrilocal residence rules (that is, requirements that a married woman leave her family home and reside in the home of her husband or his family). Such arrangements can lead to extreme and dangerous inequalities. Mary Elaine Hegland describes an Iranian village in which women have virtually no rights whatsoever. Everything in this society favors men, who are raised to be violent and domineering; they learn early on "to devalue women and their activi-ties, to use violence to get what they want, and to demonstrate the power and strength required for political survival." The control over women's lives is nearly total. A woman is required to be a virgin at the time of marriage. She is under the authority of her male relatives until she marries, at which time that authority transfers to her husband; so complete is it that her own father cannot intervene to minimize the husband's abuses against her. Men beat their wives as well as their own sisters if they dare to challenge the patriarchal system. Women are so little valued that, as one informant told, "When I was born, the minute they told my mother it was a girl she began to cry bitterly."[34]

Eunice Uzodike tells an even more horrifying story about the consequences of institutionalized patriarchy. It is a tale of a twelve-year-old girl who was married to a much senior man (a Fulani pastoralist in Nigeria) and repeatedly ran away from him. After the final escape attempt, the husband was determined to end her defiant behavior. He cut off one of her legs, causing her to bleed to death. When her father learned of the husband's action, he saw no fault in the husband. Before a woman is married, she is the responsibility of the father; after marriage, all rights over her, including the right of life and death, pass to the husband.[35] Lest the reader think that such comportment is restricted to "primitive" and "savage" societies, it is salutary to remind ourselves of ancient Roman custom and law, specifically the institution of *patria potestas* that granted men the right of life and death over their families. Marriage as an institution awarded the husband rights over his wife, and childbirth established his rights over his children—the same rights he had over his other property, his slaves, and his tenants. Among these rights was the power to disinherit, to dispose, to sell into slavery, or even to kill members of his household. This is one of the origins of the familiar notion that "a man's home is his castle," where he makes the law.

Inequalities and hierarchies of all sorts contribute to the conditions that favor violence, either as oppression or resistance to oppression. Obviously an institution like slavery, which depends on a social and legal imbalance between types of humans, is abusive and violent (at least structurally violent if not always physically so). However, these imbalances have been explained and justified by everything from nature (e.g., Aristotle's "natural slave" theory, or more modern "racial inferiority" ideas) to history to economics to religion. Short of slavery, hierarchical and stratified relations are common between economic, political, racial, ethnic, and other categories, providing causes for grievance, complaint, competition, and often enough conflict. For instance, class inequalities were the motivator for much violence in the nineteenth and twentieth centuries, from labor unrest in the United States to workers' revolutions in Russia and China.

In earlier times, peasant uprisings against conditions such as serfdom and the privileges of the nobility sparked violence and were met with violence.

Not only political differences but the highest level of political institutions have been sources of violence. Premodern political systems, including chiefdoms, have often been capable of violence because of the leader's ability to call upon and even coerce followers to take up arms at his command: from the Zulus to the Hawaiians, powerful chiefs could inspire or compel violent efforts of their people against other peoples. However, virtually all analysts agree that the modern centralized political system called the "state" achieved unprecedented heights in mobilization and performance of violence. In fact, the great sociologist Max Weber defined *state* precisely as "a human community that (successfully) claims the *monopoly of the legitimate use of physical force* within a given territory."[36] In other words, the main function if not the very essence of the state is to control and perform violence.

In the state, but by no means exclusively in the state, are specific "institutions of violence," such as the police, the military, and the prison system. Other societies have had their own institutions of violence. Cheyenne traditional society, for example, contained a set of "warrior societies" like the Bowstring and the Crazy Dogs, each of which was organized to conduct raids against other groups, to defend against raids from other groups, to police the buffalo hunt, and so on. Elsewhere, societies have included age-based groups (technically known as *age-sets*) that were often commissioned as the protectors of the society and as the aggressors against neighboring societies. Male initiation rituals often functioned to harden young men against pain and to bolster their bravery and toughness. At the extreme, institutions like the Spartan *agoge* served as literal training grounds for the next generation of fighters (and, not inconsequentially, oppressors of the local enslaved *helot* population).

All these sorts of institutions are normally set within a much wider context of social concepts and values. One crucial example of such a concept is honor. Honor is some socially conceived and socially relevant evaluation of the worth or quality of individuals, families, and broader categories (the village, the nation). Honor is often a competitive or combative commodity, and it is also often the province of men. One illustration comes from the description of traditional and post-Communist Albania by Stephanie Schwandner-Sievers. In the absence of effective national-level politics, she found local Albanians turning to their *kanun* or traditional systems of rules and values. *Kanun* is fundamentally concerned with honor—the honor of a man, his family, and his village. If honor is threatened, violence is not only appropriate but probably necessary. Much of *kanun* morality is expressed in proverbs, such as "Blood for blood," "The soap of a man is his gunpowder," and "The wolf licks his own flesh but eats the flesh of others." Accordingly, if another (out-group) man or family or village starts a conflict, especially if in-group blood is spilled, revenge attacks are reasonable and required to restore the "balance of blood." Alternately, young men may organize attacks on other villages simply to acquire prestige and prove their honor, guaranteeing feelings of dishonor in the subject village and possibly a counterattack. Individuals and groups who have been so dishonored are fair targets for public ridicule, ostracism, and assault. If honor is lost, there are two main ways to recover it. The first is a ritual of forgiveness, in which the dishonored family or group must show extreme generosity. By making such a gesture, their honor rises in the eyes of witnesses. The other obvious course is counterviolence, in which the dishonored party "washes his blackened face," especially killing a member of another group during a feud.[37]

In Albanian society and outside it as well, other psychological and cultural values promote violence too. Closely tied to honor is masculinity, especially what Beatrice Whiting called "protest masculinity."[38] Manliness is often a limited and contested commodity that must be achieved in contrast to, and at the cost of, women. Unsurprisingly, combative and bellicose notions of masculinity are directly associated with aggressiveness and violence. These hostile attitudes and values have been embodied in practices from the Yanomamo chest-pounding challenge to medieval European jousts to early modern sword or pistol duels to contemporary organized sports: quite literally, George Gilder called competitive sports "possibly the single most important male rite in modern society," "a religious male rite," and "an ideal of beauty and truth," while John Carroll stressed "the military and political values inherent in sport . . . [which] should not be muzzled by humanist values: it is the living arena for the great virtue of manliness."[39] More than a few societies have gone so far as to praise the beauty of violence and death itself, from the Spanish bullfighter to the Japanese samurai.

Many other institutions exist in the human world, some of which are conducive to nonviolence, some to violence. One last feature of institutions that bears comment is, once again, the role of leadership. Some institutions have very formal positions of power and authority, including a complex and rigid hierarchy of statuses. Institutions tend in their very nature to be conservative, to want to preserve and perpetuate themselves, and they also attempt to lock individuals into more or less circumscribed roles in relation to each other and to

authority. When these roles, and these authorities, call for violence, the forthcoming actions may not been taken as improper at all—not even as "violent."

Interests

Individually, humans have a capacity for violence. Groups unleash or exacerbate
that capacity, and institutions regularize and legitimize it. But interests are
largely what motivate it. It would be hard to imagine a human group that was
not at least potentially if not actually an interest group as well.

An *interest* is some more or less specific and intentional goal or aim or purpose that an individual or group pursues. The most primary of interests involve
practical, material ends, such as food, money, land, and other resources, as well
as more abstract or socially defined ones like jobs, access to education, and political power. However, interests need not necessarily be quite so concrete; they can
also include symbolic resources dear to an individual or group, such as honor,
rights, equality, "truth," "morality," and culture itself (that is, the survival of
and freedom to practice one's culture, language, religion, styles of dress, and
other customs). When individuals—and more so groups—come into conflict
over interests, or when one feels that another is a obstacle to its interests, the
prospect for violence is increased by another dimension.

Groups seldom fight each other openly over mere groupness. Northern Irish
Catholics and Protestants, for instance, have not warred for the last few decades
over the sheer existence of divergent groups, nor even over doctrinal differences
between the two sects of Christianity. If that were the case, we would expect
American Catholics and Protestants to fight openly as well, which they do not
(see chapter 6). Integrated groups, identity, and institutions provide the parties
and the organization for violence, but it is interests that provide the reasons and
justifications—some desired outcomes and the barriers impeding them, namely,
some other group and its identity and institutions. In another social context, where
either the interest-issues did not exist or were not associated with group membership, we would expect that the difference between the groups would not escalate into a conflict between them. In other words, group identity differences
alone are not enough to account for conflict and violence; other factors must
merge with those identities to transform *identity groups* into *interest groups* and
subsequently into *conflict groups*.

Even more significant, the identity groups need not exist prior to and be
constitutive of the interest groups. In the reverse, some collection of humans

may find themselves with shared interests and assemble themselves into an identity group. Such was the hope and aim of Marxism, in which workers would realize—literally become conscious of—their common interests as workers and organize themselves accordingly. Marx said that other forms of identity, including nationality and ethnicity, were either anachronisms in a modern world or else a "false consciousness" perpetrated on them to divide them and disguise their "true" identity as a class. It was "workers of the world" to whom Marx called, not to Englishmen or Americans or Germans. That most individuals never answered this call suggests that identities are not infinitely malleable, or at least that some sources of identity seem to have more valence than others.

At any rate, when interests enter the picture, the cleavages between groups become more concrete and sometimes more intractable. The out-group is not just different, not just strange, but now "in our way." Louis Kreisberg has proposed a model to explain how these kinds of issues can contribute to the escalation and/or resolution of group conflicts. In fact, he defines social conflict as the situation "when two or more parties believe they have incompatible objectives."[40] In a cyclical fashion, the first phase of any such struggle is the "basis for conflict," when the two parties "are likely to come to believe that they have conflicting goals."[41] Dishearteningly but significantly, "almost any division of people into two or more sets can be the basis for collective identification and organization of conflict groups";[42] in other words, the groups need not be ancient or "authentic" in any serious way. In many cases, the conflict creates the group rather than vice versa. Thus, many different kinds of interest groups can coalesce and conflict, including class, race, ethnic, political, and religious ones. He notes that political/national groups are particularly prone to such confrontations because of the institutions they contain, especially their central governments and standing armies. Governments, he writes, "are ready-made adversaries in international conflicts. Each claims absolute sovereignty, and each has specialized subunits to conduct conflict. The cleavages, however, do not simply pit each government against every other. Governments are linked together into many cross-cutting alliances, which are based on ideology, economic interests, and military concerns."[43]

If the bases of conflict are there, and the leaders and the members of the relevant groups act in certain ways, then the second phase of "emergence of conflict" follows. This entails three factors: (1) self-consciousness as collectivities with interests, (2) a grievance against the other group on the part of one or both, and (3) the determination that their grievance can be reduced or eliminated and their interests achieved through some change in the other, up to and including its destruction. One key message is that for there to be interest-based conflict, there must be, besides an interest, a *claim* and a *grievance*. The claim is what the group wants and why it should have it: "We are the Xs and we demand and deserve Y." The terms of the claim may well be the identity of the group—its history, its antiquity, its "authentic culture," its "purity" or "morality" or "goodness," its prior possession of the resource (especially land), and so on. The grievance is its complaint against the other group—how the out-group has deprived it of its rightful possessions, mistreated it in some way, or blocked it from achieving its goals. The grievance can also include previous harm done by the out-group, for example, past violence and conflict.

Even at this point, violence is not inevitable. Kreisberg insists that there are various courses of action available, including persuasion, reward, and ultimately coercion. Ironically, groups ideally if not usually settle their differences of interest with violence when it is in their interest to do so. That is to say, groups may have tried other methods to no avail, or they detect a weakness in the opposition, or they may hunger for a "final solution." When this moment arrives, the third phase of "escalation of conflict" appears. The conflict turns violent, with a certain self-propelled quality:

> Once conflict behavior has started, mechanisms are triggered that tend to increase its magnitude. Having expressed hostility and coercive action against another party, the alleged reason for it assumes importance commensurate with the action taken. . . . Under such circumstances, fewer alternative courses of action are considered than in periods that are not viewed as a time of crisis. . . . Each side tends to persist in the course of action already undertaken. In addition, crisis decision making tends to rely on stereotyped images of adversaries and on historical analogies and to view possible outcomes in terms of absolute victory and defeat.[44]

For a variety of possible reasons, the conflict may eventually begin to deescalate. The goals of one or both groups may change, or one group may achieve its main goals. Leaders may adopt new policies, or members may tire of or withdraw support from the struggle. Outside forces (e.g., other countries) may intervene; the warring groups may reach a compromise; or one of the sides may be defeated or liquidated. The final phase is "termination," in which conflict ends, either permanently or temporarily. This may constitute a genuine resolution of the problem, a momentary respite in a protracted struggle, or a fundamental shift in the terms of the competition, including the replacement of the leadership or policies of one or both combatants or the disappearance of one or both. We should be fully aware, though, that a cease-fire is not the same thing as a true and sustainable peace.

Ideology

All groups of social significance consist of individuals sharing some identity organized by institutions to pursue interests. However, not all groups—and only human groups—add the sixth and most incendiary ingredient of ideology. We do not mean here ideology in the negative or Marxist sense, that is, of a false and even deliberately misleading façade of ideas intended to obscure the real qualities of nature or society. Ideology is simply the "contents" of a worldview or belief system, the ideas and beliefs and values shared by a group or movement. The "truth" or "falseness" of an ideology is not the issue here and often cannot be determined, or rather does not apply at all. An ideology includes factual claims about the world, but it also includes values and judgments and perspectives that are not "truth claims" (for instance, "We are the master race" or "The proletariat should control the means of production") and cannot be treated as such. Of course, members typically consider their ideology to be true, or at least profoundly important.

An ideology is a set of ideas, but it is much more than that. It is "doctrine" and "theory," sometimes if not usually an ostensibly complete "view of reality"—a sort of "theory of everything." Jonathan Fox has listed five properties of ideologies:

1. They "provide a meaningful framework for understanding the world."
2. They "provide rules and standards of behavior that link individual actions and goals to this meaningful framework."
3. They "are usually derived from an external framework."
4. They "link individuals to a greater whole and sometimes provide formal institutions [that] help to define and organize that whole."
5. They "have the ability to legitimize actions and institutions."[45]

Actually, what Fox says is that these are the five properties shared by religion and ideology, failing to grasp that religion *is* an ideology.

Not all ideologies are religious by any means, and nonreligious ideologies can be just as productive of violence as religious ones. In the twentieth century, political, economic, and ethnic/cultural/nationalist ideologies have been the source of unprecedented aggression and destruction. What all these systems had in common was a notion of what was real, good, necessary, and even inevitable, and of the steps required to bring about certain desired ends. For instance, perhaps the first modern ideological struggle was the French Revolution, in which parties clashed not just over who would rule the society but over exactly what kind of society it would be. The goals of the most ideological of the revolutionaries, like Robespierre who oversaw the Terror in 1793–1794, were a total revision, a total *perfection*, of society—what he called a "republic of virtue." He and his comrades sought the absolute victory of their ideas and beliefs and therefore the absolute defeat, the absolute eradication, of any competitors. As Robespierre himself stated in announcing the republic of virtue:

> We desire an order of things in which all base and cruel feelings are suppressed by the laws, and all beneficent and generous feelings evoked; in which ambition means the desire to merit glory and to serve one's country. In which distinctions arise only from equality itself . . . ; in which all minds are enlarged by the continued conviction of republican sentiments and by the endeavor to win the respect of a great people. . . .
>
> We must crush both the internal and foreign enemies of the Republic, or perish with it. And in this situation, the first maxim of your policy should be to guide the people by reason and repress the enemies of the people by terror.[46]

This sublime aspiration of the revolution and the attainment of perfect virtue of course required an instrument, and that instrument was the guillotine, invented in 1792 and carrying the inscription "THE JUSTICE OF THE PEOPLE."

Subsequent ideological revolutions and social movements, from Marxist communism to Nazism to various ethnic and nationalist ones, including some anticolonialist struggles, bore the same marks as the French Revolution. These marks include, among others, idealism and a sense of moral superiority distinguished by absolute certainty in the rightness and ultimate success of the movement and its leadership. The aims of the French and Soviet upheavals were not merely a better society but a perfect one; they proposed to solve all problems, eliminate all vices, secure all blessings. While they often engaged in contradictions like "freedom through terror," they tended to deny contradiction, imagining overly simple and absolute answers.

Idealism of this sort perhaps cannot exist without a supporting structure of moralism. In other words, the leaders and members of the group must feel that they are doing a good thing, indeed the best possible thing. They, the insiders, are the good people with the good intentions. Part of this moralism comes from and is propped up by the claim to be acting in the name of something higher; Robespierre would never allege that he was working on his own behalf, perhaps even on his own volition. Rather, the vanguard of the ideological movement is acting "in the name of the people" or "in the name of the nation" or "in the name of the class" or "in the name of the god." Therefore, those who do not belong to and oppose the group, the outsiders, are not just bad but immoral—"counter-revolutionaries," "enemies of the people," "infidels," and "demonic," the very impediments to the perfect future. Nothing good can come from them, and nothing is too horrible to be used against them. The stakes are too high.

Finally, given their idealism and moralism, it is sensible that the actors would find themselves absolutely certain of the truth and the eventual success of their position. In the throes of ideology, "uncertainty and ambivalence, always painful to experience, are banished. There is no room for the other side's point of view."[47] Probably no one could struggle so incessantly—and savagely—without such certainty. Here, Hoffer makes the important point that the details of the doctrine are not as critical as the conviction of their correctness:

> The effectiveness of a doctrine does not come from its meaning but from its certitude. No doctrine however profound and sublime will be effective unless it is presented as the embodiment of the one and only truth. . . . It is obvious, therefore, that in order to be effective a doctrine must not be understood, but has to be believed in. We can be absolutely certain only about things we do not understand. A doctrine that is understood is shorn of its strength. . . . The devout are always urged to seek the absolute truth with their hearts and not their minds. . . . If a doctrine is not unintelligible, it has to be vague; and if neither unintelligible nor vague, it has to be unverifiable. . . . To be in possession of an absolute truth is to have a net of familiarity spread over the whole of eternity.[48]

Two serious implications flow from this fact. First, if the actors feel that they are absolutely right and absolutely good, the potential for compromise with other groups is strictly reduced; we do not bargain with evil or error, we destroy it. Second, if the ultimate good and truth is so valuable, so inevitable, yet so threatened, there is no sacrifice too great to make on its behalf. We are clearly ready, even eager, to sacrifice the opposition on the altar of tomorrow's perfection; we are often equally ready to sacrifice ourselves, since the end is so much greater than any individual human life.

While Hoffer may be correct that certitude means more in the final analysis than the specifics of the doctrine, still the doctrine can make a huge difference. Some of the most perilous items or themes of ideological doctrine, which reappear in many even diametrically opposed ideologies, include *dualism*, *war*, and *the purifying quality of violence*. Ideological groups tend to see the world in very dualistic, us-versus-them, terms. Dissenters are not "loyal opposition" but total enemies, sometimes the very incarnation of evil. They may be demonized and dehumanized, especially if "we" are really the people or are acting in the interests of the people. "They" must not be the people—or people at all. Some ideological systems have an inherent concept of war or destructive conflict as a tool if not a good. Marxism is fundamentally based on a view of society as the product of competitive and conflictual processes; all hitherto societies therefore have been the product of conflict, namely, class conflict. Class conflict in their theory is a scientific fact of social evolution. Therefore, conflict and violence are not only natural but desirable. Later Marxists like Georges Sorel argued this point precisely: "Proletarian violence has become an essential factor of Marxism."[49] In fact, he overtly invoked the notion of war—that is, a disciplined military campaign, as opposed to the disorganized destruction of the French Revolution or the medieval Inquisition—when he demanded that the violence of the proletarian revolution must be "purely and simply acts of war; they have the value of military demonstrations, and serve to make the separation of classes. Everything in war is carried on without hatred and without the spirit of revenge." Any other approach, especially gentler methods and compromise, represents "not a little stupidity."[50]

When the fight is a merely human and earthly one, the capacity for violence is high enough. However, when the struggle takes on cosmic proportions—when it is sewn into the very fabric of reality—then all weapons are unsheathed and all negotiations are called off. Marxism makes conflict a part of society and nature, but only religion can make it a part of supernature: the universe itself may be divided into a pair of armed camps, with humans the (sometimes unwitting or unwilling) foot soldiers in a cosmic epic in which there is no neutral ground.

Violence, in such cases, can become not only a necessary evil but a noble and purifying act in its own right. Perhaps Frantz Fanon, the anticolonialist activist, expressed this best. For him, the end of colonialism meant not just a shift in politics and economics but, as in the French and Soviet and other revolutions, "the veritable creation of new men."[51] These new humans will be cast in the crucible of violence:

The violence which has ruled over the ordering of the colonial world . . . will be claimed and taken over by the native at the moment when, deciding to embody history in his own person, he surges into the forbidden quarters. . . . The destruction of the colonial world is no more and no less than the abolition of one zone [in a dualistic system of colonizer versus colonized], its burial in the depths of the earth or its expulsion from the country.[52]

In fact, in line with Sorel, he saw more peaceable paths to decolonization as a kind of "detached complicity" with the oppressive system. Instead, he literally recommended violence as the method that would restore dignity and authenticity, even mental health:

There are no limits—for in reality your purpose in coming together is to allow the accumulated libido, the hampered aggressivity, to dissolve as in a volcanic eruption. Symbolical killings, fantastic rides, imaginary mass murders—all must be brought out. The evil humors are undammed, and flow away with a din as of molten lava.[53]

CONCLUSION: HURTING WITHOUT FEELING BAD—OR FEELING ANYTHING AT ALL

It is evident now how the independent variables of the individual, integration into groups, identity, institutions, interests, and ideologies accumulate to lay the foundations for violence. It is also evident how these variables are interrelated and how ideology provides a source for the others. If a belief system or theory of nature, society, or reality contains specific assertions or propositions, those items can become internalized in the personality of the individual and established as the basis for the group's existence. The interactions, history, and symbols of the ideological group are raw material for its identity; in fact, such is the hope and plan of the movers of the group. The beliefs and values of the ideology institutionalize themselves within the group and seek to expand, at the farthest extent to encompass the entire society, perhaps the entire world. The ideological group has its interests, from the mundane, such as more wealth, living space, rights, and opportunities for itself, to the abstract, such as the preservation, perpetuation, and triumph of the group as a group and a movement. Thus, while there are certainly nonideological groups and identities and institutions and interests, ideological ones most thoroughly fulfill and focus all the qualities that support violence into an effective system.

The grounds of violence converge on a single point, which has also been identified and emphasized by other observers and experimenters in the field of human violence. This point is the possibility and the methodology for removing or undermining the innate inhibitors of harmful actions. As humans mature, they tend to develop a capacity for intersubjectivity, that is, for understanding and sharing each other's experiences. If I see you cry, I know that you are sad, since that is how I would feel if I were crying. And I would not like that feeling myself, so I am inclined to avoid causing it in you. If I see you wince or hear you scream, I know that you are in pain, since that is how I would feel if I were wincing or screaming. And I would not like that feeling myself, so I am inclined to avoid causing it in you.

The simple term for this awareness is *empathy*, "feeling with" the other. We say in English that "I feel your pain," that it will "hurt me as much as it hurts you." When this is true, it is a powerful restraint on giving injury. However, when it is not true, one of the most powerful restraints against violence has been withdrawn.

Evidence suggests that a lack of empathy is a highly dangerous thing. One investigator of the most violent of criminal offenders, the psychopath, has developed a list of characteristics of psychopathy. Among these are several that indicate a failure of human empathy: lack of remorse or guilt, shallow affect (little emotion of any kind), callousness, and impulsivity.[54] Brain scans of violent offenders have shown that they literally do not experience the discomfort and revulsion that most of us feel when we encounter suffering.

I am not suggesting that all violent people, let alone all violent religious people, are psychopaths. The message is much more disturbing than that. A person does not *have* to be a psychopath to feel good about causing harm and suffering—or to feel little or nothing at all about it. Rather, what we have discovered is that a human needs only a belief system that teaches that he or she is acting for a good reason (even a "higher cause"), under someone else's authority, as a member of a (threatened) group, in pursuit of interests. Along the way, if the individual can learn, by way of gradual escalation, to commit violence against someone who is worth less—or completely worthless, less than a human being—then violence becomes not only possible but likely, if not certain.

CHAPTER 2

UNDERSTANDING RELIGION

If the first obstacle to clarifying the relation between religion and violence is a failure to understand the nature and diversity of violence, the second is a failure to understand the nature and diversity of religion. Most people take religion to be what their own religion is: as Parson Thwackum in the Henry Fielding novel *The History of Tom Jones* said, "When I mention religion I mean the Christian religion; and not only the Christian religion, but the Protestant religion; and not only the Protestant religion, but the Church of England."[1] For Americans and Christians, religion then specifically means first and foremost *theism* or even *monotheism*, the belief in some kind of, but definitely a single, god. That is simply and unequivocally inadequate as a description or definition of religion, since most religions throughout human history have not been theisms at all, let alone monotheisms. We cannot presume that all religions are like the one we are familiar with; to make that presumption is to risk profoundly misunderstanding the entire subject.

Along with the presumption of theism comes a whole list of other presumptuous errors committed by popular and scholarly writers alike. Charles Selengut, in his otherwise interesting book *Sacred Fury*, makes a variety of such overgeneralized assertions. For example, he claims on the first page, "At the center of all religions is the yearning for the *eschaton*, an end-time when all peoples of the world will live together in peace and harmony, without war or conflict."[2]

That is wrong on two counts. First, not all religions have a concept of *eschaton* or end-time at all. Second, not all religions that do have the concept believe in a time when "all the peoples of the world" will live in peace; that does not even quite characterize the Christian version, since *most* of the peoples of the world will have been destroyed along the way, leaving only *one* kind of people—Christians. He also claims that all religions "have versions of an eternal life for their religious martyrs who die a sacrificed death on behalf of the tradition."[3] This too is wrong, since most religions have never had a martyr tradition, and many do not even believe in "an eternal life." A third mistake comes in his claim that "the earliest and most elemental expression of religious violence [is] holy wars."[4] Actually, most religions have never had a concept of holy war (some have lacked the very concept of war!), and there are many other kinds of violence that preceded that concept, which will compose the following chapters of this book.

I do not mean to select Selengut for special criticism. The literature on religion in general and religious violence in particular is full of such ethnocentric assumptions: *my* religion has these characteristics, therefore *all* religions have these characteristics. Or even worse, the characteristics of *my* religion are the *essential* characteristics of religion. If we want to see religion or anything else clearly, we must see it as it really is, in all its complexity and variety, not as we want to see it. And it is necessary to see religion as it really is—or better yet, *religions* as they really are—in order to grasp the relation between religion and violence.

WHAT IS RELIGION?

The only way to comprehend religion is to examine it in all its diversity and internal complexity, that is, as *religions*. In fact, there may be no such thing as "religion" at all; it may be nothing more than a category in which different cultural systems are placed. But what makes something a religion as opposed to some other kind of phenomenon (a theory, a science, a philosophy, an opinion, etc.)?

This question raises the issue of definition, which we encountered in the first chapter. Defining violence, we saw, is a problem, and we did not attempt to solve it, rather to point out the parameters and consequences of any particular definition. Writers have attempted to define religion from many different perspectives. Most definitions that we are likely to meet involve some notion of *god(s)*, by which is meant some all-powerful, creative, and moral supernatural being(s). One huge problem with this approach, aside from the fact that not all religions have god(s) of any kind, is that not all religions with god(s) believe the god(s) to be all-powerful or creative or moral. Ancient Greek religion included many gods, each with certain powers and not others: some created things and others did not, and some were moral and others were not. As a necessary and sufficient condition, neither god(s) nor omnipotence nor creativity nor morality will do as the essence of religion.

Some definitions of religion have emphasized one or more elements of religion. That is, some researchers have suggested that ritual or belief or symbol or myth is the core of religion. Perhaps the tersest definition of religion ever offered came from the nineteenth-century ethnologist E. B. Tylor, who described it as belief in spiritual beings.[5] He and others of like mind further regarded religion basically as an explanatory system, an intellectual activity intended to account for particular facts and experiences, especially dreams and visions—even if these religious explanations are ultimately wrong. Thus, from this point of view, religion is not totally unlike science; it merely starts from false premises (that is, supernatural premises) and arrives at false conclusions.

A different set of thinkers has also traced religion to its psychological roots but emphasized emotion over intellect. Rudolf Otto, for example, in his *The Idea of the Holy*, suggested that religion arises from a primal experience of "the holy" or what he calls "the numinous," characterized as "creature-consciousness" or "the emotion of a creature, submerged and overwhelmed by its own nothingness in contrast to that which is supreme above all creatures."[6] This sensation of an Other, a presence "felt as objective and outside the self," leads to the *mysterium tremendum*—the awe, fear, fascination, and reverence—that "may at times come sweeping like a gentle tide" or "burst in sudden eruption" as the source of religious ideas.[7]

Finally among the psychological approaches, observers from Lucien Lévy-Bruhl to Sigmund Freud and Carl Jung have attributed religion to a unique mode of thought, explicitly nonlogical and even irrational. Lévy-Bruhl argued that all "primitive cultures" functioned on the basis of prelogical mentality, one that did not recognize the basic principle of exclusion—that a thing cannot be itself and something else simultaneously. Instead, he opined, prelogical thought operates on the principle of participation, in which contradictions and opposites can coexist—in which a statue can be a spirit or a wafer can be a bit of flesh. Freud and Jung too found the source of religion in a more primitive and less rational mode of thought. Freud called it the "primary process," the spontaneous, unconscious, and therefore non-reality-based mentality of the infant, as well as of the primitive culture, the neurotic patient, and the religious person. Found in dreams and symptoms, the primary process works through substitution, indirect reference, and above all symbolism. Jung, originally a follower of Freud, concurred in own essay "Concerning the Two Kinds of Thinking," distinguishing between "reality thinking" (which is logical, practical, and discursive) and "fantasy thinking" (which "turns away from reality, sets free subjective wishes, and is, in regard to adaptation, wholly unproductive").[8] Such thinking, Jung insisted, lay at the foundation of ancient and primitive societies, of the mentality of children and neurotics, and of dreams and religion. In a more or less similar vein, Max Mueller considered religion to be a disease of language, the result of taking symbols or metaphors literally: for instance, it is fine to use the moon to rhapsodize on supernatural forces, or to take breath (*spiritus* in Latin) as a symbol of life, but to insist that the moon *is* a supernatural being or that spirit *is* an actual thing or entity is a mistake.

A completely different approach to religion is practiced in sociology and anthropology, which propose social rather than mental/emotional definitions and explanations for religion. Perhaps the most influential social theorist was Émile Durkheim, who defined religion in his seminal *The Elementary Forms of the Religious Life* as "a unified system of beliefs and practices relative to sacred things, that is to say, things set aside and forbidden—beliefs and practices which unite into one single moral community called a church, all those who adhere to them."[9] For Durkheim, as for the psychologists, the basic question was why religion exists in the first place or, in more Durkheimian terms, where the idea of religion originally came from. His assertion is that society exists prior to all thought or speculation, and therefore that religion is a symbolic representation of social relations. The important contribution of religion to society is integration and cohesion, that is, the establishment and perpetuation of the "moral community" or group with shared norms and values. This is crucial to remember: contrary to William James's opinion that religion is "the feelings, acts, and experiences of individual men in their solitude, so far as they apprehend themselves to stand in relation to whatever they may consider the divine,"[10] religion is collective and social through and through, and the "solitary" feelings, acts, and experiences of individuals have been inculcated in them as, in Durkheim's terms, collective representations. Religion in this view is not only representational but also constitutive: it forms and transforms individuals into certain kinds of people and binds them into a certain kind of community. For him, ritual plays the crucial role, providing an occasion for collective ideas and feelings to be experienced, performed, and deeply instilled.

While Durkheim saw religion as a (more or less) accurate representation of society, Karl Marx criticized it as not only an inaccurate but also an intentionally misleading representation of society. Famous for equating religion to opium, the complaint of Marx was that it is a system to justify and literally disguise or invert unjust social and economic arrangements and to keep the oppressed masses in their place. For instance, in Hinduism each person is led to believe that he or she has earned his or her caste position through past lives and actions and therefore deserves whatever status he or she occupies; resistance to the system would be futile and self-defeating. Similarly, in medieval Christianity the believer was instructed that feudal class arrangements were God given, so peasants should accept their lot and direct their efforts to otherworldly rewards, not to seeking rewards, let alone changes, in this world.

In recent years, a symbolic approach to religion, without the theoretical baggage of Freud and Jung and Marx, has emerged. One of the most frequently quoted recent definitions of religion was thus suggested by the American anthropologist Clifford Geertz, who called it "a system of symbols which act to establish powerful, pervasive, and long-lasting moods and motivations in men by formulating conceptions of a general order of existence and clothing these conceptions with such an aura of factuality that the moods and motivations seem uniquely realistic."[11] His point, which will be significant as we proceed, is that through religion human beings are rendered likely to think, feel, and act in particular ways precisely because they think that the (natural and supernatural) world works in particular ways—that is, because the religious account of the world is *true*, certain courses of human behavior are *necessary and good*.

The Building Blocks of Religion

These and many other definitions and theories of religion have been offered, and there is no benefit in trying to settle on one. Religion is all these things or can be seen from all these perspectives. Quite possibly, like violence, religion does not have an essence, a single distinguishing quality, but rather is a varied, internally diverse, composite, and sometimes ambiguous and even contradictory phenomenon. We might be better served, then, to think about the kinds of components that religions can include rather than the one essential factor that they supposedly all share.

For instance, the *Encyclopedia of Philosophy* offers a list of features that commonly occur across religions, without asserting that any or all of them are universal to religions. These include (1) belief in supernatural beings; (2) a distinction between sacred and profane objects; (3) ritual acts focused on sacred objects; (4) a moral code believed to be sanctioned by the spirits; (5) characteristically religious feelings (awe, sense of mystery, sense of guilt, adoration), which tend to be aroused in the presence of sacred objects and during the practice of ritual, and which are connected in idea with the spirits; (6) prayer and other forms of communication with spirits; (7) a world view, or a general picture of the world as a whole and the place of the individual therein, which contains some specification of an overall purpose or point of the world and an indication of how the individual fits into it; (8) a more or less total organization of one's life based on the world view; and (9) a social group bound together by all of the above. Any actual religion, then, would be a system of thought that contains some of or all these elements.

The anthropologist Anthony Wallace was one of the first to elaborate such a view of religion. In his theory, religion starts from a fundamental premise; it is then built up out of blocks or elements or modules of religious behavior that are aggregated into bigger and bigger systems until they emerge as "a religion." The absolute foundation of religion, he says, is the "supernatural premise," the idea that supernatural things exist; without this, there would be no religion. Next, potential units or atoms of religious behavior are selected and combined in various ways. He identifies thirteen such "elementary particles" of religion, including

- prayer, or speech directed to supernatural entities
- music and dancing and singing
- physiological exercises, including substance use and physical hardships and trials
- exhortation or orders, encouragements, and threats
- myth, or narratives about supernatural entities
- simulation or imitation such as magic, witchcraft, and ritual
- mana, or ideas about the power one gets from contact with powerful or sacred objects
- taboo, or prohibitions against contact with certain things
- feasts
- sacrifice
- congregation, or group gathering and activity
- inspiration, such as hallucination and mysticism
- symbols

Particular assemblages of these behaviors form "ritual complexes," which are subsequently explained and justified by myths (for Wallace, ritual is primary over myth, and action generally over thought or meaning). Ritual complexes are further combined to form "cult institutions," which are ultimately combined to form a religion. A *religion*, therefore, he defines as "a loosely related group of cult institutions and other, even less well-organized special practices and beliefs."[12]

More recent work by Pascal Boyer, Scott Atran, and Lee Kirkpatrick has taken the modular approach to religion in another direction. All three agree that religion is not a discrete or independent thing but a "by-product" of more general, preexisting, and not uniquely religious psychological and social processes. Kirkpatrick, an evolutionary psychologist, emphasizes the factor of attachment, the psychological tendency to reach out to and bond with an "other," ideally one who will care for us (the first and major attachment figure is the mother). Religious beings then become abstract or superhuman attachment figures.[13] Boyer, an anthropologist, stresses the evolved mental predispositions of humans, the nature of social living, the processes of information exchange, and the generation of knowledge by deriving inferences from experience. Central to the latter is the concept of agency, that is, that there is an "agent" or mind—humanlike in many ways—behind phenomena or events.[14] (Kirkpatrick calls this "psychological animism.") All three share a focus on what Atran, also an anthropologist, calls "mental modules," the functional components of perception, emotion, and conceptualization that underlie all human thought and experience. In Atran's words, "Religious beliefs and practices involve the very same cognitive and affective structures as nonreligious beliefs and practices—and no others—but in (more or less) systematically distinctive ways."[15] Likewise, from Boyer's perspective, religion is a distinct way of thinking or acting but is entirely constructed out of "mental systems and capacities that are there anyway. . . . [Therefore] the notion of religion as a special domain is not just unfounded but in fact rather ethnocentric."[16]

In this view, when general-purpose cognitive, emotional, and behavioral traits are mixed and deployed in certain ways they are "religion," and when they are mixed and deployed in other ways they are not "religion." This suggests a number of important implications. First, as we said above, religion is not a thing but rather a composite; no one element or module is essential. Second, the modules that compose religion are not themselves essentially "religious"; even William James, a defender of religion, had to admit that there is nothing essentially religious about religious emotions:

There is religious fear, religious love, religious awe, religious joy, and so forth. But religious love is only man's natural emotion of love directed to a religious object; religious fear is only the ordinary fear of commerce, so to speak, the common quaking of the human breast, in so far as the notion of divine retribution may arouse it; religious awe is the same organic thrill which we feel in a forest at twilight, or in a mountain gorge; only this time it comes over us at the thought of our supernatural relations; and similarly of all the various sentiments which may be called into play in the lives of religious persons. . . . As there thus seems to be no one elementary religious emotion, but only a common storehouse of emotions upon which religious objects may draw, so there might conceivably also prove to be no one specific and essential kind of religious object, and no one specific and essential kind of religious act.[17]

The same is true of Wallace's particles of ritual: every one of them has a nonreligious corollary (with the possible exception of sacrifice, although there is a metaphorical kind of secular sacrifice that does not usually involve killing). In other words, there is religious music and nonreligious music, religious exercise and nonreligious exercise, religious narrative and nonreligious narrative, and so on. Therefore, and third, there is little if anything that separates religion from nonreligion, other than the supernatural premise that there are nonhuman entities or agents at work in the world. In fact, these nonhuman agents are surprisingly, often disappointingly, human in their attitudes and actions. Finally, since religion is a modular and composite phenomenon whose modules are not uniquely religious, it follows that all sorts of other normal human traits and tendencies could also become connected and enmeshed with religion. Among these would be politics, economics, gender, technology, popular culture, and of course violence. Normal human violence, directed toward religious objects and goals or related to religious groups and beliefs and causes, becomes religious violence.

POPULATING THE RELIGIOUS DOMAIN: BEINGS, FORCES, AND "TYPES" OF RELIGION

The foregoing discussion suggests a different, more inclusive, and more productive view of religion than is usually found. As I stated at the opening of this chapter, monotheism—a religious belief system premised on the existence of a single god—is the most familiar form of religion to most Americans and Westerners, but as we are about to learn, it is not the only or in fact the most common one. Even worse, Christian or Judeo-Christian monotheism carries with it a language—of *sin* and *hell* and *heaven* and *salvation*, and so on, including the very concept of *god* itself—that is not universal to and therefore not applicable to all or even most religions.

In the following section we will see that a religion can function perfectly well (and most have) without a concept like "god." What religions cannot seem to function without is some concept of other-than-human agents—beings or entities that are dissimilar to humans in some ways (they may live longer or forever, they may be at least sometimes disembodied, and they may have extraordinary powers) but similar to humans in other ways, particularly in having mind or will or intention. This is why anthropologist Robin Horton concluded that

> in every situation commonly labeled religious we are dealing with action directed towards objects which are believed to respond in terms of certain categories—in our own culture those of purpose, intelligence, and emotion—which are also the distinctive categories for the description of human action. The application of these categories leads us to say that such objects are "personified." The relationship between human beings and religious objects can be further defined as governed by certain ideas of patterning and obligation such as characterize relationships among human beings. In short, Religion can be looked upon as an extension of the field of people's social relationships beyond the confines of purely human society. And for completeness' sake, we should perhaps add the rider that this extension must be one in which human beings involved see themselves in a dependent position vis-à-vis their nonhuman alters.[18]

In other words, the specific kinds of nonhuman and superhuman entities or agents could be and actually are quite diverse, but they share cross-culturally two qualities that make them interesting to and relevant to humans: they have minds or personalities that are recognizable and at least partly knowable, and they interact with us humans in recognizably social ways. In short, they are like—or they *are*—"persons" in our social world.

Graham Harvey has summed this position well in his *Animism: Respecting the Living World*. In the animistic/religious worldview,

> the world is full of persons, only some of whom are human, and . . . life is always lived in relationships with others. . . . Persons are beings, rather than objects, who are animated and social toward others (even if they are not always

sociable). [Religion] may involve learning how to recognize who is a person and what is not—because it is not always obvious and not all [religions] agree that everything that exists is alive or personal.[19]

Persons, or personal agents, are inherently and almost necessarily social. They are "those with whom other persons interact with varying degrees of reciprocity," not to mention respect and deference (especially if they are singly powerful persons). "Persons may be spoken *with*. Objects, by contrast, are usually spoken *about*. Persons are volitional, relational, cultural, and social beings. They demonstrate intentionality and agency with varying degrees of autonomy and freedom."[20] It is of little concern that "some persons look like objects"—such as animals or plants or mountains or moons—or, for that matter, that some cannot be seen at all.

From this analysis, religions share an agentive-personal perspective on reality, namely, that humans are not the only "persons" or volitional, relational beings in existence. Where religions diverge is in what particular kinds of non-human agents they posit. Some religions have many, others have few. Some have powerful, creative, and moral agents; others do not. As Harvey reminds us, these nonhuman agents need not be particularly pleasant or kind: they may be angry, mischievous, irascible, or indifferent, too. And finally, these nonhuman agents are not mutually exclusive: it is absolutely not the case that religions that include one kind of agent (say, gods) always exclude any other kind. In fact, investigation shows conclusively that religions are modular here, too, such that the various kinds of religious entities and agents can be mixed in endless ways. Ultimately, it makes no sense to talk about "types" of religion (as in "theism" as a type of religion) but rather about "components" of religion, of which god(s) are one.

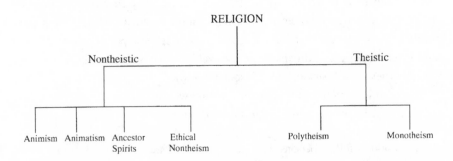

Fig. 2.1. "Types" or Components of Religion

Religious Beings (Nonhuman)

As we have stressed several times in this chapter already, gods are the most familiar and, for many people, the paradigmatic religious beings. However, across religions there are many different kinds of nonhuman and superhuman beings, with an almost infinite array of personalities and powers. These beings are typically referred to as "spirits" and include gods as well as other kinds of disembodied or immaterial agents. However, the distinction between gods and other spiritual beings is imperfect at best and not universally true in all religions. For instance, Levy, Mageo, and Howard argue that "spirits" and "gods" fall at opposite ends of "a continuum of culturally defined spiritual entities ranging from well-defined, socially encompassing beings at one pole, to socially marginal, fleeting presences at the other."[21] They would have us understand that gods are among the former, while spirits are the latter. Gods and spirits allegedly differ in four ways: structure, personhood, experience, and morality. By *structure* they mean that gods are associated with more elaborated social institutions, including priesthoods, shrines, and festivals, as well as with specific territories; spirits are less elaborated and more "fluid," "emergent, contingent, and unexpected."[22] In terms of personhood, gods are more physically and socially human, while spirits are "vague . . . only minimally persons."[23] Gods, they insist, are also less directly experienced than spirits, which are more commonly encountered and often more immediately the objects of human concern, since they are lower and more accessible beings. Finally, the authors suggest that gods are more likely to be agents and paragons of the moral order than spirits, which tend to be "extramoral" or evil. Gods instead "are clear models for social order"[24] who ordain and sanction human morality, but spirits "are threats to order and frequently must be purged so that order may be reestablished."[25]

As lucid and appealing as this case is, it is not supported by the cross-cultural evidence. Many religions include gods who are not at all elaborated nor represented by priesthoods nor attached to any particular spatial locations (in fact, the Christian god is not spatially situated but global and universal; see p. 65, section on world religions.) On the other hand, spirits are often quite highly elaborated, with individual names, histories, and personalities, and if anything spirits are more commonly associated with particular places (mountains, lakes, waterfalls, etc.) than gods are. Further, spirits are frequently more humanlike than gods, with appetites, grudges, families, homes, and such. While it is true that "lower spirits" often act as intermediaries between humans and "high gods," not all gods have this kind of midlevel spirit rank to call upon (e.g., Catholic Christianity has a rank of intermediary saints, but Protestant Christianity does not). Finally for our purposes, gods are often not moral agents nor moral exemplars, like the Greek gods, whose immorality was the cause for much consternation and speculation among early philosophers.

So, rather than making a hard distinction between gods and other spirits, let us regard gods as a type of spirits and then consider some of the diversity in religious notions about nonhuman agents. The religions of the world include anywhere from a few to a vast number of spirits. Some are named and well known, while others are vague and mysterious. Some have humanlike personalities, and others are quite foreign or inhuman. Some are good to or considerate of humans, others are malicious, and still others are capricious or apathetic. All of them can have an impact on human life for better or worse; the very existence of spirits means that humans must conduct themselves in different ways—in more circumspect ways—than if spirits did not exist.

Some spirits are associated with or take particular material forms. Frequently these forms include animals and plants, as well as natural objects (rocks, mountains, rivers, the sun and moon) and forces (wind, thunder); they may also be connected to particular sites and locations. It is the idea that spirits give life to such material and often inanimate objects that accounts for the common term for this religious belief: *animism*. For instance, Australian Aboriginal societies, sometimes held up as the model of animistic religions, believed that plants, animals, and other natural phenomena had or possessed spirit essences that they shared with physical locations as well as with humans; hence, certain places were "snake" or "kangaroo" or "fire" sacred sites, at which the proper myths and rituals had to be performed. Failure to perform human religious duties could result in various kinds of misfortune. The Anutans in the Solomon Islands had a category of spirits called *atua* or *atua vare* who inhabited the area outside the village; they did not have individual names or personalities, but they did have bodies, and they caused accidents and difficulties, although more to scare than to harm.[26] Nukulaelae islanders spoke of spirits called Te Lasi or "the Big Ones" with known names and identities. Powerful and evil, with wills of their own, they took various forms, including babies, animals, or sea creatures; they were typically female and killed out of their anger, mostly by strangulation, suffocation, or "consumption" of the victim.[27] Among the Ainu of northern Japan, virtually all plants, animals, and even humanmade objects were "spirit-owning" or "spirit-bearing" beings. During their "life" there were restrictions on how humans could interact with them, and even in "death" these restrictions continued; for instance, people had to keep a separate location for the disposal of each type of spirit-owning being, called *keyohniusi*, or otherwise these beings could bring sickness or worse.[28]

In Melford Spiro's research in Burma, he found various demons, such as the *bilus* or ogre that eats humans. However, the most elaborated part of the religion was the set of *nats*, which included (1) nature spirits, (2) *devas* or Buddhist and therefore benevolent beings, and (3) the "thirty-seven nats." Nature spirits were associated with and guarded their particular locations, taking the form of such beings as *taw-saun nat* or *taung-saun nat*, the guardians of the forest or hill, respectively. Collectively they made the world a treacherous place. But worse were the thirty-seven *nats* or powerful beings called *thounze khunna min nat* or "thirty-seven chief *nats*." They were distinctly malevolent, each with a name and its own mythical story, and they had to be propitiated with gifts of food.[29]

Often more powerful, but not always more benevolent, are the gods. Many religions include gods, often along with other spiritual beings, but many others do not, and among those that do include gods, their conceptions of gods vary widely. Asked to define *god*, most Westerners and Christians would likely give an answer similar to the one given by the theologian Richard Swinburne: "a person without a body (i.e., a spirit) present everywhere, the creator and sustainer of the universe, able to do everything (i.e., omnipotent), knowing all things, perfectly good, a source of moral obligation, immutable, eternal, a necessary being, holy and worthy of worship."[30] However, as can be seen and must be seen, this is not the definition of *god* but *the description of a particular god*, namely, the Christian god. Indisputably, not all gods fit this description.

The !Kung, a foraging society in Africa's Kalahari desert, would be most people's candidate for a nontheistic religion. Yet the !Kung believed in two gods, the great god Gao Na and the lesser god Kauha (among other things; see below). Each had a wife and children and lived in the sky. Gao Na had the form of a human and brought both good and bad to humans through the dead ancestors and other intermediary spirits. He was known for having human emotions and enjoyed food and sex; he was not a moral paragon but performed immoral acts like incest and cannibalism.[31] In this and other ways, the !Kung gods resembled the ancient Greek gods, some of whom were good and some of whom were bad, but none of whom was morally perfect and all of whom could be dangerous to humans.

The Konyak Nagas of India believed in a morally active god called Gawang or Zangbau who was a highly personal being and the creator of the universe. He had the form of a gargantuan human and was called upon in daily life and the main social occasions in culture; he was a protector of morality who punished wrongdoing. On the other hand, the Azande of Africa had a god named Mbori or Mboli who was morally neutral and not terribly interested in human affairs. The people of Gopalpur in India had both helpful and harmful gods, based on their gender: male gods were benevolent, but goddesses punished as well as protected. Between these extremes are all sorts of complex variations on the god theme. The god of the Kaguru of East Africa, named Mulungu, was a universe creator, but the religion did not contain the story of this creation nor did people care very much; Mulungu himself was imagined as humanlike but with only one foot or arm or eye or ear. The islanders of Ulithi in Micronesia knew about several gods, none of whom were creators, and their religion contained no creation story. There was a high god, Ialulep, who was described as very large, old, weak, and with white hair, and who held the "thread of life" of each person and decided when a person would die by breaking the thread. Under him were numerous sky gods and earth gods, including ones with more or less specific natural and social juris-dictions, like Palulap the Great Navigator, Ialulwe the patron god of sailors, Solang the patron god of canoe builders, as well as the high god's son Lugeilang, who liked the company of human women and fathered the trickster god Iolofath.

Clearly then, not all gods are good or at least purely good. Mboli was a morally ambivalent or passive god, like many Greek gods. Such gods either do both good and evil or are unconcerned about the distinction (not all religions possess a concept of "evil" like that of Judeo-Christianity). Even the Judeo-Christian god is associated at moments with good and evil alike: in the Torah/Old Testament, the Judeo-Christian god Yahweh states, "I form the light and create darkness: I make peace and create evil: I, the Lord, do all these things" through his prophet (Isaiah 45:7). Exodus 15:3 maintains, "The Lord is a man of war: the Lord is his name." And the book of Job, which is centrally concerned with the problem of evil, offers no real solution; when questioned by Job about the goodness and morality of letting Job suffer, Yahweh merely thunders back that Job has no right to ask the question.[32]

Monotheisms (religions with only one god), especially omnibenevolent monotheisms (whose one god is purportedly all good) have the most intense problem with evil. One perennial solution is dualism, that is, the claim that there is a second being or force of malevolence opposing (but presumably not equal to, since that would make him/it a god as well) the all-good god. Christianity takes this approach, positing a Satan (from the Hebrew *shaitan* for adversary or enemy) or devil as the foil for its god; just as Yahweh is all good, Satan is all evil—or still worse, an apostate angel, a traitor to heaven. Maybe the most famous and histor-ically influential religious dualism was that of Zoroaster or Zarathustra, whose religion depicted a universe with two equal forces—light (Ahura Mazda) and darkness (Ahriman or Angra Mainyu)—in continuous conflict and struggle. Angra Mainyu was a kind of countercreator or anticreator who was responsible for bringing the serpent, plagues, "plunder and sin," unbelief, "tears and wailing," and the 99,999 diseases into the otherwise perfect creation of Ahura Mazda. Accordingly, the two gods and their forces were perpetually at war, making all creation a battleground and humans soldiers in this cosmic war.

Religious Beings (Human)

In addition to the extrahuman spirits and gods, most if not all religions see humans themselves as spiritual beings in some sense, that is, as having an aspect or component of spirit to them. Christianity is certainly such a religion. Its god gave life to lifeless matter by breathing spirit into that matter. Thus humans in this religious view are composite beings, with material bodies and immaterial spirits. At the end of their lives, their spiritual component will survive, even eternally, and enjoy reward or suffer punishment in a spiritual realm.

The Judeo-Christian notion of human spirit, or "soul," has a set of distinct qualities. It is, for instance, personal (i.e., it retains at least some of the nature or "personality" of the individual), nonmaterial, unitary (i.e., there is only one, and it does not contain parts), indestructible, yet detachable from the body. Not all religions contain such a concept. The Tausug people of the Philippines tra-ditionally believed that the soul was a composite of four parts. The "transcen-dent soul" was not even in the body but always in the supernatural realm, and was all good. The "life soul" was associated with the body, especially the blood, but could detach and roam during dreams. The "breath" was the life force and was always attached to the body, while the "spirit soul" was a kind of shadow that could also roam. The Dusun of Borneo held that humans had seven soul-bits, one lodged inside the other and ranging in size from the thickness of the thumb to the thickness of the pinky finger. The six outside souls or *magalugulu* looked like a shadow of human shape, but the innermost soul or *gadagada* was invisible and shapeless. The Konyak Nagas spoke of several invisible parts to humans that separated and went different ways at death; the *yaha*, containing much of the individual's personality, went to the land of the dead, the *hiba* would become a ghost if the person died a violent death, but the *mia* stayed connected to the head—one reason why headhunting made sense in their culture. Even in Buddhist teaching, the spiritual part of a person is not eternal and unchanging or entirely personal; in fact, a key concept in Buddhism is *anatta* or "no self/soul," that is, that there is no unchanging essence of a person.

If humans have a supernatural or spiritual facet while they live, it is conceivable that it would remain active after they die as well. In the Christian and many other views, the soul part(s) go(es) somewhere out of communication with the living (although not all Christians completely share this opinion, as psychics and séances illustrate); in other religions, however, the deceased continued to interact with and affect the living, often for the worse, giving us the term *ancestor worship* (despite the fact that societies did not always "worship" or even like their dead). The !Kung said that their dead ancestors, called *//gauwasi* or *//gangwasi*, represented a danger to the living not out the ancestors' evil but out of their loneliness; aware of and sad for their living loved ones, the dead would try to bring the living to the afterlife with them, with undesirable results for the living. The Burmese villagers that Spiro studied saw the spirits of their dead or *leikpya* as potential mischief makers that remained around the house or village and haunted its living inhabitants. More worrisome than the ordinary dead were the spirits of those who lived wicked lives, for they were transformed into *tasei* or *thaye*, evil ghosts. Villagers recounted that these beings were usually invisible but could become visible, with a "flimsy and resilient materiality." They were enormous (over seven feet tall) beings, dark or black, with huge ears, tongues, and tusklike teeth—"repulsive in every way"—that camped on the edge of the village, especially near burial grounds, from whence they would eat corpses or attack and consume the living.[33] According to the Navajos, a ghost was the evil part of the deceased person, so ghosts were all evil by definition. The Dani of New Guinea also claimed that most ghosts were malevolent beings, who tended to attack living adults from the front.

Normal humans after death can be harmful to their living peers intentionally or unintentionally. However, many religions also teach that there are certain kinds of living humans who are dangerous and malevolent, such as witches and sorcerers. The broad but not totally consistent distinction between these two types of beings is that sorcerers tend to depend on skill and technique while witches tend to have a (super)natural talent or even physical capacity for malice. In fact, a great many societies have believed that misfortune, including sickness, death, and bad luck, was never really a random or natural occurrence but that there was always some agent involved, human or otherwise. The Bunyoro of Africa insisted that a sorcerer deliberately inflicted harm on victims through a mixture of natural and supernatural means, usually targeting those fairly close to him in proximity and kinship.

> A sorcerer is a person who wants to kill people. He may do it by blowing medicine toward them, or by putting it in the victim's food or water, or by hiding it in the path where he must pass. People practice sorcery against those whom they hate. They practice it against those who steal from them, and also against people who are richer than they are. Sorcery is brought about by envy, hatred, and quarreling.[34]

On Ulithi, people actually hired sorcerers secretly to do evil to those "whom they feel are guilty of ill will or overt action against them."[35] The materials employed included "magical starfish, live lizards, and coconut oil" that had been sung over and planted in or near the victim's house; also potions might be poured on the victim's comb or clothing. Apache sorcerers used an array of techniques, including poisons, spells, and "injection" of a foreign substance into the person's body. Males were more often sorcerers because they were held to be more prone to *kedn* or "anger" than women.

Witches cross-culturally bear no resemblance to the American image of an old woman in a pointed hat riding a broom. Among the Menomini Indians, all elders were believed to be witches; hence, younger members of society observed the morals and norms out of fear of the power of the elder witches. In most religions, witches have been perceived as more specific, usually particular individuals, although again, often most or all adversity is blamed on them. The Azande of the Sudan saw witches at work everywhere:

> If blight seizes the ground-nut crop it is witchcraft; if the bush is vaingloriously scoured for game it is witchcraft; if women laboriously bale water out of a pool and are rewarded by but a few small fish it is witchcraft; if termites do not rise when their swarming is due and a cold useless night is spent in waiting for their flight it is witchcraft; if a wife is sulky and unresponsive to her husband it is witchcraft; if a prince is cold and distant with his subjects it is witchcraft; if a magical rite fails to achieve its purpose it is witchcraft; if, in fact, any failure or misfortune falls upon anyone at any time and in relation to any of the manifold activities of his life it may be due to witchcraft.[36]

The Swazi of southern Africa believed in both witches and sorcerers, which together made up the class of *batsakatsi* or "evil-doers." Witches had an innate physiological and psychological potential for evil, the capacity for which belongs to men and women but is only passed along by women. The Kaguru of eastern Africa also said that witches (*wahai*) were congenitally evil people, the ontological opposite of normal human beings. The Dani of New Guinea maintained that they did not engage in witchcraft because they lacked the ability. However, their neighbors practiced it, by physical (e.g., poison) or supernatural (e.g., pointing a stick at a victim) means. They were known to hunt down and kill suspected witches among their neighbors—a form of justifiable homicide.

Witches and sorcerers can thus be seen as a source and a target of much human evil. They were believed to cause harm, often on the basis of negative emotions like anger or jealousy but often because it was simply their nature. Since they were understood to cause harm, they were also subjected to harm, resisted and opposed sometimes by magical and ritual means and sometimes by physical force. Even the Judeo-Christian scriptures order that believers should "not suffer a witch to live" (Exodus 22:18), and many believers throughout history have taken the order seriously (see chapter 5). More people have (we can safely assume) died from witchcraft accusations than from witchcraft.

Before pressing on, it is worth noting that, just as the line between spirits and gods is vague and porous, so is the line between humans and "nonhuman" spirits. Dead humans often ascended to god status, and living humans (such as the Egyptian pharaohs or Mayan kings) were sometimes regarded as gods on earth. In other cases, gods or spirits might take human form or descend or decline into human status. According to Stanley Tambiah, for instance, villagers in northeastern Thailand believed that the Buddhist gods could only advance in their spiritual quest by reincarnation as humans.[37] Among the Sherpas of Nepal, the gods could not empathize with humans enough to grant them favors unless the gods took corporeal form, dwelling temporarily in "bodies" made of dough.

Religious Forces

Depending on the religion, instead of or in addition to spiritual beings, there may be forces that impinge on or determine the quality of human life as well. This religious idea is known as *animatism*. The main difference between supernatural beings and forces is that the former tend to be "personal" or even persons (that is, they have minds and wills and personalities), whereas the latter tend to be "impersonal." Supernatural forces are energies or principles, like a kind of spiritual electricity or gravity. Some of the most familiar of these include the Chinese concept of *chi* and the Polynesian concept of *mana*. Each has its own properties, though not personalities, and the humans who understand and use those properties thrive and succeed while those who do not struggle and fail. Other such forces or principles that Americans and Westerners often refer to, with varying degrees of seriousness or of awareness of their supernatural connotations, are *fate*, *luck*, and *destiny*.

There are many permutations of this idea. The Dusun believed in and fretted about a kind of luck that was a finite spiritual resource of each individual; a person could expend his or her quantity of luck in one area of life and so endanger other areas (e.g., acquisition of property, success in disputes, etc.). Also, luck was finite in society, making one person's gain in it another person's loss; this naturally led to arguments about attempts to steal or damage each other's luck. The Apache organized their actions around a power known as *diyi*, which was in infinite supply. Many forms of this power were recognized, related to different animals or natural phenomena. In a twist, diyi did have some personal attributes, including the ability to seek out people to attach to (individuals could also seek diyi) and to experience anger, which could of course be harmful to humans. The Menomini of North America also spoke of a power that they called *tatahkesewen* ("that which has energy"), *meskowesan* ("that which has strength"), or *ahpehtesewesen* ("that which is valuable"). They described it as nonmaterial and invisible but like a bright light. This form of power could also be sought and mastered, through dreams, vision quests, and the guidance of guardian spirits.

Ideas about spiritual forces can be particularly important in terms of religious roles like the shaman and religious activities like curing illness or preventing or recovering from misfortune. In !Kung religion, which includes gods, ancestor spirits, and nature spirits, there was also a type of energy called *n/um*. Richard Lee defines it as a "substance that lies in the pit of the stomach of men and women . . . and becomes active during a healing dance. The !Kung believe that the movements of the dancers heat the n/um up and when it boils it rises up the spinal cord and explodes in the brain."[38] With this power under control, the shaman could perform supernatural feats like traveling to the spirit world and curing disease (on the assumption that the cause of the disease was spiritual in the first place).

Finally, the Tallensi in Africa had a concept that is similar to the Western notion of destiny. In the Tallensi version, humans were born with a good or evil destiny that determined the course of their lives. An evil destiny was indicated by the person's refusal or inability to perform his or her social roles and obligations; a person's successful performance of social expectations was proof of a good destiny. Interestingly, destiny and the dead ancestors were interrelated, since it was the spirits of ancestors who gave a person his or her fate. But fortunately the person born with an evil destiny could be helped, on the premise that ancestors were potentially amenable to reversing their original assignment of destiny through rituals and supplications.

Another form that nonpersonal supernatural influences on human life can take is that of a principle or the very order of the universe. This is perhaps best represented in the Hindu and Buddhist traditions, which are historically related. Hinduism, a complex and diverse religious worldview, includes a vast array of gods, many of them ambivalent in numerous ways (in terms of benevolence, gender, etc.). However, even the gods themselves are subject to a universal order or *dharma* in which life and death, creation and destruction, move in an unending cycle. All things—humans, animals, the gods themselves, and the universe as a whole—arise and decline, only to arise again. The human life cycle is short (a few decades), the cycle of the gods is longer, and the cycle of the universe is millions of years, but all things are eventually destroyed and recreated. The principle that underlies this system is *karma*, the spiritual cause and effect that links the present cycle to the last and to the next.

One manifestation of karma is reincarnation. Humans, and all other creatures, struggle through an indefinite number of incarnations on their path to enlightenment and release from *samsara*, the cycle of life and death. These various incarnations constitute steps or stages along the path, the higher stages being more spiritually aware and purer than the lower ones. Within the human domain, there are different levels of spiritual attainment, the castes. Individuals are assigned to castes by birth and occupation, but most fundamentally by spiritual condition: those who lived virtuous past lives move up the caste system, and those who did not live virtuous lives move down. The terrestrial ramifications of this spiritual progression are major: lower-caste individuals do harder and dirtier work and enjoy lower status than their social and spiritual superiors. Humans who are sufficiently wicked can sink below the human level to animals, plants, insects, or worse. Each stage on the progression has its particular duty or dharma, so there is theoretically no remorse for those who are on lower levels: they are working their way either up or down, by their own deeds. One of the most interesting aspects of the dharma is the role or caste of *kshatriyas*, the nobility and warrior caste. One of their duties is to make war, which necessarily involves killing (see chapter 7).

Buddhism starts from some similar premises but develops them in different ways. According to the Buddha, the unenlightened person is also doomed to reincarnate again and again until he or she achieves enlightenment and becomes a buddha or enlightened one. However, a person does not have to wait an infinite number of lifetimes to complete this project; it can be accomplished in this lifetime. The secret is the knowledge and the method for doing so. The knowledge takes the form of the discovery that the first Buddha made, namely, the Four Noble Truths. The first truth is that existence is *dukkha* or suffering, literally "broken" or "flawed." This condition cannot be changed, and it cannot really be explained. It just is. To live is to suffer, and to die is to suffer. To lose the things you want or to have the things you do not want is equally suffering. The second truth asserts that the cause of this suffering is attachment, or desire. Attachment to our wealth, our loved ones, and our own body and life exposes us to suffering. We cannot eradicate suffering, but we can avoid it by the third truth, detachment, or lack of desire. If we do not love our wealth, we cannot be pained at its loss. The same is true with our family and our own self: detachment from them removes the opportunity to suffer. The means to achieve this state is the fourth truth, known as the Eightfold Path. It teaches the correct behaviors and attitudes and thoughts for becoming enlightened, one of the central of which is *ahimsa*, or nonharm, and expresses itself in various ways, including vegetarianism.

"LOCAL" VERSUS "WORLD" RELIGIONS

The human world has been and continues to be characterized by a multitude of religious beliefs and practices, all of which make a place for and give explanations for violence. However, as Ernest Gellner has designated it, one of the "big divides in human history" is the consolidation of a few "world religions" out of the world's multitudinous traditional or tribal religions.[39] Not only are the world religions larger and more widely distributed around the globe, but also they have a distinct set of qualities—ones that also tend to promote violence more extensively.

Until a few thousand years ago, all religions were "local" or small-scale ones. Essentially, each was the belief of one particular society: the Piaroa of Venezuela had their own religion, the Warlpiri of Australia their own, the !Kung of Africa their own, and so on. Such a religion—often called a "folk" or "traditional" religion—was local in two senses. It belonged to or applied to one specific group of people, as well as to one specific territory. In fact, often if not ordinarily these two factors were interdependent: spirits or forces pertained to definite spatial locations, and humans inhabited those locations along with them. Both spirits/forces and humans were often seen as autochthonous, literally sprung from the ground they occupied. Naturally, ancestors of present humans also dwelled in those locations, since the group had occupied the same space for generations.

Accordingly, local religions really were and are local—relevant or "true" only for the local society. This is critical in two ways. First, such a religion cannot spread or expand, for it is tied to place; it is limited in its possible scope. It would be quite pointless to try to proselytize the religion. Second, and related to this, such a religion is not very troubled by the existence of other, even contradictory, religions. Virtually all traditional societies were aware of neighbors with divergent religions (as well as other customs). Sometimes they even disapproved of the beliefs and practices of their neighbors. But essentially, those foreign religions were of no great concern to them; each group, each region, had its own spirits or gods or forces, and what was true or important for one group or region would not necessarily be true for another. Multiple, diverse, and contradictory "truths" were the order of the day.

One other factor acted to constrain the contentiousness of local religions: they were usually preliterate. Without writing, there was no set scripture, no authoritative word. Religious knowledge depended on malleable human memory, and it was also *distributed* among the society. No single individual, even in a small society like an Australian Aboriginal one, could—or had the right to—know all knowledge or perform all practices. Individuals were charged with responsibility for the knowledge of their personal or family sites or spirits or of the visions and revelations they received. This did not mean, of course, that there was no disputation within the society over the details and meanings of religious phenomena; there certainly were. But it did mean that there was no "ultimate authority" to which people could appeal or the interpretation of which they could fight about.

Thus, Gellner has summarized the nature of local religions as

- concrete, that is, not particularly given to "speculation" and intense philosophical introspection. Rather, they "take for granted" the truth of their beliefs and the efficacy of their actions as "self-evident";

- ad hoc, in the sense that they deal with specific spiritual or practical problems when they arise rather than establishing a permanent self-sustaining "institution" and "orthodoxy";
- noncodified, especially not written down and "settled" into a "canon" of official dogma; and
- "patently social." The religion and its society are tightly interwoven. People do not so much *believe* their religion as *do* it. The "beliefs" of the religion mirror and reinforce the "morality" or behavioral imperatives of it. In other words, the realm of ideas or beliefs is also the world of action and value.

Societies with such religions were not necessarily nonviolent; in actuality, some were intensely violent. Some even practiced particular well-established forms of religious violence, whether sacrifice or sorcery or the killing of witches. However, other, more "modern" and large-scale manifestations of religious violence were lacking.

Less than five thousand years ago, and then only gradually, a new kind of religion began to emerge. The key contributors to this new development were writing, centralized political systems, and plural or multicultural societies. In the first couple millennia, religions were still predominantly local: Mesopotamian or Greek cities had their own unique local gods, priests, and rules. Even ancient Hebrew writings suggest that their god was precisely that— *their* god, one god among many gods but the one who had formed a bond with their nation among the many nations and their land among the many lands. The other gods were not false; they were merely the gods of other people (a religious position known as *monolatry*).

The advent of writing, political centralization, and extensive cultural contact and mixing had profound consequences. Slowly, as a body of writings, a *canon*, settled, a single uniform—or at least official—doctrine or dogma took shape. Individuals or groups who did not accept the canonical truth were deviants and heretics; worse, the canon itself became a subject of argument and hostility, in terms of what should be included in it and how it should be interpreted. Conflicts over who had the "true" knowledge or interpretation became possible and then common. The existence and weight of centralized political institutions made religious issues and disputes much more serious. The leadership could impose official religious rules and interpretations and could use the apparatus of state to enforce them. Religion started to be as centralized as politics. Finally, prolonged contacts between groups and societies with different religions—in markets and trading situations, in multicultural empires, and in wars—brought religions into competition and conflict in unprecedented ways, causing some to shrivel and disappear and others to organize and advance.

Out of this novel social and intellectual context developed a novel approach to religion, to which a handful of religions successfully adapted. Those religions that would go on to become "world religions" detached themselves from place; while still typically having their sacred sites, they became portable: one could be a Christian, a Muslim, or a Buddhist, for example, anywhere. At the same time, or perhaps because of this change, the religion was *true everywhere*. It no longer had only local applicability; the rules, rituals, beliefs, and gods were not local but *universal*. Since the religion was not tied to place, it could be everywhere. The next logical step was that it *should* be everywhere. Proselytization now made sense.

Hence, the world religions claimed and claim to be relevant and true for the whole world, that is, they assert universalism. The problem, obviously, is that they confront other religions—other world religions that also claim to be universally true as well as surviving local religions that claim to be locally true. Universalistic religions must necessarily be hostile to other religions, both universalistic and nonuniversalistic ones. So, they are also *exclusivistic*: only those people who follow their religion are right or good. A dualism emerges between "us believers" and "you nonbelievers" that makes conflict and violence more likely and acceptable—even noble. Two familiar forms this takes, as we will see later (chapter 7), are the Christian "city of God" versus "city of man" and the Muslim *dar al-Islam* (realm of peace) versus *dar al-harb* (realm of strife). In both systems, the first of the pair is the good domain, the domain of "true religion" and of believers in true religion; the second is the bad domain, the domain of false religion or of no religion. This necessarily sets up a struggle against unrighteousness and unbelief, which becomes a central feature of the religion. The more or less explicit goal is to eliminate the worldly, godless domain by conversion to the true and good religion, through proselytization if possible and force if necessary. In both religions—and others like them—this duality and clash between domains can be projected far beyond the earth, to the very cosmos itself, creating a context of cosmic opposition and struggle in which humans must take sides and be active participants.

World religions, then, aim to establish new communities (literal or figurative), but they are not communal or "patently social" in the sense in which local religions were. In fact, one other aspect of the environment of world religions is the shattering of old authentic communities—whether Greek city-states or Western Christian neighborhoods and villages—and their dissolution into large, relatively anonymous, and multicultural societies, states, and empires. As a result, while world religions are universalistic, they are simultaneously *individualistic*, inviting individuals to join the religion and often requiring an individual choice of, commitment to, and confirmation of membership. It would make little sense for an outsider to "convert to" !Kung or Warlpiri religion; it would make little sense to become a member of a world religion any way other than conversion. Local religions are or purport to be autochthonous; world religions are almost by definition *voluntary*.

In the end, world religions are almost everything that local religions are not: formal, institutionalized, canonical, universalistic, dualistic, exclusivistic, "artificial," and individualistic. These qualities make them hostile and combative in ways that would not be possible for local religions. For the latter, the presence of other religions is somewhere between a matter of indifference and of curiosity, but not an affront. Instead of a dualistic view—which is really a monistic one ultimately (the truth versus the rest)—theirs is a pluralistic view: many peoples, many religions. Their religious reality is at least somewhat taken for granted. For world religions, the presence of other religions—and even of other versions of its own religion—is somewhere between a problem and a cosmic insult. Their innate monism (one and only one truth) inevitably leads to a kind of division of humanity, a profound and absolute us-versus-them, which is very self-conscious and very defensive—and offensive.

THE FUNCTIONS OF RELIGION: EXPLANATION, CONTROL, AND LEGITIMATION

Whatever specific form it takes—and it takes literally thousands of forms—religion supposes that there are (at least somewhat humanlike) nonhuman agents sharing the world with humans. Moreover, humans must interact with or take into account these agents, and to a greater or lesser extent we depend on them (and sometimes they on us). Another way to express it is that they shape our lives. There may be many agents or few. They may be material, immaterial, or something in between. They may be nasty or nice. They may be powerful or pitiful. They may be engaged with us or indifferent to us. There may be an unbridgeable gulf separating us and them, or a porous border. But the one thing that is sure is that they are there.

Descriptions of religions, and their relation to the everyday lived lives of human beings and societies, are interesting and important, as are theories about the origins and sources of religions. However, another and perhaps more significant question is the *function* of religions: what do they do for humans, how do they contribute to and influence human life? Thinkers have identified and discussed various functions, but we can distill these ideas down to three main areas. They are *explanation*, *control*, and *legitimation*.

The explanatory aspect of religion is clear enough. Some early scholars like Tylor thought that explanation was the original and essential function of religion: humans have questions, and religion offers answers. What are dreams, visions, and hallucinations? What is the difference between a living body and a dead one? Where does life come from, and where do the dead go? How did humanity, the earth and the very universe, as well as particular social institutions and practices—language, kingship, marriage, farming, cities, and so on—begin? These are among the questions that religions frequently purport to answer, but not always: religions can only answer the questions they ask, and different religions ask different questions. Christianity does not, for instance, answer the question of how to get a better reincarnation, since it does not—and cannot—ask the question. Nor does Warlpiri religion answer the question of how to get to heaven, since it does not—and cannot—ask the question, lacking a concept of heaven. Further, even religions that raise the questions do not always explain phenomena but only suggest or insist that there is an explanation, maybe one that we cannot see or understand. In other words, sometimes the answer is "We don't know, but we are sure there is an answer" or "You should not/may not ask that question."

Of course, religion is not the only source or type of explanation; science, for example, explains things, too. The difference between a religious and a scientific explanation is that religious explanations entail (usually nonhuman) agents as the primary explanatory device. And, as mindful and volitional entities, agents act for "reasons," not from "causes." That is to say, the behavior of (religious and other) agents cannot be completely predicted from antecedent conditions, because they are not completely determined by conditions; they are more or less "free" to act—and to act for their own purposes. And their purposes refer either to their particular "personalities" and "natures" or to the particular *future condi-*

tions, that is to say "goals" or "ends," they are trying to achieve—exactly as human purposes do. Therefore, to the extent that their personalities or natures or wills are known (somewhat, at best), and that the future can be known (not at all), things can be more or less explained.

Among the questions often addressed by religions are those concerning suffering, sickness, and misfortune. Why does suffering exist at all? And even more so, why am *I* suffering? The religious answer to such questions is, characteristically, an agentive answer. Christianity as an example offers a variety of possible agentive solutions. One is the concept of human "free will": humans with freedom of choice and action can and too often do exercise that freedom in ways that are negative and destructive to themselves and others. Sometimes, as in the concept of "original sin," we may suffer for the poor decisions of other and ancient humans. But human agency cannot explain all misfortune (such as the damage caused by hurricanes), nor do human agents operate in a vacuum. In most variations of Christianity, an agent of evil (and perhaps his minions of demonic agents) tempt humans to do destructive and self-destructive things or even literally attack us and cause suffering directly. And the agent of good, the Christian god, may impose suffering for such reasons as punishment, warning, and testing—all purposive, goal directed, and essentially just.

Other religions have offered these and other explanations. As we saw above, witches or sorcerers may be the source of the trouble. It may be obnoxious, offended, or mischievous spirits. It may be angry or lonely ancestors. It may be a force like chi or mana. Or, in the Buddhist view of the world, it may be the very nature of existence: suffering is simply one of those things woven into the fabric of reality, and there is nothing we can do short of disengagement from the world. It may be our individual "fate" or "destiny."

Explanation is a potent and popular function of religion, but it is hardly the end of religion's power and may be its least interesting power. For humans want more than answers to questions; they want solutions to problems. They want control.

The question, "Why am I sick?" naturally leads to the question, "How can I get well?" The quest here is not an intellectual one but a practical one, literally a behavioral one: What should I/we do? What *works*? That is—and this is a highly overlooked aspect of religion—religions are not only, perhaps even mostly, about ideas but about effects. Humans want to bring about certain effects in the world: health, wealth, a good crop, fertility, success in a venture, a good rebirth, or what have you. We want to influence the outcome of events and activities. In such circumstances, we are not looking for information, let alone "meaning," but *results*. If, as it claims to do, religion represents what is "real," then it should bring about real consequences.

Humans attempt to control the natural world, the supernatural world, and the social world simultaneously. In terms of the natural world, humans at various places and times have aimed to control the weather (e.g., make it rain, turn aside hurricanes, calm the seas, etc.), their own physical health and that of their plants and animals, the sturdiness of their buildings and ships, and so on. Accordingly, humans use their religious knowledge and resources to achieve their own goals and purposes. (As we will see in the next two chapters, blood sacrifice and self-harm have been two recurring "methods" for getting things done.) At the same time, humans also try to control supernatural beings and forces, either to attract supernatural agents to good purposes or to repel them from bad purposes. Sometimes religions teach that supernatural agents can be convinced with words or placated with offerings. In other cases, like Aztec religion, humans must literally feed the gods to keep them alive and vital—specifically, to keep the sun rising every day.

Humans use these same techniques to control the social world as well, that is, the actions of other people and the success and well-being of their institutions. From love magic to curses, from praying for their country to praying for their football team, humans use words, gestures, and objects to influence social behavior and the outcome of social events. Religious rituals have attempted to strengthen contracts and treaties, guarantee truthful testimony in court, and affect the outcome of wars, not to mention transform children into adults and single people into married people.

In this sense, religion is not merely or even primarily "symbolic." When a shaman is conducting a curing ceremony over a sick patient, he or she is not "symbolizing" anything, let alone (as Durkheim would suggest) representing social relations to himself or herself. Rather, the shaman is trying to cure the patient. Whether this manner of control actually works is a separate question, although in some instances—such as marriage—the "success" of the ritual is purely social, in other words, there is no physical change in the participants, but they are "married" if we humans say they are married.

Finally and most consequentially, religion provides the function of legitimation. Legitimation is different from explanation or control and yet potentially encompasses or recruits both. The basic issue in legitimation is not knowledge or control but *justification*. To put this another way, the question addressed by legitimation is not the explanatory one ("Why are things this way?") nor the practical one ("How do I achieve this effect?") but the validation one ("Why *should* things be this way?" "Why *should* I do this?"). In a word, the question is, why is this *good* or *right*?

There are many possible approaches to the legitimation problem. One, of course, is not to question at all but rather to think that this is just the way it is, that there is no other way it could be. People suffer, men wear pants, the speed limit is fifty-five miles per hour, and that's just how it is. But this is not a satisfying answer for an inquisitive mind, nor is it factually accurate: people do suffer, but men do not wear pants everywhere, and the speed limit is other than fifty-five miles per hour in some places. And even the inevitability of suffering leaves unaddressed the question of why I or my loved ones are suffering *now* and whether it is *legitimate* suffering.

In other words, one could argue, and some have argued, that the ways of the world are simply natural; they are there like gravity. On the other hand, since Rousseau's time, it has been possible to argue that at least the ways of humans are not natural but social, that is, that we have created our own social reality through a "social contract." So, the speed limit is fifty-five miles per hour because we voted it into effect, and our men wear pants because that is our historical-cultural habit or norm. We could institute a different speed limit, we could start different clothing norms, but we choose these. But this view leaves two profound problems: *why* did we choose those, and why should *I* obey them? Of course, as a society we can offer arguments (like the speed limit protects lives or saves fuel) and impose penalties (like fines and jail for speeders), but these do not get to the heart of the legitimation issue.

The religious contribution to legitimation is neither natural nor social but, characteristically, supernatural and agentive. In most variations, some not altogether typically human agent(s) did or said something that established the way things are. This agent may be a god, or spirits of different kinds, or ancestors (like Adam and Eve) or culture heroes (like Gilgamesh or Hercules or, for that matter, George Washington). In Australian Aboriginal religions, for instance, the first beings (often part human and part animal or plant) traveled across a featureless landscape, having adventures. Their exploits produced the hills (where perhaps a being's body turned into a mound) and rivers (where perhaps a dragged spear carved a waterway), as well as human beings and human institutions like language, marriage, and of course songs, symbols, and stories. Humans did not invent or institute such things; they were established before us and given to us.

In other traditions, the establishment of the facts of life may be more acci-dental (as in Adam's and Eve's transgressions in Judeo-Christianity) or more intentional (as in the provision of laws by Yahweh in that tradition), but either way, nature and culture alike are "settled" by the actions of powerful and prior beings. The great scholar of comparative religions, Mircea Eliade, called these "paradigmatic acts," the behaviors or events that set the pattern or paradigm that we follow today. Malinowski referred to the stories of such actions and events, usually preserved in myth, as a "charter"—not merely a symbol or an explanation but "a living reality, believed to have once happened in primeval times, and continuing ever since to influence the world and human destinies."[40]

The lessons in this religious understanding of origins are twofold. First, humans are in fact not the designers of their own reality. Life is not a social con-tract but a fait accompli presented to humanity. Therefore, it cannot be altered by humans, except in trivial ways. Second, and essential to the first, the legiti-mation of this reality comes not only from its "utter factuality" but also from the authority of its founder(s)—and the latter in a quite literal sense: the god(s) or spirits or ancestors or culture hero(es) were the *authors* of the story that put the world in place. As agents, they made it. And they had the authority to do so because they were here first (and therefore closer to the seat of power) and/or because they *were* the seat of power. For humans now, the work of authoring is done; the situation for humans is thus not one of agency than of *obligation*. Finally, nature and culture both derive their ultimate qualities—and their ulti-mate duties—from supernature, from the actions and choices of agents earlier and greater than humans.

The paradigmatic ("this is the way it is") and therefore obligatory ("this is what we must do") quality of reality flows from three sources in religion: *models*, *mandates*, and *metaphysics*.

Models

Humans, as imitative creatures, need examples of what they should be and what they should do. Other humans, especially older humans, provide some of these models. However, the ultimate models are the first in time and in power, the ones who were, again, the very authors of the world that people inhabit. For Christians that means first and foremost Jesus, which is why Christians often arrive at their own decisions and actions by asking, what would Jesus do? or what did he actually do?—that is, by consulting scriptures. But Jesus is in no way the only model. Paul serves as a model, as well as, consequentially, the early martyrs, not to mention many figures like Abraham (who was prepared to sacrifice his son on divine command). For Muslims it means first and foremost Muhammad, whose sayings, doings, and rulings offer the image to emulate. Additionally, for at least some Muslims it may also be Muhammad's descendants Ali or Husayn, who were "martyred" in the years after Muhammad's death. For Hindus it may be the gods Vishnu or Ram/Rama or Murugan (see chapter 4), the culture hero Arjuna (who learned to make war as a caste duty), or Sita (wife of Rama, who was willing to give up her life for him). For other traditions, as we will see below, it is their own gods/spirits, ancestors, and founders. What they did, we should do. What happened to them should happen to us. There is no nobler and "truer" path than their footsteps.

Mandates

In some religions (but not all), the authors left explicit orders or instructions. Sometimes these commands are moral, sometimes practical or ritual. The directions can concern anything from the criminal laws that members must follow (e.g., outlawing murder or robbery), to standards for their dress and diet, to guidance in their ritual activities (e.g., how to arrange an altar or slaughter an animal), to rules for war. These commands may also include how to treat nonmembers, including avoidance, conversion, or extermination. Because the authors are either still active in the world today or left such a deep impression on that world, there are naturally consequences for following or deviating from the mandates. The specific positive (rewards) and negative (punishments) sanctions vary across religions, but it is widely held that accepting and performing one's obligations—whatever those obligations are—leads to happiness, serenity, long life, good health, success, wealth, and other desirable states. Conversely, rejecting or violating one's obligations brings misery, turmoil, sickness, and death, failure, poverty, and an undesirable "afterlife."

Metaphysics

As in the Hindu/Buddhist case, sometimes the nature of reality is such that we simply must act in certain ways. The order of the universe, which is perhaps nobody's choice or doing (that is, not "authored" in the final analysis but just primordial), dictates our options and outcomes. If there is karma and dharma in the world, then that's that. If there are witches or ancestor spirits or supernatural forces around, then we must accept it and act appropriately. Even agentive religions like Christianity still establish a fundamental metaphysics, with the "reality" of heaven and hell and of the cosmic struggle between good and evil. We can choose, but we always choose in full view of the metaphysical realities and ramifications.

Specifically what religions ask, or demand, that humans do is surprisingly diverse—and not always particularly nice. But if this is what the gods/spirits/ancestors/founders/heroes did, and this is what we are commanded to do, and this is just the way it is, then we know what we must do.

CONCLUSION: SOCIETY, SUPERNATURAL AGENTS, AND VIOLENCE

Clearly, there are abundant and diverse religions in the world, with little in common other than a premise of supernatural or spiritual beings and forces that share the universe with us. Not all contain gods, and when they do, not all contain gods of the familiar sort that we might regard as powerful, knowledgeable, or moral. More important, very few reject violence outright as a human and supernatural possibility or reality, and even those who do forbid it in theory or in doctrine often do not abstain from it in practice. Religion can be, like all other human institutions, a force for help or harm—or often both simultaneously, depending on who is being helped or harmed. In fact, our categories of "help" and "harm," of "peace" and "violence," of "good" and "evil" may not always apply.

As we have insisted previously, religion is not inherently and irredeemably violent; it is certainly not the essence and source of all violence. However, as we have clearly seen now, religion can and frequently does particularly effectively provide the conditions that satisfy the six dimensions or levels in our model of violence. To begin, religion is a group phenomenon, although—or especially because—it is supported by or arises from certain human innate or instinctual traits (e.g., agency attribution, social interaction, reciprocity, and so on). As such, it is subject to all the (many negative) features of group phenomena, including exclusionary membership (us versus them), collective ideas and values (Durkheim's "collective representations" or, less kindly, group-think), and the leadership principle, with the attendant expectations of conformity if not strict obedience. Indeed, now the leaders, or it might be appropriate to say the "authorities," are not only human but extrahuman and superhuman, with the additional degree of respect, deference, fear, and love that this implies.

Next, religion is, or at least strives to be, ingredient to identity. While not all individual members take their identity equally from their religion, any religion offers an identity (both personal and collective), but goes much further. A religion, like the general culture of which it is a part, contributes to the formation or production of individual members, of personality, of moods and motivations. A religion provides symbols and stories that function like lenses to shape perception, interpretation, and, most critically, action. Even more pervasive, a religion infiltrates and colonizes experience—not just at those powerful ritual moments so dear to Durkheim but also or arguably mostly in the small and insignificant moments, accomplishing what John and Jean Comaroff called the epiphany of the everyday, the "epic of the ordinary," the revolution in habits, and the "quest to refurnish the mundane."[41] This penetration and saturation of everyday life with the dictates—not so much the ideas and doctrines as the norms—of religion, as any observer can see, includes issues like what food to eat, what clothes to wear, how to groom hair and beards, how to marry and have sex, how to count and divide time, and many, many more.

Moving on, every religion contains its institutions, the "cult" in Scott Appleby's alliterative list of features of a religion ("a creed, a cult, a code of conduct, and a confessional community").[42] Among the institutions are the established rituals and liturgies, as well as the offices or specialist roles in the system. These include not only positive roles, like shaman or oracle or prophet, but also negative roles, like witch and sorcerer, as discussed above. There may be formal positions or groups, like judges or a hierarchical priesthood, which may be more or less integrated with political institutions; as mentioned, the chief, king, or emperor may be the high priest. Of course, religious institutions, as they penetrate society, entangle with other institutions, including marriage and the family.

Penultimately, a religion has its interests, both individually and collectively; a religious group is not only a community of confession but also a community of interests. The most basic interest is the preservation and perpetuation of the group and its doctrines and norms; this it shares with all types of groups. However, the particular beliefs of the religion establish other, more specific, and often more powerful interests, such as attaining heaven or avoiding hell. In other religions, personal interests may be achieving a good reincarnation, relieving karma or making "merit" for oneself and one's kin and ancestors, and recruiting the supposed agents to one's health, wealth, good luck, and long life. Collectively, the community may find it in its interest to form and maintain social boundaries, to discourage or punish dissent and deviance (as "heresy"), to expand itself through proselytization and conversion, and to oppose its "enemies," including nonmembers ("infidels" or "pagans" or "disbelievers") and especially apostates.

Finally, as seen throughout the previous points, a religion has its ideology. In fact, rather than Jonathan Fox's claim that religion and ideologies share certain qualities, we should emphasize that a religion *is* an ideology: as he explains, both religion and ideology provide, or rather religion-as-ideology provides, a meaning framework derived from an external (here, extrahuman) source, rules and standards linked to that framework, bonds between individuals and between individuals and the group crystallized in institutions, and a discourse of legitimation for the group's actions and institutions. In fact, religion may be the ultimate ideology, since its framework is so totally external (i.e., supernaturally ordained or given), its rules and standards so obligatory, its bonds so unbreakable, and its legitimation so absolute.

The specific ideological assertions of religions vary, but regardless of the details, these ideologies are *religious* (rather than political or philosophical, etc.) precisely because they start from and depend on the supernatural premise—the belief that there are nonhuman agents who interact socially with humans and who *authorized* (because they *authored*) the terms of human social and physical existence. This provides the most effective possible legitimation for what we are ordered or ordained to do: it makes the group, its identity, its institutions, its interests, and its particular ideology good and right (even righteousness) by definition. Therefore, if it is in the identity or the institutions or the interests or the ideology of a religion to be violent, that, too, is good and right, even righteous.

As we suggested in the first chapter, religion need not be inherently violent in order to be violent. First, insofar as it meets the conditions that promote violence, it will be violent. But arguably no other social force observed in human history can meet those conditions as well as religion. Second, the particular doctrines and worldview of a religion may encourage or advocate violence beyond those basic conditions; notions like holy war or the efficacy of blood sacrifice virtually cry out for violence. Third, as a modular thing, religion easily attracts and integrates other phenomena, like nationalism, class, race, gender, ethnicity, and even elements of popular culture, as well as violence *qua* violence. That is to say, even if religion were a purely nonviolent phenomenon on its own, it would still have the potential to absorb violent influences from its surroundings; instead, it has its own violent capacities *and* the potential to absorb those influences.

In summary then, religion as a social and ideological system has the capacity and the tendency to

- create a reality in which violence is acceptable, necessary, and even desirable;
- attribute the authority for the violence to the greatest possible good, whether that is the believing community, the authorizing god(s) or spirit(s), or the cosmos itself;
- set leadership, at the human and superhuman level, that cannot be questioned or opposed;
- totalize identities in exclusive ways—an absolute "us" against an absolute "them";
- demonize "them" literally, since a nonhuman and subhuman category of "demons" becomes a metaphysical reality;
- provide an ideology that specifically calls for struggle, combat, resistance, and destruction against the human and subhuman others;
- raise the stakes, with ultimate rewards and ultimate punishments for our behaviors, based on religious rules and expectations; and
- establish an ultimate goal or end that cannot and must not fail and that can and must be pursued by any means possible. Nothing can be higher than this goal, so all actions—and all humans, and even the world itself—are less than the great purpose that awaits.

Not all religions meet all these conditions. But when they do, and the more of them they meet, violence becomes not only likely but comparatively minor in the light of greater religious truths.

CHAPTER 3

SACRIFICE

According to Judeo-Christian tradition, before any other form of violence had appeared in the newly created world—before holy war, before persecution, even before murder—there was sacrifice. The first progeny of human parents, Cain and Abel, offered the first sacrifices, and it was over these sacrifices that the first human-on-human violence occurred: God did not "respect" (the term used in the King James version) the offer of plants as much as the offer of animals, and the resulting jealousy led to homicide. The next reference to sacrifice in Judeo-Christian writings is Noah, who made a "burnt sacrifice" of every "clean" species (Genesis 8:20). The most famous case of sacrifice came generations later, when Abraham was ordered and prepared to kill his own son "for a burnt offering" (Genesis 22:2) but instead, in the original instance of "substitutive" sacrifice, was allowed to kill a ram.

Despite the fact that holy war and faith-inspired terrorism preoccupy us in the present day, these particular forms of religious violence are actually less common and more recent than other forms. They have also, arguably, resulted in less total suffering in the world—especially if we admit nonhuman suffering. On the other hand, a wide assortment of societies and religions for a vast span of time have tormented and killed animals as well as humans for religious purposes. The total carnage perpetrated on the living beings of the planet—the sheer quantity of agony inflicted and blood spilled—can never be calculated. The "guilt" of the victims of such devastation, the extent to which they "deserve" their fate, is beside the point of the act of victimization and in fact would in many cases defeat the point.

Sacrifice is a critical place to start our discussion of religious violence, not necessarily because it is the first or most universal manifestation (although it is one of the first and one of the most universal) but because it has been so very widespread and so very overlooked in recent treatments of violence. Yet it sheds a valuable light on religious violence, that is, injury and destruction that is committed in the name and service of religion. Whether or not it is the essence of religious violence, as René Girard argues (to which we will return below), it is certainly distinctly, even wholly, religious. Nigel Davies defines sacrifice precisely as "killing with a spiritual or religious motivation, usually, but not exclusively, accompanied by ritual. Normally it was performed in a sacred place or one that had been made sacred for the occasion."[1] It may be the only form of violence for which there is no real secular correlate: we may speak of sacrificing to pay for a new house or sacrificing our life for our country, but no one seriously thinks that killing a chicken will get them a new house, nor even that giving up their life will automatically save their homeland. These latter are modern-day metaphors of a literal practice of causing pain or taking life as a means to some goal. Religious sacrifice is, as we will see, "purposeful" or "instrumental" behavior, intended and believed to have some empirical effect. It may be the *only* way to achieve the effect: as Davies goes on to argue, practitioners of sacrifice "lived in the knowledge that it was both necessary and right"[2]—a kind of knowledge that religion alone can guarantee.

WHAT IS SACRIFICE?

Despite the comparative lack of attention in recent literature, there have been various attempts in anthropology and religious studies to define and explain sacrifice as a religious activity. Davies suggested a definition above. Bourdillon widens the definition to include the "slaughter of an animal or person, or the surrender of a possession, in ritual,"[3] since sacrifice does not always involve killing. But neither approach will quite do, for a number of reasons. One is that animals and people are not the only sacrificial objects: plants, liquids (e.g., wine or oil), artifacts, and almost anything else might become a sacrificial offering instead of or in addition to a living creature. Further, when living creatures are included, they are not always destroyed; sometimes simply drawing blood or inflicting pain in some manner constitutes the ritual. Nor is all killing of animals or humans sacrificial; no one would call an abattoir a sacrificial site, nor hunting a sacrificial act, nor war a type of mass sacrifice. Also, the forms that sacrifice takes and the behaviors it entails can be very diverse: in some instances there may be an emotional frenzy, in other instances a calm, almost festive atmosphere; in some instances the remains may be eaten as a feast or sacrament, in other instances the flesh may be immolated beyond use; in some instances the execution may be quick, in other instances it may be prolonged to maximize the torment of the victim. Ultimately, Nancy Jay warns us, our familiar use of the word "lumps together . . . actions that sacrificers themselves do not call by one name"[4] and would perhaps not recognize as "sacrifice" at all.

The English word *sacrifice* derives from the Latin *sacer*, "holy" or "sacred," and *facere*, "to make or do." The victim of sacrifice is damaged or destroyed but also changed, made sacred, in the process; it is diminished but also enhanced. Often if not always, so is the person or cause for which the sacrifice is made. That is, the benefit of the sacrifice is not usually for the victim but for the person who *provides* the victim or for the person who *performs* the sacrifice (frequently not the same person) or for the community in general or some greater "purpose" (as we will discuss below). The sacrifice is often thought of and spoken of as a "gift" or an "offering," which naturally suggests the social and interpersonal quality of the action—a human giving some of or all of a possession to a nonhuman partner in exchange for effects that humans themselves cannot achieve. It is an act, at least in some sense, of reciprocity. The anthropologist Meyer Fortes thus suggests that sacrifice

> is a special ritual procedure for establishing or mobilizing a relationship of mutuality between the donor (individual and collective) and the recipient; and there is generally, if not always, an implication of mutual constraint, and indeed of actual or potential mutual coercion in the act. . . . Sacrifice is more commonly a response to a demand or command from supernatural agencies or else a rendering of a standard obligation, than a spontaneous offering; and whether or not it is thought of as an expiation or propitiation or purgation, there is commonly an element of demand, certainly of persuasion, on the donor's side.[5]

One of the first modern scholarly explications of sacrifice was given by Henri Hubert and Marcel Mauss, the latter being the well-known collaborator of the renowned sociologist Émile Durkheim. In their work, they define *sacrifice* as "a religious act which, through the consecration of a victim, modifies the condition of the moral person who accomplishes it or that of certain objects with which he is concerned."[6] Their approach, like Durkheim's, depends on the distinction between the "sacred" and the "profane." The sacred is the powerful, the supernatural, which simultaneously attracts and frightens; it is that which one cannot approach casually or in an everyday condition. The profane is the ordinary, the worldly, the mundane, that which should not touch the sacred without endangering itself and perhaps endangering (profaning, desecrating) the sacred as well. For Durkheim, and thus for Hubert and Mauss, this absolute distinction is the essence of religion; without the sacred there would be no religion, and without religion there would be no sacred.

In such a dualistic universe, it is hazardous to be too far from the sacred—or too close to it. And since the sacred and the profane can never cross the boundary that separates them, a mediator is necessary; this mediator must first be *consecrated*, made sacred or "with the sacred," and such is the function of sacrifice, "making sacred." Hubert and Mauss write that "the thing consecrated serves as an intermediary between the sacrificer, or the object which is to receive the practical benefits of the sacrifice, and the divinity to whom the sacrifice is usually addressed. Man and the god are not in direct contact."[7] Destroying the sacrifice is one method of permanently detaching it from the mundane and profane; it cannot return to normal use. Burning is one recurrent technique that transforms the "material" into the "spiritual" or at least the rarified and vaporous.

Hubert and Mauss note that the benefits of the sacrifice may not be intended directly for the human sacrificer or provider of the sacrifice. While an effect is almost invariably sought, the effect may be intended for "the sacrificer's [house], field, the river he has to cross, the oath he takes, the treaty he makes, etc."[8] But in spite of the "diverse forms it takes, it always consists in one same procedure, which may be used for the most widely differing purposes. *This procedure consists in establishing a means of communication between the sacred and the profane worlds through the mediation of a victim, that is, of a thing that in the course of the ceremony is destroyed*" (emphasis in the original).[9] And, ultimately, like all communication, it is mutual and reciprocal: "There is perhaps no sacrifice that has not some contractual element. The two parties present exchange their services and each gets his due. For the gods too have need of the profane."[10] This last idea raises a tantalizing specter to which we will return and that will cast a critical new light on sacrifice.

As plausible and influential as this theory is, it is hardly the only interpretation of sacrifice available, nor is it without its critics. Luc de Heusch, in his survey of sacrifice in Africa, explicitly countered that the "sacred/profane opposition is clearly a misleading starting point for the analysis of ritual,"[11] including sacrifice, if only because "sacred" and "profane" are not cross-culturally universal concepts. (Likewise, he criticized the concept of "sin" and the expiation of sin as central to the existence and function of sacrifice.) Other interpreters have emphasized other qualities of the sacrificial act. For E. B. Tylor, it was primarily a gift to divinity. For Robertson Smith, it was more than anything else a communal meal. James Frazier perceived it as a ritual means of controlling death, while Edward Westermarck, like many before and since, stressed its substitutive or "scapegoating" nature. We will return to the matter of explaining sacrifice later in the chapter, including the dominant ideas of René Girard and Walter Burkert, whom we will have occasion to criticize. No doubt, all these suggestions have their merit, and each may apply more appropriately to some cases of sacrifice than others. At this point, however, let us only evoke John Beattie's declaration that "almost always sacrifice is seen [by its perpetrators] as being, mostly, about power, or *powers*."[12]

THE DIVERSITY OF SACRIFICE

Despite the fact that sacrifice always entails damaging or destroying some material beings or objects for religious reasons, its forms and functions have been remarkably diverse across cultures. This is why we must reject the notion that any one religion's sacrificial system—or even worse, one particular aspect of one religion's sacrificial system—can sum up or stand for the worldwide practices of sacrifice. In particular, that means being circumspect about Judeo-Christian ideas and terminology like *sin* and *salvation* and *scapegoat* and even *god*. Therefore, this section will examine in some detail the specific sacrificial practices, concepts, and motivations from a range of different societies. We will see that no single experience is typical of all instances of sacrificial violence. At the same time, we can identify two main categories across cultures—animal sacrifice and human sacrifice—with considerable further internal diversity but nevertheless some fundamental unity. It is worth repeating that virtually any object or substance might be and has been sacrificed (from fruits, vegetables, and grains to bread, oil, wine, wood, gold and other metals, ad infinitum). However, while some loss and hardship may result from this behavior, no literal "violence" or pain and suffering is inflicted by these practices, and so we will not discuss them here.

Animal Sacrifice

Without doubt, the single most common version of sacrifice has involved animals, especially large-bodied mammals like cows, goats, sheep, pigs, and so on, although any animal is a potential object of ritual destruction. For the typical Western reader, the most familiar illustration will be ancient Hebrew/Israelite sacrifice, perhaps especially the story of Abraham and Isaac, which has led many thinkers to take the "scapegoating" or *aqedah* (the technical term for the near-sacrifice of Isaac) as paradigmatic not only of biblical sacrifice but of all sacrifice. However, this would be ethnocentric and inadequate, even within the context of Judeo-Christian practice; interestingly, in the Judeo-Christian scriptures (King James version), the term *scapegoat* only occurs three times, all in Leviticus 16, and this scapegoat was not killed but released into the wilderness.

Animal sacrifice has actually been practiced by many religions, in many different ways and for many different reasons. In this section we will explore some of the variety of animal sacrifice and see how scapegoating often, if not ordinarily, had little to do with the religion's ideas and practices of the ritual.

Sacrifice in Ancient Judaism

Sacrifice was arguably the first ritual act of humanity according to the Judeo-Christian scriptures, and, according to Christian Eberhart, "sacrifice is the basic category of Israelite religion."[13] At the time of the original biblical sacrifices (Cain and Abel in Genesis) and for chapters and years to come, no explanation, reasoning, or rule for sacrifice was given. However, as the religion developed, not only slaughtering animals but, as Eberhart stresses, *burning* animals became a, if not the, central ritual act; he even ventures the opinion that *"the burning rite determines whether any cultic ritual qualifies as an 'offering for God.'* It is, therefore, the constitutive element of a sacrifice."[14] The first reference to "burnt offerings" comes in the story of Noah (Genesis 8:20), and by Moses's time (Exodus), animal sacrifice was clearly frequent and important; one of his objections to Egyptian rule was that the people were unable to sacrifice to their god.

It is only after the exodus from Egypt, as religious law is established, that sacrifice begins to take on specific characteristics. We see, for example, for the first time a mention of different types or occasions of sacrifice—"burnt offerings" and "peace offerings" initially (Exodus 20), then "sin offerings" (Exodus 29), "wave offerings" and "heave offerings" (Exodus 29), and others such as "trespass offerings" (Leviticus 5:19), "sacrifice of thanksgiving" (Leviticus 22:29), and "jealousy offerings" (Numbers 5:15). The book of Leviticus finally begins to lay out the procedures for various kinds of sacrifices. For instance, Leviticus 1:3–17 describes the method for burnt sacrifice:

> If his offering be a burnt sacrifice of the herd, let him offer a male without blemish: he shall offer it of his own voluntary will at the door of the tabernacle of the congregation before the Lord.
>
> And he shall put his hand upon the head of the burnt offering; and it shall be accepted for him to make atonement for him.
>
> And he shall flay the burnt offering, and cut it into his pieces.
>
> But his inwards and his legs shall he wash in water: and the priest shall burn all on the altar, to be a burnt sacrifice, an offering made by fire, of a sweet savor unto the Lord.
>
> And if his offering be of the flocks, namely, of the sheep, or of the goats, for a burnt sacrifice; he shall bring it a male without blemish.
>
> But he shall wash the inwards and the legs with water: and the priest shall bring it all, and burn it upon the altar: it is a burnt sacrifice, an offering made by fire, of a sweet savor unto the Lord.
>
> And if the burnt sacrifice for his offering to the Lord be of fowls, then he shall bring his offering of turtledoves, or of young pigeons.
>
> And he shall cleave it with the wings thereof, but shall not divide it asunder: and the priest shall burn it upon the altar, upon the wood that is upon the fire: it is a burnt sacrifice, an offering made by fire, of a sweet savor unto the Lord.

Many such instructions follow, in minute detail. Also, here we see the notion of atonement, which first appears in Exodus 29:36, without explanation of how sacrifice is meant to achieve it. It suggests, nevertheless, some undesirable social or spiritual condition that sacrifice removes. It also states that the smell of sacrifice is a "sweet savor" to their god, something that he enjoys.

The objects of sacrifice in the tradition are disproportionately animals, particularly domesticated animals, although doves and pigeons are included. More often and preferably, cattle and oxen and goats and sheep are used, perhaps in combination: Numbers 7 specifies two oxen, five rams, five he-goats, and five lambs as the prescribed peace offering. Note the preference for male sacrificial victims. The disposition of the sacrificial remains is spelled out and varies by victim and occasion. A peace offering (Leviticus 9) required burning the flesh on the altar and sprinkling the blood on the altar. The breast of the sacrificial ram was to be waved in the air, and the shoulder heaved up, giving us the terms *wave offering* and *heave offering* (Exodus 29:27). Some sacrifices were consumed by the group, others by the priests. According to Leviticus 7:15, the meat of peace offerings should be eaten the same day it was sacrificed but not the next day; the following verse orders that a vow or voluntary offering could be eaten on both days. Eating the peace offering on the third day was an abomination. And the fat, which was burned on the "outer altar," was exclusively for the Lord and not to be eaten by humans at all.

It is more than obvious that sacrifice in ancient Hebrew religion was rampant, diverse, and central to ritual activities; Michael Bryson goes so far as to insist that the "formation of community is inextricably bound up with violence in the Hebrew scriptures."[15] To the question of whether communal identity *must* be forged in sacrificial violence, Bryson answers yes, or at least it *is* so forged: "Communities are formed, communal actions are undertaken, and communal identities are reinforced through sacrificial violence and the violence (often war) that follows."[16] Gray, on the other hand, disagrees with the analysis of Hebrew sacrifice as strictly communal, at least in Robertson Smith's sense of a communal meal or an occasion for religious fellowship. After considering Hebrew sacrificial terminology and practice, he concludes that Hebrew sacrifice was predominantly a matter of gift-giving to their god; in fact, he argues that scriptural instructions like those in Numbers 28 portray sacrifices as virtual "food of the god" (a common motif across cultures). Other "effects" of sacrifice may have been simultaneous: Gray insists that a sacrifice could be a gift at the same time as a propitiation and an expiation, not to mention an act that makes the god "merry." However, he downplays the propitiatory and expiatory aspects of the ritual, especially early on:

> While propitiation and expiation as the end of sacrifice were in the earlier periods of the history of Israel anything but unknown or even exceptional, it was also far from being constant or even relatively frequent. Sacrifice was more often Eucharistic than propitiatory, and it was more often offered with feelings of joy and security than in fear and contrition.[17]

In the end, he decides, the "reason" for sacrifice was comparatively unimportant. "Widely and largely the entire ritual was simply accepted as ordinances of God; God willed them so; and that was enough."[18]

That animal sacrifice continued into New Testament times is clear from the presence of the sellers of animals at the temple in Jerusalem. However, as early as the Psalms and the subsequent prophets, the meaning of sacrifice began to change, in particular to become more symbolic and allegorical or psychological. Psalms 51 states: "For thou desirest not sacrifice; else would I give it: thou delightest not in burnt offering. . . . Then shalt thou be pleased with the sacrifices of righteousness, with burnt offering and whole burnt offering: then shall they offer bullocks upon thine altar." Isaiah 1:11 marks the radical break, however: "To what purpose is the multitude of your sacrifices unto me? saith the LORD: I am full of the burnt offerings of rams, and the fat of fed beasts; and I delight not in the blood of bullocks, or of lambs, or of he-goats." Although sacrifice by no means ended, nor was it ordered to end, sacrifice alone was coming to be seen as insufficient. Sacrifice did not erase sin or guarantee salvation.

Sacrifice in Hinduism

Hinduism is a historically and regionally diverse religion, but it is fair to say that literal sacrifice was a key component of classical priestly (Brahminic) Hinduism and that sacrifice persists today, if in symbolic or metaphorical senses. Hinduism began to take shape after the Aryan invasions of India circa the fifteenth century BCE. A rigid class or caste system formed, with a caste of Brahmins who had the sole and essential task of performing sacrifices for the people. Some of the early literature, the Vedas, contains extensive hymns and instructions for sacrifice. For instance, the very first hymn in the Rig Veda, to the fire god Agni, mentions sacrifice three times:

> I laud Agni, the chosen Priest, God, minister of sacrifice,
> The hotar, lavishest of wealth.
> Worthy is Agni to be praised by living as by ancient seers.
> He shall bring hitherward the Gods.
> Through Agni man obtaineth wealth, yea, plenty waxing day by day,
> Most rich in heroes, glorious.
> Agni, the perfect sacrifice which thou encompassest about
> Verily goeth to the Gods.
> May Agni, sapient-minded Priest, truthful, most gloriously great,
> The God, come hither with the Gods.
> Whatever blessing, Agni, thou wilt grant unto thy worshipper,
> That, Angiras, is indeed thy truth.

> To thee, dispeller of the night, O Agni, day by day with prayer
> Bringing thee reverence, we come
> Ruler of sacrifices, guard of Law eternal, radiant One,
> Increasing in thine own abode.
> Be to us easy of approach, even as a father to his son:
> Agni, be with us for our weal.[19]

Agni, as the personification of the fire that made burnt sacrifice possible, was thus viewed as particularly significant, the mediator between humans and the other gods.

The Hindu term for sacrifice is *yajna,* and it is one—and one of the most important—of the external forms of Hindu religious practice. Hinduism has long valued both external or ritual and internal or contemplative paths—"action" as well as "knowledge" and "devotion"—to spiritual accomplishment and enlightenment. However, as in the Hebrew tradition, the action/ritual aspect predated the knowledge/contemplative aspect. Correct performance of the rituals, including the sacrificial rituals, was paramount; in fact, as Octavian Sarbatoare argues, "*Yajna* in itself is to be seen as the very essence of Veda."[20] Accordingly, a large literature accumulated, known as *srauta,* as guidebooks and manuals for correct sacrifice. Derived from the Sanskrit word *sruti,* or revelation, the manuals provided instructions for the placement of the sacrificial fires, the roles of various priests, the timing of rituals, and the particular animals to be offered and techniques to be performed.

> The basic shrauta [*sic*] rite involved the participation of four Vedic priests, each one having specific attributes. They were known as *hotri, adhvaryu, udgatri,* and *brahman (brahmin)*; each priest could have three helpers if necessary. The Vedic priests were all chanting priests. As tradition stipulates, *hotri* was the priest chanting the hymns of Rig Veda while performing the oblation into the fire, *adhvaryu* was the one chanting the hymns of Yajur Veda while performing *adhvara,* i.e., his duties before the sacrifice itself. *Udgatri* priest was the one chanting the Sama Veda hymns, while *brahman* priest, seen as the most learned, was the supervisor of the entire ceremony and the one chanting the hymns of Atharva Veda. Yet, the central figure of the sacrifice was seen to be the *adhvaryu* priest for the fact that he was the one measuring the sacrificial ground, building all that was necessary and preparing the materials to be used, like articles of oblation, utensils, woods, and water. He also used to kindle the fire for expected offerings. Thus, the *adhvaryu* priest's skills to perform correct

[*sic*] his duties were of utmost importance for the rituals of fire sacrifice. The very sucess of *yajna* was dependent on having the right setup before the ceremony of chanting and offering could start.[21]

Over time sacrifice continued but also transformed. The Bhagavad Gita, a much later composition, still praises sacrifice: Krishna, the deity in the story, warns that "for him that makes no sacrifice, he hath nor part nor lot even in the present world. How should he share another?" Even so, it is clear that sacrifice, just as in the Torah/Old Testament, is changing and that it alone is insufficient: "O Arjuna, neither by study of the Vedas, nor by sacrifice, nor by charity, nor by rituals, nor by severe austerities, can I be seen in this cosmic form by any one other than you in this human world."[22] Like later Judaism, if sacrificial behavior was still required at all, it had to be supplemented with, if not subordinated to, proper thought, attitude, and belief. Righteousness began to replace ritualism as the real base of religion.

As the priestly form of sacrifice weakened (but never quite disappeared), sacrifice could become a more domestic affair. According to Sri Swami Sivananda, the yajna tradition includes five daily sacrifices that should be performed by all men. These include *Brahma yajna*, *Deva yajna*, *Pitri yajna*, *Bhuta yajna*, and *Manushya yajna*. He insists that these actions are beneficial for the "spiritual evolution or growth" of humans. Since a person is dependent on five sources—the sacred texts, the gods, the ancestors, nature (the plants, animals, and elements), and one's fellow man—a person builds up a debt to these sources. "He must pay back his debt by performing these five sacrifices daily. Further, numerous insects are killed by him unconsciously during walking, sweeping, grinding, cooking, etc. This sin is removed by performance of these sacrifices." Brahma yajna involves the act of reading the texts, growing in knowledge, and sharing that knowledge with others. Deva yajna includes sacrifices, such as food, for the deities, a mundane version of Vedic practices. Pitri yajna and Bhuta yajna entail making offerings to the ancestors and the animals, respectively. Finally, Manushya yajna means feeding and comforting the poor and suffering. By performing these actions, the person learns and changes: "Man has no separate individual existence. He is connected with the world. He is like a bead in the rosary. His whole life must be a life of sacrifice and duties. Then only he will have rapid evolution. Then only he will realize the supreme bliss of the Eternal. Then only he will free himself from the round of births and deaths and attain immortality."[23]

Hindu sacrifice lives on today in one of the most sacrifice-intensive religions in the world, that of the island of Bali. According to Sidarta Wijaya,

> Animal sacrifices or using animals in religious ceremonies is obligatory in Bali.
> Most of Balinese ceremonies require one or more animals to be sacrificed.
> Killing animals in this way is not considered a cruelty. When an animal is killed
> in sacrifice, it acquires karma, enough perhaps, to allow it to be reincarnated at
> [a] higher level. The body is not important to the Hindu faithful. It is a shell.
> An animal that is killed for a sacrifice is always treated with a great reverence.[24]

Wijaya goes on to explain that thousands of animals, from chickens and ducks
to pigs and dogs and tigers, are sacrificed every month, usually by cutting their
throats or drowning; in "auspicious" months, twice as many may die. And in the
once-every-century festival of Eka Desa Rudra (last conducted in 1979), a vast
sacrifice or *tawur agung* including every living species on the island is performed.

Sacrifice in Pre-Christian Europe

At the same time or even before the ancient Hebrews were sacrificing animals
to their god, cultures in Europe were sacrificing lives—among them human
lives (see below)—to their spiritual superiors. Prehistoric archaeological sites
dating back tens to hundreds of thousands of years ago reveal animal bones, such
as bear skulls, in the burial sites of humans. We cannot conclude that these
beings were the victims of sacrifice, but we can conclude that the placement of
animal remains in context with human corpses had some meaning to those who
placed them.

Of the classical sacrificial cultures, the best known is the Greek. In fact,
Walter Burkert has based much of his theory of sacrifice on the Greek example.
In Athens, he writes, "almost every day had its festival or sacrifice. Out of all
these sacrifices, one stood out by virtue of its singular, even grotesque, features:
the Buphonia, 'ox-slaying,' for 'Zeus of the City.'"[25] At midsummer, a group of
oxen were led up the Acropolis to the altar of Zeus. A procession accompanied
the animals, with carriers bearing sacrificial water and grain and a special sacrificial knife. The sack of grain was set on the altar, around which the oxen were
led in a circle. A ceremonial axe, stored at the shrine, was cleaned with the water
brought up to the site. All paused until an ox began to eat the grain, which was
regarded as a sin or taboo; at that point, a sacrificer killed the ox and fled. Cutters skinned and butchered the ox, removing its internal organs, and the meat
was roasted and eaten; the bones were burned on the altar. After completion of
the ceremony, a trial was held at the center of town "for the crime of having

killed at the altar."[26] The actual ox-killer, who had escaped immediately upon completing his duties, was unavailable to try, so the ultimate guilt fell upon the tools of sacrifice—the axe and knife. The axe was found not guilty, but the knife was convicted and disposed of in the sea. An interesting point that Miranda Green makes in regard to Greek ox sacrifice is that it was felt important that the animal "volunteer" for its death—by taking the grain (committing a violation) and lowering its head to expose its neck to the blade—thus transforming the sacrifice from an act of human cruelty to an act of animal self-offering.[27]

Beyond this one dramatic sacrificial performance, Dennis Hughes catalogues seven different varieties of Greek ritual killing:

1. "Olympian sacrifice" or *thysia*, like that described by Burkert but including other occasions such as weddings and the presentation of children or brides to the kindred (Jay notes that in the second century of the Christian era, the sacrament of the Eucharist was referred to as *thysia*.)
2. Sacrifice offered to heroes
3. Funeral sacrifice for the dead
4. Sacrifice prior to battles or to crossing frontiers and rivers
5. Sacrifice as part of oaths (votive sacrifices)
6. Purification sacrifice
7. Scrifice of burnt offerings as part of the cult of various gods[28]

Roman religion also integrated sacrifice as a fundamental element. According to John Scheid's study of the religion of Rome, there were many, even dozens, of sacrificial practices based on their performance, their goals, and the gods addressed.[29] The major forms included the public cult that was conducted at the temple, household sacrifice held in an individual's home, and private sacrifice carried out in a remote spot for purposes of divination or magic. Sacrifice was part of regular calendrical ceremonies and other prominent events:

> The anniversary of the foundation of a temple began with a sacrifice. . . . Certain major rituals, such as the regular vows at the beginning of the year, great festivals such as the Roman Games of 13 September and the Plebeian Games of 13 November, extraordinary ceremonies such as those involving vows, triumphs, *lecisternia* [rituals to restore harmony between humans and gods], dedications, purifications, and the Secular Games all featured sacrifices or often even culminated in them.[30]

Sacrifice also played a part in everyday social interactions: not only did people offer animal victims as "gifts" to the gods but also as "gifts from fathers of families, gifts from children when they passed into adulthood, . . . gifts from the city, gifts from the Senate and from individual military units, gifts from one of the tribes of the Roman people or from a college, and so on."[31]

Scheid provides the most complete account of public/temple sacrifice. The ritual usually began at dawn with the participants ceremonially washing and dressing themselves. The victims, usually adult domesticated cows, pigs, sheep, or goats, were also washed and decorated. (Male gods were normally offered gelded male beasts, and female gods were presented with females.) The sacrificial party marched to the altar of the appropriate divinity and, pouring wine and incense on the fire, greeted the god with a welcome or *praefatio* (preface). The victim was then rubbed with a mixture of salt and flour, before a ceremonial knife was traced along its back, symbolically transferring it from human property to divine property ("sacra-ficing" or making it holy). The animal was killed and drained of blood, usually by slashing the throat, but only after it was determined that the victim had "volunteered" for annihilation by lowering its head as if to display its neck, as in the Greek practice. The slaughtered animal was placed on its back and opened for an inspection of its entrails (normal organs representing the god's approval). The carcass was sectioned, with the god's portion (the internal organs) boiled or grilled. For most gods, the meat was then dropped onto the fire; for water gods it was cast into the water, and for nether gods it was buried or left on the ground. Once the burnt offering was made, the remaining portions were considered profane and fit only for humans, who accepted and ate it as a gift *from* the gods.

Sacrifice in Africa

Some of the best-documented cases of animal sacrifice are found in the literature on Africa, where especially cattle sacrifice was an important and recurring theme. The practice was widespread on the continent but particularly associated with pastoral (animal-herding) societies. Perhaps the classic description of traditional African sacrifice comes from the anthropologist E. E. Evans-Pritchard's book on the Nuer, an East African people, for whom "the most typical and expressive act . . . [is] the rite of sacrifice."[32] Evans-Pritchard notes that the Nuer performed sacrifices for many different reasons:

when a man is sick, when sin has been committed, when a wife is barren, sometimes on the birth of a first child, at the birth of twins, at initiation of sons, at marriages, at funerals and mortuary ceremonies, after homicides and at settlement of feuds, at periodic ceremonies in honor of one or other of their many spirits or of a dead father, before war, when persons or property are struck by lightning, when threatened or overcome by plague or famine, sometimes before large-scale fishing enterprises, when a ghost is troublesome, etc.[33]

He condenses these myriad occasions into two main categories—the prevention of danger or misfortune, and the limitation and elimination of misfortune that has already happened. Further he identifies two general forms of sacrifice, individual and collective.

Despite what seems like daunting diversity, Evans-Pritchard argues that the processes of sacrifice "are almost always the same and performed in the same order [although] they are much more elaborate on some occasions than on others."[34] Needless to say, the standard sacrificial victim was the ox. In fact, in Nuer religion all cattle were "reserved" for sacrifice; *kwoth*, their conception of divinity, created cattle expressly for the purpose of sacrifice. So, even when other animals (or occasionally a vegetable like a cucumber) were substituted, they were still referred to as *yang* or "cow."

The proceedings opened, as we have come to expect, with an invocation, which was explicitly not a prayer or a magical spell; the language of invocation "is more definite and particular; and its clauses are mostly affirmations, formal statements, rather than petitions."[35] That is, the invocation for a sacrifice on occasion of illness declared that the action would cure the disease. This was followed by the kill, accomplished by spearing the ox on its right side (smaller animals received cuts to the throat). Ideally the victim would "fall well," on its right side with its head pointed toward the village; a bad fall might invalidate the ritual and require another attempt. Despite the seriousness of the event, Evans-Pritchard notes a "certain air of casualness and lack of ceremony about the whole sacrificial procedure"—not the extreme emotion that some scholars would expect (see below). With the deadly act, the sacrifice was complete, and kwoth "took" (the Nuer word was *kan*, not their word for eat [*cam*] or drink [*madh*]) the "life" (*yiegh*) of the victim in the form of the blood and chyme that flowed into the earth.

Godfrey Lienhardt discusses sacrifice among the neighbors of the Nuer, the Dinka. Like the former, the Dinka sacrificed for numerous reasons, including natural events, sickness, and regular annual cycles. For instance, oxen were routinely killed at the end of the harvest season, in November/December, when settled villagers were about to disperse into their dry-season camps—a time "when social life is in the villages at its most concentrated and intense. People thus sacrifice for prosperity and strength just at the time when they are most experiencing the fullness of social life and, in the temporary abundance of the harvest, are at the peak of their physical well-being."[36] The process of immolation itself followed a mostly familiar pattern, with a setting-aside of the victim(s), an invocation, a kill by cutting the throat, a performance of hymns of honor, and finally the consumption of the body.

Luc de Heusch's survey of African sacrifice gives many other examples. The Zulu, for instance, trapped a live hornbill, suffocated it or broke its neck, and tossed it into a lake or river in order to combat drought; the logic was that the sky would cry for its dearest animal, thus delivering rain.[37] The Thonga possessed a concept of *mhamba* or "offering," of which sacrifice (here, of a chicken or goat) was one special type, employed on particularly significant occasions, such as marriages, funerals, initiations and other "collective rites of passage," and exorcisms. Overall, Heusch states, "blood sacrifice accompanies a dramatic situation that involves a temporary rupture of fundamental social bonds, between groups or between men and the ancestors. . . . Blood sacrifice simultaneously affirms and conjures away a danger inherent in the articulations of the social body."[38] Among the Dogon, every sacrificial moment began with slicing the throat of a chicken and then moved on to a second animal, often a cow, sheep, or goat. One indicative occasion for the practice was before the rainy season and the planting of fields, when *bulu* (the sacrifice ritual, literally "to make alive again/resuscitate") was performed for Lebe Seru, the ancestral spirit of agriculture—and the mythical first victim of sacrifice (see p. 111).

Human Sacrifice

Clearly, any living being with blood to spill and flesh to burn can make an adequate sacrifice, and countless lives have been lost, copious amounts of blood have been shed, and inestimable pain and anguish have been inflicted on the nonhuman world in the practice. However, piety-fired slaughter has hardly stopped with animals; often enough, humans have provided, sometimes in prodigious quantities, the objects of ritual destruction. In fact, in some interpretations, humans provided the ultimate or ideal victim: as Heusch suggests, "the most perfect sacrificial debt is that which a man must pay with his own blood. . . . The animal victim is only a substitute"[39]—just as a ram was substituted at the last minute for Isaac.

In this section, we turn to human sacrifice across culture and history. Frequently, the processes of sacrifice were similar whether the victim was animal or human. However, there were two major recurring differences. The first was scale: religions have seldom called for the mass sacrifice of cows or sheep but often for the mass sacrifice of humans. The second was intensity of suffering. Seldom did societies go out of their way to torture and prolong the agony of animals. But, as Davies reminds us, "man was often deliberately made to suffer as a preparation for death. No one thought of scalping a ram, though in Africa animals were sometimes ill-treated."[40]

Human Sacrifice in the Judeo-Christian Tradition

Animal sacrifice was a key component of the cult of ancient Judaism, up to and including the time of Jesus. Modern Jews and Christians little note nor long remember that human sacrifice was also at least sometimes practiced by ancient Hebrews, even if the ancients did not completely condone the behavior. After all, Abraham did not balk at the (belayed) order to sacrifice his son. Davies alludes to a number of other circumstances in their scriptures. In the Book of Judges, an Israelite king named Jephthah, in exchange for victory in a battle against Ammon, swore to seize "whatsoever cometh forth of the doors of my house to meet me . . . and I will offer it up for a burnt offering" (Judges 11:31). Unfortunately, it was his own daughter who met him at the door, but he "did with her according to his vow which he had vowed" (Judges 11:40). One of the builders of Jericho, Hiel the Bethelite, buried his firstborn son Abiram under the foundations and his youngest son Segub under the gates (1 Kings 16:34)— a common use of sacrificed bodies or body parts. In 2 Kings 16:3, Ahaz "made his son pass through the fire," although admittedly this was "according to the abominations of the heathen." The "fire" mentioned in this passage refers to a Canaanite custom of child sacrifice, specifically at a site called Tophet. According to Davies, when the Hebrews came under the cultural influence of Canaan after Abraham's time, the practice spread among them; "records of the eighth and seventh centuries [BCE]. demonstrated beyond all doubt that the Israelites of the period made burnt offerings of their sons in the Tophet fires lighted in the Valley of Geninnon outside Jerusalem."[41] Whether it was still foreign influence, Moses did utter in Exodus 13:15 that since his god killed "all the firstborn in the land of Egypt, both the firstborn of man, and the firstborn of beast: therefore I sacrifice to the Lord all that openeth the matrix [i.e., womb] being males; but all the firstborn of my children I redeem." The ultimate vanquishing of the practice does not change the fact that it existed.

As we saw earlier, the prophets came increasingly to condemn all sacrifice not so much as cruel but as ineffective. Humans were sinful, and sacrifice had not managed to alter that failing. No amount of animal blood and burnt flesh appeared to be able to rectify the situation. God himself had become tired of sacrifice without repentance: "In burnt offerings and sacrifices for sin thou hast had no pleasure" (Hebrews 10:6). However, Christianity presents the solution to the problem of sacrifice as an even greater sacrifice—the greatest sacrifice of all. In a venerable tradition encompassing such gods as Tammuz, Zeus, Odin, Herakles, Melkart, Dido, Artemis, Erigone, Adonis, Mithras, and others, the deity allowed himself to be killed as the sacrifice to end all sacrifices. "Christ our passover is sacrificed for us" (1 Corinthians 5:7). Christ "hath given himself for us an offering and a sacrifice to God for a sweetsmelling savor" (Ephesians 5:2). By this supreme sacrifice, a self-sacrifice of the greatest life, of Life itself, the greatest possible benefit for humans was obtained. As Hebrews 9:26 puts it, God in the form of Jesus "appeared to put away sin by the sacrifice of himself." The final triumph over sin and even death was achieved through sacrificial death.

Human Sacrifice in Pre-Christian Europe

"All over pre-Christian Europe every imaginable form of human sacrifice was to be found: infanticide, fertility rites, immolation of war prisoners, live burials under buildings, sacrifice of the god or of the ruler in his stead."[42] As we approach the Iron Age in Europe (after about 1000 BCE), the evidence of intentional killing and use of the bodies of human victims becomes more abundant and clear. We have two main sources on the subject of ancient European sacrifice, archaeology and ancient texts, both of which are controversial but compelling. Iron Age excavations at Gournay and Danebury have yielded animal and human remains, according to Green.[43] That this is not a coincidence, and in fact that it is sacrificial, is suggested by what she calls the "overkill violence" that many such sites illustrate. "Lindow Man," who died in ancient Europe, was found in a marsh where he had been left, garroted and with his skull fractured. A male at Hudremose had his right arm chopped off, while a male from Borremose had his face mutilated. A female unearthed at Danebury evidenced a butchered pelvis, while a young boy was dismembered. Even more striking finds include an adolescent male in northern Germany who appears to have been drowned while blindfolded, his head half-shaved, and made to sink with rocks and branches.[44] A boy from a neighboring region was uncovered in a peat bog where he had been left, ankles tied together, hands tied behind his back, and a rope tied around his neck that ran between his legs.[45]

Observers and writers at the time also commented on such practices. In his *Pharsalis*, Lucan wrote that the southern Gauls worshipped gods who demanded "hideous offerings" and that every tree showed signs of human blood on it. Tacitus in *Annales* reported that the natives of Britain poured human blood on their altars and practiced divination with human entrails. Strabo, author of *Geographia*, claimed that the people of the mountainous areas of Spain sacrificed horses as well as human prisoners and that the right hand of human victims was consecrated to their gods. Norse/Germanic peoples offered sacrificed war captives to Odin (see below), while Celts and Druids burned alive their prisoners and criminals inside an enormous likeness of a human, the "wicker man"; Vikings "bound victims to the rollers over which a new ship slipped into the sea and reddened the keel with human blood."[46] Human sacrifice was practiced in Carthage as late as 146 BCE, with children serving as burnt offerings.[47]

Greek sacrifices typically employed animals, especially the bull or ox. However, there is evidence of human sacrifice as well. The writer Porphyry, of the third century CE, recounted sixteen cases of human sacrifice in his *De Abstinentia*, half of them in Greek civilization. An annual human victim was provided to the god Kronos at Rhodes. At Salamis, he claimed, a human was offered to Agraulis and later to Diomedes. "The one who was to be slain, led by the ephebes, would run three times around the altar, whereupon the priest would strike him on the throat with a spear, and so would he burn him entirely on the pyre which had been heaped up. But Diphilus the king of Cyprus . . . abolished the rite, changing the custom into an ox sacrifice."[48]

Perhaps the most famous and curious of the Greek sacrificial victims was the *pharmakos*. Every year in Athens, two people were selected to be *pharmakoi* for scourging, ostracism, and, according to some sources, death. The Athenian ritual occurred at the time of the Apollo festival of Thargelia, a spring preharvest event. The victims were ceremoniously dressed and decorated and then paraded, during which they were whipped with branches from the fig tree. Curses and stones were hurled at them. They were finally chased from the city and perhaps killed. Plutarch mentions a similar ritual in another city, which he called the "driving out of *boulimos*." The head of the city would beat a slave and run him through the gates of the city; private citizens would hit their own slaves and chase them through the door of the house, crying "Out with famine, in with wealth and health." There is no evidence that anyone was killed, but such rituals clearly served a purification function, with the victim symbolically carrying away the illness and misfortune of the year.

Human sacrifice was legal in Rome until 97 BCE, although this does not mean that it was commonly practiced that late. However, according to Scheid, even if they were not actively killing people as sacrifice, "the Romans would solemnly dedicate a besieged town to the gods of the underworld or, at the private level, their own personal enemies, using magical rites."[49] And a revival of human sacrifice apparently happened in the first century CE due to the arrival of Oriental mystery cults, many of which spoke of the death and resurrection of their man-god savior figure.

Human Sacrifice in Hawaii and the Pacific Islands

Sacrifice in the premodern Hawaiian kingdom took many of the familiar forms. Beings of every sort were offered up to the relevant deity, on the premise that each god was defined by, embodied in, and therefore related to "a number of natural manifestations, mostly species, which are said to be his *kina lau*, 'myriad bodies' (literally '400 bodies'), or 'interchangeable body forms.'"[50] Thus, as Valeri explains, "the offering consecrated to a deity must include species considered its 'bodies.'"[51] Also, sacrifice seemed obsessively frequent: occasions deserving a taking of life included human life-cycle events (birth, arrival at manhood, betrothal, marriage, death, as well as postmortem ritual and ceremonies for the dead), important economic or political activities (apprenticeship in an art or craft, construction of a house or irrigation canal or field, deployment of a new fishing net, agriculture, war and peace, or undertaking a voyage), purification (of sickness, ritual violation, or immorality), requests to the spirits (for rain, fertility, protection, or victory in battle), and sorcery and divination. There must have been a constant stream of blood from the islands.

According to Valeri, the central idiom of Hawaiian sacrifice was satisfying the hunger of the gods: "The god is supposed to be fed by the offerings; that of these offerings he eats either the 'essence' or the 'first portion' or both." The god's portion was ideally scorched—charred on the outside, raw on the inside—

a condition unfit for human use and therefore wholly divine. Other parts of the victims, or other methods of preparation, left the food edible for humans, in which case "they are supposed to absorb divine mana."[52]

Human beings were regular and superior sacrificial victims. The future victim was segregated from society inside a house or temple, often with his arms and legs bound or broken and his eyes gouged out. So began the torture of humans the likes of which we do not usually encounter with animals. He was also stripped naked and often genitally abused. By the moment of sacrifice, the victim might already be dead: as Valeri reminds us, "sacrifice is defined in Hawaii by the consecration of the victim to the god rather than by the actual execution."[53] Uncharacteristically, blood was not spilt or even allowed in the temple. So the body was washed to remove any blood released during torture and death. The purified body was brought to the inner sanctum of the temple, where it was first singed of skin and hair and then scorched in the customary way. Finally, it was laid on the altar to decompose—the gods taking the flesh—until the bones, especially the skull and most especially the teeth, could be collected and presented to a person of prestige, like the king. Such body parts were typically fastened to the clothing, utensils, and other artifacts like drums of the nobility. In fact, as we will see below, the king was regarded as the supreme sacrificer and often if not ideally the primary beneficiary of the act.

Human sacrifice was by no means restricted to the Hawaiian Islands. The practice of infanticide throughout Polynesia was associated with kingship and ancestor worship: "Babies would be promptly sent back to the nether world shortly after birth, because they were thought to be the best intermediaries between the living and the sacred dead."[54] On Tonga, the onset of adulthood of the chief's successor called for ten human victims, while the Tahitian god Oro demanded human lives on the accession of a new chief as well as the start or end of a war, the opening of a new temple, or the launching of the chief's flagship. On the Marquesan Islands, "No major event was allowed to pass without at least a few human offerings."[55]

Human Sacrifice in Dahomey and Other African Kingdoms

The African kingdom of Dahomey had one of the most extensive documented systems of human sacrifice, related both to notions of soul, gods, and ancestors, and to the office of king. The Dahomeans of course practiced animal sacrifice in addition (especially of oxen and goats), but human victims were common and more valuable.

In the religion as in the politics of Dahomey, status and hierarchy were key. Melville Herskovits, one of the main chroniclers of the kingdom, tells that the king occupied an unprecedented, essentially sacred, status and that the ancestor-spirits were also stratified into lower dead, princely dead, and royal dead. As in many traditional kingdoms, the king not only ruled the society but virtually embodied or symbolized it: his power was its power, his health was its health, his life was its life. Therefore, sacrifice to or for the living king and the dead kings was necessary. For instance, Dahomean religion and politics "daily required a sacrifice as a matter of routine thank-offering for the King's awakening in health to the new day."[56] This daily ritual required the lives of two slaves, one male and one female. Deaths were also caused as a gift to noble ancestors, ten or more at any typical ceremony. Other of the many occasions for human sacrifice included

> whenever the King gave food to his ancestors, when he authorized a new market to be established, before he went to war, and on his return from a campaign. Sacrifices were also made when a King's palace was built, the heads of these persons being cut off and the blood mixed with the earth of the palace walls. When a well was dug a man and a woman were killed to ask permission of the earth to dig.[57]

However, human sacrifice was most prodigious at the death of a king, "who was said to require a sufficient retinue for the next world to establish in miniature a replica of his kingdom."[58] This called for a representative of each office, craft or occupation, and village to be interred along with him, in addition to his wives (who could number more than one hundred), as well as pallbearers and funeral officiates.

It is safe to say that human sacrifice was intimately tied to the monarchy. In fact, Herskovits calls it "a royal prerogative" and also essentially "an economic phenomenon." This follows from the logic of Dahomean politics, economics, and religion. Ancestors, gods, and sacred events required sacrifice. A poor citizen sacrificed vegetables or perhaps a small animal. A wealthy man offered a larger animal (a goat or sheep), while a nobleman could give cattle.

> The most expensive "animal," however, was a human being, hence it was to the richest and most powerful person in the kingdom, the King, to whom the right to make this costly sacrifice was reserved. . . . [So] when "blood" offerings are required of a King, then he must offer the costliest of all "blooded" creatures—human beings.[59]

In some African (and other) kingdoms, the king himself might become a sacrificial victim, on the assumption that a weak or sick or old king was a danger to the entire society, if not to the very natural world. Kings might serve a specific term of office and then be executed, or they might be killed when they showed signs of degeneration or illness (sometimes nothing more than a cough or sneeze). On the other hand, given this preoccupation with health, human body parts were often incorporated into charms and medicines: Davies mentions how a high-born woman of Lesotho in 1948 ordered flesh to be cut from a living man (who had to be ceremonially killed afterward) for the purpose of making a medicine called *diretlo*.[60]

Human Sacrifice in Mesoamerican Civilizations

Of all the known instances of human sacrifice, probably none is grander in scale and more macabre in practice than that of the Aztec and Maya. Yet some scholars like David Carrasco have been stumped as to why it has not played a more prominent role in the analyses of sacrifice, which instead have tended to focus on ancient Hebrew and Greco-Roman materials. In fact, he notes that "all significant theories of ritual sacrifice . . . *completely ignored* the most thorough record of real, historical sacrifice while favoring either distant reports of animal sacrifices or literary sacrifices from Western Classics!" (emphasis in the original).[61] This is certainly the case in the two major theories we will consider shortly.

Sacrifice was as complicated as it was prodigious in Mesoamerica, where "almost every living thing and many inanimate objects were offered in sacrifice," including all kinds of animals—domesticated and wild—and plants, as well as such substances as honey, wax, water, pottery, textiles, precious stones, shell, coral, and so on.[62] But humans too were sacrificed, in epic proportions unrivaled by any other documented society. The victims came from many different sources—war captives certainly, but also adults of their own society (especially orphans and slaves), and, naturally, children (again, especially orphans, illegitimate ones, or those "donated" by their parents). The search for war prisoners meant the prosecution of wars simply for the purpose of obtaining prisoners— a further violent side effect that probably took more lives than the sacrifice itself. Among captives, the most valuable were high-ranking officials, including rulers of defeated enemies. Sometimes, the priests who presided over sacrificial rituals themselves fell victim to the rituals.

As is well known, Mayan/Aztec sacrifice emphasized blood and especially the heart. While the sacrificial removal of still-beating hearts was common, many other techniques existed, including beheading, slitting the throat, piercing with arrows, beating with thorny branches, and falling or pushing off the top of buildings, as well as nonlethal methods, such as removal and burial of fingers or drawing blood from the tongue, arm, ear, or penis. One description of the less-familiar arrow sacrifice ritual, based on pre-Columbian drawings, indicates that

> the victim, stripped naked, was painted blue, a color associated with sacrifice. After dancing with him, the participants in the ceremony tied the victim to a stake. Dancing, they circled around him, and each man, as he came into position, fired an arrow at the victim's heart, previously marked in white.[63]

Eye-witness accounts, like that of Spanish contemporary Diego de Landa, present the same picture "in which the victim was painted blue, tied to a post, cut in the genital area, and finally killed by arrows shot by dancers."[64]

Some of the most gruesome treatment came after the death of the victims, when their bodies had perhaps been tossed down the stairs of the temple. The dead (or occasionally still living) body might be flayed, the intact skin then worn by an attending priest. According to Robicsek and Hales, "Flaying the victim and later donning his skin was carried out in honor of the god Xipe Totec, whose feast, Tlacaxipehualiztli ('the flaying of man'), was celebrated in Central Mexico."[65]

The justifications for human sacrifice were many and familiar, including annual ceremonies (particularly for fertility), the laying of foundations for buildings, and the provision of attendants to follow a dead lord into the afterlife. However, the most unique but central motivation for Mesoamerican human sacrifice was to feed the sun god. The present sun, the fifth incarnation or iteration of the solar light, was a precarious deity (like its prior incarnations, destined to expire in the cosmic cycle of birth and death) and a hungry deity (draining its precious power as it gave off its light). This created great anxiety in humans, who considered it their duty and burden to preserve the sun by funneling life back to it:

> The fundamental principle was the need to strengthen a hungry god, one in need of food, a god whose existence depended on humans. This was the Fifth Sun, who was condemned, like the sun that had preceded him, to die in a cataclysm. As long as men could offer blood and the hearts of captives taken in

combat, his power would not decline, and he would continue on his course above the earth.[66]

Thus, symbolic images of the sun abounded portraying it in its cruelly needy condition. The Aztec Calendar Stone, for instance, placed Tonatiuh, the Fifth Sun, in the center, "whose open mouth yields a tongue in the form of a sacrificial knife symbolizing the imperative to acquire human beings for sacrifice and divine food in the form of blood."[67] Other designs presented the sun god "lavishly dressed and seated on a throne, drinking a rich stream of blood."[68]

The sun was hardly the only deity that demanded a meal. Xipe, the deity of agriculture and fertility, required nourishment. Spirits of lakes and other bodies of water received offerings as well.

THEORIES OF SACRIFICE: GIRARD AND BURKERT

A practice as widespread and extensive as sacrifice must have some, or more than one, rationale. What is the sense behind destroying what is generally regarded as innocent life in pursuit of some religious goal? As we have seen, a number of suggestions have been made—a gift or payment to divinity, a communal feast, scapegoating, and so on. Two recent and highly regarded theories, by René Girard and Walter Burkert, have generated renewed interest in the phenomenon of sacrifice but have also, it will be argued, taken the analysis of sacrifice—and religious violence in general—in the wrong direction.

Girard, perhaps the leading contemporary scholar on religion and violence, in his hugely influential book *Violence and the Sacred*, virtually equates religion with violence—or at least with the human struggle to contain violence—and therefore virtually equates religion with sacrifice. According to him, "sacrifice is the most crucial and fundamental of rites; it is also the most commonplace."[69] The origin and function of sacrifice, he posits, is essentially related to nonreligious violence, ordinary social violence or "internal violence—all the dissensions, rivalries, jealousies, and quarrels within the community that the sacrifices are designed to suppress."[70] The basis of this ubiquitous and unavoidable human violence is "mimetic desire," that is, the pursuit of the same goals or objects by members of a group in conformity with each other. "Man is the creature who does not know what to desire, and he turns to others in order to make up his mind. We desire what others desire, because we imitate their desires."[71] The ultimate cause of violence, then, is *culture*, the very fact that humans have and share culture: because members of a society learn by mimesis to desire and pursue the same things, humans are necessarily rivals and obstacles to each other, which necessarily spawns ambivalences, hostilities, and outright conflicts. Thus, the very process of becoming a member of one's society breeds violence, and violence breeds sacrifice—and religion itself.

Human communal violence, left unchecked, would be fatal not only to individual humans but also to the very existence of the community. Violence leads to more violence—revenge, feuds, vendettas, civil wars, and so on—in "an interminable, infinitely repetitive process" that would be ultimately disintegrative.[72] In societies with formal political or judicial systems, Girard opines, individuals and groups can submit their complaints and conflicts to third-party authorities, breaking the cycle of violence. In the absence of these institutions, humans manage their violence themselves, but they do so ritually. Rather than kill each other, they select a substitute victim. Onto this victim (the "scapegoat") the society projects all its animosities and grudges; by killing it, they express their violence without killing each other. Thus, they are able to release their aggressive tendencies and contain them at the same time; they can be destructive without destroying each other and society. Even so, the violence of human social life cannot be permanently exorcised, so another sacrifice will eventually be required.

Thus, another key concept for Girard is sacrificial substitution, or what we commonly call scapegoating. One takes on the burden of all—unfairly, in the end, because one cannot be guilty of the sins of all, and the victim may actually be absolutely innocent (what guilt could a cow bear?). But not just any substitute will do: for Girard, the effectiveness of the substitution only works when members conceal from themselves its symbolic quality. The act must *seem* real. That is why "for a species or category of living creature, human or animal, to appear suitable for sacrifice, it must bear a sharp resemblance to the *human* categories excluded from the ranks of the 'sacrificeable,' while still maintaining a degree of difference that forbids all possible confusion."[73] The ideal target of my violence would of course be the actual individual who caused me pain. The next best target is some other human, one without a close association to me or to the society at large. This could include slaves, war captives, young children, the disabled or deformed, the mentally ill, the illegitimate—anyone who is in some way "outside" normal society. After a human being, the next best choices are large-bodied mammals, then smaller animals, then plants, then inanimate objects. Hence we see across cultures (that do not conduct actual human sacrifices) the recurring sacrifice of cattle, sheep, goats, dogs, and so on.

Sacrifice, in this view, is not about communicating or mediating between humans and divinity; if anything, the introduction of divinity in the equation is part of the concealment. We do not sacrifice to expel our internal hostilities, the mythology of sacrifice asserts, but to comply with the demands or orders of some supernatural entity. Religion as such becomes "another term for that obscurity that surrounds man's efforts to defend himself by curative or preventive means against his own violence."[74] In other words, humans are violent first and religious second, and the latter is a thin cover for the former. One last point is that Girard sees sacrifice not only as the essence of religion but also one specific form of sacrifice (scapegoating) as "the generative principle" not just of religion but of all belief, ritual, and "even culture as a whole."[75]

Burkert too concludes that "sacrificial killing is the basic experience of the 'sacred.' *Homo religiosus* acts and attains self-awareness as *Homo necans* [killer]."[76] His theory, originally published in the same year as Girard's seminal work, resembles the latter in two ways: in its interest in origins and in its emphasis on violence as a defining social experience. For Burkert, the original act of violence is the hunt. He imagines a time when humans did not hunt: "Man became man through the hunt, through the act of killing."[77] However, beyond its economic necessity, the kill is thrilling and horrifying: he believes that prehistoric hunters felt shock and anxiety at the death they wrought. These intense experiences— "the shock of the deadly blow and flowing blood, the bodily and spiritual rapture of festive eating, the strict order surrounding the whole process"—were the very fount of the religious sentiment, the "*sacra* par excellence."[78] "Thus," he concludes, "blood and violence lurk fascinatingly at the very heart of religion."[79]

Yet, as for Girard, religion is not the *cause* of violence but the *response* to or *effect* of violence. Violence is natural and endemic to humans; it is also socially generative. Indeed, it is the very reason for society and for the success of particular societies:

> The only prehistoric and historic groups obviously able to assert themselves were those held together by the ritual power to kill. The earliest male societies banded together for collective killing in the hunt. Through solidarity and cooperative organization, and by establishing an inviolable order, the sacrificial ritual gave society its form.

As ethology has shown, a sense of community arises from collective aggression. Finally, the hunt as a ritualized and sacred act of killing becomes a displacement of human aggression onto a nonhuman victim. In short, the hunt was the source of sacrifice, and sacrifice was the source of religion.[80]

TOWARD A BETTER UNDERSTANDING OF SACRIFICE

The now-standard interpretations of Girard and Burkert do not stand up well against the data. Both would lead us to expect that sacrifice is a universal human practice, which—despite its frequency—is not quite the case. In fact, both suggest that "simpler" societies ought to manifest more sacrifice than "complex" ones; Burkert goes so far as to opine that hunting societies should evince the most sacrifice since they are in most direct contact with the horror of killing. But this is clearly false. First, hunting societies are actually the *least* likely to engage in sacrificial action; we saw no examples of them in our survey above, and Jonathan Z. Smith, a critic of the Girard-Burkert approach, reminds us there are "no unambiguous instance[s] of animal sacrifice performed by hunters."[81] Second, Burkert's analysis would indicate that wild animals make the best sacrificial victims, whereas in reality wild animals are uncommon offerings. Rather, as Smith scolds, "Animal sacrifice appears to be, universally, the ritual killing of a domesticated animal by agrarian or pastoralist societies."[82] Third, Girard's catharsis dynamic seems to have little to do with most actual occasions of sacrifice; there is often little evidence of or reference to pent-up social animosity. Fourth and perhaps most significant, Girard predicts that sacrifice should be most prevalent in societies that lack formal politics and legal-judicial institutions, but instead it is in highly formalized political systems—the Greco-Roman states, the Hawaiian and Dahomean kingdoms, and the Mayan and Aztec empires—that we find the most extensive and elaborated sacrificial traditions. Finally, it appears that both scholars are basing their positions on limited, ethnocentric models of Western (namely, ancient Hebrew and Greco-Roman) behavior without adequate cross-cultural facts.

Rather than accepting these flawed and simplistic views, let us suggest that there are three distinct but interrelated bases for sacrifice as a religious and social act. They are (1) specific religious doctrines, including and especially emulating models provided in mythology; (2) political processes, in particular the legitimation of hierarchical and exploitative social arrangements; and most fundamental, (3) a religious metaphysics in which life is a finite commodity and must be "invested" or "circulated" in order to make or control life—what I will call "the religious economy of life."

Religious Doctrine and the Reenactment of Myth

It is not facetious to assert that people commit sacrifice because they believe that they must. The compulsion to sacrifice comes from two aspects of religious ideology—mandates set down by supernatural or ancestral agents, and models established by those agents. For instance, the Torah and the Vedas ordained and gave detailed directions for sacrifice; it was never explained what the sacrifice was "for" or how it was supposed to "work." It was simply what members were told to do, and they did it as they were told. In such cases, Frits Staal may be correct in regard to the "meaning" of ritual action: writing in the context of Vedic ritual, he insists that ritual, which would include sacrifice, is "pure activity," the point or "meaning" of which is simply *to do it and to do it correctly*.[83]

Beyond the explicit commands inherent in religion are the claims and beliefs that compose its "content." Mesoamerican sacrifice was related to the belief in a dangerously hungry sun god, one who had emerged originally out of an act of self-sacrifice. As Carrasco retells the myth, for fifty-two years after the end of the previous age, there had been no light, for there was no sun. The gods assembled to ask, "Who will carry the burden? Who will take it upon himself to be the sun, to bring the dawn?" For four days the gods did rituals, with a sacred fire burning in a holy hearth. Finally, two gods offered to throw themselves into the fire to become the new sun. Tecuciztecatl was too scared to try, but Nanauatzin succeeded. The *Florentine Codex* describes the result:

> Onward thou, O Nanauatzin! Take heart! And Nanauatzin, daring all at once, determined—resolved—hardened his heart, and shut firmly his eyes. He had no fear; he did not stop short; he did not falter in fright; he did not turn back. All at once he quickly threw himself and cast himself into the fire; once and for all he went. Thereupon he burned; his body crackled and sizzled. . . . Then the gods sat waiting to see where Nanauatzin would come to rise—he who fell first into the fire—in order that he might shine as the sun; in order that dawn might break. When the gods had sat and been waiting for a long time, there-

upon began the reddening (of the dawn); in all directions, all around, the dawn and light extended, and so, they say, thereupon the gods fell upon their knees in order to await where he who had become the sun would become to rise.[84]

Likewise, Hinduism often portrays the god Shiva in terms of the belief

> that God is always hungry . . . and riddled with desire. That he is exiled in his divine world, hence driven in longing toward this, human one. That his consequent impact upon our world inevitably entails violence and destruction, particularly focused on those who are closest to him here. That this violent impacting, in which God's hunger seeks a human victim, offers the only possibility for deep transformation in that victim's self-knowledge. That such transformation generally proceeds through paradox.[85]

This may seem like a strange notion to Christians who believe in a self-sufficient god with no needs, let alone the need for human blood. But not all religions are like Christianity, and not all gods are like the Christian god.

Other less spectacular cases of sacrifice stand on a similar foundation: the gods/spirits/ancestors were believed to need or demand or deserve gifts or payment. Recall that from the religious perspective, humans are in a reciprocal-dependent relationship with nonhuman agents—subhumans (animals and plants) and superhumans. The Buid of the Philippines were a prime illustration. They thought that humans received pigs from the good *andagaw* spirits, who deserved a return offering. At the same time, humans preyed on pigs, and evil spirits preyed on humans; literally, the Buid said that "'humans are the pigs of the evil spirits,' and that the death of a human provides the evil spirits with a feast in the same way as the killing of a pig in sacrifice provides humans with a feast."[86]

Finally, in addition to explicit instructions and general beliefs, religions provide models or exemplars of behavior: so it was done in the beginning, so it shall be done now. For example, in order to understand Mesoamerican sacrifice, we must understand what happened in mythical time. The Mother Goddess Coatepec had four hundred children, including the goddess Coyalxauhqui, who led a conspiracy to kill her. As the combatants ascended the sacred mountain, Coatepec gave birth to a male, Huitzilopochtli. Born fully grown, Huitzilopochtli took up arms, fought Coyalxauhqui, and slew her, cutting off her head and throwing her body down the mountain. As Carrasco explains, the central Aztec temple, the Templo Mayor, was a reproduction of that mountain and that event, complete with a carving of Coyalxauhqui's broken body at the bottom of the staircase. Like Huitzilopochtli, the sacrificial priests rolled victims' bodies down the incline, even posing the dead bodies in the likeness of the dead goddess—an intentional reenactment of the divine killing.

Similarly, Dogon sacrifice was modeled after events in their sacred history. The supreme god Amma originally created the cosmic order, which included two pairs of androgynous twin beings. One member of the lower twin-pair, Ogo, disrupted the divine design, so Amma ordered the death of Ogo's twin, Nommo Semu. One of the higher twins, Nommo Titiyayne, was given the task of conducting the sacrifice, which began with castration of Semu; then the executioner tied him to a tree "in order to prolong his agony" and ultimately slit his throat, releasing torrents of blood upon the earth.

> The Dogon say that Nommo "showed men their first example of sacrifice." All ritual immolations are inspired by this model, "whatever the place, the purpose, the officiants [*sic*], or the procedure." The ritual always starts with slitting the throat of a young chick or a pullet, which "represents" Nommo's castration. . . . Thus a second animal is immolated to commemorate Nommo's sacrifice, properly speaking.[87]

The Legitimation of the Political Order

Part of the answer to the riddle of sacrifice can be found, not unreasonably, outside of religion, in the realm of politics and social order. Critically contrary to Girard's expectations, sacrifice was not only practiced but also perfected in highly organized, stratified societies with formal political institutions. At first thought, this might seem confusing, since sacrifice appears "primitive" or "anachronistic" to us. However, if we associate the problem of sacrifice with the problem of *power* more generally, the confusion dissipates.

The crucial relationship between political power and sacrifice takes at least three forms—sacrifice for the benefit of the king, king as sacrificer, and king as sacrifice—all informed by the premodern notion of the "sacred king." This notion can be seen in many variations on the office of king: the Egyptian pharaoh as deity himself, the Shilluck (African) king as reincarnation of the first king Nyikang and mediator between humans and divinity, the Hawaiian king as the closest human being to the gods, the European kings as rulers "by divine right," ancient Chinese emperors as bearers of a "mandate of heaven," and so on. In other words, in addition to political powers, they possessed or literally were supernatural powers as well; they were often symbols or living representations of their realms—both the social and the physical components of their realms. It was therefore essential that such leaders demonstrate and maintain their own strength and vitality, since theirs not just symbolized but also literally embodied, personified, the strength and vitality of the kingdom. As E. O. James explained, there are diverse ways to ensure that the king does not decline, dragging the health of the kingdom down with him. One is the execution of a substitute, often a family member, removing death from his surroundings. Another is a limitation on the term of the king, sometimes including killing him before he can show weakness. A third is some type of ritual renewal, such as (sometimes divine) marriage. A fourth is sacrifice.[88]

In many traditional kingdoms and empires, the king or emperor also had the role of principal or sole sacrificer. The ruler, as a semidivine being himself, might be the only human powerful enough, or intermediate enough between nature and supernature, to control sacrifice. In performing, or at least authorizing and overseeing, sacrifice, he also expressed and reestablished his authority over life and death in his domain. Sacrifice was thus a "political" act, indeed the very performance of politics itself: as in Hawaii, "The king is king . . . because he is the head of the cult, the supreme sacrificer. . . . It is precisely this that gives him authority over men, since it makes his actions more perfect and efficacious than theirs."[89] It was a sign to the members of the society—and to members of other societies—of the leader's monopoly of power and his awesome willingness to use it. The sacrifice of prisoners of war or the killing of servants and relatives as a royal retinue in the afterlife was a public demonstration of the terrible importance and power of the royal personage. Human sacrifice in particular, as the most "expensive" and valuable offering that could be made, was often especially the prerogative of kingship. Wilkerson, writing from the Aztec context (which perhaps best exemplifies our point), says that rituals including sacrifice

> are not purely religious in nature. They also allow public reaffirmation of power and demonstrate the prerogatives of status. . . . These actions are not simply the result of the dual civic and religious duties of Precolumbian rulers; they also serve a decidedly secular purpose in making the ruler visible doing what only he [is] permitted to do.[90]

The sheer spectacle of sacrifice, the burial of dozens or hundreds of courtiers, and the centralization of control over political, social, and religious "production" were part of the theater of power, which created and reaffirmed "the two highly structured and essential institutions of rulership and religion."[91] This is why Girard is so critically wrong about the social location of sacrifice.

The Religious Economy of Life

The fact that sacrifice is fundamentally *not* a "primitive" and hunting-culture behavior is patently obvious. Rather, it is most often found, and mostly extensively developed, in "advanced" societies or at least those based on domestication, not hunting, of wild animals. Further, as we have seen, the typical victims of sacrifice are domesticated, not wild, animals, including that most domesticated of all animals, humans. Jonathan Z. Smith seems to pick up the clue, that sacrifice, *"in its agrarian or pastoral* [as well as or especially its urban civilized] *context, is the artificial (i.e., ritualized) killing of an artificial (i.e., domesticated) animal"* (emphasis in the original).[92]

Let us consider again and finally the situations in which sacrifice was likely to appear. In many cultures, sacrifice was associated with agriculture and fertility: blood was sprinkled on or body parts were buried in fields, and so on. It was also closely associated with construction: blood was poured or rubbed on or body parts were buried in or under foundations, walls, bridges, and the like. Dangerous or merely socially significant occasions like births, marriages, initiations, and funerals frequently called for sacrifice. Threats from nature, moments of illness, negative "spiritual" conditions (sin, pollution, and such), embarkations on or completions of major activities like wars or business ventures or agreements, not to mention anything at all concerning rulers, were regular sacrificial occasions. Additionally, when the spirits needed appeasement or payment, and especially when the gods were hungry or weakened—when the whole world seemed to be tiring and wearing down—sacrifice was practiced.

What do these circumstances have in common? They are all, if you will, "creative" times, situations in which humans are making something, literally *producing* something, whether it is a field of grain, a building, a healthy person, a successful contract, or a good king. All these outcomes are "artificial" in Smith's sense of the word: without the effort, without the *investment*, there would be no production. In a serious way, all these situations are occasions of augmenting power, of augmenting *life*, of making things stronger and more vital. But how can humans generate strength and increase life? One means, from a certain perspective—perhaps the only means available to finite creatures like ourselves—is to transfer strength, vitality, or life from one place to another. In a "closed system" of power and life, in which humans can neither create nor destroy life, the only option is to circulate life in an *economy of life*.

What I mean by "economy" is that for everything that is produced, something else must be consumed. We cannot build a house without cutting down some trees. The consumption of wood in the production of houses is economic. Hunters do not "make" the animals they hunt (there may in fact be and often are "increase rituals" in hunting societies to enhance the fertility or supply of animals, but these do not tend to be sacrificial); hunted animals are not *artificial* animals. But societies based on farming or animal herding—that is, on domesticated species—do "make" those species in not only figurative but also literal ways. Domesticated plants and animals are artificial in this sense; they are products of human action or artifice. Houses and walls and temples and gates are also products of human action, as are (at least in some cases or from some perspectives) recovery from illness, prevention or containment of natural disaster, and achievement of fertility, victory, stability, and political power.

The clues have been everywhere, yet observers have consistently missed them. As Ian Bradley puts it, victims "were not slaughtered in these rituals to be offered as a gift to the gods but rather to release the life-blood which had a unique and mysterious sacrificial efficacy."[93] Many societies have been quite explicit about this. The Nuer believed that blood, whether bovine or human, was potent such that divinity "takes the life (or breath) or that he takes the blood—the blood and the breath being symbols of the life."[94] The Dogon were said to "maintain life" through the repetition of the primordial sacrifice which established life in the first place. Even the Judeo-Christian tradition holds that "the blood is the life" (Deuteronomy 12:23), and Christians believe that through the sacrifice of Jesus—literally through his blood—not just life but eternal life is gained. In other words, as Davies expresses, the object of sacrifice can be seen "more to preserve than to destroy life."[95] That may be why the process of sacrifice among the Aztec entailed shedding as much blood as possible or why a Hawaiian sacrifice was just as suitable if the victim was already dead.

Instead of Girard or Burkert, the writer who has come closest to this understanding is E. O. James, who wrote in 1933, "In the ritual of shedding blood it is not the taking of life but the giving of life that really is fundamental, for blood is not death but life. The outpouring of the vital fluid in actuality, or by substitute, is the sacred act whereby life is given to promote and preserve life, and to establish thereby a bond of union with the supernatural order."[96] In other words, the "fundamental principle throughout [instances of sacrifice] is the same; the giving of life to promote or preserve life, death being merely a means of liberating vitality. . . . Consequently, the destruction of the victim, to which many writers have given a central position in the rite, assumes a position of secondary importance in comparison with the 'transmission' of the soul-substance" to whatever being or purpose it is intended.[97]

What was formerly seen as pointless cruelty and misdirected sublimation of human aggression now becomes a kind of "conservation of energy"—energy being located in the life, often specifically the blood, of a sacrificial victim. There is only so much life force in the world. If humans want to make something, or to make something firm or fecund, then they must transfer energy (life force) from where it is to where they want it. And since the release of life energy entails at least spilling blood if not death, the result is sacrifice as we know it. Sacrifice represents a conservation of life, in which life or life force cannot be created nor destroyed but simply circulated. But we can see now how violence might be perceived as incidental to the act of harming or killing—indeed, how the bleeding, beating, or killing of a victim *might not be perceived as violence at all* but as a necessary and even wonderful celebration and promotion of life.

Sacrifice comes into focus under this new light. For example, one of the most often cited reasons for and forms of sacrifice—especially in Christianity—is *expiation*, the removal of evil or sin as the source of human suffering; it may also involve the payment of some penalty or debt. In at least one interpretation, being in a state of sin or evil influence is a sign or result of weakness. But how is bleeding or killing an animal (or a man or a god-man) supposed to help? In this new interpretation, a sacrifice would be one method of gathering or restoring strength to purge and resist the negative forces: the life energy of the sacrificial victim is transferred to the benefactor. In situations when misfortune is based on misdeed (violation of a religious rule or neglect of a religious obligation, etc.), the energy of the sacrifice might be the stuff of reconciliation. Even in situations of good fortune, the life force of the victim might be a compensation or thankful offering. Finally, if the sacrificer were seeking some specific instrumental result, a reciprocal "gift" of life to the beings who can deliver the result would be appropriate. As James phrases it, such sacrifice was "essentially a transference of life to enable the gods to continue their beneficent functions on earth."[98]

Finally, while this interpretation of sacrifice earns a modest place for humans (as circulators or "entrepreneurs" of life but not creators of life), it also suggests that humans may have claimed a somewhat grander role for themselves. In a way they *were* creators, if only cocreators, and in particular they had discovered a second process of production or reproduction. According to Nancy Jay, this new productive power was appropriated not just for humans but specifically for *men*, rendering sacrifice as a process of male power. She notes firstly that sacrifice is "beautifully suited for identifying and maintaining" male identity and corporateness. "Sacrifice can expiate, get rid of, the consequences of having been born of woman (along with countless other dangers) and at the same time integrate the pure and eternal patrilineage."[99] In many traditional societies sacrifices were lineage activities performed for their ancestors and as such renewed the vitality of the group and purged it of undesirable forces.

Even more, she sees sacrifice by male groups to male ancestors as a kind of symbolic "self-reproduction" that shifts the very power of creation from women to men. If sacrifice is the manipulation and transmission of life through death, such that those who perform sacrifice make life as they take life, then sacrifice is one means by which men co-opt for themselves the power of production and reproduction. One of her most compelling examples is the very case of Abraham and Isaac, with which we began: "Isaac, on the edge of death, received his life not by birth from his mother but from the hand of his father as directed by God (Elohim); and the granting of life was a deliberate, purposeful act rather than a mere natural process, a spiritual 'birth' accomplished without female assistance."[100] Clearly, the male appropriation of creation manifests not only in the taking of life but in the withholding of the taking of life. In her view, it is no surprise that the ultimate act of creation, the creation of the universe, is performed in the Judeo-Christian tradition without the aid of a female divinity and that the creation of woman comes as a "birth" out of (and as a sacrifice of a part of) a man.

CHAPTER 4

SELF-INJURY

Mayan kings spilled not only the blood of sacrificial victims but their own as well, pulling barbed strings through their tongues to draw out royal blood. Turkish Sufis (Muslim mystics) pierced their tongues and cheeks with skewers, as well as standing on swords, sticking knives in their eyes, and chewing and swallowing glass. Australian Aboriginals circumcised young men, fully awake, and opened veins in their genitals repeatedly in adulthood. The Nuer of East Africa cut scars (called *gar*) so deep into the foreheads of boys that the marks were permanently visible on the bone beneath. Christian ascetics denied themselves food, sleep, medical care, or even basic hygiene, allowing sores to fester, while martyrs walked confidently to their deaths.

As ubiquitous and profligate as sacrifice was, there is another more fundamental and more universal form of religious violence—violence directed against the self. Arguably, there is no society or religion, including hunter-gatherer societies, that did not practice some form of self-mutilation or self-deprivation for serious religious reasons. The reasons offered for this behavior were of course as varied as the behaviors themselves and the religions underlying them. In fact, while the range of sacrificial action was fairly wide, the range of self-destructive action was dramatically wider. There are so many ways to hurt oneself, from depriving simple comforts like soft beds and normal conversation, to undergoing painful and disfiguring physical operations, to torturing oneself, to killing oneself or allowing oneself to be killed.

In this chapter, we will examine the self-injurious violence performed in the name of religion or for religious purposes. Significantly, Ariel Glucklich has declared that "specific studies of religion and physical pain are rare"[1] although not totally absent: we have already seen a great number of studies of sacrificial pain, and we will see many more of varieties of suffering in this and subsequent chapters—and actually a number of quite important texts have been written on

117

the subject of pain, including Piero Camporesi's *The Incorruptible Flesh: Bodily Mutilation and Mortification in Religion and Folklore*,[2] Judith Perkins's *The Suffering Self: Pain and Narrative Representation in the Early Christian Era*,[3] and the frequently mentioned book by Elaine Scarry, *The Body in Pain: The Making and Unmaking of the World*.[4] There is also a multitude of work on wounding and suffering in specific historical and cultural contexts, such as the Native American Sun Dance or Australian Aboriginal initiation rituals.

Even so, given the epic scale of self-inflicted pain, insufficient attention has been paid to it. There are a variety of potential explanations for this lack. One is quite likely the desire to dissociate religion from such destructive behavior: surely religion, at least "real" or "healthy" religion, does not sanction or motivate this way of acting. Another is perhaps the tendency to dismiss self-injurious behavior as deviant, even pathological. After all, self-harm is a category of psychological disorder in modern medicine. It is difficult for many people to imagine any circumstance in which hurting oneself is justified or even sane. It seems like sheer masochism. Yet, contrary to Girard, self-directed violence may be the original and essential form of religious violence.

As indicated, self-destructive religious violence falls along a continuum from minor inconvenience to major torment to death. Such deeds include fasting or denying oneself particular foods, sleep deprivation, isolation or silence, enforced celibacy, hitting, cutting, scarring, piercing, burning, whipping, castration or amputation of body parts, holding awkward or painful poses, carrying weights, ingesting drugs or poisons, drawing blood, and subjecting oneself to beating or torture and ultimately suicide or presenting oneself for execution. All these acts, and many more, have been performed by humans in the pursuit of religion. Indeed, the one unifying factor of this spectrum of self-abuse is its religious genesis.

Human inhumanity to itself is truly breathtaking. At the same time, as we have argued previously, every one of these types of religious self-abuse has a nonreligious counterpart: people hurt themselves for religious as well as nonreligious reasons. There is religious fasting and secular fasting. There is religious and secular celibacy, religious and secular self-hitting or self-cutting or self-amputation. There is religious suicide and secular suicide. Granted, most of these "mundane" expressions of self-injury are regarded as mental illness, and many have technical names. All modern readers are familiar with anorexia and bulimia, in which people (commonly young girls) make normal eating a huge source of anguish. Trichotillomania names a condition in which people pull out their own hair and seem to enjoy it. In Munchhausen syndrome, people seek as much attention as they can get from medical professionals, often by literally harming or poisoning themselves to simulate an illness (and more sadly, individuals with "Munchhausen syndrome by proxy" will use other people, including their own children, to get attention, even if this requires injuring or poisoning the child). Most gruesome of all is apotemnophilia, in which patients want to, and sometimes do, destroy perfectly healthy body parts (usually arms or legs). Potentially a subtype of "body dysmorphic disorder" related to a distorted sense of their own body (perceiving themselves as fat when they are dangerously thin, etc.), sufferers of apotemnophilia seem to experience the offending body part as "wrong" or unnecessary or out of place; one sufferer said that in her mind her otherwise normal leg ended at the knee. Naturally, doctors are generally opposed to removing healthy limbs, but some patients have resorted to damaging it first (by cutting, shooting, or freezing in dry ice) to force amputation.

It goes without saying that not all methods of self-mutilation are so extreme. In fact, what might be considered "self-mutilation" in some cultures, or in some segments of its own culture, is regarded as normal or desirable in another: ear-piercing or body-piercing or tattooing or even infant circumcision, Botox injections to the face, and operations to remove bones from a woman's foot (to fit into narrower shoes) seem minor to many Westerners, not "injurious" at all. Nevertheless, it is obvious that humans have devised an infinite number of ways to manipulate, mutilate, or simply manage the body. No culture leaves the body alone; it is sensible, then, that no religion would leave the body alone. Humans hardly seem to need spiritual justifications to damage themselves, but they certainly have found them.

We turn now to examples of religion-motivated self-inflicted harm. The great diversity in such behavior can be organized into three main categories. First, there is self-mortification of an episodic and "amateur" kind: individuals who are not religious specialists or full-time practitioners may seek out or submit themselves to specific experiences of pain or injury, sometimes during collective rituals, sometimes on key personal occasions. Despite their lay status, such persons may still be grievously hurt, even killed—and death may be the practical goal. Second, there is asceticism, in which specialists devote themselves to ordeals of deprivation and suffering for religion; the point here is often to stay alive and maximize one's discomfort. Finally, there is martyrdom, the acceptance if not pursuit of death in the name of some religious cause. Interestingly, in most if not all cases, victims of religious self-harm would either claim that there is no pain or that the pain is not only bearable but worthwhile—or even that there is no "harm" occurring despite the pain. Like many secular self-injurers, they may not simply dismiss the accusation of self-destructiveness but actually enjoy the experience: as one source on self-cutting describes, "Many cutters report that when they harm themselves, they feel relief rather than physical pain. 'I cut because all the pain flows out with the blood and I feel relief,' [a self-cutter said]. . . . She echoes what many others self-injurers frequently report feeling when they harm themselves—a release of tension, pain, and confusion."[5] In all cases, a message is clearly being sent—that there is something better, more valuable, than comfort or than life itself.

RELIGIOUS SELF-MORTIFICATION: A CRY OF PAIN TO THE SPIRITS

Across cultures and religions, there is simply no more common practice than inflicting or accepting the infliction of some degree of pain upon oneself. Many rituals require it; many individuals resort to it. In any event, religion teaches that there is some good to come from it—literally, no (physical) pain, no (spiritual) gain.

Australian Aboriginal Initiation

Australian Aboriginal societies, foragers for whom animal—let alone human—sacrifice would have seemed absurd, nevertheless practiced various forms of self-injurious behavior, many of them associated with male initiation. Aboriginals consisted of as many as several hundred different linguistic and cultural groups spread across the continent, yet there were certain recurring themes in their religious practices. According to the anthropologist A. P. Elkin, as well as my own field research in Australia, the initiation of young men into adulthood (usually in their late-teen years) involved an assortment of painful physical operations. One practice, called *cicatrization*, involved cutting deep and long scars across a youth's chest, even packing the cut with dirt and other material to create a permanent raised welt. In tooth avulsion a healthy tooth (usually an incisor) was removed. The nasal septum was pierced, allowing a bone or feather to be worn through the nose. Arm ligatures were tied tightly around the upper arm, restricting blood circulation. And most famous and important, circumcision was performed on the young men, which was only a prelude to the later and repeated subincision (cutting along the underside of the penis) that they would experience at higher stages of initiation.

As Elkin explains, these operations were often interconnected, with blood as the dominant theme: "The tying of arm ligatures is but a preparation for the duty of blood-letting, and subincision prepares the genital organ for a similar purpose; blood is drawn from it for ritual use, to express emotions in a prescribed ritual manner both in initiation and totemic ceremonies."[6] As he continues:

> Arm-blood is sacred, and is used for sticking ornamental material (bird's down and ochre) on the body in preparation for a ceremony, for anointing the candidates, and for sacramental drinking by the candidates and the elders. It gives strength to the young fellows so that they will be able to bear the sight of the sacred symbols and rites which are to be revealed.[7]

Blood from arms and genitals, mixed with water and ochre, was also used for painting sacred symbols and was dripped onto sacred stones and other objects as if anointing them.

Blood rituals were only a part of the initiation process, which began with the symbolic violence of "abducting" the initiate from his often tearful mother, this kidnapping understood as a symbolic death of the youth. Prior to circumcision, the boys were subjected to seclusion, demands of silence and obedience, tooth avulsion, and long treks through the desert. During the weeks-long ceremony, they were shown sacred objects and taught esoteric knowledge before being returned to their families, changed forever by the experience—literally made into new men.

One revealing aspect of this behavior is that, while Aboriginals did not practice sacrifice, some of their attitudes resembled and anticipated sacrificial ones. Blood was power, power that could be—and had to be—transferred from adults to youths, humans to objects, and natural beings to supernatural ones. In Elkin's words, "just as human blood gives physical strength to the weak and aged, just as it gives spiritual courage and sacred life to the newly initiated, so in these ceremonies it gives life to the [supernatural or ancestral] hero or to the totemic species."[8]

The "Training" of Shamans

In many religions that contained the role of shaman or ritual healer, becoming a shaman or practicing shamanic powers involved numerous painful ordeals. Among these the great historian of religion Mircea Eliade mentioned "beatings, feet held close to fire, suspension in the air, amputation of fingers, and various other cruelties,"[9] including sleep deprivation and long hours of chanting, fasting, drug ingestion, sexual abstinence, isolation from the community, physical exertions, and insect bites, to name but a few.

In such shamanic apprenticeships, Eliade saw a cross-cultural theme of "suffering, death, resurrection"[10] from which the trainee emerged a changed and more powerful person. The conceptual death of the future shaman often involved a symbolic (from our point of view; shamans seemed to claim that it was real) dismemberment and replacement of their internal organs with new supernatural ones and/or insertion of supernatural substances like crystals into their bodies. Shamans might come to experience themselves as dead, enabling them to travel to or commune with the spirits and the dead. In the case of Eskimo shamans, "a long effort of physical privation and mental contemplation [was] directed to gaining *the ability to see himself as a skeleton*"[11] (emphasis in the original). Elkin confirms that the Aboriginal shaman was "made" through a process of creative destruction in which "the postulant dies to his old life and rises a new person" with "new 'insides.'"[12] Across cultures, it was typically either a spirit or a senior shaman who did the "killing."

Shamans were sometimes "called" to their vocation, but in other instances they pursued the shamanic power. The !Kung bushmen of the Kalahari desert employed a spiritual energy they called *n/um* that was located in their lower spine and that "boiled" up their body as they danced the shaman dance, a painful sensation that many attempted but few mastered. Among Native American societies of the Great Plains, the "vision quest" was often associated with "isolation and self-mortification," although Ruth Benedict noted that this varied considerably by tribe. In the Cheyenne version of the quest, the seeker

> goes out to a lonely part of the prairie on the day selected, accompanied by the person who is to tie the thongs for him. . . . He is then tied to the pole by means of wooden pins driven through the flesh. All day long, after he is left alone again, he must walk back and forth on the sunward side of the pole, praying constantly, and fixing his eyes on the sun, trying to tear the pins loose

from the torn flesh. At night the helper returns, and pieces of the torn skin are held toward the sun and sky and the four directions and buried. That night he sleeps on the prairie and gets his power.[13]

However, she notes that self-torture was most intensely integrated into vision-questing for the Dakota, quoting several sources that emphasized "the part played by lacerations in the securing of any sort of vision among the Dakota."[14]

One unique ritual that seems to be closely connected to the shamanic pursuit was the Sun Dance; in fact, Benedict argues that "the final tortures of the sun dance . . . were reserved for those who desired to become shamans, and the ultimate purpose of the ordeal was the obtaining of the vision."[15] Generally known to the Western public, the Sun Dance often (but not always: Linton reported that the Comanche version included no torture and little discomfort)[16] required a firm commitment to pain:

> The dancers are pierced in the skin above the pectoral muscles or scapulae where wooden skewers are inserted. These are attached to thongs leading to the Sun Dance pole. Other skewers may be attached at the back or upper arms and tied to buffalo skulls. The dancers move toward the pole, then run backward with great force, tearing themselves free.[17]

Benedict cited a previous observer named Riggs who wrote in 1869 that Sioux Sun Dancers were not only attached to but also hung from the pole: "'Thus they hang suspended only by those cords without food or drink for two, three, or four days, gazing into vacancy, their minds fixed intently upon the object in which they wish to be assisted by the deity, and waiting for a vision from above.'"[18]

Ritual Self-Torture in Malaysia

Readers may be familiar with some of the exertions undertaken by "professional" yogis and mendicants in Hinduism. However, the extremities of Hinduism are not limited to India nor to religious specialists. Colleen Ward recounts the self-mortifications practiced in the Malaysian ceremony of Thaipusam in which members of the Hindu minority of that country engage in activities reminiscent of the Sun Dance but also consistent with practices in India and Sri Lanka like the Kumbha Mela (see below).

In Thaipusam, Hindu devotees of the god Murugan give prayers, sacrifices, and thanks involving two particular forms of self-abuse. First, they "allow their bodies to be pierced and decorated with needles, hooks, and skewers in an expression of faith and loyalty. Despite extensive piercing, most devotees rely on ritual trance for control of pain and bleeding and are able to complete the pilgrimage to Murugan's temple."[19] Second, they lift and carry burdens called *kavadis* weighing as much as forty pounds. The latter practice is once again a celebration or reenactment of a mythical event, when the giant named Idubam was defeated by and thus "became a special devotee of Murugan. Instructed to perform penance and show respect, Idubam fulfilled his religious obligations; the kavadi is now thought to be symbolic of the hills that the giant once slung over his shoulder and carried away on poles."[20] Therefore, carrying kavadis is considered meritorious for a follower of the god, who by bearing the burden "demonstrate[s] purity of heart, . . . receives praise and support from family and friends, . . . displays invincibility and power . . . , and experiences self-satisfaction over a job well done and a bargain completed." [21] Even preparations for the ritual impose hardships on the followers, for, as in many ritual situations, they have to approach the occasion purified:

> The preparation period . . . is usually set at one week although some may impose rigorous self-discipline for up to a month before the Thaipusam celebration. During this time the devotee restricts diet and sleep patterns, fasting and limiting him/herself to one vegetarian meal per day and decreasing the hours of sleep per night. She/he also abstains from alcohol, smoking, sexual intercourse, and social activities.[22]

Sambia Masculinity Rituals

In some cultures and religions, the spiritual struggles are not limited to human versus spirit or good versus evil. Many, like the Sambia of eastern New Guinea, found themselves struggling ritually with the tension between male and female—with painful results for both sexes.

Like a number of societies in New Guinea, the Sambia were highly sex stratified, with men in the dominant status. This distinction and inequality was manifested in economic and political, symbolic and ideological, and religious and ritual ways. Men held the prime positions of power; social organization was based on male lineages and a central men's house where unmarried adult males resided as a group ready to engage in their most valuable activity, war. They also promoted what Gilbert Herdt calls "idioms of masculinity," including "secret traditions of knowledge and belief (enforced by social taboos)" that separated and elevated men over women.[23]

However, males were not merely or primarily natural beings but social creations; that is, Sambia men worried that boys would not become men, or at least strong men (*aamooluku*) as opposed to weak or soft men (*wusaatu*, "rubbish"), more effeminate than masculine. Accordingly, the Sambia believed that "it is a matter of utmost urgency that a boy be initiated and masculinized" to produce a real man out of a potential man. The problem for male children was that they were necessarily and unavoidably polluted with female substance, as a consequence of being born from a woman, being in physical contact with a woman, and being nurtured and suckled by a woman. This was a threat, even a contradiction, to *moyu*, which Herdt defines as a "mystical notion referring to male substance, [which] is linked to semen."[24] "A boy's body has female contaminants inside it that not only stymie his physical development but, if not removed, will weaken and eventually kill him."[25]

The problem could be solved in two ways. First, the female substance had to be expelled. This involved a set of ritual practices to get the femaleness out and off of the youth. One type of ritual Herdt calls "stretching rites," in which the boy's skin was rubbed coarsely with sticks, switches, and other scratchy materials to "open" or "stretch" the skin; the resulting bleeding was good, for it purged womanly poisons from his system. "Egestive rites" were intended to purge the boy's insides; he was made to vomit and defecate out the antimale stuff, and his nose was made to bleed. In fact, adult men would continue throughout their lives to induce nose-bleeds, especially after their wives' periods. A third type of behavior, called "ingestive rites," introduced the proper male substances into his body. This included taboos on "soft foods" and even water, along with literally hundreds of dietary rules on what could and could not be eaten. A final, and to many Westerners especially distasteful, aspect of "supplying" boys with maleness or moyu was inseminating the boys by having them perform oral sex on young adult men, thereby transferring some of the adult male substance to the "empty" immature males.

Penitence and Self-Flagellation

Religions with certain concepts and worldviews have engaged in behavior that is not only self-injurious but self-punitive. Not all pain is punishment: none of the forms of self-mortification we have seen so far involve a notion of punishment. Punishment necessarily presupposes guilt, and self-harm under a condition of guilt (or "sin") can be construed as a type of penitence, an expression of sorrow or regret at one's faults or weaknesses—or perhaps at the faults or weaknesses of others or of the world as a whole.

Penitence has been a part of Christianity for centuries and follows from the sense of guilt or sin—even "original sin," inexpungeable by any act of sacrifice or charity—that the religion has tended to instill in believers. Christians are told explicitly that Jesus died for *their* sins, a gesture of "grace" that no human could possibly deserve. Early Christian ascetics took the suffering of Christ quite personally and attempted to emulate his model (see below). However, in the second Christian millennium, the practice of whipping oneself, also referred to as *scourging* or *self-flagellation*, began to develop and spread, first among monastic orders like the Franciscans and Dominicans and gradually to the general membership. Self-punishment for wickedness was only exacerbated by the crises in Europe of the 1200s and 1300s, like the Black Plague. Writes Michael Carroll, "This is why public processions of flagellants in the Middle Ages so often followed upon natural disasters," which Christians tended to blame on themselves.[26] If they were culpable, then presumably some demonstration of guilt and some acceptance of punishment would assuage divine anger.

In his two-volume history of Christianity, Justo Gonzalez describes how flagellation emerged as a popular movement in 1260 and grew over the following century. And he finds that the decision to scourge oneself "was not a momentary or disorderly hysteria"[27] but rather a sober commitment. Flagellants had to undergo "a rigid and sometimes even ritualistic discipline" for thirty-three and a half days and then continue to beat themselves annually thereafter. The flagellation process itself proceeded as follows:

> Twice a day they would march in procession to the local church, two by two, while singing hymns. After praying to the Virgin in the church, they would return to the public square, still singing. There they would bare their backs, form a circle, and kneel in prayer. While still kneeling, they resumed their singing, and beat themselves vigorously, until their backs were bloody. Sometimes one of their leaders would preach to them, usually on the sufferings of Christ. After the flagellation they would arise, cover their backs, and withdraw in procession. Besides these two public flagellations every day, there was a third one, to be done in private.[28]

According to Carroll, the practice spread to Italy in the 1400s and to Spain in the 1500s, where flagellants assembled into penitential clubs or fraternities or "brotherhoods." By the 1600s, "the public processions staged by flagellant confraternities in Spain had become among the most elaborate such processions in the Catholic world."[29]

Naturally, where Catholic Christianity spread in that era, self-scourging also found a home. By 1527 there were already flagellant brotherhoods in Mexico. In part this was a simple diffusion of European practice, but in part it was something much different—namely, a dramatic means of attracting and retaining native converts. The contemporary missionaries overtly understood and admitted that

> theatrical techniques were often necessary in order to secure the emotional involvement of rural populations in the mission experience. As a result, during the course of their sermons missionaries often held up skulls, cut their own hair, passed their arms through flames, and so on. The most efficacious techniques, however, were always those that involved what Luigi Lombardi Satriani [1981] has called the "theatricalization of blood." In other words, rural activities that were public and that involved much shedding of blood—including, but not limited to, flagellation—were seen to be (and were) a form of visual entertainment that best secured the involvement of onlookers in the mission as a whole.[30]

The bulk of Carroll's study examines a penitential brotherhood, the Hermandad de Nuestro Padre Jesus Nazareno, in New Mexico in the 1800s and possibly early 1900s. The Penitentes were again not a spontaneous or irrational mob but an organized and traditional institution. There was a hierarchy of officers, headed by the *mayor* and including senior brothers (Brothers of Light) and junior brothers (Brothers of Blood). A man was first initiated into the brotherhood by being "sealed," that is, having the seal or symbol of the group carved into his bare back with broken glass or a sharp stone. It was the juniors, the Brothers of Blood, who undertook the self-whipping, particularly during the Easter season. As in Europe, they marched in procession, shirtless and flogging themselves or being flogged by another brother with the *disciplina*, a whip made of yucca strands. In some cases they also carried heavy wooden crosses, dragged carts (called *carreta de la muerte*, "death cart") loaded with a wooden statue, knelt on jagged rocks, or tied tight tourniquets around their legs. Finally, observers have documented other mortifications like being buried upright with only one's head above the ground; having one's arms tied to a pole across the shoulders while the hands held two swords, each positioned downwards so that as one walked, the swords pricked the thighs; having cactus strapped tightly to various parts of one's body and/or beating oneself with cactus pads; and allowing oneself to be bound and pulled over rough ground or cactus by others.[31]

Self-mortifying brotherhoods formed in other Catholic colonies as well, such as the Philippines, where self-whipping was introduced in 1590. It quickly became popular, although as European attitudes changed, colonial policies changed too: bloody penance was banned in 1771. Interestingly, a revival in penitential practice occurred in the 1950s, with a remarkable twist—*self-crucifixion*, which first appeared in 1961. One or more volunteers would allow themselves to be suspended on, bound to, or even nailed to a cross in imitation of Jesus. By 1992, twelve "victims" from the area of San Pedro Kutud were participating as *kristos* or self-crucifiers, and every indication is that the practice survives and grows to this day.

Christianity, while it distinguishes itself in penitential and self-flagellatory behavior, does not monopolize that behavior. Islam also has a flagellation tradition, despite the fact that some Muslims argue that the Qur'an forbids self-harm. Nevertheless, just as (some) Catholic Christians employed self-flagellation while (most) Protestant Christians condemned it, so some Shi'ite Muslims employ it while (most) Sunni Muslims condemn it.

The most dramatic occasion for self-mortification in Shi'ite Islam comes on the day of Asura, the tenth day of the Islamic month of Muharram. It is a commemoration of the defeat, even the martyrdom, of the early Muslim leader Husayn (also spelled Husain or Hussein, etc.) at the battle of Karbala in 680 CE. Husayn was a direct descendant of Muhammad, and for many Muslims the family line of the founding prophet is the only legitimate leadership of the religion. Therefore, for devotees of the ancestral line of the "rightly guided prophets" (also known as the *Shi'a* or "partisans"), the faith went wrong with the killing of Husayn and his kinsman Ali.

Practitioners gather on their day of mourning to beat themselves across the back with chain-whips and to cut themselves over the head and face, often resulting in great flow of blood. In more minor cases, participants may merely pound their chests. Such behavior is performed not only in the Karbala region but also wherever there is a significant Shi'ite population, including in Iran and in Pakistan. Hegland describes the practice in Pakistan:

different circles and rows of men, bared to the waist, were energetically beating themselves on the chest in rhythm with their chanting. They stayed in place for some time and then moved up a short way before stopping again. Whenever the sound of clanging metal arose, people ran in the direction of the noise to see men striking their backs with chain flails ending in knives, for the few moments before others forced them to quit their bloody self-mortification. As men cut away at their backs, blood ran down, soaking their *shalwar* sometimes even to the ankles and showing up in striking red contrast against their pure, white cotton pants.[32]

Mothers of course were proud to have their sons demonstrate their faith and courage so. Perhaps most interesting in this case, the women were beginning to participate as well, if only through comparatively mild chest-beating behavior—smacking themselves "right hand to left side, and left hand to right side—in time to the chanting."[33]

Sati (Widow Self-Immolation) in India

While the exertions discussed above seldom resulted in more than pain and bloody scenes, some religion-inspired self-violence not just culminated in but actually aspired to death. One stark example is the fate of widows in classical— and sometimes contemporary—India. Related to this tradition are two other modern phenomena: first, "dowry death" in which a husband or mother-in-law may abuse or even kill a woman in order to extort a higher dowry payment from her father or to free the husband from the marriage altogether so that he can collect another dowry; second, the abandonment and impoverishment of widows, who were not supposed to survive their husbands' deaths in the first place.

In Hinduism, the ideal manner of disposal of corpses is cremation: a pyre is constructed and the body burned ceremonially on it. When the deceased is a male, a tradition exists (though it is hardly followed in all cases) that the widow should join him in death. As Narasimhan cites from the ancient text called *Shuddhitattva*: "All the actions of a woman should be the same as that of her husband. If her husband is happy, she should be happy, if he is sad she should be sad, and if he is dead she should also die. Such a wife is called *pativrata* [loyal/pure/chaste]."[34] Likewise, the *Parasara Samhita* urges, "She who follows her husband in death dwells in heaven for as many years as there are hairs on the human body—that is, thirty-five million years."[35] The practice is known as *sati*, another word that connotes purity. Narasimhan explains that the term is derived from *sat* meaning truth, and a *sati* was a woman who was "true to her ideals." Since Indian tradition holds chastity, purity, and loyalty to the husband (*pativrata*) as the highest ideals for a woman, there appears to be an inexorable logic behind a decision to give up one's life on the death of a husband as proof of chastity or the ultimate expression of a wife's "fidelity."[36]

Surprisingly, Narasimhan argues that the early Indian texts, the Vedas, do not refer to sati and that the practice seems to originate much more recently. By the first to third centuries CE, sati was offered as an option: kill yourself or accept a life of celibacy. In the fifth century CE, the *Vedavyasasmirti* recommends it as the best option. The Puranas, composed in the sixth century CE, went further:

> Tell the faithful wife of the greatest duty of women: she is loyal and pure who burns herself with her husband's corpse. Should the husband die on a journey, holding his sandals to her breast let her pass into the flames.
>
> When the widow consigns herself to the same pile with the corpse of the deceased, whoever performs *kriya* (rites) for her husband shall perform it for her.[37]

Finally, around 700 CE, the Hindu scholar Angirasa urged that "for all women there is no other duty except falling into the funeral pyre when the husband dies."[38]

Understandably, not many modern wives follow these injunctions, and some attempts have been made to eliminate the practice. However, in 1987, an eighteen-year-old bride named Roop Kanwar suffered the loss of her new husband. She ended up on her husband's pyre, under suspicious circumstances: some witnesses claim that she was dragged or drugged onto the flames. The local response was not outrage but quite the opposite: she was celebrated and sainted as *Sati Mata* ("pure mother"), and a cult quickly grew around her great self-sacrifice. Mala Sen reports that some locals attributed miraculous curative powers to her, and believers gathered and chanted at her funeral site for weeks afterward.[39] Narasimhan completes the story:

> Reasoning that only a woman endowed with divine strength would have chosen an end through fire, [the faithful] converged on the *chabutra* (funeral platform) with offerings of coconut and incense. . . .
>
> "We believe that this was an act of God," insisted a paternal uncle of the deceased [husband].[40]

According to Sen, critics—including women's rights activists—who protested the death and its celebration were branded as "modern, corrupt, and godless."[41]

Collective Suicide

Doctrines and traditions like those concerning sati have led to the loss of many lives, but at least ordinarily only one at a time. In more than a few cases—especially but not exclusively in modern times—religions have perpetrated mass self-destruction, dozens or even hundreds in one spasm of communal suicide. On some occasions, this has been associated with an actual, or more likely a perceived or anticipated, persecution of their group, and it has also been entangled with specific beliefs, particularly those predicting an (imminent) end of the world. Many of these groups possessed a millenarian attitude, often but not always inherited from Christianity.

Probably the most famous mass suicide occurred within the "People's Temple" at Jonestown, Guyana, in November 1978. Headed by a man named Jim Jones, the People's Temple, or more fully the People's Temple Christian Church, was founded in 1955 in Indianapolis. One of the interesting and controversial aspects of the early Jones church was its openness to African Americans, which led him to relocate the congregation of eighty members (about half African American) to the more tolerant environment of California in 1965. In 1974 Jones acquired four thousand acres of land in Guyana, a South American country with a multiracial population. At first, fifty members settled there, but it eventually grew into a utopian community of over nine hundred. Criticism subsequently emerged of the group's practices, both religious and financial, leading to an inspection by a team including US congressman Leo Ryan. While things seemed positive at first, a member secretly slipped Ryan a note asking for help escaping from Jonestown. When the Temple's leadership discovered this, they assaulted Ryan's party as the visitors were leaving, killing Ryan and four others and wounding dozens of Ryan's staff, reporters, and defectors. At this point, Jones declared the world of the People's Temple Christian Church at an end, and nine hundred nine (including about three hundred children) followers were given a Kool-Aid-like beverage laced with cyanide and tranquilizers to drink. Parents reportedly served their children first, before poisoning themselves. Jones shot himself in the head.

In the late 1990s the pattern repeated itself with the group called The Evolutionary Level Above Human (TELAH), better known as "Heaven's Gate."

Another millenarian religion, TELAH, founded by Marshall Applewhite (who called himself "Do") and Bonnie Lu Nettles ("Ti") around 1975, taught that extraterrestrial aliens had seeded the primitive human species with computer chips, creating a higher form of human being that the aliens tended like a garden. Periodically teams arrived from the home planet to harvest the more evolved humans and to attempt to improve additional humans. Of course, whenever earthly rulers and religions discovered this activity, they opposed it and executed the team if possible; as it happens, Jesus and his disciples had been a previous alien team. Applewhite was the current team leader, struggling to spread the message of higher humanity and to prepare those evolved humans for transport to the homeworld, aboard a spaceship that was believed to hover behind the Hale-Bopp comet. One step in the preparations was shedding the primitive trait of gender, inducing some of the male members to have themselves castrated. Then, on March 28, 1997, thirty-nine members of the group were found dead, identically dressed, in their house in California. There were allegedly no signs of desperation or disaster; rather, they apparently believed that the time had come to depart from their physical bodies and "upload" their memory chips onto the alien spacecraft. As the Religious Movements Project of the University of Virginia puts it, "In the end, the deaths of the Heaven's Gate group were acts of faith; they were graduating to the higher level from which Do and Ti had descended."[42]

The conflagration at Waco, Texas, in 1993 is more controversial. The Branch Davidians, an offshoot of the Seventh Day Adventists, had been founded in 1929 but were led after 1988 by Vernon Howell, who changed his name to David Koresh. Koresh envisioned himself as the fulfillment of the prophecies written in the Book of Revelation, literally the one who would arrange for the second coming of Jesus. As a group in preparation for the end-time, it formed into an isolationist commune at its compound in Waco, dubbed "Ranch Apocalypse." Marriages were conducted within the community, money collectively owned, and, in anticipation of conflict with the outside world and/or the tribulations of the end, guns stockpiled. In early 1993 the US Bureau of Alcohol, Tobacco, and Firearms raided the compound on suspicion of illegal weapons possession. Four federal agents and six group members died in the raid, and two dozen other agents were injured. A fifty-one day standoff followed, culminating in a fire (whether started by tanks shooting into the building or by arson from inside the building, no one is sure) that killed Koresh and over seventy of his flock.

Certainly there are other cases that are less known or even currently unknown. A faction called the Order of the Solar Temple (also the International Chivalric Organization of the Solar Tradition) committed mass suicide in 1994. Founded in 1984 and primarily settled in Switzerland, the movement had roots in the Rosicrucian tradition. Its founder, Joseph Di Mambro, with a partner named Luc Jouret gave lectures and held workshops about so-called spiritual masters and the esoteric knowledge they possessed. However, distrust in the group led to defections and an increasingly apocalyptic tone to its rhetoric. On the morning of October 4, 1994, fifty-three loyal members were found dead in their Swiss town, as well as in Quebec where a cell resided. In March 1997, five additional Quebec followers killed themselves. The world knows almost nothing about the congregation calling itself Restoration of the Ten Commandments of God, an apocalyptic group in Uganda with ties to Catholicism. Its leader, Joseph Kibweteere, convinced that the end was near and the righteous would be saved, shepherded some four hundred seventy members to kill themselves, the bodies found in the ashes of their burnt church. In 1986 several women in the Japanese religion Friends of Truth were found dead, having apparently killed themselves to accompany their recently deceased leader. In 1993, fifty-three Thais in a Vietnamese millenarian group directed by Ca Van Lieng committed suicide rather than face the predicted Armageddon in 2000.

ASCETICISM: RELIGIOUS ATHLETES

In the preceding examples of autoviolence, the participants have largely been the regular rank-and-file of the religion. This has not meant, notably, that the self-injury is always minor: the ordinary followers of a faith may be called upon, or may eagerly volunteer themselves, to give their blood and their very lives. When we turn to ascetics—sometimes also referred to as monks or mendicants—we are not so much at a different point on a spectrum as at a different dimension of the same phenomena. The main difference between ascetics and ordinary self-mortifiers is that the former are "professionals," often "full-time" or official or ordained representatives of the religion; they may, therefore, take on their self-destructive duties more regularly or even permanently, as well as more enthusiastically. The main similarities between the two are the range of austerities they may accept—from light to onerous to fatal—and, of course, their spiritual motivation.

Asceticism is essentially a formal, even lifetime, commitment to some degree of self-privation and self-mortification. The word derives from the Greek verb *askein* for "to work/exercise," giving us the nouns *askesis* for "work/exercise" and *asketes* for "one who works/exercises." We might do well to take this idea seriously: for the practicing ascetic, the rigors of asceticism *are* in a real sense his or her work, and they certainly do constitute a form of exercise and are frequently understood as such by the practitioners. The specific kinds of exercises that are typically included in the ascetic regimen are "dieting, vegetarianism, fasting, sexual abstinence, sexual control, sexual continence, virginity, physical retreat from society, general dissipation of the body, wearing of rough clothing, flagellation, political quietism, prayer, night vigils, martyrdom, and abstinence from bathing."[43] Gillian Clark places poverty at the center of the ascetic experience, arguing that many "aspects of the ascetic life could also be interpreted as consequences of the choice of poverty: hunger, dirt, extremes of heat and cold."[44]

Asceticism is among the most dramatic expressions of religious self-injury and among the most dramatic expressions of all religion. Max Weber used the term "religious virtuosity" to describe the behavior: just as some of us are amateur musicians while a special few are musical virtuosi, so some of us are amateur religionists while a special few are religious virtuosi. The virtuoso is the highest and fullest achievement in the field, and if the field is religion generally, or religious self-destruction particularly, then a minority will truly stand above the rest.

Weber went on to suggest that there are two main approaches to asceticism, namely, "inner-worldly asceticism" and "world-rejecting asceticism." In the first approach, the practitioner continues to participate in the mundane world, perhaps through the institutions of the religion, and "may have the obligation to transform the world in accordance with his ascetic ideals."[45] In the second approach, the ascetic calling "may entail a formal withdrawal from the 'world': from social and psychological ties with the family, from the possession of worldly goods, and from political, economic, artistic, and erotic activities—in short, from all creaturely interests."[46] Ultimately, he is led to conclude that asceticism is associated with certain kinds of religions, specifically those with a "salvation" theology of some sort: it is, quite literally, "a methodical procedure for salvation."[47] Therefore, we would expect to encounter it in some religious contexts and not others, and in fact, we do find it most fully expressed in two major religious traditions—Christianity and Hinduism (and the offshoots of Hinduism like Jainism and Buddhism). It is to these two ascetic traditions that we turn.

Asceticism in Christianity

From its earliest days, Christianity has had a distinct "other-worldly" quality to it: Jesus said that his kingdom was not of this world and urged believers to reject wealth, career, and family in order to follow him. Paul even more clearly warned followers of the dangers of sexuality and urged abstinence on them. And from the days of the early church, many followers took these admonitions to heart, at the very least living simple and chaste lives and sometimes literally withdrawing into separatist communities or individual isolation to await the end of the world.

As Gonzalez states, a certain degree of disengagement, even monasticism, existed in the first centuries of Christianity, but it was Anthony (ca. 250–ca. 355) who developed the role of the solitary desert monk. From the Greek *monos* for "solitary/alone," monks like Anthony retreated into the Egyptian desert in a "search for solitude. Society, with its noise and its many activities, was seen as a temptation and a distraction from the monastic goal,"[48] that goal being knowledge of God and attainment of salvation. Hermits like Anthony determined that this goal could not be reached through timid or part-time effort, after work and on weekends. It required a full commitment of one's time, mind, and body. The body in particular, it seems, was a problem for Anthony. Samuel Rubenson, after studying the saint's writings, concluded that Anthony saw asceticism as

> a necessary first step in the human being's return to God. The human being is torn apart by passions attacking through the senses and ideas attacking through the mind. He or she has no power over self, but has become a seat of unclean motions and demons. The latter must be driven out and the body and the soul cleansed. Ascetic practice is the method of cutting short the influences of the motions and demons. There is, however, no specific teaching about various ascetic practices in the letters, only an emphasis on the need to purify each member of the "body," and the need to be guided and strengthened by the spirit.[49]

Others heeded the call or felt the same imperative, as hundreds or thousands adopted the privations of solitude, few possessions, minimal diet, and long hours of prayer and meditation.

So was founded the *eremitic* tradition of Christian asceticism, which Geoffrey Harpham in his important treatise on the culture of asceticism describes as "the heroic fanaticism of the early desert solitaries such as Anthony, who lived essentially alone in remote settings like Egypt or Syria, torturing themselves and confronting demons in an improvisational, unregulated, and ecstatic warfare."[50] Many since have chosen that path. However, as the movement grew, as novices sought out experienced monks (Gonzalez mentions that Anthony had to escape from the fans and imitators who wanted his advice and assistance), and as monks began to band together to work and study and pray, a second tradition, the *cenobitic*, coalesced. Attributed originally to Pachomius, who probably initiated it around 320 CE, it refers to a communal monasticism, the kind of *monastery* with which most Christians are familiar. Rather than improvisational and unregulated, it was

> a more corporate and stable form of asceticism, an institutionalization of the primary charisma of the eremite. . . . [In the cenobitic life] a number of monks and even nuns submitted themselves to extraordinary regulation, discipline, and obedience, living under a Superior in strict adherence to a Rule which prescribed their conduct, their food, and even their thoughts.[51]

The cenobitic system flourished in Christianity, given further structure by Benedict (480–547), Francis (1182–1126), and Dominic (1170–1221), each of whom established lasting monastic communities. Benedict in particular is remembered for laying down the rule, which did not demand great deprivation but did demand great discipline. The two main components of the discipline were "permanence and obedience."[52] Monks were bound to a single monastery, and they were compelled to obey their superior, the abbot, immediately, willingly, and energetically. The rule also required communal labor, shared poverty, and a busy schedule of religious devotions including eight collective prayers each day.

While the monastic life often legislated a routine of privations from solitude and silence to meager nourishment, long hours of work and prayer, and almost always celibacy, some groups and individuals took the self-mortification much further. We already noted above how self-flagellation emerged in the second Christian millennium. Piero Camporesi, in his study of medieval Europe, discusses how "worry, dread, and insomnia, anxiety and insecurity, terror of an unfathomable end, miniature apocalypses wrought by famine and epidemic" led to extravagant self-punishments.[53] He quotes a source on one ascetic who

> would fast on bread and water, kneeling on the bare ground as he ate, after a long penance performed in the public refectory . . . no matter how weary he might be from an exacting journey or the weakness of old age, even though he

practically always observed harsh abstinence by eating stale bread dipped in rank water from washed crockery in the cellar, to which he added ashes. . . . He would treat himself with harshness by letting his appetite for food be whetted and then refusing to eat it by way of mortification.[54]

He further cites Johannes Climacus, whose 1570 *Santa Scala* ("the holy ladder" to monastic perfection) delighted in his vision of the self-destructive saints:

> Their eyes are dull, concave and sunken deeply into their heads, and all their lashes had fallen out; their cheeks were wizened, burned and full of sores. . . . Their faces were thin, dry and pale, not unlike the faces of the dead. Their chests likewise had sores and contusions from self-inflicted bleeding and they suffered great pain from the beatings they had given themselves. From their mouths there came forth blood rather than saliva, because of their beaten and broken torsos. . . . Their clothes were all ragged, full of filth, flea and lice-ridden. . . . [They begged that upon their deaths they should] be thrown like beasts into some river or in some field so that they should be devoured by wild animals. . . . [They] gave forth an intolerable smell from their decayed and blistered bodies. . . . They ate their bread rolled in ashes. They were dried out like hay, so their skin stuck to their skeletons.[55]

Guiseppe de Copertino excelled most in self-harm, to the level of what Camporesi calls "a bloodthirsty butchering of self":

> Twice a week he beat himself so ferociously that thirty years later the walls of his cell still bore not merely marks, but veritable encrustations, of blood upon them. . . . Not satisfied even with this, he would ask others to flog him so that he was sensible only of pain. If ever he was assailed by impure thoughts or vain fancies, or some distraction, he would flog himself to the very bone. His favorite instruments of self-torture were ropes tipped with crooked needles, followed by steel rowels with sharp points which tore his flesh so that the blood streamed down and he would fall into the deepest of swoons. . . . His many wounds had only his rasping hairshirt to dress them; and the fearful chain that he wore about his loins made the wound stick to his hairshirt and the hairshirt to the chain, so that his soaking and wounded body resembled more a corpse than a living human being.[56]

To bring this macabre catalog to a premature close (for Camporesi offers many more examples), take Francesco di Girolamo, who wore permanently next to his skin a jerkin of chain-mail, embroidered with sharp steel points. . . . In calculating the number of times a day that he subjected himself to his many merciless penances, whether publicly or in private, by night or by day, once with iron chains, another time with scourges tipped with nails, tearing at his innocent body (some of these punishments lasted a full half hour), it can be said with certainty that at least three times a day he inflicted so harsh a torture on himself as to draw blood every time. Nor were these the only instruments he used to torture his body. Many others of his own invention were discovered in his room after his death, causing repugnance to at the mere sight of them.[57]

Asceticism in Hinduism and Related Traditions

Asceticism was and is a recognized component in the major south Asian complex of religions starting with Hinduism and extending to Jainism and Buddhism. As the root of this set of traditions, let us look at Hinduism first and longest.

Within Hinduism, there are two major sources or streams of the ascetic imperative. One is open to everyone (or at least every man), while the other is limited to dedicated "professionals" who make deprivation a way of life. Common to the two streams is the basic concept of dharma, the religious order of existence. Humans are trapped in a cycle of birth, death, and rebirth (samsara). One's next birth is determined by one's spiritual achievements in this life, namely, the condition of one's karma or spiritual purity or impurity. One cannot evade the law of karma nor the suffering that rebirth brings. The goal, then, is to be released from the endless cycle, to achieve *moksha*. For most people, this will be an effort of many, perhaps thousands, of lifetimes. For those who actively undertake the quest for release, for salvation, the process may be accelerated.

For most individuals (again, this means most males), the course of life requires participation in the affairs of everyday life—working, marrying, raising children, and so on. Hindu doctrine thus viewed the life cycle as divided into several distinct stages, each with its particular duty (dharma). The first stage (*brahmacharya*) applied to youth and carried the role of learner or student. Upon reaching adulthood, a man got a job and a family and became a householder (*grahasthin*). Once his children were grown and his social duties fulfilled, he (and his wife if she desired) could become a retired "forest-dweller" (*vanaprastha*), renouncing the pleasures of the world and devoting himself (and herself) to religious improvement. The final stage, if a man could achieve it, was sannyasin, the highest condition of renunciation that a layman could reach while alive. As described by Alter, a sannyasin "is one who has renounced all material possessions and is no longer encumbered by social and ritual obligations. As a free individual he pursues divine knowledge on his own terms. To engage in this pursuit, a sannyasi [*sic*] must develop a categorically asocial attitude and style of life: he must go through life naked, alone, wandering, celibate, begging, fasting, and silent."[58] The sannyasin marks his body with the ashes of sacred (including funeral) fires and may shave off his hair or wear it uncut and unwashed. Of course he should observe absolute celibacy. And he may engage in other extreme exercises known as *tapas*, including fasting, self-flagellation, self-cutting, walking on shoes of nails or lying on beds of nails, and so forth. It must be understood that the religious motives of the sannyasin are not identical to those of the Christian ascetic. The Hindu does not, Alter supposes, "do penance" or "expiate sin." Instead,

> he engages in a form of self-control—in the most extended, corporeal sense of this term—that is directed at a manifest mastery of the very substances of life. . . . When a sannyasi [*sic*] sits under cold running water for days on end during the dead of winter or meditates while lying on a bed of nails, he is not making atonement or abusing himself. He is, rather, extending sensory control to the end of self-realization by way of reconstituting the individual substantial self on a transcendental plane.[59]

In conventional Hinduism, the path of the sannyasin is not open to women, but Lynn Denton discovered a community of female ascetics or *sannyasinis* who also forsook or rejected traditional social roles, in this case the role of wife and mother. Some of these women had voluntarily refused a woman's place (e.g., declined to marry), while others were widows or "unmarriageable" for reasons of poverty, age, deformity, physical unattractiveness, or mental illness. In Denton's survey, more than half of sannyasinis were young women whose families could not afford a dowry.

Becoming a female ascetic means, as it often means for men (see below) and in other religions like Christianity, becoming a member of an ascetic institution. In other words, while there are solitary wandering mendicants, many if not most ascetics attain and practice their rigors in a group. And this means finding a sponsor or teacher or master: "No one legitimately enters a community without first requesting a fully initiated ascetic to accept him or her as a disciple."[60] The disciple then assumes the burdens or discipline (*sadhudharma*) of an ascetic-in-training, including subordination and strict obedience to the guru. These vows include *vairagya* (desirelessness or detachment), *tyag* (renunciation, self-negation), *tapasya* ("the practice of particularly unnatural and awesome austerities"),[61] and *sannyasa* (commitment to the ascetic way of life). The woman who can fulfill this discipline, this *sadhudharma*, becomes an ascetic, a *sadhu*.

Among the traditional male renouncers, the same two main options exist as in Christianity—a solitary itinerant path and a communal settled path. Taking the Ramanandi sect of Vaishnavite (that is, dedicated to the god Vishnu) Hinduism as an example, Peter van der Veer reports that each would-be sadhu must "choose a guru who will initiate him into the celibate 'Clan of God.'"[62] Celibacy is indeed a key if not the key to Ramanandi life, since they believe that semen contains a supernatural power (*shakti*) that they desire to retain for themselves. In fact, they model themselves after their mythological hero and progenitor, Ram (or Rama), who "is the ideal, detached husband who puts the socio-religious order (dharma) and his ties with his family above his love for his wife. Sita, on the other hand, is the ideal submissive wife who shows unquestioning loyalty to her husband (pativrata)."[63] They view themselves as the slaves (*das*) of Ram.

Once initiated, the sadhu may subsequently choose to be initiated into one of three subdisciplines, *tyagis*, *nagas*, or *rasiks*. Tyagis are the epitome of the homeless monk: *tyag* means "abandonment" or "renunciation," and tyagis practice it through abandoning as much of the normal pleasure of clothing, food, shelter, and sex as possible. They wear their hair long and matted, cover themselves with ashes, and smoke hashish as they sit by fires in the heat of the sun. Nagas are not only ascetics but wrestlers who train mind and body. They practice many of the renunciations of the tyagis but not for the same purpose: while the tyagis aspire to supernatural energy through their discipline, the nagas seek physical strength and success in combat. In fact, Van der Veer asserts that nagas not only wrestle but organize themselves along paramilitary lines and have even participated in military activity in the past:

> "Recruits" have to pass through ten stages of service, before they attain the full status of naga, leader of a group of "recruits." Their training refers to the army of monkeys in the Ram-story. Hanuman, their tutelary deity, is not only the image of masculine prowess, but also of self-effacing devotion to Ram. . . . The "regiments" of nagas have evolved out of the itinerant groups of tyagis. They

have developed the body techniques, which characterize the lifestyle of the tyagis, not to generate heat . . . but to build physical strength. Their military training and organization have made them a political group that uses physical force to attain its ends. The Ramanandi nagas are organized in regiments (*akhara*) and armies (*ani*) which protect the life and property of their unarmed brethren.[64]

Finally, the rasiks, who comprise the majority of Ramanandis, differ from the other two in their selection of the path of devotion and theological knowledge over heat and strength and are the most sedentary and communal. They do not necessarily practice celibacy, but, interestingly, they see themselves at least ritually as females (as *sahki* or "girlfriend" of the god) and even dress as women.

Some of the types of self-mortifications practiced by Ramanandis and similar sects in India may be familiar to Westerners as the extreme behaviors (tapas) of yogis or holy men. Individually or in groups, they strike complicated and painful physical poses, standing on one foot or on their heads sometimes for hours at a time; they may wear piles of smoldering cow-dung on their heads and exercise until the pile burns away. Some eat little (and almost all are vegetarians), with Ramanandis often eating only "jungle fruits" and wild rice or even nothing but milk. In the *panch agni* or "five-fire" ritual, they sit between five fires during midday. In what must be one of the most arduous ordeals, a "standing baba" (*khareshwari*) undertakes to remain in a standing position continuously for twelve years. This being strictly speaking impossible, they will truss themselves up in harnesses and swings so that they do not and cannot fall, but this can cause sores, swollen legs, and ulcers. Particularly during the festival of Kumbha Mela, sadhus may attach hooks to their skin from which they suspend themselves in the air or pull carts (sometimes bearing other sadhus suspended in the air). Finally, they may conduct punishing pilgrimages in which they prostrate themselves fully on the ground, rise to take a few steps and prostrate themselves again, all the way to their destination.

The Jain tradition emerged from Hinduism in the sixth century BCE, rejecting much of Hindu social organization but retaining certain core concepts, like *ahimsa*, nonviolence (see chapter 9). Jainism too promotes an ascetic path; in fact, in a sense all Jains are ascetics, since they severely restrict what they may eat. The laity may also accept other disciplines, including abstaining from alcohol and butter and honey, limiting the amount of clothing and shoes they wear, confining their use of perfume and furniture and cars and bath water, restricting their travel, and naturally avoiding sex as much as possible. But individuals may also become full-time ascetics, with women predominating in the vocation: "Twice as many women as men pursue the ascetic path, and women are considered better suited to monastic life," although ideologically asceticism is still a male prerogative.[65]

Jainism divides ascetics into "white clad" (*Suetambar*) and "sky clad" (*Digambar*). The white clad adopt somewhat milder austerities: they wear clothing, for example (a white robe that gives them their name). Women can only belong to this type, since the "sky clad" monk or *muni* goes naked, which would not be appropriate for women. Carrithers focuses on the more austere Digambars, who besides forsaking clothing pledge to wander on foot, to eat only one meal a day, and to engage in various means of self-mortification. They progress through the ranks of monkhood, from novices who make a few minor vows to fully initiated munis who take the great vows to eat standing up, never bathe or clean their teeth, and perform tapas like those listed previously. Most harshly, they vow *sallekhana*, to take their own lives eventually by fasting to death. Jain ascetics are "selfless" in a sense, but this does not mean that they are civic minded. As in Buddhism below, they are on a solitary salvation quest that cannot benefit their fellow humans: "Munis are concerned only with their own liberation. As a Digambar layman put it to me, 'We feed the munis, but they are completely independent (*svatantra*). They owe us nothing.'"[66] According to Vallely they are seen as "heroic" by society but still utterly committed to their own personal spiritual advancement.

Buddhism appeared around the same time as Jainism and resembles it in many ways. The first Buddha, Gautama, allegedly tried the paths of severe self-mortification as well as of luxury and comfort and found both lacking. He advocated a "middle path" of detachment without self-punishment for freeing oneself from the cycle of rebirth. One could—indeed, should—be in the world but not of the world. In the end, every person was to be a monk, to abstain from sex and meat and emotional attachments to anything, including other humans. One could feel compassion, certainly, but attachment exposed one to dukkha, the pain of existence. Those who could devote themselves seriously to the quest for *nirvana* abandoned their homes and families and become monks (*bhikkhu*). From a certain perspective, such monks were already in another world, "'homeless' (*anagirika*), gone forth (*pabbajita*) from the world of the householder."[67] However, as in the other cases cited, bhikkhus soon formed into communities and monasteries to share their search. Nevertheless, whether the life of the monk is to be "peripatetic, or whether it is to be sedentary . . . in any case the clear message of both the Buddha's sermons and the monastic rule is that the Sangha [community of monks] is to be morally pure and, by contemporary Western standards, unremittingly ascetic."[68] The laity can and often does participate in these renunciations, especially on ritual occasions, and they can improve their spiritual lot by supporting the monks with food, but like the Jains, religion is every person for himself or herself.

PAIN, BUT WHAT GAIN?

In the modern Western world, it is difficult to see any virtue in suffering. In fact, we do all that we can to alleviate and prevent pain and even mild discomfort. Pain seems to us at best undesirable, worse yet almost unnatural, and at worst pathological: no one in their right mind would actively choose or passively accept agony. This view is indisputably not shared by all religions; quite the opposite, religions find ways to normalize, valorize, and aggrandize not only suffering but also voluntary suffering. Indeed, during the February 2000 "Jubilee of the Sick Persons and Health Care Workers," Pope John Paul II spoke explicitly and effusively of the "saving value of suffering":

> Since then all suffering has *a possibility of meaning*, which makes it remarkably valuable. For 2,000 years, since the day of the Passion, the Cross shines as the supreme manifestation of God's love for us. Those who are able to accept it in their lives experience how pain illumined by faith becomes a source of hope and salvation. . . .
>
> The Church enters the new millennium, clasping to her heart the Gospel of suffering, which is a message of redemption and salvation. Dear sick brothers and sisters, you are exceptional witnesses to this Gospel. The third millennium awaits this witness from suffering Christians. . . .
>
> Through your suffering you are especially close to Christ. In this suffering may Christ always be your strength, he who redeemed the world through his passion and death on the Cross. Dear suffering brothers and sisters, we are indebted to you.[69]

Sixteen years earlier, he praised pain again, asserting, "The joy comes from the discovery of the meaning of suffering. What we express with the word 'suffering' seems to be particularly *essential to the nature of Man*. . . . Christianity is not a system into which we have to fit the awkward fact of pain. . . . In a sense, it creates, rather than solves, the problem of pain."[70]

It seems that every religion ever practiced by humans has integrated some painful practices. Often, the extreme acts of self-mortification have been reserved for the "specialists." Still, the ordinary members of the religion have also been welcomed if not expected to bear some burden too and to accept privations from fasting to sexual abstinence to bloodletting to flagellation. Why? The answer is as complicated and diverse as the phenomenon of self-directed violence itself. There is no one reason common to all religions for the deliberate, frequently eager pursuit of self-harm, but there are many reasons that, in combination, make discomfort unto death a regular feature of religion.

Imitation of a Religious Role Model

As with sacrifice, self-mortification is routinely an emulation of a mythical or ancestral paradigm: the god or ancestor or founder suffered, therefore the follower should suffer as well. (This is the mimesis that Girard should have spoken of.) There is no religion for which this statement is truer than Christianity. Many Christians have enthusiastically sought suffering, even death, because of the careers of Jesus and his early disciples. As with the flagellants and the self-crucifiers, if Christ was scourged, Christians should be scourged, and if Christ was crucified, Christians should be crucified. Early teachers like Paul made the point clearly:

> We are the children of God: And if children, then heirs; heirs of God, and joint-heirs with Christ; if so be that we suffer with him, that we may be also glorified together.[71]
>
> It is for your consolation and salvation, which is effectual in the enduring of the same sufferings which we also suffer: or whether we be comforted, it is for your consolation and salvation.[72]
>
> For unto you it is given in the behalf of Christ, not only to believe on him, but also to suffer for his sake.[73]
>
> [I, Paul] now rejoice in my sufferings for you.[74]
>
> If we suffer, we shall also reign with him.[75]

By bearing the pain that the exemplar bore, we not only make ourselves exemplary but also closer mentally and emotionally to him.

While Christianity is the religion of the suffering paradigm par excellence, other religions have also offered their visions of the model-in-misery. The other prime case is the example set by Husayn in Islam. An article in the *Shia News* made precisely this point: "Thus the act of self-flagellation is nothing more than the believer trying to feel as his Master felt and more, realizing he cannot be at Karbala, the anguish this causes him—the anguish of separation—the helplessness creates this phenomenon of self-flagellation."[76] Even the Ramanandis deny themselves as their hero Ram denied himself, and Malaysian Hindus bear the burdens that Murugan and Idubam once bore.

Ideology and Doctrine

Apart from the mythical/historical models of their founders and progenitors, religions include specific ideas, concepts, and doctrines that demand and value self-harming behaviors. The Australian Aboriginal concept of the power of human blood and the role of that blood for rituals necessitated the fact that men ritually bleed themselves. The Sambia beliefs about gender, bodies, and mystical substances led inexorably to the tortures that men inflicted on themselves and their sons. Hindu views on women have driven women to kill themselves and observers to celebrate the deed. Many religious groups like the People's Temple and TELAH have destroyed themselves because their leaders told them to or because they believed the end was near anyhow or because they believed they were going to a better place.

In the Judeo-Christian context, one of the critical ideologies has been sin and guilt. In this worldview—not shared by Aboriginals or Sambia or Hindus, and so on—self-mortification is often *self-punishment*, which is righteous because humans inherently deserve it. Christians in particular have been moved to excessive self-violence by the excessive self-condemnation they feel, and, as we have seen, they have often delighted in the rough justice they administer to themselves. It does, I am sure, make their beliefs and their god seem more real and nearer, since they are experiencing their just reward here and now.

One particular doctrine or value, which is not shared by all religions but which is powerful within the ones that do possess it, is a profound loathing for the body. There is a strand of this view in Hinduism, as echoed in the words of the *Maitreya Upanishad*:

> Lord, this body is produced just by sexual intercourse and is devoid of consciousness; it is a veritable hell. Born through the urinary canal, it is built with

bones, plastered with flesh, and covered with skin. It is filled with feces, urine, wind, bile, phlegm, marrow, fat, serum, and many other kinds of filth. In such a body do I live.[77]

Other texts like the *Narada Parvrajaka Upanishad* have shared this contempt for the human form:

It is foul-smelling, filled with feces and urine, and infested with old-age and grief. Covered with dust and harassed by pain, it is the abode of disease.

If a man finds joy in the body—a hope of flesh, blood, pus, feces, urine, tendons, marrow, and bone—that fool will find joy even in hell.

Those who take delight in this collection of skin, flesh, blood, tendons, marrow, fat, and bones, stinking with feces and urine—what difference is there between them and worms?[78]

Clearly people with such attitudes are not going to be kind to themselves, using self-injury to castigate and even free themselves from their disgusting physical cage.

Camporesi also argues that medieval Christianity was filled with a "hatred for one's own physical body, considered foul and corrupt."[79] Life itself, bodily existence, was a kind of torture, of imprisonment:

For the men of God . . . *caro* (flesh) and *putredo* (decay) were essentially the same thing, and life but camouflaged death. Putrefaction was not a postmortem process but one which ran concurrently with life, was inherent in life, inside life itself, for life was but corruption and stench, disguised and beautified.[80]

Even when the body was not despised so completely as this, religions often taught that certain normal human functions and activities were unmeritorious or spiritually dangerous. The best example is sex, which has been a problem for many religions: in Christianity it is sinful by nature, while for Hinduism it is the source of samsara as well as a waste of the spiritual energy that men could invest in higher pursuits.

Achievement of Altered States of Consciousness

Religion is the nonordinary, the "sacred," the *mysterium tremendum et fascinosum*. Scholars from Max Mueller and Rudolf Otto to Sigmund Freud and William

James have commented on the experiential element of religion, its quality of "otherness" or transcendence. One goal of self-mortification, and of the practices that get humans into a state where self-mortification is possible (i.e., where pain is bearable or altogether absent), is to bring about an altered state of consciousness that feels transcendent and supernatural.

One of the leading scholars of altered states of consciousness, Arnold Ludwig, has noted that these conditions can be induced by a number of different methods, including reduction of mental stimulation and/or bodily activity, increase in such stimulation and activity, decreased mental alertness, increased alertness and attention, and "somatophysiological factors," such as hyperglycemia, dehydration, fever, toxins, sleep deprivation, hyperventilation, and brain seizures, to name but a few.[81] And while these methods may sound contradictory, they are in fact quite complementary. Practices like meditation may simultaneously relax or decrease mental activity and increase alertness. Repetitive behaviors like chanting or beating drums at once reduce and increase stimulation. Certain chemical substances produce such religionlike experiences that they have actually been dubbed "entheogens" (god makers) by scientists. Notice that the somatophysiological factors listed by Ludwig are precisely those that one might generate through fasting or ingestion of foreign substances (like food rolled in ashes) or long hours of sleepless chanting. And of course, quite possibly the most mind-altering experience of all is pain.

As some nonreligious self-injurers have admitted, pain actually makes them feel better. One explanation is probably the release of endorphins to fight the pain. But pain also means stimulation, *hyper*stimulation, of the body, providing exactly one of Ludwig's key processes for establishing altered mental states. In other words, from this perspective, self-mortification is not about the body or the pain directly, but rather about *using pain* to achieve other ends. Glucklich's study of "sacred pain" suggests precisely this function:

> Religious pain produces states of consciousness, and cognitive-emotional changes, that affect the identity of the individual subject and her sense of belonging to a larger community or to a more fundamental sate of being. More succinctly, pain strengthens the religious person's bond with God and with other persons.[82]

The key, of course, to "the psychological transformations that take place" is the careful application of "regulated pain."[83]

Discipline and Focus

As we have seen, far from being a purely negative and life-diminishing experience, self-torment can from a certain perspective be interpreted as a positive and life-enhancing one. It is not even, from this perspective, necessarily "anti-body" but may actually value and glorify the body as the vehicle for humanity's highest mental and spiritual achievements.

Most religions agree on one point: in our everyday mundane life, we are not very disciplined, very focused, very aware of the world—or the "otherworld"—around us. Our minds wander, our passions drag us along, our attention is undirected. What many religions offer, as we asserted in chapter 2, is *control*—control of self, control of nature, and control of supernature. This entails, however, a concentration of our energies—and an invoking of energies that we did not know we had.

Students of religious pain like Geoffrey Harpham and Elaine Scarry suggest that, while pain "reduces" our humanity in a way, it also intensifies it. Scarry writes that "in serious pain the claims of the body utterly nullify the claims of the world," and the entire world for the sufferer becomes his or her suffering.[84] This urgent bodily pain blocks or "obliterates" even psychological and spiritual pain—often the pain that the religion, through its beliefs and concepts, induces in the first place—"because it obliterates all psychological content, painful, pleasurable, or neutral."[85]

> Another manifestation of this power is its continual reappearance in religious experience. The self-flagellation of the religious ascetic, for example, is not (as is often asserted) an act of denying the body, eliminating its claim for attention, but a way of so emphasizing the body that the contents of the world are cancelled and the path is clear for the entry of an unworldly, contentless force. It is in part this world-ridding, path-clearing logic that explains the obsession of pain in the rituals of large, widely shared religions as well as in the imagery of intensely private visions, that partly explains why the crucifixion of Christ is at the center of Christianity, why so many primitive forms of worship climax in pain ceremonies.[86]

This intense, voluntary, purposive mortification "destroys a person's self and world," resulting in a "contraction of the universe down to the immediate vicinity of the body or as the body swelling to fill the entire universe."[87] However, while this sounds like a negating or at best solipsistic act, Harpham insists that it is transformative, even creative. Self-violence, like asceticism, "both denigrates and dignifies the body, casting it at once as a transgressive force always on the side of 'the world' and as the scene or stage for discipline, self-denial, ascesis."[88] Recall that the root of the word *asceticism* is "work" or "exercise," and in an important sense not only asceticism but also all self-directed violence is exercise, technique, work-on-the-self. It is training the self, via the body, to feel and respond in certain ways. No wonder Harpham concludes that autoviolence "is not merely capable of assuming a multitude of forms; it is the form-producing agent itself."[89]

Richard Valantasis summarizes this position when he claims that the focal point of self-mortification "is a self who, through behavioral changes, seeks to become a different person, a new self; to become a different person in new relationships; and to become a different person in a new society that forms a new culture."[90] It achieves this ambitious goal by pressing religion into the very skin, by em-bodying it—which must necessarily be an excruciating process, as we are breaking the body to remake the body (and the person). The body, thus, is the ultimate religious object, the ultimate "natural symbol,"[91] indeed the ultimate work of art. Through what Thomas Csordas calls "somatic modes of attention," culturally elaborated ways of attending to and with one's body in surroundings that include the embodied presence of others, humans learn not only to attend *to* their body but to attend *with* their body—a "turning toward," a conversion, a becoming that is not merely cognitive but visceral.[92] Of course if the body is a work of art, and suffering is a kind of "performance art" of the body, then the highest art form of all would be the final destruction of the body.

MARTYRDOM: DEATH ON PRINCIPLE

Each act of self-mortification or asceticism (and every act of self-mortification is a kind of asceticism) is a "small death," which sometimes culminates in actual death. But self-mortification or asceticism does not usually aim at final death. In a few religions, however, a tradition that willingly accepts, welcomes, or even seeks death has evolved.

The word *martyr* derives from the Greek *martys* for "witness," related to the Latin *memor* for "mindful." The martyr then is one who gives his or her life as a witness to and of a religion, as mindful of a religion—keeping that religion in mind until death. As with other forms of religious violence, martyrdom need not be strictly in the cause of religion. In Lacey Baldwin Smith's major study of martyrs, he credits Socrates as the first great martyr, who did not embrace death for his religious principles but for his philosophical ones. Smith also includes John Brown, the nineteenth-century American abolitionist who hoped to precipitate a civil war with a raid on Harper's Ferry, Virginia; Brown was certainly a devoutly religious man who saw his mission as righteous, even though it was not a religious mission proper.[93] But both victims "died for what they believed in," and to have flinched from death—especially given Socrates' opportunity to do so—would have in some way diminished the cause.

Humans have been willing to die for almost any cause imaginable: many have given their lives for their country, for their party or political ideology, for their family, for their philosophy, or presumably for their favorite sports team. Not all deserve the title of martyr. Many more have simply committed suicide but have not so earned the title. Dying does not automatically confer on one the status of martyr, nor does dying "for a cause." That is why Smith calls his book *Fools, Martyrs, and Traitors*: an American who lets himself be killed for al Qaeda is deemed a traitor, and one who lets himself be killed for the New York Yankees is regarded as a fool.

Martyrdom, thus, is clearly a judgment, and a relative and postmortem one at that: one cannot declare oneself a martyr, only posterity can bestow the honor. Many a would-be martyr is no doubt lost in the dustbin of history. To understand martyrdom, we must therefore recognize its necessary components. One is surely a cause or principle of some sort; moreover, it must be, from somebody's point of view, a "good" or "noble" or even "true" cause. Religion certainly provides that motivation for humans, since members of religions necessarily hold those religions to be true. But not all religions have asked members to become martyrs; in fact, most have no such conception or role at all. Martyrdom in traditional Australian Aboriginal religions would have been a nonsensical idea.

Second, there must be, in most cases, a threat or challenge to that cause or truth. While some traditions might valorize self-destruction on a good day, more often martyrdom is not just "for" something but "against" something as well. Smith characterizes martyrdom as "an act of symbolic protest,"[94] a refusal to compromise or capitulate. It depends on and sustains what Michael Gaddis, in his substantial study of violence in early Christianity, calls an "oppositional mentality."[95] In other words, the cause is the motive, but the threat is the catalyst. Third, there must, obviously, be a person willing, even eager, to place himself or herself in harm's way. This may include a religious/cultural ideal of dying for the cause or merely a personal commitment to do so (Socrates was under no religious compulsion to die). Finally, and most often overlooked, there must be an audience. Martyrdom is not an act that one can perform in private: it must be a public event, and the more public and the more spectacular, the better. The eyes of the world must be upon the martyr, or no message is conveyed, no lesson learned, no glory won. (This may be true as well in the case of self-mortification and asceticism: while a few self-injurers do so in utter privacy, many desire to be looked at, to be seen, if only by their god.) An unseen death is, in the end, a meaningless death, and a meaningless death is not a martyr's death. The martyr must feel not only that his or her death is for a cause but also that it will *advance* the cause.

Not many religious traditions have provided all these circumstances for martyrdom, so accordingly martyrdom is a comparatively rare form of religious self-harm. However, it is a particularly dramatic form and one with which Western audiences are familiar. Therefore, let us turn finally to this great self-destruction in its most common, Judeo-Christian-Muslim, context.

Martyrdom in Judaism

Early Judaism offers few instances of, and arguably little justification for, martyrdom. With a bit of stretching, one can identify perhaps a handful of cases in the early Hebrew scriptures; Droge and Tabor count among them the suicide (or rather ordered homicide) of Abimelech in Judges 9, the death of Saul in 1 Samuel 31, the death of Samson who killed himself and his tormentors in Judges 16, the suicide of Ahithaphel in 2 Samuel 17, and the self-conflagration of Zimri in 1 Kings 16.[96] However, for the most part, there was nothing to gain from self-destruction, since no doctrine of eternal life or salvation had yet emerged: as Ecclesiastes 9:5–6 teaches, "The dead know not any thing, neither have they any more a reward; for the memory of them is forgotten. Also their love, and their hatred, and their envy, is now perished; neither have they any more a portion for ever in any thing that is done under the sun."

Throwing oneself into the jaws of death for religion begins to make sense after the eschatological concepts of salvation and resurrection and messiah appear in later centuries, and especially after the conquests by Persia, Macedon, and Rome. Martyrdom comes to maturity in the acts of the Maccabees, those religious patriots of the Hellenistic period. In the mid–second century BCE under the ruler Antiochus IV, an onslaught against Jewish practices and sensibilities began:

> The Law of Moses . . . was now abolished; circumcision, the observation of the
> Sabbath and the dietary code were outlawed; a high altar to Zeus was con-
> structed in the midst of Yahweh's own sacred house; and throughout Israel,
> Jews were ordered not only to sacrifice to Zeus with swine meat but also, as a
> final act of oblivion, to no longer confess themselves to be Jews.[97]

Naturally, many Jews refused, some fleeing Jerusalem, some passively protesting, some aggressively defending tradition and truth. When ordered to cooperate, many resisted, even under threat of death: in a text known as the *Testament of Moses*, a man named Taxo even urged his sons: "There let us die rather than transgress the commandments of the lord of lords, the God of our fathers. For if we do this, and do die, our blood will be avenged before the Lord."[98]

In 165 BCE a revolt led by Judas Maccabee broke out, as recounted in the Books of Maccabees. These books contain numerous stories of martyrs, like Eleazar, who

> was being forced to open his mouth to eat swine's flesh. But he, welcoming
> death with honor rather than life with pollution, went up to the rack of his
> own accord, spitting out the flesh, as men ought to do who have courage to
> refuse things that it is not right to taste, even for the natural love of life.[99]

Likewise, a mother and her seven sons gladly died rather than eat the abominated pork: "We are ready to die rather than transgress the laws of our fathers," they declared.[100] The Fourth Book of Maccabees claims that the youngest son and the mother actually leapt into a fire to commit suicide over the unbearable demands. An elder named Razis also killed himself to avoid blasphemy, "preferring to die nobly rather than fall into the hands of sinners and suffer outrages unworthy of his noble birth."[101]

During the Roman occupation (the decades preceding and following the birth of Jesus), self-chosen death in opposition to foreign authority and practice was revived. Josephus, a contemporary chronicler, tells how temple priests killed themselves when Pompey besieged the temple in 63 BCE. However, the classic case of Jewish martyrdom occurred at the hilltop stronghold of Masada in 73 CE. Facing imminent defeat after a long siege, some nine hundred sixty believers took their own lives, with only seven survivors—a happening reminiscent of Jonestown. For Droge and Tabor, all these incidents illustrate the nature of martyrdom:

> First, they reflect situations of opposition and persecution. Second, the choice to die, which these individuals make, is viewed by the authors as necessary, noble, and heroic. Third, these individuals are often eager to die; indeed, in several cases they end up directly *killing themselves*. Fourth, there is often the idea of vicarious benefit resulting from their suffering and death. And finally, the expectation of vindication and reward beyond death, more often than not, is a prime motivation for their choice of death.[102]

Martyrdom in Christianity

Martyrdom, along with the lesser mortifications as described above, has always been a central aspect of the Christian religion. One obvious reason is that its founder himself was martyred, establishing the precedent that many would follow. Another reason is the martyr tradition that already existed in its Jewish roots. A third reason is the persecution that Christians experienced in the first centuries of their movement, which constituted an immediate and continuous threat and insult to their faith. However, even once the mortal danger was passed, even once Christianity was in power in the Roman Empire, the martyrdom mentality persisted, into the early modern period if not beyond.

We have just seen the precedent of dying for religious principles in the case of Jewish martyrdom. The death of Jesus might be construed as a (self-)sacrifice or a martyrdom, or both: Jesus was given ample opportunity to recant his claims and escape his fate, but he declined, so in a sense he chose his death, or at least accepted it willingly. As we have also seen repeatedly, one of the imperatives of religion is to emulate the model of the founder/ancestor. Subsequent devotees of Jesus believed that they should follow him even—or especially—into death. Jesus and his early disciples helped foment this opinion. The gospel writer Mark has Jesus himself declare, "Whosoever will come after me, let him deny himself, and take up his cross, and follow me. For whosoever will save his life shall lose it; but whosoever shall lose his life for my sake and the gospel's, the same shall save it."[103] Paul exhorted Christians to be "willing rather to be absent from the body, and to be present with the Lord,"[104] and Revelation reports a "voice from heaven" claiming, "Blessed are the dead which die in the Lord."[105]

The early disciples and teachers of Christianity provided additional models.

John the Baptist had essentially been martyred for standing up against Herod. Stephen was stoned for his beliefs, the first documented Christian to die for the new religion. Paul was probably beheaded in Rome around 66 CE for his years of preaching the doctrine. On the other hand, the great model of the coward who retreated from his martyr's role, who blanched when asked to stand by his faith, was Peter and his denial of knowing or being associated with Jesus after the master's arrest.

During the persecution of Christians by Rome, Christians were given plenty of chances to die for their beliefs, and many accepted the situation with strength, cheer, and even gladness. One of the most famous stories is of a woman named Vibia Perpetua, who gave her life in 203 CE in the arena as did so many others. As shown in the medieval source *The Passion of Saints Perpetua and Felicity*, Perpetua was a twenty-two-year-old woman of noble birth who had taken to studying the new religion. She was arrested, brought before a tribunal, and—like the Jewish martyrs before her—asked to perform the sacrileges of a "false religion" (in this case, Roman sacrifice), but she refused and answered, "I am a Christian." She was condemned to face the lions and held in a dungeon, where she had dreams and visions that convinced her that "I should fight, not with beasts but with the devil; but I knew that mine was the victory." On the day of the execution, she attempted to fortify her fellow convicts by saying, "Stand fast in the faith, and love you all one another, and be not offended because of our passion." As the animals sent to kill her failed to do so, she was finally dispatched by the thrust of a sword, the narrator explaining, "Perchance so great a woman could not else have been slain (being feared of the unclean spirit) had she not herself so willed it."[106]

There is no tally of the martyrs who died for Christianity, although many records and collections of "acts of martyrs" and "lives of martyrs" have been assembled and celebrated in the religion. Indeed, dying for the cause was seen, at least by some, as not only grand but also necessary. Ignatius, a first-century bishop, wrote of his death sentence: "I am dying willingly for God's sake. . . . Allow me to be eaten by the beasts, through which I can attain to God. . . . Then shall I be truly a disciple of Christ. . . . For in the midst of life I write to you desiring death."[107] Even Celsus, a Roman polemicist against Christianity, wrote:

> If you happen to be a worshipper of God and someone commands you to act blasphemously or to say some other disgraceful thing, you ought not to put any trust in him at all. Rather than this you must remain firm in the face of

all tortures and endure death rather than say or even think anything profane about God.[108]

Of course, he was referring to other gods, including Helios and Athena.

Others took the role of martyr much further—not just as a protest but as a duty or even preference—like Origen whose *Exhortation to Martyrdom* insisted that Christians actually benefit from death: "If we wish to save our life in order to get it back better than a life, let us lose it by our martyrdom."[109] In fact, martyrdom was a gift from God, the only way to attain salvation: "It is impossible according to the laws of the Gospel to be baptized again with water and the spirit for the forgiveness of our sins. And that is why the baptism of martyrdom has been given to us."[110] Cyprian opined similarly when he declared that "death makes life more complete, death rather leads to glory."[111] However, the master of martyr rhetoric was Tertullian, who wrote such lines as:

The only key that unlocks the gates of Paradise is your own blood.

Those whose victory is slower and with greater difficulty, those receive the more glorious crown.

Seek to die a martyr.[112]

God therefore appointed as a second supply of comfort, and the last means of relief, the fight of martyrdom and the baptism—thereafter free from danger— of blood.

I strongly maintain that martyrdom is good, as required by the God by whom idolatry is also forbidden and punished. For martyrdom strives against and opposes idolatry.

He [God] has chosen to contend with a disease and to do good by imitating the malady: to destroy death by death, to dissipate killing by killing, to dispel tortures by tortures, to disperse in a vapor punishments by punishments, to bestow life by withdrawing it, to aid the flesh by injuring it, to preserve the soul by snatching it away.[113]

Perhaps no better statement of the reverse (if not perverse) logic of religious self-destruction could be formulated.

Martyrdom in Islam

Finally, the third Abrahamic religion continues many of the trends and attitudes of its predecessors. It is monotheistic, absolutist, and "orthodox" (that is, based on or committed to a set of "true beliefs"—although Islam has often been called more "orthoprax" than "orthodox"). It also has, at least in certain of its sects and interpretations, a model of martyrdom in the persons of Ali and Husayn (see p. 128). As Kermani suggests, Husayn in particular plays a similar role in Shi'ite thinking as Jesus in Christian thinking—not as a savior but as a sufferer. In his passion and death, "the suffering of the entire human race is expressed. His death became a synonym for the betrayal of humanity's hope of a better future."[114] One expression of identification with and emulation of the suffering imam is the self-flagellation of Asura described above (see p. 128). Another is martyrdom: Shi'ism at least centers on "the concept that while each Shi'ite shares in guilt for the death of the martyrs, one can nevertheless find redemption through a properly repentant attitude—above all through the intercession of an imam, that is to say: a martyr. And naturally also by following Hussein into martyrdom itself."[115]

In Islam, martyrdom is known as *shahada* and a martyr as a *shahid*, the root, consistent with the English form, deriving from "witness" or "model." In fact, in Ali Shariati's *Martyrdom: Arise and Bear Witness*, he insists that martyrdom for Shi'ites is much more than death: "So instead of martyrdom, i.e. death, it essentially means 'life,' 'evidence,' 'testify,' 'certify.'"

> Martyrdom, in summary, in our culture, contrary to other schools where it is considered to be an accident, an involvement, a death imposed upon a hero, a tragedy, is a grade, a level, a rank. It is not a means but it is a goal itself. It is originality. It is a completion. It is a lift. It itself is midway to the highest peak of humanity and it is a culture.
>
> In all ages and centuries, when the followers of a faith and an idea, have power, they guarantee their honor and lives with jihad. But when they are weakened and have no means whereby to struggle, they guarantee their lives, movements, faith, respect, honor, future and history with martyrdom. Martyrdom is an invitation to all ages and generations that if you cannot kill, die.[116]

Ezzati explains how the concept and practice of shahada is inextricably entwined with the core concepts of Islam and therefore incumbent on believers:

The concept of martyrdom (*shahada*) in Islam can only be understood in the light of the Islamic concept of Holy Struggle (*jihad*) and the concept of *jihad* may only be appreciated if the concept of the doctrine of enjoining right and discovering wrong (*al-amr bi'l-maruf*) is properly appreciated, and good and bad, right and wrong, can only be understood if the independent divine source of righteousness, truth, and goodness (*tawhid*), and how the Message of the divine source of righteousness and truth has been honestly and properly conveyed to humanity through prophethood, are understood. Finally the divine message may not be fully appreciated unless the embodiment of this divine message, or the Model of Guidance, and the Supreme Paradigm (*imama* or *uswa*) is properly recognized. . . .

A *shahid* is the person who sees and witnesses, and he is therefore the witness, as if the martyr witnesses and sees the truth physically and thus stands by it firmly, so much so that not only does he testify it verbally, but he is prepared to struggle and fight and give up his life for the truth, and thus to become a martyr. In this way, and by his struggle and sacrifice for the sake of the truth, he becomes a model, a paradigm, and an example for others, worthy of being copied, and worthy of being followed.[117]

The way of shahada, then, and of the shahid depends on the condition "that he stays loyal to the divine truth and stands ready to fight for the truth and to defend it at all costs, even at the cost of his own life. He is a *mujahid* while he lives, and a martyr if he dies or is killed for it."[118]

Therefore, as in Christianity and Judaism, the idea of martyrdom in Islam is related to religious notions of truth, of suffering, of following exemplary models, and of transforming the self and the world by witnessing it. This may and frequently does entail self-destruction, as Taleqani emphasizes. "Islam is a religion aimed at reforming humanity," he reminds us, and "if it is a true religion, it must take up the sword and advance."[119] But this advance is often blocked by ignorance or evil; when the religion meets such resistance, the resistance must be removed, in *defense* of religious truth. The shahid is only the actor, the soldier, in this defense:

> The shahid is the one who has experienced the *shuhud* (vision) of truth. The sacrifice of his own life is not based on illusion or agitation of his emotions. He has seen the truth and the goal. That is why he has chosen to wallow in the blood and the dust. Such a person does so with the intention of intimacy with God, not on the basis of fantasies and personal desires. He is above these worldly matters. He has understood the value of truth in a deserved way. This is why he annihilates himself, like a drop in the ocean of truth.[120]

Certainly, then, as in Christianity and Judaism, martyrdom is a great good, perhaps the greatest good:

> Al-shuhada (pl. of shahid), that is to say, the ones who die in the cause of God, have a great status. *Salihun* (the righteous) are those who follow them. There are altogether four groups upon whom God has completed his blessing. Those who obey God are one of these. Because they have experienced an internal revolution and have envisioned the truth, the shuhada, once martyred, have been guaranteed the sure gift of eternity by God.[121]

This is no doubt why many Muslims today are willing to give their lives in what appears to them a tremendous religious struggle, as we will see in our discussion of jihad later. It also clearly illustrates the relationships between *dying* for religion and *killing* for religion—as a soldier for religion or a spiritual warrior—which blurs the line between martyrdom and war (see chapter 7).

THE SELFISH SELFLESSNESS OF MARTYRS AND OTHER SELF-MORTIFIERS

From a certain perspective, those who commit atrocities on themselves seem like the most selfless of human beings. Literally, they seem to value themselves, or at least their bodies, little and are willing to burden themselves, even obliterate themselves, for something "higher" or "greater" than the self. They are evidencing the fact (not unique to religion) that there are some things more valuable than comfort or life itself, some things worth trading one's health, happiness, and existence for.

We might expect self-mortifiers to be not only selfless but self-effacing, meek, and kind people, people who put themselves last. Instead, Lacey Baldwin Smith claims that "on close examination" martyrs and other self-abusers

> are found to be twisted, harsh, unyielding people, possessed of what used to be called before the days of psychiatric terminology "cranky" minds—moody, unpredictable, opinionated, and self-absorbed. Almost without exception they are people who are willing to do unto others what others have done unto them because they believe themselves to be the possessors of truth for which they are not only willing to die but also willing to have others die.[122]

He goes on to list the traits of serious self-renouncers:

- They possess "a sense of uniqueness and destiny."
- They feel that they are "obliged to take upon themselves the burdens of mankind."
- They are "incapable of accepting compromise or accommodating to the needs of others."
- They feel "driven to act upon the knowledge that they are God's or history's instrument for achieving or defending absolute truth."
- "Apathy is alien to them, and so, therefore, is tolerance."
- "[T]heir determination to sacrifice themselves is accompanied by an equal willingness to sacrifice others."
- "They have no need of friend, family, or community."
- "They make no concession to the world. They recognize a higher allegiance and on occasion are happy to betray the loyalties that lesser men and women hold sacred."[123]

The ultimate worth and ultimate good of the cause, the principle, the "truth" behind self-mortification makes it unyielding and, ironically, self-important. And if Scarry, Harpham, and others are correct, the fact that in the experience of pain the self expands to block out the world and become the sufferer's universe makes self-destruction the most selfish act of all.

CHAPTER 5

PERSECUTION

Infliction of pain, suffering, and death on others (especially but not exclusively animals) and on oneself are common and nearly universal aspects of religions; if anything, self-infliction of harm is the most universal of all forms of religious violence. Both sacrifice and self-mortification then are *for* something, that is, they are seen to have some religious value or purpose or *effect*. They strengthen the crops and buildings, they feed or please the spirits, they provide blood for ceremonies, they test or purify or intensify the religious experience, or they discipline or vanquish the unruly or vile material body. In a word, although it may be a troubling word to many, sacrifice and self-mortification are "positive" forms of religious violence.

However, other forms are "negative" not in the sense that they are more violent, more harmful (sacrifice and self-mortification may be lethal), or more objectionable, but that they are *against* something—or some*one*. Sacrifice and self-harm target a *victim*, often (but not always) without a sense of the victim's evil or guilt. To put this another way, sacrificers do not kill cattle because they hate cattle; they actually quite like cattle. In the case of persecution, perpetrators target an *enemy* (almost always and necessarily human) who is bad or wrong in some way, and they pursue those adversaries with great energy and great organization.

In this chapter we turn in a new direction, then, one that will shape the discussion of most of the subsequent types of religious violence. Sacrifice and self-directed violence can reach a grand scale, as in Aztec and Dahomey society, and they can be institutionalized, but neither normally achieves the level of duration, coordination, destructiveness, and sheer animosity of religious persecution, ethnoreligious conflict, and religious war, which probably fall on a spectrum roughly in that order.

Persecution can range from relatively mild pressure and inconvenience (forcing people to wear distinctive clothing or to live in a segregated part of the community) to physical threats, torture, and gruesome death. Persecution also is not restricted to religion; people have been persecuted for all sorts of reasons or on the basis of all sorts of traits—cultural, racial, political, sexual, and many others. But the common feature is that people are selectively violated *on the basis of some trait*, one that they do not share with their persecutors. In short, wherever persecution is found, it is a matter of one kind or group of person abusing another kind or group of person *because of the difference between them*. For our purposes, that means a religious difference, although other differences may be merged with the religious ones. And while, in the outstanding historical instances of sacrifice many people have suffered and died, large-scale suffering and death are frequent if not normal—if not the whole point—in the instance of persecution.

WHAT IS PERSECUTION?

As we can already see, persecution is diverse and difficult to define. The word derives from the Latin *per sequi* for "to pursue" (literally, "through-follow"), which appropriately suggests that the target is being pursued or sought for some particular characteristic that he or she possesses, almost like a criminal. In fact, the English words *pursue* and *prosecute* derive from the same general root, completing the association. It will be useful to keep this "legal" association in mind.

There is no single official definition of *persecution*, although a helpful approach is to conceive of it as "the infliction of suffering or harm upon those who differ (in race, religion, or political opinion) in a way regarded as offensive" to those who conduct the persecution.[1] Characterizing persecution as "oppression which is inflicted on groups or individuals because of a difference that the persecutor will not tolerate" emphasizes the role of tolerability and intolerance (see below).[2]

At the same time, "persecution is an extreme concept that does not include every sort of treatment our society regards as offensive."[3] Thus, there is a distinction between, or perhaps a continuum along which fall, *discrimination*, *harassment*, and *persecution*. One element of the distinction/continuum is obviously the degree of the harm inflicted: "While persecution is not restricted to 'threats to life or freedom,' it requires more than 'mere harassment or annoyance," opined the judges in *Manzoor v. US Department of Justice* in 2001.[4] Even brief periods of imprisonment may not qualify as persecution, while direct physical abuse ordinarily does. On the other hand, *Gonzalez v. INS* in 1996 determined that "deliberate imposition of substantial economic disadvantage" could also be considered persecution, extending it beyond actual bodily injury. The US Bureau of Citizenship and Immigration Services, which handles many claims for asylum on the basis of alleged persecution, specifies interference with a person's privacy, family, home, or correspondence; relegation to substandard dwellings; exclusion from institutions of higher learning; enforced social or civil inactivity; passport denial; constant surveillance; and pressure to become an informer as potential manifestations of persecution.

The methods of persecution thus are quite diverse and often simultaneous. That is, a target group may be subjected to residential restrictions, job discrimination, ridicule and insults, public harassment, economic privations, surveillance, interrogation, torture, and execution at the same time. Three main qualities seem to separate persecution from lesser forms of bigotry:

- It is severe, even if not lethal.
- It is "official" or "institutional," condoned by some official(s) or institution(s).
- It is persistent or cumulative, consisting of a pattern of abuses.

All these qualities, naturally, are related to some social, political, racial, sexual, or religious opinion or identity of the persecuted.

Persecution, Prejudice, and Power

Two of the crucial aspects of persecution are its group nature, or better yet its group-versus-group nature, and its relation to power. As we stated at the top of this chapter, persecution is always carried out by members of one group against members of another group *as* members of those groups; in other words, persecution is never an entirely "individual" phenomenon but rather presupposes contrasting and exclusive group identity and membership. Persecution, in short, always involves "otherness," even if—or especially if—that "other" is in our midst or was formerly one of our own.

As an intergroup phenomenon, persecution falls within the broader category of intergroup dynamics, which we know (see chapter 1) can be the source of the greatest incidence and intensity of violence. One of these dynamics is prejudice. Gordon Allport described prejudice as the hostility and aversion that members of one group feel for members of another group on the basis of the real or purported qualities of that group, the members of which are assumed generally or universally to possess. Thus, each individual in the "other" group supposedly holds all the good—and bad—qualities of the entire group. This is why Allport called prejudice a consequence of "faulty and inflexible generalization"—inflexible because it is often resistant to contrary facts.[5]

Erroneous and stubborn preconceptions about other groups, mixed with the tendency (as identified by Tajfel) to prefer and positively judge one's own group and to dislike and negatively judge the other, frequently leads to intergroup animosity. Such groups, once apart, tend to remain apart, although their specific relationships can vary from insulting and critical talk to avoidance to discrimination to physical violence to extermination. Even worse, once this separation is established, it tends to be embellished, with all sorts of exaggerated or false failings, vices, and crimes ascribed to the other group. And of course, social separation—refusal to live together, work together, intermarry, and so on—does not necessarily remove all the points of contention, competition, and conflict between the two groups; they may still be, or imagine themselves to be, disadvantaged or blocked or oppressed by the other in matters of practical and symbolic interest like housing, jobs, wealth, political power, pride, and, not insignificantly, "truth."

Under these conditions, prejudice can easily escalate into violence: what was a minor or dormant difference becomes a major motivating factor. But negative attitudes and conflicting interests alone do not cause violence. First, Allport argued, the group tensions must reach a crisis: members who perceive (real or putative) disadvantages or affronts to their group "no longer feel that they can or should put up with the unemployment, rising prices, humiliations, and bewilderment. Irrationalism comes to have a strong appeal."[6] At this point, some "organized movement" emerges to play on and supposedly address the complaints of the group—a party, an institution, a cult, or even just a mob. "From such a formal or informal social organization the individual derives courage and support. He sees his irritation and his wrath are socially sanctioned. His impulses to violence are thus justified by the standards of his group—or so he thinks."[7] Finally, some "precipitating incident" transpires that puts the match to the tinder of irritation and organization. This incident can be an actual event, a rumor, an error, or a lie, but once violence erupts, the violence becomes self-sustaining and self-justifying; for instance, the very existence of inquisitorial courts seems to prove the existence and sedition of heretics, and the very existence of witch hunters (and manuals for witch hunters) seems to prove the existence and evil of witches.

The role of the party/institution/cult/mob raises the issue of power. Persecution depends on the possession and application of power, and unidirectional power at that. Persecutors, for their actions to rise above "mere" personal harassment or discrimination, must have social and/or political power at their disposal and must use that power in the sustained and orchestrated victimization of the other, who is comparatively powerless. The persecutor's power may literally be the power of the government, or it may be the power of other agencies (such as a religious institution like the Catholic church or an arm of a religious institution, like the Inquisition), or it may be both in concert. A main difference between persecution and ethnoreligious violence (chapter 6) and religious war (chapter 7) is that the victim of persecution ordinarily lacks power and thus *cannot fight back*. So not only the power but the violence is unidirectional; it is not common to find mutual persecution. If the victim is able to respond to violence with violence, then we have not persecution but combat.

Persecution, Morality, and Truth: Violence against the Intolerable

The dynamics of group identity, difference, and power alone are sufficient to unleash violent persecution by one group against another. Thus, whites have persecuted blacks, heterosexuals have persecuted homosexuals, and the lower classes (as in revolutionary socialism) have persecuted the upper classes. In all these cases, and myriad more like them, persecution has arisen because the group in power felt threatened (in its interests or in its very existence) by the group it decided to persecute. Such conditions are probably completely sufficient to produce persecution. However, often one or both of two additional conditions converge with identity, difference, and power to generate unprecedented persecution. These can be summarized as the "badness" of the persecuted group and their "falseness" or "wrongness," which are highly interrelated—and highly related to religion.

As much as politics or race or class or gender has fueled conflict, violence, and even persecution, David Heyd suggests that there are three "main spheres" or subjects in which persecution is likely to result—"religion, sex, and expression."[8] It is on these subjects that individuals and groups are likely to have the strongest opinions and to experience the strongest reactions. Some forms of expression, some sexual attitudes or practices or identities, and some religious beliefs and behaviors seem just not "right." John Horton finds then that persecution occurs when one group uses compulsion on another group "to prohibit or seriously interfere with conduct that [it] finds objectionable."[9] Of course, there are many things that we might object to, or even "find objectionable." A neighbor's loud noise or foul language might bother us. However, such behavior does not ordinarily lead to persecution. This is partly because the behavior does not rise to a level at which persecution seems an appropriate response. But that is not a sufficient explanation: it is not the case that even louder noise or even fouler language *would* merit persecution.

Bernard Williams suggests that the root of persecution is not how annoying some conduct is but how *unacceptable* or *offensive* it is: "If violence and the breakdown of social cooperation are threatened in these circumstances, it is because people find others' beliefs or ways of life deeply unacceptable. In matters of religion, for instance . . . one of the groups, at least, thinks that the other is blasphemously, disastrously, obscenely wrong."[10] In other words, persecution—at least the more exquisite kind that we encounter in inquisitions and torture chambers—entails more than threat or dislike but real, often intense, disapproval. The persecuted group is literally "intolerable"; they cannot be allowed to hold those beliefs or practice those behaviors.

Thus, in the most important cases of persecution, the targets of persecution are morally and "factually" wrong. Even more so, their wrongness is an *offense* to the persecuting group: it violates that group's deeply held values and beliefs (as well as their interests and power). It may even threaten the persecuting group's very world (drawing down divine judgment on them or the like). So, as some of the examples below will suggest, the persecutors may actually see themselves as acting in *self-defense*, even in concern—they sometimes even say "love"—for the victim. Violence, deprivation, and torture are not persecution in their eyes but *correction, discipline, and justice.*

There are, of course, various possible grounds for taking the position that the beliefs, behaviors, and values of others are intolerably bad and false, but certainly none is as convincing nor as common as religion. If religion is the "really real" and its claims and strictures are absolutely true and absolutely binding, then those who deviate are more than wrong; they are unbearably wrong. More, they have already brought down punishment on themselves: what little a mortal magistrate can do to them pales in comparison to what the supernatural authorities have in store for them. Of course, not all religions take the position that there is only one truth and one good or take an interest in what practioners of other religions—or what the nonreligious—think and do at all. Some religions find others strange, perhaps distasteful, but not so objectionable or offensive that they must interfere with, suppress, and eliminate the others. But when a religion holds absolutist and universalist kinds of beliefs and values, and when it shares social space with another religion, and when it possesses the power to enforce its claims, then persecution is a real possibility.

Therefore, certain religions or religious attitudes will tend to be more susceptible to outbursts of persecution than others. The historian Will Durant blames intolerance and the violence that flows from it on the *degree* of religiosity: "Intolerance is the natural concomitant of strong faith; tolerance grows only when faith loses certainty; certainty is murderous."[11] While this may be so, it does not distinguish religious persecution from any other strongly held commitment: one can have murderously strong political or racial beliefs, too. Others, like sociologist Rodney Stark, attribute violence and persecution not merely to religious faith but to specific religious ideologies, such as monotheism and its associated dualism. A highly dualistic religious worldview, in which good struggles against evil, is prone to persecute dissidents and nonbelievers as necessarily evil. And, as even religious sympathizers like Stark have had to admit, monotheism is especially disposed to persecution. "Particularism," he writes, "the belief that a given religion is the *only true religion*, is *inherent in monotheism*" (emphasis in original).[12] Thus, what Stark calls "the belief in One True God" makes intolerance more likely, if only because there is so much more to be intolerant of: all other religions, and all other interpretations of one's own religion, are false or worse—ungodly, sinful, evil. At the same time,

> if monotheists believe there is only One True God, they have been unable to sustain One True *Religion*. Rather, from the start all of the major monotheisms have been prone to splinter into many True Religions that sometimes acknowledge one another's right to coexist and sometimes don't. Hence, *internal* and *external conflict* is *inherent* in particularistic religion.[13]

In other words, monotheisms have a much harder time dealing with the inherent diversity of human beings. Of course, dualistic monotheisms also often breed and demand a fervor of belief that makes persecution seem necessary and valuable (see below). In this regard, they fulfill both Stark's and Durant's conditions. The hotter the fire of "true religion" burns, the more people who are consumed by it.

Even worse, and at the heart of persecution, is the essential relationship between monotheisms and governments, which unites the two characteristics introduced above. As Stark finds, "Because religious monopolies depend on state coercion, to the degree that religious monopoly exists, religious conflict will involve *a political challenge to the state*,"[14] such that disagreement with the religion is disagreement with and even disloyalty to the state—treason itself—and the state puts its coercive muscle at the disposal of religion. That, as many of our cases will illustrate, is the very recipe for persecution.

RELIGIOUS PERSECUTION IN THE ANCIENT/NON-CHRISTIAN WORLD

While religious persecution has been especially intense in the medieval and modern world, the first instances date back much further. According to Mary Jane Engh, the earliest but comparatively mild persecution occurred in ancient Egypt over the introduction of the new religious vision offered by Akhenaten around 1350 BCE. Akhenaten, born Amenhotep IV, rejected the polytheism of his ancestors and promoted the monotheistic worship of a single god, Aten, the Sun. He therefore withdrew funding of the temples of other gods, abolished their rituals and holidays, and put many priests out of work. He ordered a new capital city to be built (Akhentaten or "Horizon of Aten") and old sites of "false" gods to be defaced, including chiseling away inscriptions to them. While there are no records of imprisonment or violence, nonbelievers of his new religion were excluded from official jobs and promotions. As Engh writes, "With one divisive stroke, Akhenaten had created religious intolerance."[15] When Akhenaten died, his religion received the same treatment it had given its predecessor: its buildings were torn down and its city destroyed, the name of its founder removed from public artwork.

In the kingdoms of Israel and Judah during the seventh century BCE, there was a "revival" of the old religion that persecuted foreign and "false" elements. Hundreds of years prior, in the time of Moses, Jews had been warned that harm would come to those who betrayed their religion: "He that sacrificeth unto any god, save unto the Lord only, he shall be utterly destroyed."[16] For instance, the altars and images of other gods were to be smashed. Despite these warnings, contact with non-Hebrew peoples had led to absorption of their gods and their practices, including the worship of local spirits or *baals* and (possibly) child sacrifice; 1 Kings 18:19 mentions four hundred fifty "prophets of Baal" and four hundred "prophets of the grove" eating at the royal table. Many years later, a purification or purge of these nontraditional practices took place under the reign of Josiah after a book of traditional religious law was allegedly discovered during renovations on the temple. Artifacts and utensils used in the worship of baals were burned, the priests of the baals were "put down" (whether that means demoted or killed), property was seized or destroyed, altars were pulled down, idols were demolished, and human corpses were exhumed and their bones burned on altars to intentionally defile them. Engh continues:

> Next, Josiah's soldiers took the purge throughout the country, and even across the northern border into what had been the kingdom of Israel and was not an Assyrian province. Everywhere, Josiah's troops smashed and burned altars, images, and holy places, not only of Baal, Asherah, Chemosh, Moloch, and Milcom but altars and holy places of Yahweh too—for Yahweh's worship henceforth was to be highly centralized.[17]

In ancient Greece and Rome, "impiety" or disrespect toward or disbelief in the traditional gods was not only abnormal but criminal. In the early fifth century BCE, a priestess named Ninos had been accused of the crime of bringing foreign gods into the society, for which she received a death sentence. The vandalism of sacred images of Hermes all through Athens in 415 BCE led to several convictions, exiles, or executions. The 432 BCE decree of Diapeithes outlawed nonbelief in the gods or teaching sacrilegious doctrines, such as that the planets were natural objects: Anaxagoras was duly charged with impiety for suggesting that the sun was a burning stone, and he was fined and exiled. Many other philosophers and scientists were also persecuted, including Protagoras, Diagoras (who was sentenced to die for doubting prayer), Zeno (who was tried but acquitted), Aristotle (who fled Athens to avoid possible charges), and of course Socrates, who was executed for impiety and corrupting the youth with his questioning attitude.

At Rome, where power was much more centralized, persecutions were much more intense. The year 186 BCE saw the banning of the Bacchanalia and the arrest of priests and participants. The Bacchanalia, a foreign and allegedly immoral celebration, was believed to encourage promiscuity, drunkenness, nakedness, and other debauchery. As many as seven thousand people were arrested for joining the ritual, and the Roman historian Livy claimed, "More people were killed than imprisoned."[18] With Rome's rule expanding, it necessarily came in contact with other foreign religions, many of which were seen as enemies of the state. Druids in Britain were suppressed, both for their violent sacrificial practices and their anti-Roman organization. The Jews had always been viewed with suspicion, partly for their odd religion and partly for their refusal to submit to Roman practices like sacrificing to the gods and to the emperor. Claudius finally had the Jews banished from the city of Rome for "continually making disturbances at the instigation of Chrestos"—whether this name referred to Jesus or another political or messianic figure.

Farther east, the Persian Empire in the second through sixth centuries CE was undergoing a religious revival of its own. Persia, with an ancient religion involving priests (*magi*) and sacred fire, had followed the teachings of Zoroaster or Zarathustra for almost a millennium. Zoroaster had believed that a single good god, Ahura Mazda or the god of light, was in a cosmic struggle with his adversary, Angra Mainyu, the spirit of darkness. When Mazdaism took hold in the mid–fifth century BCE, the king Xerxes I demolished the temples of daeva worshippers, a "daeva" being any false or pre-Zoroastrian god. With Greek, Roman, and Indian influence, Mazdaism had declined over the years, so the new Persian rulers attacked these new and foreign religions. The famous innovator Mani, whose message was radical dualism and the absolute evil of the body and the material world, was arrested and died in jail, and his religious teaching was suppressed. Eventually, all religions were forbidden in the realm except Zoroastrianism, and any heretical leader or group that dared to emerge, like Mazdak in the fifth century CE, was stamped out.

EARLY PERSECUTION OF CHRISTIANS

Christianity emerged in the first and second centuries CE in an environment that was familiar with and often hostile to "new" religions. It too was the object of negative reactions from ridicule to violent oppression, particularly but not uniquely in the Roman Empire, which left a profound mark on the faith. Peter was martyred early on in Rome, where Paul also died. James, brother of Jesus, was killed in Palestine by Herod Agrippa. In fact, as Justo Gonzalez and Elaine Pagels[19] both remind us, it was the Jews whom many early Christians saw as their prime persecutors rather than the Romans, but that situation was soon to change.

Roman policy on religion was generally quite tolerant: as long as people obeyed Roman law and honored the Roman gods too (by sacrificing to them), members of other religions were fairly free to practice their own religions. Long experience with the Jews, a singularly obstinate group who refused to acknowledge any god other than their own (see chapter 4), had earned the Jews a special exemption, and since Christianity "first appeared in the Roman State as a sect of the Jews . . . it shared with Judaism not only the tolerance but even the protection of the Roman Government."[20] However, that tolerance and protection grew thin quickly. One reason was that Christians were seen as innovators and dissidents *within* Judaism: "To conservative Roman eyes, it seemed that Christians had abandoned their ancestral [Jewish] faith for a new, 'invented' religion."[21] Another reason was that Christians were even more obstinate than Jews about sacrificing and otherwise bowing to Roman gods, which was akin to treason in Rome. A third reason was the aggressive proselytizing of Christians, which caused conflicts between Romans and Christians and between Jews and Christians. This is one explanation for why Claudius expelled Christians along with Jews during his reign: the trouble between Christians and Jews seemed to him like squabbles between two sects of the same religion and he "decided to expel the lot."[22] In other words, much of the very earliest resistance to Christianity was not about Christianity at all. In fact, as Gaddis reminds us, much of what appears to posterity (and to Christian polemicists at the time and since) as specifically *religious* persecution

> simply involved the regular workings of the Roman state's machinery of coercion, aimed at a new target. Judicial torture and spectacular public executions were the normal violence one would expect to be directed against those perceived as disobedient or dangerous. Because religious dissent—unlike more conventional crimes such as murder or assault—could be undone by a simple change of mind, the persecutors' aim was fundamentally coercive rather than punitive. Arrested Christians typically received numerous invitations to sacrifice and opportunities to reconsider—and their refusal to take advantage of this leniency made them all the more infuriating in the eyes of the authorities.[23]

In short, Christians (with many others) were sanctioned for breaking the law and disturbing the peace rather than persecuted for their religious beliefs. While

Rome was tolerant of religious difference, that toleration ended "when the cults were reputed to be immoral or were a danger to the good order and security of the state"[24]—whether that cult was Bacchanalian or Christian.

However, there was some overtly anti-Christian sentiment as well. Roman understanding of Christian belief and practice led Romans to conclude that the Christians were atheists (since they worshipped an invisible god and rejected the official state gods) and immoralists: their "love feasts" smacked of sexual orgies, their "last supper" sounded suspiciously like human sacrifice and cannibalism, and their clandestine meetings at night in private homes had the scent of sedition. Plus, they came across as rabble rousers, appealing to and inciting the poor. In other words, as Gonzalez points out, there was a class aspect to Christianity in ancient Rome that disturbed authorities: it seemed to be "made up of credulous women and gathered from the very scum of mankind."[25]

History records several bursts of persecution during the first three hundred years of Christianity in Rome. The earliest came in the time of Nero, after the fire that seared much of the city in 64 CE. According to the Roman chronicler Tacitus, Nero blamed the fire on Christians and launched a purge against them that possibly cost the lives of Peter and Paul. Opinions vary on the extent of the persecution: Engh suggests that Nero "had hundreds of suspected Christians crucified, buried alive, or killed by wild beasts"[26] while Gonzalez concludes that there is "no mention of any persecution outside the city of Rome, and therefore it is quite likely that this persecution, although exceedingly cruel, was limited to the capital of the empire."[27] Canfield takes the most skeptical view, arguing that the emphasis on Nero's persecution is "wholly out of proportion to its importance," a product of activists painting a much darker picture of the period than it really was.[28] No matter what the evaluation, after Nero's fall in 68 CE, Christians were largely ignored for a time. Domitian conducted a persecution against Jews after 70 CE that entrapped some Christians too, and this persecution was not "uniformly severe throughout the empire."[29] In fact, Gonzalez can name only two victims, Flavius Clemens and Flavia Domitilla, who were executed for "atheism."

In 111 CE the emperor Trajan laid out his policy toward Christians. The government should not waste time searching for Christians, yet Christianity was classified as a *religio illicita*, an illegal religion, profession of which was a capital offense. If a person was accused of being Christian, he or she should be made to recant or suffer. Thus, while the approach was a sort of hand-off, don't ask/don't tell attitude, Christianity was a crime as such for the first time, and Christians could be punished merely for being so, whether or not they were engaged in treasonous, immoral, or antisocial behavior. Several persecuted/martyred Christians from the era have left writings, including Ignatius of Antioch and Polycarp.

From 180 until the 190s Christians lived in relative peace in Rome. Then an emperor reminiscent of Akhenaten in Egypt ascended the throne. Septimus Severus attempted to institute the worship of the sun, Sol Invictus (Unconquered Sun), as a unifying state religion, with all other gods accepted below the sun god. Jews and Christians naturally resisted, and their religions were banned in 202; it was during this period that the famous martyrdom of Perpetua transpired (see p.154). The passing of Septimus Severus delivered Christianity from persecution for about fifty years, until the "traditionalist" Decius came to power in 249. Decius inaugurated a campaign, like the later Persians, for the return to ancient Roman religion, which meant opposition to any nontraditional, non-Roman gods. His decree that all Romans must worship the city gods once again exposed Christians, as well as all other nontraditionalists, to scrutiny and persecution. The important early churchman Origen was tortured under Decius's reign as well as were hundreds of others throughout the empire in what was arguably the first systematic and prolonged persecution in Rome.

The emperor Valerian ordered exile, confiscation of property, slavery, and death for Christian priests and others who refused to honor the gods, but it is Diocletian who is remembered as the worst enemy of Christianity. As early as 295 some Christians had been executed for refusing to participate in the army or for desertion. The year 296 saw the persecution of Manicheans (who were also persecuted in Persia; see above). Finally, 303 brought the Great Persecution, in which Christian buildings and books were destroyed, followers were prohibited from public office, leaders were imprisoned, and all who refused to sacrifice to the Roman gods were arrested, tortured, and sometimes killed. "For the first time, imperial agents, court officers, and soldiers sought out and arrested Roman citizens, purely on the grounds of their religion."[30]

EARLY PERSECUTION BY CHRISTIANS

Christians had for the most part adopted a passive, long-suffering (even *pro-suffering*) stance in the opening three centuries of the religion. This is not to say that all Christians were pacifists; indeed many served nobly in the Roman and other armies (see chapter 7). However, their general powerlessness gave them a sort of "virtue of the weak." It might have been hoped that, if they ever achieved power, Christians would remember their own persecution, as well as their savior's admonition toward meekness and peacefulness, and restrain themselves from reciprocal persecution. This was not to be the case.

The Invention of Christian Heresy

A decade after Diocletian's persecution began, emperor Constantine issued the Edict of Milan (313), calling for an end to persecution of Christians. In fact, Constantine himself became a supporter of Christianity, although hardly a steadfast Christian, as he continued to worship Roman gods, to imprint those gods on Roman coins, and to act as their high priest. However, as the first and greatest patron of Christianity, he gave the religion two things that it had never had before—power and orthodoxy. Church and state were now united in a single institution, literally a single figure, since Constantine regarded himself as head of church as well as head of state. This meant that the religious branch of society had the apparatus of the secular/political branch at its disposal. Equally important, the beliefs or doctrines or "creed" of Christianity were "settled," although not to everyone's satisfaction. A variety of conflicting opinions had swirled on theological issues like the identity of Jesus (whether he was man, God, or both), the relationship between Jesus and God (whether Jesus was *created* by God or *was* God), and the "trinity" (whether God was one person or three-persons-in-one). At meetings like the Council of Nicaea in 325, under the stewardship of Constantine, these controversies were answered in favor of trinitarianism, the simultaneous humanity and divinity of Christ, and the consubstantiality of Christ and God.

One obvious consequence of orthodoxy is the creation of unorthodoxy, heterodoxy, or heresy. Other opinions than the "official" opinion would and could be banned, and with the power of the state in its hands, religious heterodoxy could be overtly criminalized. "Under the Christian empire, the imperial authorities often used their coercive power against Christian dissidents at the behest of Christian bishops."[31] One such case involved a bishop named Arius, whose doctrine (Arianism) was unitarian—God was one, not three—with Jesus as a lesser, "created" being. Contrary to the Nicene creed, Arianism was suppressed: "The leading Arian bishops were deposed, and the emperor decreed that anyone caught with Arian books would be treated as a 'criminal' and suffer 'capital punishment.' Thus, for the first time, Christians began to persecute one another for differences of opinion and faith."[32]

Emperor Theodosius, coming to the throne in 379, furthered the coalescence of Christian orthodoxy and with it Christian persecution. His Council of Chalcedon reaffirmed and fixed the Nicene position as the official one and "made those transgressions against the faith acceptable as crimes against church and state."[33]

> Religious intolerance soon became a Christian principle. . . . Within fifteen years of 380, imperial edicts deprived all heretics and pagans of the right to worship, banned them from civil offices, and exposed them to heavy fines, confiscation of property, banishment, and in certain cases death. By 435, there were sixty-six laws against Christian heretics plus many others against pagans. The purpose of persecution was to convert the heretics and heathen, thus establishing uniformity.[34]

And the death penalty was invoked early, when bishop Priscillian of Spain and six others were tortured and beheaded in 385. Unorthodox Christians and non-Christians alike were targeted, including the Platonist scholar Hypatia, who was kidnapped and torn to pieces. Yet, as efforts to eradicate heresy and "establish uniformity," they were doomed to fail.

The Persecution of Medieval Heretics and the Medieval Inquisition

Nonconformist beliefs continued to appear throughout the "Dark Ages" of Europe. For instance, many of the Germanic tribes that fought Rome and eventually occupied the continent were Arians, who considered the "official" doctrines of Christianity—which we can now call "Catholic"—to be heresy. The Vandals in North Africa expelled Catholic priests and seized their churches or used force to prevent their own people from entering the buildings. Nuns were tortured to extract confessions of sexual perversity with priests, and priests were executed. Of course, non-Christians in their domain were chastised with destruction of their shrines and sacred sites. Indeed, one of the primary subjects of Gaddis's study of early Christian violence is the "holy men" who intentionally violated pagan property and persons. Motivated by "a righteous anger against enemies of the faith,"[35] good Christian men smashed or mutilated idols, invaded homes, and beat nonbelievers. The most illustrative case gave Gaddis the title of his book: when a fifth-century Egyptian monk named Shenoute was arraigned for attacking a pagan's house, his defense was that "there is no crime for those who have Christ."[36] Surrounded by all this social and religious chaos, the church father Augustine endorsed stern, even deadly, force to compel Christians to believe the correct way—that is, his way (see below).

From one perspective, the Crusades of the early second millennium (roughly 1096 to 1204) were an attempt to unify European Christianity under one faith, one authority, and one cause (see chapter 7). If so, this merely indicates that by the eleventh century, Christendom felt the strains of heterodoxy pulling it apart. What ensued was an escalating legal battle with heresy. In 1163 the Council of Tours excommunicated all heretics, seeking prison and confiscation of property for them. The 1179 Council of the Lateran categorized heresy with banditry and robbery. In 1199 Pope Innocent III pronounced dissidents unqualified for public office or for testifying in court, writing a will, or receiving an inheritance. By 1208 the same pope declared that internal heresy was a more serious threat than distant Islam, particularly in parts of France.

By this time, the Catholic church had already fought and won its struggle against the followers of Peter Waldo, the Waldensians. Waldo had founded a sect in 1170 based on his translation of the Bible that advocated extreme poverty (which was also a protest against the luxury and corruption in the official church). His teaching was first proscribed in 1179, and when that did not stop its spread, King Pedro II of Aragon ordered Waldensians out of his domain and set a date after which any stragglers would be burnt to death. A. L. Maycock, in his study of the medieval Inquisition, wrote, "The severity of this act . . . was quite unprecedented."[37] However, it established a precedent that would be followed for centuries to come.

As the opposition of the Waldensians to the Catholic church hardened (eventually rejecting most of the sacraments, doctrines like purgatory and miracles, and belief in saints), the treatment of the sect became harsher. In 1212 eighty heretics including many Waldensians were burnt at the stake in Strasbourg. Other followers were killed throughout France during the 1200s and even early 1300s. Some were imprisoned, others given punitive penances. By the 1340s the heresy was virtually exhausted, with twelve late victims murdered in 1348 at Embrun. For good measure, several already-dead heretics were exhumed and destroyed in 1338–1339. However, the passing of the Waldensian heresy led to another and more stubborn one, the "Cathar" or Albigensian.

The Albigensian heresy was more urgent and persistent than its Waldensian counterpart and was the proximate cause of the Inquisition. The Albigensian movement, named after the town of Albi in the Languedoc region of France that was one of its strongholds, took an intensely dualistic form, believing (like Manicheans before them) that matter was wholly evil and in fact had been created by Satan, while only spirit, created by God, was good. It stands to reason, then, that Jesus had not been a material being, since God could not take a corrupt physical form; thus, Jesus was not God incarnate, did not suffer on the cross, did not die, and did not resurrect. For their leaders at least (called "The Perfect Men" or "The Good Men"), and for some laypeople, celibacy, asceticism, and poverty were demanded. Their ideal manner of death was self-starvation, and more than a few did starve themselves or otherwise seek their own destruction (jumping off cliffs or drinking poison). As early as 1018 the Albigensian heresy was known in parts of France, by midcentury had spread to central Europe, and by the mid–eleventh century to England.

The aforementioned Council of Tours urged local secular authorities to combat movements like the Albigensian one, but instead some princes and even priests had embraced it. Therefore, when Innocent III assumed the papacy, he empowered his own investigators to root out and destroy the group. The year 1215 is sometimes given as the origin of the Inquisition, but really it emerged gradually from actions and legislation before and after that date: many laws were in place long before, and laws, policies, and procedures continued to develop long after. The classic means of discovering and punishing heretics was to send a papal team of "inquisitors" into unruly provinces. These inquisitors, often Dominican friars, were duly charged, as Pope Gregory IX wrote to them:

> When you arrive in a city, summon the bishops, clergy, and people, and preach a solemn sermon on faith; then select certain men of good repute to help you in trying the heretics and suspects brought before your tribunal. All who, on examination, are found guilty or suspected of heresy must promise complete obedience to the commands of the Church; if they refuse, you must prosecute them according to the statutes that we have already promulgated.[38]

In other words, as Maycock concludes, the Inquisition "was an *ecclesiastical court* and a *weapon of internal* Church discipline"—a point that must be borne in mind (emphasis in original).[39]

The first inquisitors arrived in Languedoc in 1233 where they followed what was to become an established legal process. Based on the Roman concept of *inquisitor*, suspects were hauled before a judge or panel of judges (the inquisitors) who called witnesses and performed cross-examinations. The inquisitors were, in a sense, detectives, judges, and juries in one, empowered "to find out whether the accused was or was not guilty of a certain sin, the sin of heresy and rebellion against God's truth."[40] At least at this early stage, if the alleged heretic showed any repentance, no "crime" was assigned to him, since the Inquisition "was first and foremost a penitential and proselytizing office, not a penal tribunal."[41] In other words, "Any heretic who voluntarily confessed his lapse during [the 'grace period'] had nothing to fear. . . . He appeared before the Inquisition simply as a penitent seeking absolution for sin."[42] The problems began for the supposed heretic if he or she refused to confess and/or to repent and abandon heresy. The infamous procedures of the Inquisition evolved to break these inveterate sinners.

After the initial interview (and sometimes before), the suspect was held in prison, often for long periods of time, until an actual trial was conducted; it was believed that imprisonment was frequently sufficient to get the all-important confession and promise of obedience. When the confession was not forthcoming, torture could be applied. Religious torture used the same methods as secular/legal/criminal torture of the time, particularly the rack, the *strappado*, and a form of water torture. The rack is well known as a means to stretch and break the body. The strappado was a rope-and-pulley device in which the victim was lifted off the ground by his or her wrists, which were tied behind the back, usually resulting in dislocated shoulders; as necessary, weights were attached to the feet to enhance the agony. The Inquisitorial water torture involved pouring copious amounts of water down the throat of the victim or placing a wet cloth in the victim's mouth that blocked breathing and swallowing (not unlike latter-day water boarding).

When interrogation and torture had finally achieved the goals—either a full confession or an obstinate refusal to confess—the penalties were assessed. These might range from minor to final and always, from the church's point of view, had a penitential quality. At the lower end were "penances" like wearing one or more crosses or undertaking a mandatory pilgrimage. Some guilty or recalcitrant parties had their homes destroyed and their property seized. More than a few were incarcerated, it being believed that prison was an opportunity for spiritual rehabilitation. At the extreme end, victims were executed, often by burning at the stake—the so-called *auto-da-fé* or "act of faith." Many heretics received this fate: sixty Albigensian heretics were burned at Les Casses and another four hundred at Lavaur. However, some records indicate that the majority did not receive the ultimate punishment: documents from Toulouse covering the years 1307–1323 show nine hundred thirty judicial sentences, of which forty-two convicts were burnt while one hundred forty-three were made to wear crosses, three hundred seven imprisoned, twenty-two forced to see their houses demolished, nine sent on pilgrimage, and one exiled, and many others released from penalties.[43]

Other heresies were investigated and punished as they emerged. John Wycliffe's English movement, which came to be known as Lollardy, was persecuted in the 1300s. Wycliffe himself, who died before he could be punished, had his bones disinterred and destroyed forty years after his death. In central Europe, the followers of Jan Hus offered such firm resistance to their persecution that a struggle broke out that deserves treatment in our subsequent discussion of religious war (see chapter 7). Additional conflicts, between Catholics and Lutherans or Catholics and Huguenots, will be discussed later.

The Perennial Persecution of the Jews

If there is one group that has been continuously subjected to abuse for their religion in the West, it is the Jews. Proud and stubborn monotheists and anti-idolaters, they experienced unbearable pressures in their own homeland during occupation first by Greek/Seleucid forces and then by Rome. As we learned in the previous chapter, demands that Jews worship foreign gods or engage in prohibited activities led to armed insurrections (like the Maccabean revolt) as well as individual martyrdoms. During the Greek/Seleucid occupation, "Judeans suffered hideously at the hands of Syrian troops and officials. Mothers paraded through the streets with their murdered babies hung around their necks; old men held down while soldiers forced polluting meat into their mouths; young men tortured to death before their mothers' eyes."[44] Under Roman control, Jews also suffered and responded with violence and self-destruction, leading to the demolition of the Temple in 70 CE and the dispersion of the Jews from their land.

Even before the dispersion or diaspora, many Jews had found their way to Rome itself, where they constituted a significant and prominent community. As mentioned, Roman law, generally tolerant of religious difference, accommodated Jewish belief and practice as far as possible. However, Jews found a new adversary in their cousins the Christians. Strife between Jews and Christians sometimes brought down the hammer of authority on both of them (as during Claudius's reign) for disturbing the peace. However, once Christianity became the orthodoxy of the empire, an unprecedented threat to Judaism arose.

The Christian objections to Judaism were numerous. From a doctrinal and historical perspective, Jews (at least Jewish authorities) have traditionally been blamed for the death of Jesus, "Christ-killers," notwithstanding the fact that it was Romans who conducted the crucifixion (and that Jesus, in most interpretations, was *intended* to die as a sacrifice). Another equally serious problem was the Jewish refusal to accept what Christianity saw as their own prophecy and history: Jews had expected a messiah, and he had arrived, yet they continued to deny him. As Christ-deniers, they were by definition heretics. Apologists as early as Justin Martyr in 145 vilified and ridiculed Jews and suggested that God had shifted his favor from Israel to Christendom. The stern Augustine wrote centuries later, "The Jew can never understand the Scriptures and forever will bear the guilt for the death of Jesus."[45]

Persecution of Jews was certain and quick to follow. In 305, Spain saw the first laws proscribing Judaism: Christian women could not marry Jews, and Jews were not allowed to fraternize with Christians. When Theodosius made Christianity the sole legal religion of the empire in 391, Judaism became necessarily a religio illicita, as Christianity had been only a short time before. Jews were expelled from Alexandria, Egypt, in 415, and crowds attacked synagogues in Turkey and Italy in the late fifth and early sixth centuries. The Justinian Code (528) extended prohibitions on Judaism, preventing construction of synagogues, reading of the Bible in Hebrew, celebration of Passover, and testifying in court against Christians. In 722, emperor Leo III simply outlawed Judaism and ordered forced baptism of Jews, and in 855 they were banned from Italy.

The second Christian millennium was no more pleasant for Jews than the first, rather much less. Pope Gregory VII in 1078 ruled that no Jew could hold an office over or otherwise be superior to a Christian. The Crusades (see chapter 7), ostensibly fought to liberate Jerusalem, were hardly fought to liberate Jews: twelve thousand Jews were killed in the valley of the Rhine River before the Crusaders even departed Europe, where cheers of "Christ-killers, embrace the cross or die!" were heard. When Jerusalem was conquered, Jews were rounded up into a synagogue and burned alive inside. Various rulings of the medieval church reduced Jewish status in Europe: the Third Lateran Council (1179) designated them as "slaves to Christians" and ordered them to wear special identifying clothing or symbols, and they were routinely dispossessed of their property (e.g., in France in 1180 and in England in 1189).

Three further bases for the persistent and malignant persecution of Jews in Europe must be noted. The first was their economic status: Jews were often successful professionals or merchants, whom neighboring Christians envied or blamed for their own failings. Second was the legends and lies told about Jews, of which the darkest was the supposed "blood libel," that Jews captured and killed Christian children and used their blood for sinister purposes. The third was the uneducated belief that Jews were somehow responsible for the Black Plague in the mid–fourteenth century. Even before then, Jews had been accused in France of poisoning wells, for which five thousand were burned in 1321. But the plague was the worst disaster ever to hit Europe, and people were powerless to stop it or to even make sense of it. Jews were regularly scapegoated, blamed for naturally or supernaturally bringing on the disease. After 1347, thousands of Jews were expelled, attacked, or murdered—twelve thousand in Bavaria, two thousand in Strasbourg, six thousand in Maintz, and twelve thousand in Toledo.

Initially, Jews had not been subject to the Inquisition; that institution was reserved for Christian heretics, which meant that one had to be a Christian first. However, like all persecutions, it had the tendency to expand. As early as 1240 the Talmud was literally put on trial in Paris, where it was predictably found guilty and sentenced to burn: thousands of Talmuds and other Jewish books were subsequently collected and destroyed. Live Jews were burnt at the stake in 1288. However, it was in Spain in the late 1400s that the Inquisition turned particularly nasty for Jews.

As just recounted, the medieval Inquisition was an ecclesiastical court charged to uncover, investigate, and punish Christian heresy; strictly speaking then, it was a Christian-versus-Christian institution and did not apply to other religions. This is hardly to suggest that non-Christians were not persecuted in medieval Europe, only that other means were employed for them. By a turn of fate, Jews came within the purview of the Inquisition in Spain after 1480. What is Spain today had been divided between Christians and Muslims (or Moors) since the 700s, where the two groups, and a Jewish minority, had lived in an uneasy peace that Joseph Perez considers hardly "toleration." If the diverse religions "acted with tolerance, that was because they could not do otherwise: unwillingly, they accepted what they had no means of preventing."[46] Over the centuries Christian monarchs had chipped away at Muslim holdings on the peninsula, until by the 1300s and 1400s little remained of Moorish Spain. At the same time, Christian attitudes toward Spanish Jews hardened: the Partidas legal code of the late thirteenth century had defined Jews into a sort of perpetual captivity, "so that their very presence should be a reminder that they are descended from those who crucified our Lord Jesus Christ."[47] The 1312 Council of Zamora enacted more strenuous anti-Jewish laws, banning common meals between Christians and Jews, interreligous marriages or sexual relations, or political or occupational authority of Jews over Christians. During the fourteenth century, riots and massacres occurred in Navarre and Pamplona and Barcelona, with Jewish homes and property taken in what Perez characterizes as class conflict as much as religious conflict. Hundreds or thousands of Jews were killed, and many more prosperous ones left the country. And, consequentially, many accepted baptism and official conversion to Christianity; by 1415, as many as half of all Spanish Jews had been ostensibly Christianized, so that perhaps only one hundred thousand Jews remained on the peninsula.

Now the Spanish authorities had an interesting problem: the existence of new and questionably serious Christians, or *conversos*. The conversos or "New Christians" were not only suspect in their commitment to the religion, but they continued to form a visible, prosperous, and disliked community. In 1473 riots and street fighting broke out between poor Christians and well-to-do conversos. In fact, anti-Semitism "was now directed more against converted Jews than against those who had retained their Jewish faith, because the converts—the conversos—were accused of being false Christians and of leading a double life."[48] Some were believed to practice their Judaism in secret, and others (so-called Marranos) actually did deconvert and return to their ancestral religion.

Significantly, since the conversos were now Christians, they were officially within the grasp of Christian institutions. Accordingly, the Catholic sovereigns Ferdinand and Isabella in 1478 obtained the authority from Pope Sixtus IX to appoint inquisitors in Spain to investigate and penalize apostate conversos and the Jews who tried to deconvert them, the "Judaisers." Despite the fact that this was a twist in the history of the Inquisition, which previously had not targeted any one particular form of Christian heresy, the Spanish Inquisition did its job well—so well that it is the very archetype of vicious persecution. Tomas de Torquemada was appointed Grand Inquisitor in 1482 and led a campaign that created permanent inquisitorial courts throughout the kingdom and claimed over two thousand lives by the year 1500. The tools of the Spanish Inquisition were the same as those of the medieval version, ranging from pilgrimage, fasting, and temporary monasticism (which was virtual imprisonment) to confiscation of property, whipping, forced service as a rower on royal ships, exile, and of course the auto-da-fé of public burning. Few accused victims ever escaped punishment: records from Toledo indicate that, between 1484 and 1531, there were only eighty-eight acquittals, or just over two per year.[49]

Although non-Christianized Jews did not formally fall within the jurisdiction of the Inquisition, they were hardly protected from abuses. In fact, a thriving Jewish community was considered an obstacle to Christianization of Jews, since conversos had a place and group to return to, so in 1492 all remaining Jews in Spain were officially expelled and given four months to leave. Estimates suggest that more than half did emigrate, while others accepted Christian conversion, bringing them within reach of the Inquisition.

It is worth noting that, having hypothetically achieved its goal, the Spanish Inquisition turned to other victims. In the early 1500s, Muslims were ordered to convert, subsequently referred to as Moriscos. While only fourteen Moriscos are documented to have been burnt, many more had their wealth seized, and Muslim customs like the veil, ethnic dress, festivals, and the Arabic language were banned. Next the authorities focused on Protestants and other Christian heretics. Lutherans were killed in Valladolid in 1559, and the most famous victim, Miguel Servetus, a unitarian, was forced to flee in 1532, arriving in Geneva where he was martyred by Calvinists in 1553. By the mid-1700s, the Spanish Inquisition had nearly run its course, and it was finally officially disbanded in 1834. Perez quotes an apt epitaph: "Here lies the Inquisition, the daughter of faith and fanaticism. She died of old age."[50] But she did not pass until at least one hundred twenty-five thousand trials were held, forty-nine thousand arrests made, and as many as ten thousand victims put to death.[51]

The end of the Spanish Inquisition was far from the end of the persecution of Jews in the West. Martin Luther, that champion of religious freedom, had been virulently anti-Jewish, recommending stern measures in his "On the Jews and Their Lies":

> First, to set fire to their synagogues or schools and to bury and cover with dirt whatever will not burn so that no man will ever again see a stone or cinder of them. This is to be done in honor of our Lord and of Christendom, so that God might see that we are Christians, and do not condone or knowingly tolerate such public lying, cursing, and blasphemy of his Son and of his Christians.[52]

Additionally, he advised that Jewish homes should be "razed and destroyed" and their sacred books confiscated and that Germany should "emulate the common sense of other nations such as France, Spain, Bohemia, etc., compute with them how much their usury has extorted from us, divide this amicably, but then eject them forever from the country."[53] Sadly, his counsel would be followed for centuries after.

Anti-Semitism followed the Jews to America, where Jews (along with Quakers and other blasphemers and heretics) were banned from Massachusetts in the 1650s. Peter Stuyvesant of New Netherlands (later New York) wrote that Jews should "be not allowed to further infect and trouble this new colony."[54] Even the illustrious Toleration Act in Maryland (formally known as "An Act Concerning Religion" of 1649), provided toleration for all except those who "shall from henceforth blaspheme God, that is Curse him, or deny our Saviour Jesus Christ to be the son of God, or shall deny the holy Trinity"—which of course included Jews as well as others.

Throughout the modern era, Jews have been the brunt of discrimination and persecution, from the pogroms in imperial Russia to the Nazi Holocaust to the ramblings of neo-Nazis, Christian Identity followers (see below), and conspiracy theorists of various types. In nineteenth-century Russia, major persecutions including the pogroms (from the Russian word for "devastation" or "riot") drove Jews from their homes, businesses, and villages, especially after the assassination of Czar Alexander II in 1881, which was inevitably blamed on the Jews. (The tale of one pogrom is vividly portrayed in the musical *Fiddler on the Roof*.) In 1915, six hundred thousand Jews were removed from the western region of Russia, with some one hundred thousand dying in the process. Of course, when the Bolshevik Revolution came in 1917, Jews suddenly became the source of international communism to many hostile observers.

The story of the Holocaust is too long and too well known to recount here. Adolf Hitler, often mistakenly regarded as an atheist, wrote in *Mein Kampf*, "Today I believe that I am acting in accordance with the will of the Almighty Creator: by defending myself against the Jew, I am fighting for the work of the Lord."[55] The Nazi genocide against the Jews became the perfect conjuncture of religious fanaticism, mystical nationalism, economic competition, pseudoscientific eugenics, and modern technologies of mass murder in which six million Jews perished. History shows no reason to believe that Torquemada, Luther, or Alexander II would have done differently, had they possessed the means.

PERSECUTION IN ISLAM

The other great monotheism, Islam, has alternately been a victim and a perpetrator of persecution, depending on its status in the community: when it was the minority, as in medieval Spain, it was often persecuted, and when it was in the majority, it was often persecuting. Islam was born in the early seventh century in a polytheistic and religiously diverse cultural environment; Jews, Christians, and other religious groups lived in Arabia, and the Arabs of Mecca themselves worshipped a large number of gods housed in the structure called the Ka'aba. Muhammad's revelation was that there was only one god, al-Lah or the God, and that all others were false and idols; this one god was also the same god that the Jews and Christians believed in, although some of their specific beliefs about him were incorrect (for instance, Allah never had any sons). He fully expected that Jews and Christians would welcome and embrace this new revelation, but he was to be sorely disappointed. In fact, when Muhammad's stronghold of Medina was attacked in 627, he suspected treachery among the Jewish popula-tion, and the judge he appointed to investigate the situation "ruled that all adult male Jews should be executed and the women and children sold into slavery. Again, Jewish property was distributed to Muslims."[56]

Eventually, Jews and Christians were granted a special status, as "people of the book" or fellow monotheists. They became *dhimmi* or "protected people," but this protection was a form of institutional discrimination. They were bur-dened with a tax as non-Muslims. Additionally, they suffered various social and legal inequalities:

> They could repair existing churches and synagogues, but not build new ones. Their testimony was not valid against Muslims. Crimes against them, including murder and rape, were not punished as severely as crimes against Muslims. As Islamic law developed, *dhimmis* were often forbidden to own real estate. And the special tax they paid was explicitly forbidden to humiliate them.[57]

Yet, being a dhimmi was the only good alternative to being a Muslim in their society, since the choices were "Become a Muslim, become a dhimmi (if you were eligible), leave the country, or die."[58]

Other religions fared much worse. When Islam spread into Persia, that society's ancient religion, Zoroastrianism, was persecuted: temple riches were looted, practitioners were expelled or forced to flee, and the sacred fires were extinguished. Diffusing beyond the Middle East into India, Islam encountered Buddhism and Hinduism, both idolatry and polytheism from the Muslim per-spective. In 1018 Sultan Mahmud destroyed Hindu temples and icons at the site of Mathura—reminiscent of what would happen to the Buddhist statues at Bamiyan in Afghanistan a millennium later—and in 1019 temple-goers were killed at Kanauj. Even back in the home country of Arabia, all the pagan gods were removed by Muhammad himself from the Ka'aba, leaving it the abode of Allah exclusively.

Islam's attitudes toward religion and war are vitally important and will be discussed later (chapter 7). However, these attitudes must be understood in the context of doctrines about idolatry and unbelief. On this point, the Qur'an is quite explicit. According to sura 9.28, "The idolaters are nothing but unclean." Therefore, sura 9.123 instructs the faithful to "fight those of the unbelievers who are near to you and let them find in you hardness; and know that Allah is with those who guard (against evil)." After all, sura 4.76 teaches, "Those who believe fight in the way of Allah, and those who disbelieve fight in the way of the Shaitan [satan]. Fight therefore against the friends of the Shaitan; surely the strategy of the Shaitan is weak."

Interestingly, the Qur'an construes the existence and activity of nonbelievers, idolaters, and polytheists as *persecution of Islam*, and in that sense Muslims are only fighting for their freedom of religion. The non-Muslim persecutes the Muslim, so

> fight with them until there is no persecution, and religion should be only for Allah, but if they desist, then there should be no hostility except against the oppressors.[59]

> [P]ersecution is graver than slaughter; and they will not cease fighting with you until they turn you back from your religion, if they can; and whoever of you turns back from his religion, then he dies while an unbeliever—these it is whose works shall go for nothing in this world and the hereafter, and they are the inmates of the fire; therein they shall abide.[60]

Other instances of persecution of non-Muslim religions have depended on the particular local circumstances. When Sikhism appeared in the sixteenth century in northern India as a syncretism of Hinduism and Islam, it was suppressed by the Muslim Mughal authorities; no doubt, such statements by the Sikh founder, Guru Nanak, as "There is no Hindu, there is no Muslim" earned the movement some animosity. This oppression drove an originally pacifist religion to become militarized, as we will discuss in chapter 7. For now, struggles with the Muslim government in Lahore (in modern-day Pakistan) led to a Muslim attack on the Sikh Golden Temple at Amritsar in 1746, a massacre of seven thousand believers, which Sikhs remember as the "Lesser Holocaust." The "Greater Holocaust" in 1762 claimed another twenty thousand Sikh lives.

Another new religion that has faced persecution from Islam is Baha'i. Its original source was the teachings of Mirza Ali Muhammad, known to the faithful as the Bab or Gate, who was born in Persia in 1819. Raised a Muslim—in fact, descended from the prophet Muhammad—at age twenty-five it was revealed to him that "God the Exalted had elected Him to the station of Bab-hood," meaning that "he was the channel of grace from some great Person still behind the veil of glory," a sort of messenger of a greater leader to come.[61] When he declared himself the Mahdi, the awaited leader or savior prophesied in Islam, it was too much for Persian authorities, and on July 9, 1850, he was shot to death (after a previous attempt to execute him failed). Baha'is naturally regard him as a martyr. The central figure in Baha'i came after him, Mirza Husayn Ali or Baha'u'llah, the Glory of God. He was jailed repeatedly for his religious activities, as were his followers, and although he died a peaceful death in 1892, his religion continues to be persecuted, especially in its homeland of Iran.

In other countries today, the local nonconformists face persecution. Hazaras in Afghanistan suffered a massacre in 1998 in which two thousand were killed, partly in response to the killing of two thousand Taliban prisoners by Hazaras in 1997. In Pakistan, the Ahmadiyya sect was forbidden by law in 1984 to refer to themselves as Muslims or to preach or proselytize their beliefs. More generally, blasphemy was made a capital offence, with life imprisonment for desecrating a Qur'an and ten years in jail for merely insulting religion. Sunni Muslims enjoy advantages in government employment and access to public services. School textbooks contain disparaging comments about Hindus and Jews, and discrimination and violence has been perpetrated against non-Muslims, including mob attacks on Christians in 2005 and seizures of Hindu land in 2004. A *fatwa* or religious order also banned Ahmadiyya in Muslim-majority Indonesia, where a regional office of the Ministry of Religious Affairs banned twelve other sects, including Jehovah's Witnesses, International Society for Krishna Consciousness (popularly known as Hare Krishna), and various pre-Muslim religions. Finally, the abuses in Sudan since a regime dominated by the National Islamic Front came to power in 1989 are all too well known. Human Rights Watch estimates that one hundred thousand people were evicted from the capital city of Khartoum in the first five years of the regime, and hundreds if not thousands of others were arrested, interrogated, jailed, tortured, forced into exile, or killed. The methods of torture reported by survivors include immersion of the head in cold water, hanging from the hands on cell bars, burning with cigarette ends, electric shock, mock execution, rape, and pulling out of finger nails. Forms of cruel, inhuman or degrading treatment or punishment include confinement of many people in a very small cell, insults, beatings, and humiliation by requiring a person to imitate animal sounds.[62]

All of that pales in comparison to the horrors of Darfur, where hundreds of thousands have been sent fleeing to refugee camps as (allegedly) government-backed guerrillas attack tribal villages, killing and destroying in their path—and often attacking those very refugee camps where survivors settle.

THE PERSECUTION OF WITCHES

Nobody, it seems, likes a witch. Witches in various permutations across cultures have been the very personification of antisocial behavior, the polar opposite of a good citizen or often of a human being. Throughout the world, witches (and their close cousins the sorcerers) were often blamed for some of or all the misfortune that befell their neighbors and their communities, as Evans-Pritchard remarked of the Azande (see chapter 2). The Barabaig people of Africa claimed that a witch was a person whose very presence caused adversity, while the Kaguru believed that witches were innately evil, or even worse, "the physical opposites of humans even though they may appear to be like ordinary humans [who] do not recognize the rules and constraints of society."[63]

The exact attributes of the witch varied greatly from religion to religion but were always perverse or "backward," antisocial if not intentionally evil. It is reasonable, then, that societies with a belief in witches would also have an aversion to witches and that they would combat witchcraft when they identified it. The Burmese enlisted good master witches (*ahtelan hsaya*) to battle evil ones. Many societies employed diviners or oracles to locate witches, if only to counteract their witchcraft. The Dani of New Guinea actually hunted and killed them when they detected their work, and James Smith describes a case from the late 1990s in which a Kenyan village hired a professional witch finder to determine their source of their hardships.[64] In many parts of Africa today, young children are frequently accused and scourged as witches, often by Christian missionaries.

However, few if any societies have ever systematically hunted and persecuted witches like Christian Europe of the sixteenth to eighteenth centuries.

The precedent of the belief in and condemnation of witches was old: Deuteronomy 18:10, 1 Samuel 15:23, 2 Kings 9:22, 2 Chronicles 33:6, Micah 5:12, and Nahum 3:4 all refer critically to witches, and the appropriate response is spelled out clearly in Exodus 22:18: "Thou shalt not suffer a witch to live." However, the belief in witches did not lead immediately to orchestrated persecution. In fact, surprisingly, the early medieval church was not convinced that witches even existed; rather, as Stewart and Strathern put it, "the Church at first derided the idea that witches had real occult powers, regarding them as simply deluded by the Devil."[65] St. Boniface in the eighth century had declared belief in witchcraft to be an un-Christian throwback to pagan religion, and the Frankish emperor Charlemagne had ordered execution for any who burned an alleged witch. Finally, the collection of church law known as Canon Episcopi in 906 stated that belief in witches was heresy.

All this changed, indeed reversed itself, in the heretical hysteria of the thirteenth century and beyond. Revealingly, early witch hunters worked in southern France, in the same territory where the Albigensian heresy was fought. In 1320 Pope John XXII ordered the Inquisition to extend its mission to investigating and punishing witchcraft and sorcery, and in 1398 the theology professors of the University of Paris declared witchcraft and other types of magic to be heresy since those practices involved explicit or implicit pacts with Satan. It is crucial to recognize this characteristic of late-medieval witchcraft doctrine: many religions had acknowledged witchcraft, but until this moment it was not regarded as a relationship with the devil. In fact, it could not be so regarded in most religions, since they possessed no such concept as "the devil." But witchcraft in a Christian context *must* become a kind of devil worship or at least devil relationship. And, worst of all, it was not just any relationship but a blatantly *sexual* relationship. Witchcraft became Christian heresy in a time of general concern over heresy, but "only a special definition of heresy, one that pictured women as Satan's sexual servants, could have inspired the repressions of the witch hunt."[66]

Many major analysts agree that the witch-craze, and the image of the witch herself (for most European witches were women) was an invention of the historical moment; Stewart and Strathern insist, "Witchcraft in this sense was 'produced' by the Church hierarchy itself in the context of continuing struggles to assert its overall authority."[67] The first ingredient was the ongoing battle with heresy in its doctrinal (e.g., Waldensian or Albigensian) form. Another ingredient was the struggle against Judaism. The energized Inquisition was also inclined to find enemies, including enemies in the surviving scraps of pre-

Christian religion, what the historian H. R. Trevor-Roper calls "the mental rubbish of peasant credulity."[68] However, the credulity was not the peasants' alone: inquisitors and other authorities were inclined to take seriously the claims and confessions they heard.

The two pivotal events in the institutionalization of witch persecution were the papal bull of 1484, Summis Desiderantes, which authorized the Inquisition "to proceed to the correction, imprisonment, and punishment" of witches, and the subsequent publication of a guidebook for the interrogation and treatment of witches, the infamous *Malleus Maleficarum* or *Hammer of Witches*, first released around 1486. In painstaking detail, the *Malleus Maleficarum* and similar manuals laid out the mythology of witchcraft, insisting

> that every grotesque detail of demonology is true, that skepticism must be sti-
> fled, that skeptics and lawyers who defend witches are themselves witches, that
> all witches, "good: or "bad," must be burnt, that no excuse, no extenuation is
> allowable, that mere denunciation by one witch is sufficient evidence to burn
> another. All agree that witches are multiplying incredibly in Christendom, and
> that the reason for their increase is the indecent leniency of judges, the inde-
> cent immunity of Satan's accomplices, the skeptics.[69]

In other words, not only were these authorities totally credulous, but the idea of witchcraft was self-perpetuating, and any attempts to deny or question witchcraft were further evidence of witchcraft.

Trevor-Roper, Klaits, and others link much of the witch craze to the growing intolerance in late-medieval European Christianity. The last straw was, of course, the successful "Protestant" movement of the early/mid–sixteenth century. With Martin Luther, John Calvin, and such leaders permanently fracturing the unity of Christendom, religious hatred peaked, culminating in religious wars across Europe (see chapter 7). Two facts become clear: both the time period and the geographical location of the height of the witch craze coincided with the struggle between religious partisans. Trevor-Roper explains, "We can trace it geographically, watch it, country by country, as the Protestant or the Catholic missionaries declare war on the obstinate."[70] In the words of Klaits, "Witch hunting spread with the arrival of spiritual militancy in backwoods Europe"[71] and "demonstrates the success of reforming efforts to energize the lay elites with the ideology of spiritual purification."[72]

The consequences for the bewildered witches are well known. All the old tortures of the Inquisition were employed, plus news ones especially designed for witches. The victims were disproportionately old, poor, and female; by most counts, women comprised 80 percent or more of all casualties, and more in some places. And casualties there were: more than one thousand deaths in southwest Germany, two thousand in Bavaria, and three thousand in central Germany. In Bonn, fully half of the city was implicated in witchcraft, and professionals, clergy, and even small children were burned. The height of the witch craze on the Continent, not surprisingly, corresponded to the height of religious conflict, the Thirty Years' War (1618–1648). Across the channel in England, the witch craze was never as organized or as intense, yet five hundred forty-five witch accusations and seventy-four executions were conducted in Essex alone between 1560 and 1680,[73] and the craze temporarily made an appearance in America late in the seventeenth century, claiming a few victims at Salem, Massachusetts. Then, almost as suddenly as it started, the witch craze abated.

PERSECUTION OF RELIGION BY ANTIRELIGION

Religion has been the victim not only of religion but also, occasionally, of nonreligion, too. Of course, this is not to overlook the fact that nonreligious people—atheists and skeptics and the insufficiently enthusiastic—have regularly suffered under the power of religious authorities. However, in a few instances, nonreligious or even antireligious parties have come to power, and they have often turned their fury on religion.

There are probably only three real cases of antireligious governments in recorded history, and one of those was more opposed to certain kinds of religion than to religion in general. This one, the first, was early modern England where, according to Sommerville, a more or less deliberate and systematic secularization campaign was conducted under Henry VIII. Henry had been in a struggle with the Catholic church over his marital status. However, his religious argument went much further, potentially to the total eradication of religion from everyday experience. Church land was seized by the government, and monasteries were demolished or converted to secular uses. As many as three hundred sixty village churches were torn down or abandoned, their metal fixtures melted into cannons or ammunition. The state also took direct control over religion, limiting the number and exuberance of holidays and setting their dates. Power was wrested from religious councils and vested in secular courts and offices, with laymen rather than clergy in these positions. The clergy itself was "professional-ized," transformed from charismatic spiritual leaders into mere office holders. Organizations like occupational guilds were stripped of their religious elements and changed into strictly economic institutions. Thought, literature, the arts, and even language itself were demythologized. In fact Sommerville claims that language "was among the first things to be secularized," at once changing people's "habits of perception" and creating "a vocabulary which could express real unbelief."[74] Religion was deprived of its mystical language, Latin, and set in the vernacular of English. Printing and commercial sales of Bibles "put cul-tural authority in secular hands."[75] Magical invocations, glossolalia (speaking in tongues), and religious vows and oaths were discouraged. And religion itself was objectified: words like *religion, Christianity, theism,* and *supernatural* came into use for the first time, and an entirely new vocabulary of secular and scientific terms appeared, including *atheism, skeptic, deist, rationalist, investigate, criticism, analyze,* and *consciousness.*

Over two hundred years later, a more overtly hostile regime arose in revo-lutionary France. The French Revolution began in 1789 as a revolt against arbi-trary royal power and excessive taxation, transformed into a radical social-reform movement, and ultimately ended in revived despotism (in the form of the emperor Napoleon). It was during the middle phase, when all sorts of traditional beliefs and institutions were being questioned and abandoned, that religion came under assault. Christianity in France had already been subjected to intense criticism by the *philosophes* of the 1700s, such as Voltaire and Rousseau. Pre-dictably then, as the renowned historian Alexis de Tocqueville observed, "One of the earliest enterprises of the revolutionary movement was a concerted attack on the Church, and among the many passions inflamed by it the first to be kin-dled and last to be extinguished was of an antireligious nature."[76]

When a political insurrection broke out against the king and the upper classes, the Catholic hierarchy was subjected to criticism: after all, it was the two privileged groups—the nobility and the clergy—that held the majority voting power in the legislative assembly. Further, the Catholic church, as a traditional institution, was opposed to the revolutionary and democratic tendencies of the popular government. In response, the government decreed the Civil Constitution of the Clergy in 1790, which attempted to bring the priesthood under secular authority, including an oath of loyalty to the revolution as a condition of holding religious offices. It was in 1793, with a war under way and with the "dangerous classes" in power in Paris, that the most sweeping reforms came against many social institutions, including the church. A new calendar was promulgated that detached dating from Christianity and set Year One to 1792. The seven-day week was eliminated, and with it Sunday, and the months were renamed. Worst of all, a kind of radical rationalism reigned, with its "Committee of Public Safety," its idealistic notion of "virtue," and its weapon the guillotine.

The Reign of Terror that ruled in 1793 and 1794 is most infamous for its campaign of executions of counterrevolutionaries and enemies of the people. In fact, this is the first time in history that the term *terror* was used in its modern political sense, and, as its prime champion, Robespierre, explained, it was fear and violence in the service of virtue, of establishing a republic of virtue:

> We desire an order of things in which all base and cruel feelings are suppressed by the laws, and all beneficent and generous feelings evoked; in which ambition means the desire to merit glory and to serve one's country; in which distinctions arise only from equality itself . . . ; in which all minds are enlarged by the continued conviction of republican sentiments and by the endeavor to win the respect of a great people. . . .
>
> We desire to substitute in our country, morality for egoism, honesty for mere honour, principle for habit, duty for decorum, the empire of reason for the tyranny of fashion, contempt of vice for scorn of misfortune, . . . the love of glory for the love of money . . . that is to say, all the virtues and the amazing achievements of the Republic for all the vices and puerilities of the monarchy. . . .
>
> We must crush both the internal and foreign enemies of the Republic, or perish with it. And in this situation, the first maxim of your policy should be to guide the people by reason and repress the enemies of the people by *terreur*.[77]

Of course, some of the key victims of this virtuous terror were to be members of the church. Hundreds of priests were killed for alleged counterrevolutionary activity. Thousands more were defrocked and even forced to abrogate their vows by marrying. In what J. M. Thompson calls a "de-christianizing campaign,"[78] church structures were vandalized, church bells pulled down and melted into coins or guns, and priests imprisoned or deported. The very idea of God was condemned as "jealous, capricious, greedy, cruel, implacable."[79] Accordingly, the church buildings were to be converted into Temples of Reason, and in the place of Christianity, Robespierre offered a Cult of the Supreme Being and of Nature, a supposedly secular and rational religion. This new religion, announced in May 1794, contained its own holidays (dedicated to such things as "the human race," "the republic," "justice," "agriculture," "old age," and so on) and an admonition to hate treachery and tyranny as the highest religious duty. However, Robespierre's people's religion died with him in July 1794, when the revolution finally claimed the revolutionary.

The final and greatest purge of religion came in the form of Communist revolutions in Russia, China, and other Marxist systems in the early/mid–twentieth century. Like the French Revolution only more so, the Communist revolutions were "total" revolutions, aimed at reforming much of if not all society. Unlike their predecessor, the Communist revolutions had an underlying "theory," the historical materialist teachings of Karl Marx. In Marx's view, religion was a kind of false consciousness, an "opium of the people," a "sigh of the oppressed"; it was quite literally a tool of exploitation used on the masses to distract them from practical, economic concerns and to compel them to support their oppressors with taxes, tithes, and indulgences. When the revolution came, Marx fully expected that religion would disappear—wither away, just as the state too would wither away, the two always inextricably linked anyhow. With humanity's material needs fulfilled, people would no longer need "pie in the sky."

Marxist theory was put into practice in 1917, when a Marxist party, the Bolsheviks under Lenin, seized power in Russia. Religion came under relentless onslaught but once again as part of a much broader initiative to redesign society. The Bolshevik Revolution was never a mere political movement but a plan to create a new society and a new humanity: "From the moment they seized power the Bolsheviks felt they could not project Russia's development along Marxist-Leninist lines without introducing drastic changes in family, church, and education."[80] So, a stream of orders flowed from the new regime changing or abolishing many of Russia's traditional institutions, which were deemed backward, repressive, or counterrevolutionary. All private property was eliminated and claimed by the government in the name of the people. Banks were confiscated, inheritance outlawed, and all legal institutions (courts, local governments, etc.) liquidated. Ranks, hierarchies, and honors—even in education and the military—were abolished.

Outside of political-economic institutions, the two main realms of reform were kinship and gender relations and religion. Marriage and family law were drastically changed: the sexes were made legally equal, women were granted the right to divorce, children were given legal status equal to adults (whether or not those children were "legitimate"), and formerly criminal actions like abortion, adultery, bigamy, and even incest were decriminalized. Church marriage was made optional, with only civil marriage having legal standing. But this was just the beginning of the whittling away of religious authority over everyday life. In fact, as Dmytryshyn opined, "Next to the family, the Bolsheviks considered organized religion as the significant obstacle in their attempt to project Russia's development along Marxist-Leninist lines."[81]

The party nationalized church property when it nationalized all property. It further separated the church from the state (for instance, detaching marriage from religion, as noted above). State financial support for religion ended, and education was also stripped from the church and placed under secular control. The government took possession of birth and death records formerly held by the church. Any priests who supported the enemies of the party were executed. Even the highest officials were vulnerable: the Orthodox patriarch was arrested in 1925 and exiled to Siberia, and his successor was arrested in 1926. As a consequence of this religious resistance, persecution intensified: in 1927, seventeen churches, thirty-four monasteries, fourteen synagogues, and nine mosques were shut down; and in 1928 another three hundred fifty-nine churches and forty-eight monasteries were closed.[82] Even more, "the Church had to compete with Communist party–approved antireligious propaganda spread through schools, press, and all other media of communication and education."[83] A League of Militant Atheists was formed in 1925 to advance antireligious attitudes, and a newspaper called *The Atheist* launched constant attacks on religion. As Stalin rose to power, conditions only worsened: all Catholic priests in Moscow were arrested and put on trial, with Archbishop Cieplak sentenced to ten years in solitary confinement and Monsignor Constantine Budkiewicz put to death. In 1929, a law forbade any religious activities or instruction beyond basic religious services in sanctioned church buildings, and May 1931 saw the "antireligion five-year plan" that stipulated that by 1937 "not a single house of prayer will be needed any longer in any territory of the Soviet Union, and the very notion of God will be expunged as a survival of the Middle Ages and an instrument for holding down the working masses."[84]

In other Communist states, the situation was similar if not worse. In the People's Republic of China, religion was explicitly regarded as a "historical phenomenon" that had outlived its oppressive usefulness and that would vanish as the revolution progressed. In the meantime, many religious houses—Christian, Buddhist, Muslim, tribal, and so on—were closed, and the remainders were compelled to register with the government. Officials and members of various religions were subjected to "reeducation" and harsh social criticism. Conditions were particularly bad in Tibet, which was occupied by China in 1950 and 1951. The 1959 uprising that led to the emigration of the Dalai Lama and one hundred thousand other Tibetans brought firm suppression of religion in that country: nearly all of Tibet's monasteries and nunneries were demolished, and over half a million monks and nuns were ousted. According to Ronald Schwartz, "many were tortured, killed, imprisoned, or forced to disrobe. A few years later, during the Cultural Revolution, any display of religion was prohibited, punishable by beatings and imprisonment, and all religious objects were confiscated and destroyed."[85] When Buddhism (and political activism) reemerged after 1980, it was suppressed with the arrest and incarceration of thousands of Tibetans, two-thirds of them monks and nuns; believers who continued to practice their religions in prison were beaten and tortured. In 1998, a three-year plan to eradicate religion was launched in Tibet, publicly criticizing religious leaders and ridiculing religious doctrines. In the process, more monks and nuns were ejected from their retreats, exiled, or imprisoned.

Tibet and Buddhism are hardly the exclusive targets of religious persecution in China. The Uighurs of Xinjiang Province, predominantly Muslims, have been subjected to the same treatment, particularly when they also engage in political (anticommunist) activity. According to a Human Rights Watch report, more than two hundred have been sentenced to death since 1997, and Muslim officials have been harassed and mosques destroyed. Uighur imams have, like other religious authorities, been put through "reeducation." Official education, in state-run schools, forbids the teaching of religion, the use of religious materials, the practice of religion, or any "activities that would enhance the development of religious followers."[86] The Uighur oppression briefly came into international view around the 2008 Beijing Olympics.

Christianity is certainly also restricted (it was first banned as long ago as the 1720s for its anti-Chinese doctrines). In 1955, over one thousand Catholic priests, nuns, and followers were arrested. What remained of the Catholic church was taken over by the Communist government, which appointed its own clergy and bishops without papal approval. An "official" Catholic church exists in China under state control, although an "underground" church also exists. Finally, one of the most persecuted groups in contemporary China is the new religion of Falun Gong, a variation of the ancient Chinese discipline of qigong mixed with popular Buddhism and Taoism and some apocalyptic/salvationist elements. It was founded in 1992 by Li Hongzhi and claims a worldwide membership of 100 million, with 70 million in China, although Chinese government estimates suggest less than 40 million and perhaps as few as 2 million.[87] Repression came swiftly after ten thousand members assembled in the neighborhood of Chinese authorities in central Beijing in 1999. Police began to break up Falun Gong gatherings and to condemn the movement in the media. In July 1999, Falun Gong was officially banned and legally disbanded, and it was classified as an "evil cult." A purge of Falun Gong literature followed, with over 2 million books and pictures destroyed.[88] Arrests of members and leaders came next, with a warrant for the arrest of Li Hongzhi himself. By 2001 Falun Gong was declared one of the primary enemies of the government, and by the end of 2001, official efforts to eradicate the movement were showing some success, as Falun Gong was becoming less confrontational while its ranks were shrinking.

PERSECUTION BY THE AMERICAN RELIGIOUS RIGHT

There are many premises on which one group might persecute another—religion, race, and politics, to name but three. In the American right-wing movement, these three have sometimes become virulently enmeshed.

It is frequently argued that the United States was founded as a Christian country. It is less disputable that the United States was founded as a slave-owning country. So began a long and troubled history of race relations and the religion that allowed if not enabled these relations. A major consequence of the black/white divide was the American Civil War, in which states fought states for the right to make their own laws, including the legality of slavery. The defeat of the Confederacy in 1865 settled the legal question but hardly the status of African Americans, let alone the social and political relations between the races. Out of this defeat grew the first in a long line of religiously oriented racial-persecution movements, the Ku Klux Klan (KKK). Founded sometime between late 1865 and mid-1866 in Pulaski, Tennessee, the KKK was initially conceived as a "social" club by former Confederate soldiers including Richard Reed, Calvin Jones, John Lester, Frank McCord, John Kennedy, and most notoriously, James Crow; its purpose was to "have fun, make mischief, and play pranks on the public,"[89] but these pranks soon took a sinister and racist turn. An announcement as early as 1867 contained the language, "Unholy blacks, cursed of God, take warning and fly."[90] By the spring of 1868, the Klan had become a private army to intimidate freed slaves and their Northern, Republican supporters. Violence ensued: teachers were threatened, whipped, and murdered, and schools burned; black politicians and activists, or merely blacks who attempted to use their new rights, were harassed and killed; especially offensively, a white woman named Mrs. Skates who offered refuge to three blacks was beaten, stripped naked, and violated with hot tar poured on her genitals. In response to this "reign of terror," in 1871 President Ulysses S. Grant deployed the US Army to put the KKK out of business.

The armed suppression of the Klan was successful, but the group was revived in its more familiar form during World War I by William Joseph Simmons, a Methodist minister who rode the circuit through Alabama and Florida. It was he who set the first Klan burning cross on a mountaintop in Georgia in 1915; "burning crosses," Wade informs us, "had *never* been part of the Reconstruction Ku Klux Klan."[91] This new Klan was not only racist but "nativist," that is, actively opposed to all "non-Americans," such as immigrants, Catholics, and Jews. As a Klan document of the time asserted:

> Only native-born American citizens who believe in the tenets of the Christian religion and owe no allegiance of any degree or nature to any foreign Government, nation, political institution, sect, people, or person [i.e., the Pope or Catholic organization] are eligible. . . . We avow the distinction between races of mankind as same has been decreed by the Creator, and we shall ever be true to the faithful maintenance of White Supremacy.[92]

It was clear that religion, race, and nationality/nationalism had already become intertwined.

The early twentieth century in the United States was also the period of the formulation of the religious movement known as *fundamentalism*. Some of its exponents held positions or came to hold positions amenable to Klan doctrine. The highly regarded evangelist Billy Sunday said in 1917 that "Christianity and Patriotism are synonymous terms, and hell and traitors are synonymous."[93] Simmons, it seems, had sought an alliance with Christianity, and so the Klan moved in a more overtly religious direction—so much so that sociologist John Mecklin could conclude in 1924, "A Fundamentalist would certainly find himself thoroughly at home in the atmosphere of the Klan ceremonies"—and vice versa.[94] Accordingly, around 1921 the Klan began to formally reach out to Christian fundamentalists, upon whose support the revived movement came to depend. Simultaneously, the Klan's message became more explicitly religious: a document called "The Klansman's Creed" included the statement:

I believe in God and in the tenets of the Christian religion and that a godless nation cannot long prosper.

I believe that a church that is not grounded on the principles of morality and justice is a mockery to God and to man.[95]

The Klan declined again during the Great Depression, only to reappear in the 1940s with the message espoused by Grand Dragon Samuel Green: "If God wanted us all equal, He would have made all people white men."[96] The social movements of the 1950s and 1960s—civil rights, women's rights, church/state separation, and so on—mobilized the Klan profoundly. As Southern African Americans rose up, and "liberals" traveled south to support them, violence broke out again. In 1963, the Sixteenth Street Baptist Church was bombed. In 1964, three civil rights workers—Michael Schwerner, Andrew Goodman, and Jim Chaney—disappeared and were found dead in Mississippi. Also in 1964, a black teacher named Lemuel Penn was fatally shot in the head by KKK assassins as he drove his car in Georgia. The temper of the group was expressed by Texas Grand Dragon Louis Beam: "I've got the Bible in one hand and a .38 in the other hand, and I know what to do."[97]

Violence continued into the 1980s. Klansmen shot five black women in Chattanooga, Tennessee, in 1980—four as they walked home and a fifth as she planted flowers in her yard. In Detroit, they attempted to kill a black man who moved into a white neighborhood. In 1981, a young black man named Michael Donald was kidnapped, strangled, and hanged to death in Mobile, Alabama. The policy and the justification were clearly enunciated by Bill Wilkinson: "The Klan stands for segregation. It stands for America, and it stands for God Almighty."[98]

The KKK persists to this day, but it has long since spawned other equally violent organizations whose stated enemies include blacks, Jews, immigrants, communists, liberals, and sometimes the American government itself, all of which are often seen as interchangeable or in some conspiratorial cabal: as Reverend William Potter Gale said, "You got your nigger Jews, you got your Asiatic Jews, and you got your white Jews. They're all Jews and they're all offspring of the Devil. . . . Turn a nigger inside out and you've got a Jew."[99] Further, this whole pack of Jewish/black/communist conspirators have or will soon have infiltrated the government and established a ZOG or "Zionist Occupation Government." One such group is the Posse Comitatus, founded in 1969 by Henry Beach and the aforementioned Gale, which refused to recognize the federal government of the United States and claimed the right to withhold taxes and arrest its adversaries. The Aryan Nations grew out of the Church of Jesus Christ Christian, led by Reverend Charles Conley Lynch and Richard Butler. Aryan Nations naturally idolized Adolf Hitler, down to wearing Nazi uniforms and conducting paramilitary drills. In fact, the first lines of their Web site feature a quotation of Hitler: "Those who want to live, let them fight, and those who do not want to fight in this world of eternal struggle do not deserve to live."[100] They also subscribe to the doctrine known as Christian Identity, which asserts that the white race (sometimes even more specifically, white America) is the true people of God, the true Israel, and that the Jews are descendants of the Devil. Its philosophy claims the following:

> We believe in the preservation of our Race, individually and collectively, as a people as demanded and directed by Yahweh (Aryan Nations members do not call the supreme being God because God is dog spelled backwards). . . . We believe that Adam, man of Genesis, is the placing of the White Race upon this earth. Not all races descend from Adam. Adam is the father of the White Race only. . . . We believe that the Cananite [sic] Jew is the natural enemy of our Aryan (White) Race. . . . The Jew is like a destroying virus that attacks our racial body to destroy our Aryan culture and the purity of our Race. . . . [101]

The Mountain Church of Jesus Christ, created in 1971 by a former Klan grand dragon named Robert Miles, combined elements of KKK, Nazi, and Christian Identity dogma, although George and Wilcox maintain that Miles "is as comfortable with neopagans and Odinists (those who worship the Norse god Odin) as with Christians."[102]

Unsurprisingly, many of these religious/racist/nationalist organizations have found common cause with the "militia" movement, which encourages self-arming in preparation for violent confrontation with the government and its Jewish/black/communist allies. One example is the Covenant, Sword, and the Arm of the Lord (CSA) group founded in the 1980s in Missouri. This religious, racist, militia association was strengthened with the debacles at Ruby Ridge and Waco, in which members felt that Christianity and citizenship were under direct assault. In response to such perceived affronts, Pastor Pete Peters of the LaPorte Church of Christ, a Christian Identity sect, gathered organizations of all sorts in late October 1992. This gathering at Estes Park, Colorado, dubbed the Rocky Mountain Rendezvous, agreed to moderate the racist and anti-Semitic rhetoric in order to attract more mainstream members and adopted a plan for armed but decentralized resistance. The attendees drafted a letter to Randy Weaver, the martyr of Ruby Ridge, which read in part:

> Impelled by the spirit of our Heavenly Father, We, 160 Christian men assembled for three days of prayer and counsel, at Estes Park, Colorado, . . .
>
> We have not the power to restore to you the loved ones who were cruelly stolen from you!
>
> But as Christian men, led by the word of our Heavenly Father, we are determined to never rest while you are in peril and distress!
>
> We are determined to employ HIS [*sic*] strength and to work continually to insure that Vicki and Samuel's [Weaver's wife and son] mortal sacrifices were not in vain!
>
> We call for Divine Judgment upon the wicked and the guilty who shed the blood of Vicki and Samuel![103]

The willingness of such groups to use violence in pursuit of their religiously inspired cause should not be minimized (as we will see again in chapter 8). As a supporter of Randy Weaver (who himself has since disavowed violence) said, "I'm ready to get my gun and my clips and take off my safety and pull my trigger with my finger. I don't care anymore. This is the beginning of a revolution, a war."[104] Pastor James Bruggemann of Stone Kingdom Ministries in Asheville, North Carolina, completely agrees: "No, folks, it is not a perverse joy I take in the impending doom of the enemy. It is a righteous joy!"[105]

THE VIRTUES OF PERSECUTING— AND BEING PERSECUTED

From the outside, persecution is a self-evidently bad thing: no one wants to be persecuted, and no one wants to be a persecutor. In fact, persecutors almost never use the term *persecution* to describe their own actions. There are a few exceptions, but these only shed light on what one could call, and the self-described persecutor would call, *good* persecution. For instance, Thomas Babington Macaulay wrote in his 1870 *Critical and Historical Essays*: "I am in the right, and you are in the wrong. When you are stronger, you ought to tolerate me; for it is your duty to tolerate truth. But when I am the stronger, I shall persecute you; for it is my duty to persecute error."[106]

We tend to be quick to attribute persecution to fear and low self-esteem in the persecutor, but, as Baumeister warned us (see chapter 1), that is often the victims' perspective. Persecutors see it differently. They typically explain and legitimate their actions as *punishment, correction, or hygiene*, or all at once. We must begin from the premise, as Macaulay does, that for the persecutor some things are true and some things are errors, and some of these truths and errors are overwhelmingly important. Errors, especially really grievous errors, the kind that threaten not just the errant but all those around them, cannot be left unaddressed. The fact that individuals in error do not always realize their mistakes, or that they do not always readily admit them and repent them, does not diminish their fault; rather, it may exacerbate their fault. When the stakes are greatest—as when they concern absolute truth, eternity, and immortal souls—the issues are most serious.

This is why persecutors often see their behavior not as persecution at all but as *justice*, even as mercy. The legal analogy here is intentional: persecution often has the quality, at least for the persecutor, of a legal process. The point is to discover "the truth," determine guilt, and administer punishment. In many cases, as with the Inquisition, the mechanism of persecution is literally a court of inquiry, with judges, records, witnesses, and sentences. It is not only "legal," it is *the legal system*. For instance, the great church father Augustine was altogether in favor of persecution of heretics. For him, crimes were crimes, and spiritual crimes were even graver than property or violent crimes. Capital punishment was fit for some secular crimes, especially, as Augustine rationalized, since we all die eventually anyhow. For dissidents and schismatics—people who not only make profound errors in religion but might lead others into error with them, endangering not only their own souls but the souls of others—physical pain, torture, and even death did not seem like too stiff a punishment. Far worse than bodily death, "we fear their eternal death, which can happen if we do not guard against it and can be averted if we do guard against it."[107] Thus, pain, deprivation, and death (Levy indicates that Augustine preferred flogging, confiscation of property, and exile over execution) were not persecution at all but penalty, and legitimate penalty at that, for the harm that the victim was doing to religion, God, and the community of believers: "There is an unjust persecution which the wicked inflict on the Church of Christ, and there is a just persecution which the Church of Christ inflicts on the wicked."[108]

More than a penalty, Augustine saw violence as instruction, as not just punishment of error but correction of error. More like a parent than a prison guard, the persecutor uses pain "to heal by love, not to injure by hatred" so that the victim "may learn not to blaspheme."[109] The use of force was thereby not only justified but actually precedented: Augustine referred to Luke 14:23 where Jesus is quoted as saying, "Go out into the highways and hedges, and compel them to come in, that my house may be filled," and he also argued that the church was following the model of Paul, who "was forced by Christ; therefore, the Church imitates her Lord in forcing [heretics], although in her early days she did not expect to have to compel anyone in order to fulfill the prophetic utterance."[110] Ultimately, violence was not only justified but also supposedly appreciated by the victims: "It has been a blessing to many to be driven first by fear of bodily pain, in order afterwards to be instructed."[111] And indisputably, he reasoned, whether or not they appreciated it, the victims benefited from their abuse: it forced "those who carried the standard of Christ against Christ to return to Catholic unity, under stress of fear and compulsion, rather than merely . . . leave them free to go astray and be lost."[112] In a word, as Gaddis astutely notes, Augustine and his successors saw persecution instead as religious coercion: "Their coercion justified itself through a disciplinary discourse: it employed calibrated violence not to destroy its target[s] but to chastise, reform, even educate them."[113]

The other major medieval Christian theorist, Thomas Aquinas, concurred. To him, anyone who erred in religion was guilty of blasphemy (false and insulting speech toward God), and blasphemy was the one original religious capital offense, punishable by death. Blasphemy, in legal terms, was like perjury, only infinitely worse, for it was lying about and to God. Therefore, since the victim of persecution was essentially a criminal, persecution was nothing more than criminal justice: heretics and nonconformists "by right . . . can be put to death and despoiled of their possessions by the secular [authorities], even if they do not corrupt others, for they are blasphemers against God, because they observe a false faith. Thus they can be justly punished [even] more than those accused of high treason."[114] According to Aquinas, religious error was dangerous not only to the holder of such opinions but also to everyone else; it was like an infection that could sicken other believers and the church as a whole. So, even more than justice, persecution was like medicine, a "purging" of corruption from the spiritual body, a kind of "surgery" to remove an unhealthy part of the church. That important church leaders found not only validity but pleasure in the torment of their enemies is expressed best by Tertullian:

> How shall I admire, how laugh, how rejoice, how exult, when I behold so many
> proud monarchs, and fancied gods, groaning in the lowest abyss of darkness;
> so many magistrates who persecuted the name of the Lord, liquefying in fiercer
> fires than they ever kindled against the Christians; so many sage philosophers
> blushing in red hot flames with their deluded scholars; so many celebrated
> poets trembling before the tribunal, not of Minos, but of Christ; so many
> tragedians, more tuneful in the expression of their suffering.[115]

Surely these words from the late second/early third century CE, before Christianity rose to political power, presage the reality that followed when it came into
possession of power.

The pleasure of administering persecution—that is, of being a "good persecutor"—is one thing. The pleasure of receiving persecution—that is, of being a
"good victim"—is another thing completely. Yet, in some religious worldviews,
it is virtuous to be persecuted, too. As we saw in the previous chapter, many
early Christians, like Tertullian, found great honor and opportunity in their own
persecution (although obviously Tertullian dreamed of turning the tables one
day), up to and including martyrdom. For Tertullian and others like him, there
was no path to heaven *other than* being persecuted.

Michael Pocock, writing in *Moody Magazine*, an instrument of the Moody
Bible Institute, explains that there are four reasons why Christians value persecution: "(1) They are identified with Christ. (2) They hold a position contrary to
that of the majority. (3) Satan opposes God's people and plan. (4) God uses hardship to advance His kingdom and develop Christians."[116] (Of course, these reasons do not explain why non-Christians might value persecution, or why Christians commit persecution). So, not only are Christians fulfilling a religious duty
in accepting their own suffering—"Everyone who wants to live a godly life in
Christ Jesus will be persecuted," wrote Paul in 2 Timothy 3:12—but they are
being attacked by the devil and tested by their own god. Persecution, in a word,
is good, since it indicates that the prophecies were true, the models were correct,
and the supernatural forces are at work.

A certain constituency of contemporary Christianity positively revels in its
persecution. Publications like "The Voices of the Martyrs" and Web sites like
http://www.persecution.org and http://www.christianpersecution.info (the latter
an outlet of a group called Worthy Ministries) keep the reader informed—and
agitated—about the persecution of Christians around the world. Gaddis inter-
prets that persecution was a critical element in early Christian community

building, and it still is. Persecution is also important in the identity of many religions beyond Christianity. Sikhs actively preserve a memory of their persecution throughout history and the martyrdom of their early leaders. Shi'ite flagellants too celebrate and identify with the persecution of their founder and exemplar. The experience of the Holocaust is at the heart of Jewish identity for many modern Jews. Humes and Clark find evidence in their fieldwork that the ongoing persecution of Baha'is in Iran is a part of the construction of their collective memory, including for Baha'is outside of Iran.[117]

Allport's theory of groups and prejudice sheds some light on this process. Prejudice, group hostilities, and even group violence can have several positive group-building and group-maintaining effects. There is value in perceiving one's "own kind," one's in-group, in a favorable way in contrast to those inferior or evil others; all humans derive some of their self-worth from their affiliations, whether they be family, nation, race, or religion. Persecuting and being persecuted equally allow the group to feel defensive (many groups persecute out of "self-defense"), which also gives an elevated sense of one's own importance and goodness. And more than elevation, denigration of the out-group can unite and integrate the in-group: "Hostility toward out-groups helps strengthen our sense of belonging"[118] and to strengthen the boundaries of the group, what Allport calls "re-fencing." While the group's identity and boundaries are rejuvenated, the individual member's commitment and loyalty to the group is enhanced. The individual is asked to identify with the suffering of other members, even those remote in place or time. The group, its leaders, and its doctrines can also be idealized in mutual distress, unfortunately often by ignoring or denying the faults and failings of one's in-group, endowing it instead with absolute goodness and rightness. And, as evidence has shown, the absolutely good can do anything to the absolutely bad and feel totally justified about it.

That persecution is often efficacious, for the persecutor and the persecuted, is undeniable. As the past chapters have suggested, and as the following chapters will illustrate, fighting, suffering, and dying are often goods in themselves. Martin Luther himself said that "where there is no battle for the Gospel it rusts and it finds no cause and no occasion to show its vigor and power. Therefore, nothing better can befall the Gospel than that the world should fight it with force and cunning."[119] Indeed, it can be equally beneficial to have an enemy or to be an enemy.

CHAPTER 6

ETHNORELIGIOUS CONFLICT

Around the world, religious communities have taken up arms against each other as groups—Catholic versus Protestant in Northern Ireland, Muslim versus Jew in Israel/Palestine, Muslim versus Christian in Yugoslavia, Sikh versus Muslim versus Hindu in India, Buddhist versus Hindu in Sri Lanka, and so on. Such violence, unlike sacrifice and self-mortification that tend to be personal and small scale, is necessarily collective (group-on-group) and potentially quite large scale, verging on or shading into sustained war (see chapter 7). In fact, when sacrifice reached massive proportions, as in centralized kingdoms like Dahomey or the Mayan and Aztec empires, it was still essentially a multiplication of individual acts of violence rather than a "campaign" of conflict against an opposing group, aiming at the defeat or eradication of that group (although such societies at least sometimes fought wars specifically to provide victims for their sacrifice machine). In a certain sense, even persecution, including its most organized forms like the Inquisition, is often an extended series of individual encounters—of persecuting group or institution versus persecuted person. Furthermore, and perhaps crucially, the casualties of sacrifice, self-mortification, and persecution are often defenseless victims, not armed combatants. This is why a sustained program of religious persecution and annihilation like the Nazi genocide of the Jews does not quite constitute an "ethnic conflict": it was one-way destruction, with little or no counterkilling of Germans by Jews.

Ethnic conflict may be protracted or sporadic or acute and brief; it may be comparatively mild or dramatically intense. But whatever course it follows, in its most intense form it is difficult to distinguish clearly from "war." Tanks may literally roll, bombs may be thrown, and more or less regular uniformed fighters may be battling other more or less regular uniformed fighters. A relatively small percentage of the population may be actively engaged in the fighting, but then that is true in any war. The only real difference between a major ethnic conflict and a war properly speaking (but it is an analytically significant difference) is that a war is "external" or international—between nations, or more accurately, between *states*—whereas an ethnic conflict, virtually by definition, is "internal," a "civil" struggle between two or more groups *within a state*.

In this chapter we will investigate contemporary ethnic conflicts in which religion plays a central or fundamental role. Not all ethnic conflicts are religion based, and obviously not all religious groups are embroiled in ethnic conflicts. In other words, ethnic conflict is not *inherently* religious; rather, religion is one of the types of communities or causes that may become entangled in such conflicts. And religions are not *inherently* conflictual in the bomb-throwing, armies-marching sense; rather, even when religious differences exist, there must be *other aggravating circumstances* that transform those religious differences into "ethnic" and military differences. Religion, then, as we suggested in the first two chapters, may be one module in a complex, multivariate alloy of conflict, and conflict may be one module in a complex, multivariate alloy of religion. In the end, not all ethnic conflicts are ethnoreligious conflicts, and ethnoreligious conflicts are not exclusively about religion but are about other things, too.

ETHNICITY, CULTURE, RELIGION, AND CONFLICT

Ethnic and its noun form *ethnicity* are relatively new terms in the social-scientific vocabulary. They derive from the Greek root *ethnos* for "nation" or "people," and in fact the first definition presented by Webster's is "heathen"—that is, people other than "us believers." It is, in short, a term of differentiation and separation: *we* are not "ethnic," *they* are. An "ethnic group" then is a group in some way *in distinction from other groups*, and especially from *our* group. That is, there can never be just one ethnic group in a society; there must always be two or more such groups, in some relationship of contrast and mutual exclusion. Now, there are of course all sorts of human collectivities—classes, genders, races, or simply crowds—but ethnic groups are distinguished particularly on the basis of "culture" or behavior or, occasionally and perhaps simultaneously, physical traits like skin color. George DeVos defines an ethnic group as "a self-perceived group of people who hold in common a set of traditions not shared by the others with whom they are in contact. Such traditions typically include 'folk' religious beliefs and practices, language, a sense of historical continuity, and common ancestry or place of origin"—which in combination may give the group a cultural and physical identity.[1]

An ethnic group then has a set of distinguishing characteristics that set it apart from other collectivities. For Fredrik Barth, an ethnic group is largely biologically self-perpetuating; shares fundamental cultural values, realized in overt unity in cultural forms; comprises a field of communication and interaction; and has a membership that identifies itself, and is identified by others, as constituting a category distinguishable from other categories of the same order.[2]

Andrew Greeley provides a more extensive, and less flattering, inventory of ethnic traits:

1. a presumed consciousness of kind rooted in a sense of common origin
2. sufficient territorial concentration to make it possible for members of the group to interact with each other most of the time and to reduce to a minimum interaction with members of other ethnic groups
3. a sharing of ideals and values by members
4. strong moralistic fervor for such ideals and values, combined with a sense of being persecuted by those who do not share them and hence are not members of the group
5. distrust of nonmembers, combined with massive ignorance of them
6. finally, a strong tendency among members to view themselves and their circle as the whole of reality, or at least the whole of reality that matters.[3]

It should be obvious how religions can satisfy these conditions.

In addition to the negative cast given by Greeley, both he and Barth suggest something else as well, that ethnicity involves a certain amount of "identification" or "consciousness" in addition to the empirical qualities that members share. According to Max Weber, there is a degree of subjectivity in ethnic identity above the fact of cultural differences; ethnic groups "entertain a subjective belief in their common descent because of similarities of physical type or of customs or both . . . ; it does not matter whether or not an objective blood relationship exists. Ethnic membership differs from the kinship group precisely by being a presumed identity."[4] DeVos extends this notion in his definition of *ethnicity* as the "subjective symbolic or emblematic use of any aspect of culture [by a group], in order to differentiate themselves from other groups."[5]

This definition raises a number of salient points. First, if ethnicity is subjective, then it is not entirely or simply objective or real. As Thomas Hylland Eriksen has asserted, "cultural difference between two groups *is not* the decisive feature of ethnicity" (emphasis added).[6] That is to say, there is no one-to-one correspondence between the extent of cultural difference and the extent of ethnic differentiation: two groups with small cultural—including religious—differences may perceive or promote large ethnic differences, while two groups with large cultural—including religious—differences may perceive or promote small or no ethnic differences. Certainly the cultural characteristics are available as *potential* ethnic-organizing principles, as resources or raw materials, but they must be *used by somebody* to become actual "ethnic" identifiers. In any ethnic situation, the two groups will have at least some cultural characteristics in common: in Northern Ireland, Protestants and Catholics are both Christians, and basically Caucasian, and generally English speaking. So, from a certain perspective they are two groups, while from other perspectives they are just one group.

That the cultural differences not only exist but are *used*, and are used *symbolically or emblematically*, is critical. Culture—or some particular item(s) from the vast catalog of culture—serves as an emblem, a "marker," figuratively if not literally a banner or flag of group membership. What language you speak, what clothes you wear, what food you eat, or what religion you practice can equally function as signs, badges, and organizational principles for groups; such signs are how we know if you are "one of us" or not. Finally, the idea that cultural features are actively used raises the question of what they are used *for*. The answer is twofold. First, they are used to construct the group to begin with. As subjective identities or "imagined communities,"[7] ethnic groups do not exist until, and only exist as long as, people think they do; ethnicity is a process of group identity creation. Weber referred to it in terms of humanity's "familiar tendency to monopolistic closure" (similar to Allport's notion of group processes and prejudices), to separating "us" from "them"; where such exclusionary identities occur, "they are due to conscious monopolistic closure, which started from small differences that were then cultivated and intensified."[8] And Weber was quite clear that any difference at all will suffice. This is why Barth insists that the key to ethnicity— and the violence it generates—*is not within the groups but between the groups*: "The critical focus . . . becomes the ethnic *boundary* that defines the group, not the cultural stuff that it encloses."[9] Ethnicity is, ultimately, a boundary-making and boundary-sustaining force. The very existence and persistence of ethnic groups depends on the maintenance of a boundary. The cultural features that signal the boundary may change, and the cultural characteristics of the members may likewise be transformed, indeed, even the organizational form of the group may change—yet the fact of continuing dichotomization between members and outsiders allows us to specify the nature of continuity.[10]

This is not always an entirely spontaneous process. It depends minimally on the gradual crystallization and escalation of (sometimes formerly minor) demands, grievances, and other frictions; that is, group differences do not automatically and inevitably produce group conflicts, and group conflicts do not automatically and inevitably produce group violence. Particularly crucial to the ethnic formation and mobilization process are the rhetoric and actions of cultural leaders or elites who function as ethnic "entrepreneurs"[11] to soothe or stoke cultural animosities and to give shape to ethnic identities and boundaries.

The second answer to the question of the use of ethnic identities and markers is instrumental. Ethnicity arises under two conditions—contact and competition. As stated above, ethnic groups are always contrast groups, and they only emerge where two or more (real or putative) cultural groups share social space. The fact that a group lives in a plural or multicultural setting means that members may become aware of themselves as a culture-bearing group, by exposure to others who do not possess their traits or values. Ethnicity, it must be said, is not simply culture but *self-conscious* culture. And it is not simply self-conscious culture but *mobilized* culture. Mobilization comes as a result of the second condition, the realization that we as a group are in competition with them as a group *and that cultural differences make a difference in that competition*. In any social context, there is limited availability of—and potentially differential access to—the desirable resources of the society. Citizens may notice that some people have more money or power, better housing or educational opportunities, and a generally superior standard of living than others—and that membership in one group or another seems to be a correlate or cause of these inequalities. When groups discover that their groupness seems to negatively affect their chances of acquiring wealth or status or power, and/or that another group seems to be an obstacle in that acquisition, then they may mobilize to advance their interests and to reduce or eliminate the interests of other groups—or reduce or eliminate those other groups themselves. In other words, ethnic groups are not simply cultural or identity groups but also *interest groups*, which means that they are not so much fighting *about* their culture as *with* their culture, using it as a resource and a weapon. They are certainly not trying to *convert* each other to their religion nor are they disputing each other's doctrines. What they are disputing against each other is access to or control over "mundane areas like development plans, education, trade unions, land policy, business/tax policy, [the] army," and other worldly concerns like housing, voting rights, jobs, and such.[12]

Ethnicity, Violence, and the Sacred Nation

If, as Barth and Weber proposed, ethnicity is primarily a matter of boundary maintenance, then religion is a particularly effective tool in the genesis and mobilization of ethnic attachments. First, as we have repeatedly stressed, religion is a group phenomenon par excellence. More, it provides identity—sometimes the definitive identity—to its members, and it provides institutions that embody and perpetuate that identity. The interests of the religious group can transform it into a religious interest group, and its ideologies, which may explicitly advocate violence, at least isolate it from others who do not share those ideologies. Like any "cultural isolating mechanism," religion establishes and "demands social separation from those who worship in a different manner. It creates sects and breeds sectarian violence."[13]

But because religion adds a layer of realism and legitimacy to the group and its identity, institutions, and interests, the stakes of ethnoreligious conflict can be infinitely higher than those of more specifically secular ethnic conflict. Under the influence of religion, the group may no longer be merely a "people" or a "nation"—which would supposedly entitle it to certain rights, including the right of self-determination and possibly of political independence—but a special people or what Scott Appleby calls a "sacred nation." A sacred nation, in its own eyes at least, has not only rights but also righteousness. Further, its struggles may no longer be merely for land or wealth or power but for "higher," even ultimate or cosmic goals; as such, it cannot imagine defeat or often mere compromise. As Appleby explains:

> Ethnoreligious extremists and religious nationalists may demonize their enemies, consider their own religious sources inerrant and their religious knowledge infallible, and interpret the crisis at hand as a decisive moment in the history of the faith—a time when exceptional acts are not only allowed but also required of the true believer. To the extent that they manifest these and other tendencies associated with fundamentalism, such actors replicate a fundamentalist pattern of reaction to their enemies.[14]

One example of the sacred nation, or of the "sacralization" of the nation, will illustrate our point. India is a society of incredible cultural and religious diversity. In fact, until fairly recently in history, according to many analysts, there was no such thing as a single unified Indian religion or identity; rather, there was a loosely associated but regionally differentiated variety of religious ideas and practices, sharing a few features like the caste system and beliefs in dharma and karma. However, in different locations and for different castes and cultural/linguistic groups, different gods were worshipped, different rituals conducted, different practices performed. India was literally a society of many religious paths. The coalescence of a specifically and self-consciously "Hindu" culture and identity came only in the late nineteenth century from a variety of sources, including, of course, Western colonialism and cultural categorizations. In 1871, the All-India Congress introduced a formal classification of religious and communal categories, including "Hindu." In 1875, an organization known as the Arya Samaj or Society of Aryas emerged as a sort of Vedic fundamentalist organization, calling for a strict adherence to the oldest of Hindu texts (the Vedas) and dismissing "much of later Hindu tradition as degenerate practice that is best forgotten."[15] In 1915, the All-India Hindu Mahasabha was created in association with the Indian National Congress and as a cultural reaction to the Muslim League, which was organizing Muslims and promoting Muslim identity in India, particularly in northern India (which would eventually lead, after independence, to the partition of colonial India and the establishment of Muslim-dominated Pakistan).

Out of such Hindu activism arose an ideology known as Hindutva, discussed in the 1923–1924 publication of Vinayak Damadar Savarkar that established the term. Meaning essentially "Hinduness" or "Hindu nationalism," its principles included the concept that Hindus were not only a single nation (*rashtra*) but the indigenous people of the subcontinent. All true natives of the country, regardless of their caste or sect or language, were Hindu; even more, the "fundamentals" of Hindu identity and belief were a real or "natural" thing, a racial heritage literally in the blood. Therefore, all of India was not only a home but a *sacred* home to Hindus. This ideology was institutionalized in the 1925 movement called Rashtriya Swayamsevak Sangh (National Union of Volunteers/ Servants), led by Kesnar Baliram Hedgewar. This new understanding called for a radical personal transformation, an ethnoreligious awakening, basically a "conversion," to one's true Hinduness. The RSS recruited "volunteers" or "self-servants" (*swayamsevaks*) to defend and advance the cause, an elite cadre trained in kshatriya (warrior caste) values and organized into military regiments.

By 1939, there were sixty thousand active RSS members, and by 1989, 1.8 million trained swayamsevaks in twenty-five thousand national branches.[16] The movement had become a major influence on Indian politics in the late twentieth century and was best summarized by Madhav Sadashir Golwalkar, who wrote in his 1938 *We, or Our Nationhood Defined*:

> The non-Hindu peoples in Hindustan must adopt the Hindu culture and language, must learn to respect and hold in reverence Hindu religion, must entertain no idea but glorification of the Hindu race and culture: i.e., they must not only give up their attitude of intolerance and ungratefulness towards this land and its age-old traditions, but most also cultivate a positive attitude of love and devotion instead . . . in a word, they must cease to be foreigners, or must stay in this country wholly subordinated to the Hindu nation, claiming nothing, deserving no privileges, far less any preferential treatment, not even citizens' rights.[17]

As Menon describes it, Hindutva essentially represents a massive "reconversion" (or, in some instances, a first conversion) to Hindu identity, especially overcoming or rejecting Christian conversion and reclaiming people who "have been tricked by missionaries or . . . seduced by offers of material remuneration."[18] From the Hindu nationalist perspective, the proselytization of other religions "is part of a conspiracy to destroy 'Indian' culture and to destabilize the 'Indian' polity."[19] As such, the conversion of Hindus to foreign religions, and ideally their successful reconversion to their true and native religion and identity, "is not seen as simply an individual expression of faith but rather as a political choice that necessarily implicates questions of national allegiance, patriotism, and cultural determination."[20]

In conclusion, while the invention and propagation of Hindutva is a particularly conspicuous case of ethnoreligious genesis and mobilization, it is by no means the only case. Rather, in the examples that follow, we will see similar processes at work in nearly every instance. Religion certainly exists prior to ethnogenesis, but often in fragmented and inchoate form. In the face of or in response to external and internal factors, a religious identity is not only produced and promulgated (usually but not always or entirely out of previously available religious resources) but also promoted as the identity—the true or authentic identity, and the only identity that matters—of the group. As such, the ethnoreligious group becomes "closed" and exclusionary, defensive, and often offensive—and potentially, and frequently actually, violent.

ETHNORELIGIOUS CONFLICT IN THE MODERN WORLD

Standing at the midpoint as they do between individual acts of religious violence and sustained intergroup war, and integrating religion with other forms of identity and organization such as tribal, economic/class, geographic, and political, ethnoreligious conflicts can be found throughout the world, even in locations where sects or religions previously coexisted in relative tranquility. Some such conflicts have (at least at certain moments) evinced all the qualities of a real war, and others have the potential to ignite real wars. It is unclear, then, where to categorize certain conflicts, like the one between Israel and the Palestinians. It is, in an important way, an international—even a regional—struggle, since it does not strictly take place between two religious groups within a single state. Nevertheless, religion is surely one of its many dimensions.

Similarly, the smoldering troubles in Kashmir and Punjab, the area of northern India (or southern Pakistan, since the region is in dispute) have religious qualities. India and Pakistan, two countries created out of the partition of colonial India in 1947—the one majority Hindu, the other majority Muslim—not only contain unhappy religious minorities and have experienced internal religious strife, but they have actually gone to war several times since independence. Even worse, each possesses nuclear weapons, so a major war between them would be of more than local concern. Worst of all, the Kashmir/Punjab region is claimed as home by a third ethnoreligious group, the Sikhs (see the next chapter), whose geographic concentration and martial tradition make the area a hotly contested piece of land. At partition, the majority of the territory's population was Muslim, and so Pakistan asserted ownership, but the political authority was Maharaja Hari Singh, a Hindu, giving India a valid claim to it. For Sikhs, however, Kashmir and Punjab are their primary and historical territories and their holy land: while they represent less than 2 percent of India's total population, they are two-thirds of the population of Punjab, and 80 percent of the world's twenty to twenty-five million Sikhs live there. In 1966, the Punjab area was itself partitioned to create a distinct linguistic home for Sikhs (called Punjab) attached to a non-Sikh state (called Haryana) sharing a single capital city. As this obviously did not address Sikh religious, political, and economic grievances, they radicalized in the 1970s, leading to calls for a sovereign Sikh state (to be named Khalistan) and for violent struggle against India. Growing unrest and violence led ten thousand Sikh militants to vow to fight to the death, a vow they made at their holiest of sites, the Golden Temple at Amritsar. On June 5, 1984, India conducted an assault on the temple, shelling it for five days, killing at least one thousand people, including the Sikh leader Jarnail Singh Bhindranwale, and damaging the structure. Consequently, Indian prime minister Indira Gandhi was assassinated by Sikh bodyguards on October 31, 1984, and a low-level military conflict has persisted ever since, prosecuted by groups like the Khalistan Commando Force, Khalistan Liberation Force, Bhindranwale Tiger Force of Khalistan, and All-India Sikh Student Federation.

Better known to Westerners, and on a grander scale, is the ethnoreligious violence in Sudan, particularly in the Darfur province. Related to geographic and environmental conditions (the profound difference between the north/east Nile region and the south/west desert region with its severe drought), politics, culture, and religion, the conflict has pitted northern (mostly Muslim) militias, known as the Janjaweed, against western rebels and local native peoples. It is widely believed that the Janjaweed receives support from the Sudanese government, dominated by Arabs and Muslims. A civil war beginning in early 2003 between Muslims from the north and Christians and tribal religionists from the south set the stage for the current military and humanitarian crisis, with between two hundred thousand and four hundred thousand casualties so far and over two million refugees who are constantly subject to attack by roving gangs.

Meanwhile, in the Philippines, a struggle between the Muslim southern islands and the Christian majority—a struggle that, in one form or another has continued for hundreds of years, but which has been particularly intense in recent decades—has taken as many as one hundred twenty thousand lives. In early 2000, a resistance group known as al Haratul Islamiya attacked a Catholic school, and rebels have seized hostages and are widely believed to provide inspiration if not assistance to al Qaeda. Which gives us Iraq, a state with a tormented history since its founding in 1936. Arising out of the same mandate that created Lebanon (see below), except under British authority, its first independent and pro-Western government was ousted in 1958 by the Ba'ath Party, leading eventually to the dictatorship of Saddam Hussein. Hussein's overthrow in 2003 by American forces left a power vacuum, in which Sunnis and Shi'ites began to vie for control, with Kurds in the north largely achieving a quiet autonomy from the Iraqi state. Iraqi Sunnis and Shi'ites developed a deadly pattern of attack and counterattack, Shi'ites finding champions in figures like Muqtadr al-Sadr and his Mahdi Army, and Sunnis often still identifying with the Ba'ath Party and the fallen Hussein. Both sides used stealth methods like car bombs, roadside explosives, and suicide bombers against civilian populations, the police and army, and symbolic targets like the Golden Mosque in Samsarra. A sacred shrine to Shi'ites, it was struck in February 2006 and again in June 2007, destroying its dome and minarets. In the meantime, according to United Nations sources, thirty-four thousand Iraqis died in sectarian violence—a series of revenge and counterrevenge killings, a virtual religious civil war, of the sort that extremists on both sides apparently aimed to instigate.

We turn now to an in-depth account of some of the major ethnoreligious conflicts of recent years, involving several different regions of the world—Europe, Asia, the Middle East, and Africa. In every situation, the struggles have roots in the past (sometimes a few hundred years, sometimes a few thousand years), but the current circumstances have been much exacerbated by, and therefore cannot be understood apart from, recent historical developments. Significantly, the groups involved have lived at times in peace (if only a tense peace), so that hostility and war is not their "natural," "traditional," or inevitable state. The role of religion in the conflicts must be analyzed, not taken for granted—but also not overlooked.

Ethnoreligious Conflict in Sri Lanka

Sri Lanka is a small island state (a little over twenty-three thousand square miles, or less than half the size of New York State) off the southeast tip of India. Formerly known as Ceylon during its colonial period, it has a population consisting of two main groups, a majority of Sinhalese (74 percent) and a minority of Tamils (18 percent). For probably two thousand years the two societies have shared the island in various relationships, but since 1974 they have been engaged in an at times savage conflict that has cost between forty thousand and seventy thousand lives, depending on the estimate. However, as Angelo Vidal d'Almeida Ribeiro reported to the UN Commission on Human Rights, "It cannot be repeated too often that the present tragic situation is the product of specific historical circumstances, and not, as one often hears in Sri Lanka and in the international press, the end product of a 2,500-year-old struggle between ancient enemies."[21]

The story of Sri Lanka differs depending on who tells it. From the Sinhalese perspective, they were the original inhabitants of the island, settling there in the sixth century BCE from northern India. As recounted in the Sinhalese national scripture/chronicle *Mahavamsa*, the culture hero Vijaya led a party of Buddhists to the island, which they called Lanka, arriving on the very day of the Buddha's death after granting the island to his people in these words: "Vijaya, the son of king Sinhabahu [*sic*], is come to Lanka from the country of Lala, together with seven followers. In Lanka, Oh lord of Gods, will my religion be established, and carefully protect him with his followers and Lanka."[22] In the Sinhalese version of history, the island was uninhabited except for demons (*yakkhas* and *nagas*), whom Vijaya defeated, marrying a female demon named Kuvanna and thus giving birth to the Sinhalese people. Three centuries later, King Devanampiya Tissa greeted a mission of Buddhist monks from India (at the time of the great Buddhist Indian emperor Asoka) and established a community (sangha) of monks (bhikkhus) in close alliance with the government. So began the tradition of the "political bhikkhus" on the island.

Naturally, the Tamils tell a different tale. They maintain that they were the native inhabitants of the island, the very people that the Sinhalese remember as demons. Originating from the eastern area of India (where the Indian state of Tamil Nadu exists today), they had established a Hindu society before invasion by the Sinhalese, who reduced the natives to a minority mainly located on the eastern and northern edges of the island. So began an unhappy coexistence between the two groups, a Sinhalese/Buddhist majority and a Tamil/Hindu minority—a history that is viewed by the Sinhalese "as a great apocalyptic clash between the Sinhalese, who possessed the island, and the Tamils (Dravidas), who came seeking to dispossess them."[23] The paradigmatic moment in this clash came with the contest between the usurping Tamil/Dravidian king Elara and the Sinhalese hero Dutthagamani. Although Elara was allegedly a god king, he was a non-Buddhist, so Dutthagamani and his ten champions unseated the usurper with the battle cry, "Not for kingdom but for Buddhism."[24] According to the chronicle, the Buddhist king achieved this righteous victory for religion through a savage war (earning him the name Abhaya Dutthagamani, which means "Fearless the Wicked Leader"), which raises, not for the last time, the question of how a supposedly pacifist religion like Buddhism (see chapter 9) could justify such carnage. Fortunately, the chronicle tells of how eight Buddhist saints or *arahats* flew through the air to assure the king that he had done little wrong:

> From this deed arises no hindrance in thy way to heaven. Only one and a half human beings have been slain here by thee, O Lord of men. The one had come unto the (three) refuges [i.e., became a Buddhist], the other had taken on him-

self the five precepts [i.e., adopted basic Buddhist practices]. Unbelievers and men of evil life were the rest, not more to be esteemed than beasts. But as for thee, thou wilt bring glory to the doctrine of the Buddha in manifold ways; therefore cast away care from thy heart, O ruler of men![25]

In other words, only Buddhists were truly human beings, and non-Buddhists as nonhumans were acceptable to kill.

According to Sinhalese tradition, this was the first time that the entire island had been unified under one political authority, although this unification did not last long, as it was repeatedly challenged by foreign (Indian) invasion and local Tamil unrest. By the thirteenth century CE, Sinhalese control had been reduced to the southwest portion of the island, while an independent Tamil kingdom existed in the north and east. Fatefully, the entire island was reunified under foreign colonial control, starting with Dutch occupation (from 1638) and then English (from 1794 until independence in 1948).

When Europeans arrived, they found a Sri Lanka fragmented into two major Sinhalese kingdoms (Kandy and Kotte) and a Tamil kingdom (Jaffna) separated by largely uninhabited jungle. It was only in 1815 that the last of these polities, Kandy, was subjugated and incorporated into the English Crown Colony of Ceylon. Now, for the first time in hundreds of years, Tamils and Sinhalese were forced to interact. An additional provocation was the arrival of Christian missionaries in the early nineteenth century. Significantly, Tamils embraced the new religion and learned valuable skills such as the English language much more eagerly than Sinhalese, giving the minority an advantage in the economy and administration of the colony. A third irritation to Sinhalese was the importation of large numbers of Indian Tamils to work the plantations in the central highlands of the island. During the coffee boom of 1871–1881, twenty-four thousand Indians were brought to Sri Lanka each year, and the tea boom of 1891–1900 saw another thirty-four thousand annually, seriously upsetting the "ethnic" composition of the colony. By 1953, Indian Tamils outnumbered "native" or Ceylon Tamils (984,327 to 908,705), almost all located in traditionally and strongly Sinhalese areas in the center of the country.

Both Sinhalese and Tamils were included in the colonial administration of the late nineteenth and early twentieth centuries; in fact, representation of each "community" was guaranteed. Prior to 1920, Tamils and Sinhalese held an equal number of government seats, but constitutional reforms brought that representation more into line with the groups' proportions in the society, with Sinhalese outnumbering Tamils thirteen to three. Sinhalese efforts to advance their own interests drove the Tamils to form the first ethnic political party, the Tamil Mahajana Sabha, which was soon followed by a Sinhalese party, the Sinhala Maha Sabha. However, the new constitution drafted in 1945, under which independence would be granted, offered no communal/ethnic protections of any kind, assuring that the majority Sinhalese would dominate the new state.

Independence was proclaimed in 1948 under a consensus government led by the United National Party, a modernist/Westernist party of cultural elites that did not appeal to the more traditionalist and "ethnic" segments of the population. In fact, Ludowyk suggests that it "left completely cold all of those who did not belong to the elite, particularly those who in the upper levels of the Sinhalese-speaking intelligentsia were reckoned persons of consequence: the bhikkhu (Buddhist monk), the village teacher, and the Ayurvedic physician."[26] More specific communal aggravations soon arose. The first was the fight over the national flag, which the Sinhalese wanted to feature a lion (sign of Sinhalese nationality) and Buddhist symbolism; of course, over the objections of the Tamils, they had their way. Next was a citizenship act that effectively disqualified the "Indian Tamils," who were becoming the majority of Tamils, from being citizens of the new state; this was quickly followed by a voting act that based voting rights on citizenship and thus disenfranchised the majority of Tamils. In 1951, Sinhalese was made the language of higher education in the state, and by 1956, an overtly partisan Sinhalese party, the Sri Lanka Freedom Party, appeared, which

> intended to bring the Sinhalese into a consciousness of their nationhood that would not be linked to a hybrid Ceylonese concept, which [was] dismissed as Western and middle class. The Sinhala nation were to come forward from the villages to assert themselves and wrest power from the English-educated, urban elite, who were antinational in outlook. The Sinhala language and the Buddhist religion were to be raised in status.[27]

Of course, as the final sentence suggests, Buddhists, especially the activist bhikkhus, were totally in favor of this policy.

As we noted earlier, Sri Lankan Buddhist monks had a tradition of political activity. During the colonial era, they had debated aggressively with Christian missionaries on the subject of religion. In the late 1800s, there had been a Sinhalese-Buddhist revival, with the founding of Buddhist schools and a Young Men's Buddhist Association, as well as Buddhist journals like *Sarasavi San-*

darasa, *Lak Mini Kirula*, and *Landapakaraya*. Champions of Buddhism and Sinhalese nationalism like Anagarika Dharmapala linked the two concepts, claiming the island as the one and true home of both:

> The island of Lanka belongs to the Buddhist Sinhalese. For 2,455 years this was the land of birth for the Sinhalese. Other races have come here to pursue their commercial activities. For the Europeans, apart from this land, there is Canada, Australia, South Africa, England and America to go to; for the Tamils there is South India; for the Moors . . . Egypt; the Dutch can go to Holland. But for the Sinhalese there is only this island.[28]

In the 1950s, Buddhists and political bhikkhus once again saw their hegemony under attack, and they responded. A group of monks formed the Lanka Eksath Bhikkhu Mandalaya (Lanka Union of Bhikkhus) and launched their own investigation into the condition of Buddhism in 1956. They campaigned for Sinhalese-Buddhist candidates in the elections of that year and produced a report called "The Betrayal of Buddhism."

The outcome of these activities was a greatly energized Sinhalese-Buddhist majority and eventually an ideology similar to the Hindutva of India, in the Sri Lankan case a Simhalatva or "Sinhalaness" that associated Sinhala national/racial identity with a religion (Buddhism), a land (the island of Lanka), and a state (the modern state of Sri Lanka).[29] It was only the latest expression of "political Buddhism" on the island, and naturally it created a worried Tamil-Hindu minority. Those worries were proven justified when the newly elected government adopted a Sinhalese-language-only policy and even the deportation of Indian Tamils. The government gave open aid and preference to Buddhism, and efforts to make concessions to disgruntled Tamils were condemned by Buddhist activists as treachery and met with protests. Violence was bound to follow.

And it did. In 1958 the first genuine "ethnic" violence occurred, when a mob of Sinhalese attacked a train carrying Tamils, touching off four days of rioting. In 1959, the leader of Sri Lanka was assassinated by an extremist bhikkhu who thought the government was not sufficiently pro-Buddhist (reminiscent of the assassination of Yitzak Rabin by an extremist Israeli in 1995). The two last straws for Sri Lankan coexistence came in the early 1970s. First, the government sought to rectify or "normalize" the dominance of Tamils in higher education and professional occupations by creating essentially reverse-discrimination procedures to favor Sinhalese students and workers. Second, the constitution of

1972 explicitly and officially elevated Sinhalese language and Buddhism to top status, even including a section entitled "Buddhism." The entire atmosphere in the society was tense and hostile, leading to a police attack on a Tamil studies conference in 1974. The importation of Tamil cultural materials like books and movies was banned. Not unpredictably, Tamil leaders who had once been in favor of cooperation now began to favor separation, even Tamil nationalism and independence. In 1975 the Tamil United Liberal Front was organized on a platform of Tamil nationhood and sovereignty in the north and east portion of the island, which they designated the state of Eelam. More radical factions, like the Liberation Tigers of Tamil Eelam (LTTE), the Eelam People's Revolutionary Liberation Front, the Eelam Revolutionary Organization of Students, the Tamil Eelam Liberation Organization, and the People's Liberation Organization of Tamil Eelam also appeared, some willing to use force to oppose oppression.

The armed Tamil uprising began in 1978, with the LTTE taking the lead in pro-Tamil, anti-Sinhalese violence. In 1983 the Tamil-majority city of Jaffna was convulsed by riots and fires fomented by the government and army, lasting for weeks and leaving many Tamils dead. The LTTE responded in kind. By 1987, "there was widespread Sinhalese pressure for total war against the Tamil minority."[30] To prevent this outcome, India sent a peacekeeping force of up to fifty thousand troops to the island, which was eventually resisted and targeted by both sides, and the Tigers gained in profile and status as agents of Tamil interests. In 1993, the Tigers managed to assassinate Sri Lankan president Ranasingha Premadasa and subsequently broke a cease-fire in 1995. For the past decade, Sri Lanka has been on a slow burn, with signs of greater violence on the horizon. Another cease-fire between the Tigers and the government in 2002 collapsed in 2006, leading to four thousand deaths and tens of thousands of refugees, according to Human Rights Watch. To try to prevent further Tamil Tiger incursions, police authorities in the capital city of Colombo announced on June 1, 2007, that "loiterers" would be expelled from the city, and within a week 376 Tamils had been banished. The final conflagration (for now) came in May 2009, when the Sri Lankan army surrounded the last holdouts of the LTTE and killed its leader, Vellupillai Prabhakaran. The LTTE subsequently admitted defeat, but the failure to resolve the basic problems of Sri Lanka or to establish any kind of inclusive civil society does not bode well for that country's future.

Ethnoreligious Conflict in the Former Yugoslavia

Religious communal violence has not yet led to the dismemberment of the Sri Lankan state, but it has in the case of Yugoslavia, which no longer existed as a single, unified country by the mid-1990s. Ethnoreligious groups refused to share that state any longer, and after a series of wars it decomposed into an array of small ethnic states, including Slovenia, Croatia, Serbia, and Bosnia. Perhaps the attitude that best expresses the failure of Yugoslavia was uttered by Vladimir Gligorov: "Why should I be a minority in your state when you can be a minority in mine?"[31]

Yugoslavia was from its inception an artificial state, created after World War I in the ambitious map drawing undertaken by the Allies. Of course, most states—including Sri Lanka—are artificial in the sense that their boundaries and/or political integration are recent and manmade and that they encompass multiple and often antagonistic cultural and religious groups. Many of these states are the direct product of colonialism. Yugoslavia was unique in being a voluntary creation of the several peoples of the region. The various "Slav" peoples in the area of southern Europe known as the Balkans probably arrived there in historical times, specifically in the sixth and seventh centuries CE, in the great migrations and displacements of eastern European societies. Preceded by the Illyrians, the Goths, and the Huns, the groups who would become known as Croats and Serbs may have originated from central Asia or Persia: the name *Croat*, for example, is not a Slavic word but is believed to be based on the Iranian *Choroatos* (rendered *Hrvat* in Serbo-Croatian). Both Croats and Serbs founded medieval kingdoms in the Balkans, though neither quite in its modern territory. The Croat kingdom occupied Istria (today's northwest Croatia), Dalmatia, Slavonia, and Hercegovina (today's western region of Bosnia-Hercegovina). The kingdom of the Serbs arose along the Adriatic, in present-day Kosovo and Montenegro, and expanded southeastward, where a royal seat was established at Skopje (Macedonia) in 1346. Bosnia, fatefully, never exactly referred to a polity or a people but to an area, namely, the territory around the Bosna River; furthermore, being situated centrally between Croat and Serb domains, it was often invaded and occupied by one or the other of these groups as well as by Bulgarians and Hungarians. It became something of a frontier region and a no-man's-land in the midst of larger and bellicose neighbors. There was in fact a Bosnian kingdom in the twelfth to fourteenth centuries, but it was to be short-lived, with long-term political and religious implications.

The future religious complexion of the region was determined by two great events. The first was the arrival of Christianity in the ninth century. Significantly, while both Croats and Serbs were Christianized, the more northerly Croats were introduced to Roman Catholicism while the more easterly Serbs were exposed to Eastern Orthodoxy. Bosnia, always in the middle, was never quite integrated by either and is often remembered for its generally weak Christian affiliation and for a "heresy" known as Bogomil Christianity. Whether or not either of these claims is true, they are sometimes offered to explain the second great religious event, Bosnian conversion to Islam, which would set the stage for the developments and conflicts of the 1990s.

By the fourteenth century, the regional power in southeast Europe was the Ottoman Empire, based in present-day Turkey. Expanding northwest from its base, it conquered the old eastern Roman/Byzantine Empire and the Balkans. The Slavic peoples confronted the Ottomans in the epic Battle of Kosovo Polje in 1389, in which the Slavs were decisively defeated. By 1392, all of Serbia was under Ottoman authority, with the city of Sarajevo falling in 1451. Ottoman power crept north into Bosnia through the fifteenth century, bringing all of the Balkans south of Croatia under its control. The northern-most Slavs, the Croats and Slovenes, came instead under the influence of the rival power, the Austrian Empire.

In general, Serbs remained strongly Orthodox (in fact, retreating north and east to escape Ottoman/Muslim power) and Croats firmly Catholic. However, a significant proportion of Bosnians converted to the new religion, although they never constituted a majority: between 1468 and 1485, the number of Bosnian Muslim households increased more than tenfold, with the urban centers becoming more Islamicized than the rural areas.[32] While this Bosnian conversion to Islam is noteworthy and consequential, Donia and Fine propose that "*acceptance* is a better word than *conversion* to describe what happened."[33] A large number of Bosnians adopted the new religion not so much because they were convinced of its veracity as for the benefits attached to it. Muslims enjoyed tax exemptions and legal privileges not extended to non-Muslims. There was also prestige in accepting the imperial religion, as well as access to titles like *agha* and *beg*. No doubt, some of the growth of Islam was due to immigration of Turkish and other Muslims and not local conversion. It is worth mentioning that Ottoman Bosnia was not hostile to non-Muslims, who were even welcomed into underpopulated parts of the region.

Ottoman hegemony was destined to be temporary, and by the end of the seventeenth century, the Turks had already lost Hungary and other parts of southeast Europe to Austria. In 1791, Austria wrested the title of "protector" of the Christians within Ottoman territories from the Turks. At the same time, many Slavic Muslims outside of Bosnia fled to that province to escape Austrian/ Christian influence, furthering the identification of Bosnia with Islam. By the early nineteenth century, the ethnic and religious picture in the Balkans was fractious but clearing: the northern Catholic areas were under Austrian authority, the southern Muslim remained under Ottoman authority, and (as of 1815) the western Serbian-Orthodox area had its own Constituent Assembly and elected prince. More important, communities that had formerly identified themselves by religion (Catholic, Orthodox, or Muslim) began to identify themselves "ethnically" or "nationally," as Croats or Serbs or Bosnians: literally, an Orthodox teacher in the 1860s named Teofil Petranovic traveled from village to village to convince locals to stop calling themselves *hriscani* (the local word for Orthodox) and henceforward to refer to themselves as *Serbs*.

Various and sometimes contradictory "nationalisms" coalesced in the later nineteenth century. "Ethnic" nationalists promoted "Serb" or "Croat" identity and interest, often at each other's expense: Serb activist Ilija Garasinin's 1844 *Nacertanije* (*Outline*) called for the unification of all Serbs in a "Greater Serbia," while Croat nationalists like Ante Starcevic and Josip Frank argued not only in favor of Croats but also that Croat was the only authentic identity in the region. According to Starcevic, all southern Slavs were Croats, including the Serbs. In response, Vuk Karadzic published a treatise in 1849 entitled "Serbs All and Everywhere," in which he professed that Serb identity and culture was the primary and genuine southern Slavic one and that Croats were really Serbs. Both sides squabbled with and over the Bosnian Muslims, sometimes deeming them apostate Croats or Serbs and sometimes foreign and enemy Turks. For their part, the Muslims thought of themselves as a distinct group but a religious rather than "ethnic" or "national" group. According to Donia and Fine, when they thought in terms of "national" identities at all, "Muslims changed from one national identity to another with about the same ease that an American might change political parties."[34]

However, the identity ideology that triumphed after 1918 was the pan-Slavic one, which viewed all the peoples of the territory as subnations of the more inclusive Slav, or south-Slav, nation (Poles and Russians are also Slavic peoples). Known as *Yugoslavism* (*yugo* for "south"), the movement succeeded in winning a state for itself after World War I, which it first called the Kingdom of

Serbs, Croats, and Slovenes and for which it chose a Serb family, the Karadjord-jevic, to reign as royalty. Ethnic nationalists of the Croat and Serb kind took no pleasure in this development; the minority peoples of the new state found it worrisome (since they—the Albanians and Hungarians and Macedonians, and so on—were not mentioned in the name); and the Bosnian Muslims were cautious as a religious minority (the religious composition being roughly 47 percent Orthodox, 39 percent Catholic, and 11 percent Muslim). All the various groups formed their own political and publishing fronts, including the Croat Peasant Party, the Serb Radical Party, and the Yugoslav Muslim Organization. And while Croats and Serbs picked continuously at each other, both had designs on Bosnia, as Stojan Protic of the Serbian Popular Radical Party wrote in 1917, describing his solution to the "Bosnian problem":

> Leave that to us. We have the solution for Bosnia. . . . When our army crosses the Drina, we will give the Turks [local Muslims] twenty-four hours, or even forty-eight hours, of time to return to their ancestral religion. Those who do not wish to do so are to be cut down, as we did in Serbia earlier.[35]

Despite attempts to temper ethnic animosity (changing the country's name to the Kingdom of Yugoslavia, breaking up ethnic provinces into smaller units, and banning ethnic symbols and songs), the unified state was well on the way to disintegration before conquest by Nazi Germany in 1941. At that point, the former kingdom was dismembered, with a Nazi-friendly fascist state created for the Croats under the Ustasha Party, which is still remembered for its cruelty to non-Croats. When World War II ended with the establishment of a second Yugoslavia under Communist rule, ethnic tensions were submerged for a time in favor of Yugoslav unity, "ethnic" or "national" identities being regarded as bourgeois and reactionary. Nevertheless, ethnic problems remained or increased, since "national" republics (Slovenia, Croatia, Serbia) were created within the state, Muslims were eventually declared a "nation," and economic differences between the northern/developed regions (mostly Slovenia and Croatia) and southeastern/underdeveloped regions (mostly Serbia and Bosnia) grew.

When the Communist leader Tito died in 1980, the suppressed grievances began to explode. The more prosperous northern republics were jealous of their wealth, preferring not to share with the less prosperous republics like Serbia and Bosnia. Ethnonationalisms reappeared. And fear and hatred of Muslims became overt: ugly stereotypes of Islam were advanced, as in Vuk Draskovic's 1982 novel *Noz* (*The Knife*), and concerns about the recent (1979) Islamic revolution in Iran and a rising Islamic fundamentalism led some Christians to see an international Muslim conspiracy in their midst. In 1983, a trial of Bosnian "Islamic nationalists" was conducted, including Alija Izetbegovic, author of such publications as *Islamic Declaration* and *Problems of the Islamic Renaissance* (and also future president of Bosnia). He and twelve others were convicted of "conspiring to transform Bosnia into an Islamistan."[36] Islam was declared anathema to Western civilization and Bosnian Muslims culturally and racially inferior to Western Slavs. Serb writer Dragos Kalajic insisted that they did not belong to "the European family of nations"; instead, "in satisfying their sexual impulses . . . the Ottoman armies and administrators—drawn from the Near Eastern and North African bazaars—created a distinct semi-Arab ethnic group."[37] Islamic culture was further denounced as a "darkness of the past" that advocated "the destruction of those who have another religion."[38] Calls went out to Europe and America to join in this campaign to save Western civilization.

The second disintegration of Yugoslavia and the savage ethnoreligious war between Croats, Serbs, and Muslims in Bosnia did not begin in Bosnia but rather in Slovenia and Croatia, which declared their independence in June 1991. Federal Yugoslav forces quickly invaded Slovenia and almost as quickly withdrew (departing on July 19). Fighting in Croatia ended in early 1992. Then, on March 1, 1992, Bosnia announced the successful result of its referendum on independence, and war broke out there. By that time, Serbs in Bosnia had already organized their own Serbian Autonomous Region of Hercegovina, backed by the Serb officials of Yugoslavia; likewise, Croats in Bosnia had formed a party called the Croatian Democratic Alliance and claimed authority over western Hercegovina, especially the city of Mostar. Bosnian Muslims, who had ironically always been the most "Yugoslav" of Yugoslavians—choosing the identity of "Yugoslavian" over "Bosnian" or "Muslim"—were forced to fight a two-front conflict against both Croats and Serbs. On the other hand, Muslims and Croats occasionally united against Serbs in a shifting three-way confrontation. Serbs became notorious for their policy of "ethnic cleansing," eliminating any presence of non-Serbs in Serb or Serb-held lands. And in cities like Mostar, the fighting was particularly ferocious. Not only were urban populations targeted and former neighbors transformed into enemy combatants, but also the very structures of multireligious and multicultural society that had held Yugoslavia together were marked for destruction. Medieval bridges that linked ethnic quarters of Mostar were shelled. Hundreds of mosques and other cultural buildings, like museums and libraries, were wrecked. Through actions like these, and the obliteration of the Institute for Oriental Studies, it was as if the very existence of a once inclusive multireligious society was being blotted out. In the eyes of Ali and Lifschutz, this was precisely the intention: not just to defeat or even eradicate a people but to erase the very memory of "the unique and dangerous cosmopolitanism" of multicultural, tolerant Bosnia, "which clearly had no place in the new 'pure' nation-states emerging from the ruins of Yugoslavia."[39]

Ethnoreligious Conflict in Northern Ireland

The two cases we have considered so far each involve two different religions in conflict (Buddhism/Hinduism and Christianity/Islam). However, there is no reason why two sects within the same religion cannot also degenerate into violence, as we saw in the last chapter's discussion of persecution. Northern Ireland is a perfect contemporary case of two sects or denominations of one religion turning violent, and it raises the question of when exactly we are talking about *one* religion and when we are talking about *two*. And while the doctrinal differences between Catholicism and Protestantism may not sound like—and are not—fighting words for most Christians, Carolyn Meyer in her *Voices of Northern Ireland: Growing Up in a Troubled Land* stresses that sectarian differences do make a difference there: as she quotes an Irish expatriate living in the United States, "In England, like here in America, it doesn't matter what [religion] you are. But at home it matters. You *have* to know what somebody's religion is. You have to know who you're talking to."[40]

The twentieth-century strife euphemistically dubbed "the Troubles" in Northern Ireland erupted in 1969 and has taken more than three thousand lives and caused more than thirty thousand injuries out of a population of approximately four million in 2001; as Holloway reminds us, this death rate would be the equivalent of a half-million deaths in the United States.[41] All commentators trace the roots of the conflict back four hundred years or more, although the first friction between England and Ireland (but not between Catholicism and Protestantism, since Protestantism did not exist yet) goes back over four hundred years before that. In 1169, King Henry II sent an occupying force to Dublin and seized a local area known as the Pale; by 1600, English military rule extended to most of the island, with the interesting exception of the northern region of Ulster (the location of present-day Northern Ireland), which was only integrated after a rebellion led by Hugh O'Neill was thwarted. In reprisal for the uprising, northern Irish land was confiscated and distributed among English and Scottish colonists.

Until the early 1500s, the struggle between England and Ireland was essentially political and colonial: England was attempting to absorb the smaller island into its expanding empire. But when Henry VIII broke with the Catholic Church and joined the Protestant movement in the 1530s, the clash acquired a religious dimension, of English Protestants subduing Irish Catholics. The immediate result of the conquest of Ulster was the establishment of the Plantation of Ulster, England's first real "overseas" colony, consisting of the northernmost six counties of Londonderry, Tyrone, Fermanagh, Armagh, Cavan, and Donegal. Religious and political-economic tensions between the two communities led to a rebellion in 1641 in favor of religious freedom and property rights for Catholics, which left thousands of Protestants dead.[42] Unhappily for the Irish, this was also the era of religious extremism and political revolution in England, and so Oliver Cromwell used draconian measures to suppress the heretical and disloyal rebels, sometimes massacring entire towns; Kee reports that two thousand people were killed in Wexford alone.[43] Such actions were defended and justified as "godly vengeance for Catholic massacres of Protestants at the beginning of the rising."[44] With the rebellion crushed, Irish Catholics were further dispossessed of their rights and their land: before 1641, Catholics still owned more than half of Irish land, but by 1661 that amount was reduced to 10 percent and would eventually fall to 5 percent.

As was chronically the case, Irish fortunes were tied to English political developments, so when a Catholic contender for the English throne (James II) was defeated by a Protestant rival (William of Orange), it so happens that the decisive encounter was fought on Irish soil, at the Battle of the Boyne in 1690. That date is remembered more than any other, by both sides, as the pivotal event in Irish religious and political history, since it was not only the final defeat of Catholic power on the island but also the beginning of the so-called Penal Laws that deepened the misery of Irish Catholics in their own land. They were prohibited from education, professions, and land inheritance, among other exclusionary measures.

The eighteenth century was a period of rising and falling hostility between Ireland and England. In 1720, the Parliament in London took direct control of the island, an arrangement known as "direct rule" (as opposed to local self-government, which is called "home rule"). Even at this early date, both Catholic and Protestant activists formed their paramilitary guerrilla organizations, like the Catholic Ribbonmen, Whiteboys, and Defenders, or the Protestant Peep O'Day Boys and the Orange Order.[45] Finally, in 1801 the parliamentary Act of Union formally integrated Ireland into the English kingdom, creating the United Kingdom of Great Britain and Ireland.

The struggles of the nineteenth century blended religious dissatisfaction with efforts at political independence and land reform (in the 1840s, the potato blight provoked a famine, killing perhaps a million Irish and driving two million out of the country, many to the United States). The more fervent anti-English Irish adopted not only a separatist but a republican platform and so were referred to as Republicans. The pro-English partisans desired to preserve the union between Great Britain and Ireland and so were called Unionists. Unionists like Edward Carson vowed that they would break Ulster away from Ireland if the Irish ever attained independence. Accordingly, when a home-rule bill was passed in 1912, tens of thousands of Ulster Protestants signed the Ulster Covenant denouncing the move, and a group called the Ulster Volunteer Force was assembled to resist it.

Despite these initiatives, after World War I (and after the "Easter Uprising" of 1916), an "Irish Free State" was established as a dominion within the British Empire: home rule was granted to the twenty-six southern counties of Ireland, but the northern six counties were partitioned off and incorporated as a separate administrative unit with a Unionist/Protestant majority. The two serious problems with this division were that it did not satisfy Irish nationalists, who wanted a united Ireland, and that it came after the emergence of the Irish Republican Army. A civil war between those Irish who accepted the partition and those who demanded a unified Ireland left the partitionists in command but created a disgruntled party of Irish nationalists known as Sinn Fein. Meanwhile conflict developed within Northern Ireland as well, where over four hundred people were killed in the first two years after partition.[46] Also, in response to IRA activity, a police force consisting almost entirely of Protestants was organized. As described by Holloway, "The two communities grew further apart, segregation increased and mixed marriages were few and isolated. The two communities pursued separate cultures and maintained opposed political aspirations. Their children were educated separately, taught different histories, and played different sports."[47]

In 1949, the Irish Free State seceded from the British Commonwealth and became the sovereign Republic of Ireland, or Eire. However, the soreness of the partition persisted: most of the island was Ireland, but the northern corner was still United Kingdom. And Eire was majority Catholic, but Northern Ireland was majority Protestant. Within Northern Ireland, Catholics and Protestants were not only divided along religious lines but along political (the vast majority of Protestants were and are Unionists while most Catholics were and are Irish nationalists) and economic/class lines. Most large businesses were Protestant owned, most of the high-paying jobs went to Protestants, and unemployment was much lower among Protestants. Catholics on average had lower incomes and poorer housing. Even so, by the 1960s the more educated and middle-class Catholics had abandoned their demands for Irish national unification and instead promoted a "civil rights" agenda on the model of the American civil rights movement. But civil rights protests and marches drew a violent response from Unionist/anti-Catholic crowds, which led to the further mobilization of both sides.

Triumphant Protestants had long held parades to commemorate the 1690 Battle of the Boyne. According to Meyer,

> Every year some 20-to-30 thousand Protestants gather on August 12 to march around the walls [of Catholic neighborhoods] in memory of the Apprentice Boys who slammed the gates and of Good King Billy [William of Orange] and his rescuing troops. In 1969 it was the Apprentice Boys' Parade that triggered violent demonstrations, lighting the fuse of the Troubles.[48]

Finally the annual and intentional provocations caused rioting, burning, and looting. Inevitably, ethnoreligious self-defense groups arose. The IRA was revived under the name Provisional Irish Republican Army or IRA-Provisional (the "Provos"), and various Protestant/Unionist groups and parties appeared, like a renewed Ulster Volunteer Force, as well as Ulster Defense Association, Ulster Freedom Fighters, Democratic Unionist Party (headed by Reverend Ian Paisley), the Ulster Unionist Party (under David Trimble), the Progressive Unionist Party, and the Ulster Democratic Party. The Provisional IRA adopted terrorist tactics, planting car bombs and attacking police and military posts, even within the United Kingdom; Protestant/Unionist paramilitary groups employed virtually the same methods in retaliation, bombing Catholic gathering places like pubs and executing suspected IRA members or sympathizers.

After fifteen years of continuous street fighting, the Provisional IRA announced a cease-fire in 1994, which led to talks between the UK government and Sinn Fein, which had emerged as the leading political voice of republican

Ireland. An inability to agree on disarmament, however, led to a cancellation of the cease-fire and resumption of bombing and other violence. While Northern Ireland is not in open conflict in the early twenty-first century, the issues at the bottom of the Troubles have not been resolved and seem unlikely to be resolved soon.

Ethnoreligious Conflict in Lebanon

As Kamal Sabili aptly warns in his *A House of Many Mansions: The History of Lebanon Reconsidered*, "To create a country is one thing, to create a nationality is another."[49] Few cases of multinational, multireligious nation-building suit this warning better than Lebanon, which was fashioned out of a sliver of the crumbling Ottoman Empire after World War I and was regarded hopefully as the "Switzerland of the East" for a time after World War II—a state, like Switzerland, where various nationalities coexisted in peace and even unity. Unfortunately, the course of Lebanon's history since 1975 has been anything but calm and unified; rather, the society tore itself apart for over a decade and shows dire signs of doing so again.

Lebanon is the ancient land of Canaan, "Phoenicia" to the Greeks, a tiny strip of land (only four thousand square miles) north of Israel consisting of a coastline and a series of parallel mountain ranges that striate the territory. Cities such as Tyre, Sidon, Tripoli, and Beirut have existed there for almost four thousand years, always more oriented to the western (Mediterranean) sea than to the eastern mainland. It was also, like any frontier region, constantly crossed, invaded, and settled by various surrounding groups, from the Amorites to the Egyptians to the Greeks to the Romans to the Arabs to the Turks and finally to the French.

Under Roman rule, Lebanon was one of the first areas to adopt Christianity, developing its own unique brand of Maronite Christianity from a Saint Maroun, an ascetic and hermit who took up residence in the local mountains and actively spread the faith. In the 600s CE, to the mix of pagan and Christian religion was added Islam, which was brought there in the early decades of that religion. Thus, for almost thirteen hundred years the region has had an intricately interwoven religious pattern. In fact, because of its coastal location and its rugged terrain, it became a haven for all sorts of cultural, national, and religious groups. For instance, a contingent of Greek Christians settled in the central Biqa Valley, while the south became home to Druzes, a sect of Muslims (sometimes regarded as Shi'ite) who followed the teachings of the eleventh-century mystic al-Hakim and his disciple Darazi.

Overt religious war came to Lebanon with the Crusades in the late eleventh century (see the next chapter). Through the 1200s and 1300s, European Christians, Mamluk Muslims, and Mongols contested the territory, with various shifting relations and alliances among the local communities. Finally, the Ottomans conquered the coastal strip and held it until World War I. Already by the mid–nineteenth century, Christians and Druzes were at odds, and the Ottoman administration partitioned Mount Lebanon into a northern Christian district and a southern Druze district. The partition did not solve ethnoreligious problems, as forces inside and outside the region fomented discontent (France supporting the Christians, and England supporting the Druzes). As Thomas Collelo's "country study" of Lebanon argues, "Foreign interests in Lebanon transformed these basically sociopolitical struggles into bitter religious conflict, culminating in the 1860 massacre of about ten thousand Maronites, as well as Greek Catholics and Greek Orthodox, by the Druzes. These events offered France the opportunity to intervene."[50]

As in the other examples we have investigated, the late 1800s witnessed the founding of many ethnic and religious organizations, media, and parties. However, this internal evolution was interrupted by World War I, which led to the disintegration of the Ottoman Empire and the establishment of a French mandate over Greater Syria and Lebanon in 1920 (an outcome that France had apparently pursued for some decades). The modern borders of Lebanon were set, with Beirut as the capital city, and the constitution of 1926 enshrined ethnoreligious communal representation, with a Maronite president, a Sunni prime minister, and a Shi'a speaker of the Chamber of Deputies. Independence was granted to the state of Lebanon in the midst of World War II (1941), although the Vichy French government did not at first recognize it, so independence did not officially arrive until 1943. From that date and for about thirty years, Lebanon enjoyed its tranquil, tolerant "Switzerland of the East" period under the so-called National Pact.

The National Pact, or National Covenant (*al Mithaq al Watani* in Arabic) was an enlightened agreement to recognize the historical, cultural, and religious diversity of the new state. It was premised on the willingness of ethnic and religious groups to coexist and to dissociate themselves from outside identities: both Lebanese Christians and Lebanese Muslims should think of themselves as "Lebanese" first rather than as Christians or Muslims (or even worse, as Europeans and Arabs). Also, while officially Arab-speaking, the state would maintain civil relations with domestic and foreign Christianity. Finally, political power was to be shared communally and proportionally, with the aforementioned apportionment of the three top offices and the distribution of legislative seats to follow the ethnoreligious population (that is, a ratio of six Christian to five Muslim).

Although the pact included neutrality in relation to other Arab states, it was difficult to maintain that stance after 1948 and the creation of Israel. Many Arab neighbors, and many Muslims within the state, wanted Lebanon to enter the struggle against Israel. Also, some one hundred fifty thousand Palestinian Arab refugees streamed across the southern border, making Lebanon an unwilling player in the regional events. Another provocation was the rise of pan-Arabism and the powerful figure of Egyptian president Gamal Abdul Nasser, who in 1958 succeeded in merging his country and Syria into a United Arab Republic. Nasser, Syria, and many Arabs hoped to absorb Lebanon into a united Arab state, a fate that Lebanese non-Muslims understandably did not favor. Finally, a suspicious presidential election led to riots and factional violence, including the assassination of the editor of a newspaper famous for its pan-Arab sympathies. The unrest continued into mid-1958, when the pro-Western government of Iraq was overthrown, stoking Muslim aspirations; American troops arrived on July 15, and the brief civil war claimed between two thousand and four thousand casualties.

Although neutral in the next war (the Six-Day War) between Israel and the Arab states in 1967, the repercussions of the conflict inevitably spilled into Lebanon. A primary consequence was the migration of Palestinian groups like the Palestine Liberation Organization (PLO) into Lebanese territory, from which they staged attacks on northern Israel. This not only mobilized Israel against Lebanon as a "terrorist haven," but divided Lebanese Christians and Muslims. The Lebanese army tried to oust these guerrilla groups from its land in 1969, much as it tried to do with the group Hezbollah in 2007.

Political instability, unemployment, fears of reprisals from Israel, and martial law in some parts of the state provided the tinder for the all-out multiparty war that reduced Beirut and much of the country to rubble starting in 1975. The inherent and traditional fragility of Lebanese multireligious cooperation was exacerbated by Palestinian fighters who actually outnumbered the national army, not to mention an assortment of sectarian militias that cumulatively also outnumbered the army—as many as eighteen thousand leftist/Muslim men-at-arms and twelve thousand Christian. Some of the main forces in the struggle were the Phalange Party, Amal, Guardians of the Cedars, and the Marada Brigade, with smaller or later groups joining the fray. The Phalange Party had been organized in 1936 as a Maronite militia; by 1975, it boasted sixty-five thousand members and ten thousand fighters and played a key role in the Lebanese violence and politics, including getting two of its leaders elected president of the country (Bashir Gemayel and Amin Gemayel). Amal ("hope" in Arabic and also an acronym for Afwaj al Muqawamah al Lubnaniyyah, or Lebanese Resistance Detachments) was a movement arising in 1975 among the Shi'ite community, headed by Imam Musa as-Sadr. The major force of Shi'ite interests and one of the largest organizations in the country, it sometimes turned its power against other Muslim (especially Palestinian) factions. The Guardians of the Cedars was a Lebanese nationalist group promoting Lebanese unity and opposing religious sectarianism but also opposing and condescending to Arab cultural and identity; its one thousand armed men were disproportionately important in the fighting, including defending Christian civilians. The Marada Brigade fielded thirty-five hundred soldiers, mostly in northern Lebanon, and was allied with Phalange until 1978. Two later groups of note are Islamic Amal, which appeared in 1982 and was supported by Iran, and Hezbollah (sometimes spelled Hizballah, for "Party of God"), also emerging in 1982, which still exists today and in fact is a significant force in southern Lebanon and one of the major causes of the Israeli invasion of southern Lebanon in 2007.

The factional conflict began in earnest in April 1975, when four Phalangists were shot and killed. Phalange retaliation against Palestinian Muslims led to the outbreak of widespread violence, ethnoreligious enclave against ethnoreligious enclave. What started as sporadic street fighting escalated into a virtual civil war, loosely pitting Christians against Muslims, although the sectarian picture was clearly more complicated than that. The presence of armed Palestinian refugees and the intervention of Syria and then Israel only aggravated the situation, dragging the confrontation on until 1990, when a precarious peace was brokered. But Hezbollah continues to operate in the south, constituting almost a pseudogovernment in the area, and periodic violence still occurs, especially the assassination of political figures like former prime minister Rafik Hariri on February 14, 2005, and Parliament majority leader Walid Eido on June 13, 2007.

Ethnoreligious Conflict in Nigeria

In 2002, when Christian-versus-Muslim riots erupted over the Miss World pageant, Western attention was drawn to a part of the world that it seldom thinks about and barely understands—Nigeria. This large and important West African state, a major oil producer, has been troubled by political, religious, and ethnic/tribal challenges since its founding as an independent country in 1960, including the high-profile civil war in the southern region of Biafra. Despite this troubled history, most people outside Nigeria know little about the ongoing ethnoreligious problems in this country.

Before European colonialism, the territory in and around modern Nigeria was occupied by various tribes, kingdoms, and states, including Yoruba, Benin, Hausa, Mali, and Kanem-Borno. Islam arrived in the region by the ninth century along the trade routes that linked western Africa with northern Africa and Arabia; it was especially strong in what would become present-day northern Nigeria. In the eleventh century, the king of Kanem adopted Islam, and the renowned king Mansa Musa of Mali helped secure the religion, making a pilgrimage to Mecca and importing Arab scholars and builders. What originally functioned as a kind of bonding mechanism between traders—as a facilitator of communication, a unified system of credit, a model of civil society, and a kind of "boundary of the merchant community"[51]—grew to become a central organizing and legitimating factor of political power in the alliance between state, scholar, and soldier.[52] In other words, although not all the subjects of West African kingdoms embraced Islam, the religion was well entrenched before the arrival of Europeans.

Portugal was the first European society to reach the West African coast, in the 1400s, and the slave trade quickly ensued. But it was only in Europe's "scramble for Africa" at the end of the 1800s that Nigeria was formally and completely colonized, and not by Portugal but by Britain. The most consequential aspect of this colonization was the integration of northern/inland areas with southern/coastal ones into a single administrative unit; in fact, as the documentary film *The Magnificent African Cake* narrates, Britain conquered what would become northern Nigeria, and annexed it to the south, "for no other reason than to keep it from the French," who were assembling their own Saharan empire to the north.[53] Therefore, it is, in a serious sense, a historical accident that northern provinces like Kano—some of the oldest and most deeply Islamized regions—are contained in modern Nigeria. This situation was further complicated by the typical efforts at Christian missionization, which were particularly successful in the south and southeast of the colony. Misty Bastian reports that missionaries were highly active and effective among the Igbo people of southeast Nigeria, who came to view themselves as *ndi kris* or "the Christian people."[54] Initiatives such as this introduced a new layer of social differentiation in an already mixed context.

Independence came in 1960, with Southern Cameroon exercising its option to detach from Nigeria. This left behind a state that was approximately 50 percent Muslim and 40 percent Christian, but with those religions geographically concentrated and further subdivided by many tribal/ethnic identities and allegiances. For instance, the northern Kano province, which was and remains as much as 90 percent Muslim, is all the same fragmented into a number of tribes like Hausa and Fulbe and into "traditional" Sunni sects like the Qadriyya, the Tijaniyya, the Tariqa, the Malikiya, the Ahmadiyya, the Islamiya, and the Da'awa. Subsequently, new and more fundamentalist sects of Shi'ites and especially Izala took root, which aimed to put religious authorities in political control and to impose Islamic (*shari'a*) law. In 1999, after years of strife and political instability (including military coups), eleven of Nigeria's northern states (among them Kano, Katsina, Sokoto, Zamfara, and Niger) did institute portions of shari'a law, which led to two serious problems. First, the Nigerian constitution supposedly guarantees a secular state with freedom of religion, and second, by that year many southern, especially Igbo (predominantly Christian) people had moved north, establishing a small but notable non-Muslim minority in these Islam-dominated areas.

Not content to impose religious law in the north, Muslim leaders initiated the Supreme Council for Shari'a in Nigeria (SCSN) in late 1999, which predictably touched off religious riots. In early 2000, more than one thousand people were killed in the state of Kaduna, and hundreds of Hausa people in the south were slain in revenge. Churches, mosques, homes, and businesses were reportedly burnt or destroyed. In September 2001, yet another set of riots erupted, leaving another two thousand dead. Ethnoreligious clashes continued in 2002–2003 as Christian Tarok farmers battled Muslim Hausa herders in Plateau State, resulting in seventy-two destroyed villages.

In November 2002, religious and "moral" sentiments were enflamed over holding the Miss World pageant in Nigeria. On November 1, an article appeared in the daily newspaper *This Day* that unwisely invoked the prophet Muhammad on the subject of the pageant: "What would Muhammad think? In all honesty, he would probably have chosen a wife from among them."[55] Within four days, angry protesters were in the streets of Kaduna: first they attacked the offices of the newspaper, but soon they had turned their fury on local Christians. As described by a Humans Rights Watch report:

> They advanced in large groups, armed with a variety of weapons, including machetes, knives, sticks, iron bars, and firearms. They sought out Christian homes, particularly in mixed Christian-Muslim neighborhoods, and specifically targeted people on the basis of their religion. Many Christians were killed and many were injured; others fled for their lives, leaving their homes and belongings behind, which were then looted by the rampaging youths. The attackers also destroyed or burned houses and other buildings, including a large number of churches, schools, hotels, and other properties.[56]

Christians launched a counteroffensive, of exactly the same sort. Clashes continued in Kaduna until November 23, by which time they had spread to the Nigerian capital city of Abuja, resulting in property damage but allegedly no deaths. However, the death toll in Kaduna eventually reached two hundred fifty, with another twenty thousand to thirty thousand people forced to flee their homes.

Another episode followed in 2004 in Plateau and Kano states, beginning with the murder of seventy-five Christians by armed Muslims in the town of Yelwa. In retaliation, armed Christians besieged the town and killed some seven hundred Muslims. Within a week, and hundreds of miles north, Muslims avenged the killings by assaulting Christians in Kano, leaving two hundred dead.[57] A recent incident in early 2006 in the southern Nigerian city of Onitsha left another ninety-six dead, as Hausa Muslims again assailed Igbo Christians. This particular violence was sparked by another insult to the Prophet, this time a cartoon. Christians responded, as expected, in kind, burning mosques and killing Muslims.

WHY ETHNORELIGIOUS CONFLICT NOW?

One question that nags at us is why, while religious differences have existed since the first two religions or sects appeared among humans, ethnoreligious conflict is so prominent at this particular moment in history. This is not to suggest that religious communities have never clashed in previous eras, but the emergence (some would say revival) of religion as a major motivating and aggravating force in world politics caught many observers by surprise. One reason why social scientists of all sorts assumed that religion had lost its political significance was the assumption of "secularization": from Weber to Freud to Marx to many prominent twentieth-century scholars, the sense was that religion would not find a home in the modern, urban, industrial setting and would decline or retreat or simply fade away. Another reason, specific to the latter half of the century, was the certainty of what Clifford Geertz called "the integrative revolution,"[58] the expectation that older, more local, and more divisive identities would weaken and disappear as small groups and communities were submerged into modern states with a single shared national culture. To be sure, "ethnic" cultures and identities might survive as pageantry and toothless tradition, but they—including religious beliefs and identities—would lose out to other, more inclusive and more "modern," forces.

Neither of these assumptions has proven to be true so far: the predictions of the death of religion and of local/traditional/nonstate culture and identity in general have proven to be premature at best, wrongheaded at worst. The anticipated secularization and integration have not occurred, although religion and local culture have certainly been influenced by modernization; we might say that tradition, including traditional religion, is not what it used to be. But the confidence that rationalization would triumph over religion, and state integration over "tribal" identity, has not been justified.

Why then has religion roared back, and why does it roar so ominously in so many quarters? The main reason may be modernization itself. First and foremost, as we discussed at the top of this chapter, ethnicity requires consciousness of difference, which requires contact with difference. The global colonial system that was imposed by Western societies tossed multiple cultural and religious groups together in unprecedented ways and drew artificial political boundaries around them. The result was what J. S. Furnivall, in his study of late colonialism in Burma and Indonesia, called "plural societies"—societies that not only contained numerous cultural groups but that segregated these groups into different occupations, classes, and even neighborhoods in such a way that "they mix but do not combine."[59] The effect was to bring diverse groups into contact with each other but to establish serious social differences and inequalities between them, guaranteeing dissatisfaction and social friction.

When independence from colonialism arrived, in virtually every instance the former colony retained its borders and its demographic composition (and often its name as well) as it became a sovereign state. Geertz's integrative revolution was the perceived key to the success of such a state: a common "national" culture was necessary to achieve identification with and loyalty to the new state and its government and between its citizens. In some cases, like Sri Lanka, the early days of independence seemed hopeful, as a modern integrated culture was felt to be replacing sectarian differences; in other cases, like Rwanda, the state was born out of sectarian strife. But even in the situation of Sri Lanka, as well as many other new states, local/pre-state/sectarian identities resurfaced in a new and more virulent form, as political parties, voting blocs, and, often enough, armed militias. "Traditional" culture, including religion, provided the structure and the sentiment that the national/integrated culture did not (at least not yet). So lower-level, nonintegrated or exclusionary culture (religion being one of the most exclusionary forms) persisted and acquired new properties and powers.

In the late twentieth-century postcolonial world, other processes have emerged that perpetuate and promote cultural/religious differences and identities, including "globalization," communication technologies like the Internet (and more recently, Twitter), and the failure of many new states to provide stable governance, let alone to meet the needs of their citizens. Benjamin Barber explicitly links the reality and ferocity of small, local, exclusionary, and combative identities (which he unfelicitously labels "jihad" although most are not Muslim) to the coalescence of a global system still dominated by the West and especially Western corporations (which he calls "McWorld"); ethnic/nationalist/ separatist conflict is thus seen as a reaction to or protest against globalization and integration.[60]

The state itself has also been part of the problem. In many places, the state has shown itself to be ineffective, corrupt, or oppressive. Now, Weber famously defined the state as a system that claims a monopoly on the use of legitimate violence (as in its legal and military institutions). But recent decades have seen what Brubaker and Laitin call the "decay of the Weberian state" with a "decline . . . in states' capacities to maintain order by monopolizing the legitimate use of violence in their territories and the emergence in some regions . . . of so-called quasi states" or even nonstate entities of great political significance.[61] In other words, states are no longer the only players on the world political stage; they share power and violent potential with both *substate* and *transstate entities*, that is, groups and parties that operate within and "below" the state level (like the IRA or Tamil Tigers) and/or "above" or across or outside states (like al Qaeda). Religion does not provide the only substate or transstate organizational possibility, but, as these three examples illustrate, it provides a very real and dangerous possibility.

CHAPTER 7

WAR

At one end of the spectrum of religious violence is the lone individual killing an animal or another human being as a sacrifice, or starving or beating or whipping or bleeding himself or herself. At the other end of the spectrum is the organized army of hundreds, thousands, or tens of thousands of the faithful marching to confront an opposing army (often but not necessarily the faithful of another religion). This is not to say that sacrifice and self-mortification are always small-scale, unorganized, or spontaneous actions: there were and are institutions, guidelines, and official occasions even for these types of violence, and—as in the case of Balinese Eka Desa Rudra or Aztec sacrifice—the scale of killing can be truly grand. However, there is still something that separates these forms of violence, as well as persecution and ethnoreligious conflict, from religious war, though the line between them is not always completely obvious or firm.

The difference between religious war and other forms of religious violence, then, is not the amount of death and destruction: more lives can be lost in a large persecution or ethnoreligious conflict, or even a mass sacrifice, than in a small war. The difference is certainly not the "cause," since war can serve the same religious cause as any other forms of violence. It is not entirely the weapons used, although a religious war fought only with whips and racks and sacrificial knives would be a minor war. The difference between religious war and other religious violence is primarily in the *goal* and the *conduct* of the conflict. In religious war, unlike the others, an armed and organized religious company faces *another armed and organized company*. In sacrifice, self-mortification, and persecution there is no expectation, indeed no desire, that the aggressor will meet resistance: it is usually and ideally the armed against the unarmed, or at least the less armed. Ethnoreligious conflict may fall between these two extremes, with neither side holding a total monopoly on weapons of destruction (although one side may hold a monopoly on the political system). An ethnoreligious conflict in which one group is less armed or unarmed is not a

241

war but a massacre or a genocide. If one group enjoys a significant advantage in arms, the conflict may rise to a guerrilla struggle or a terrorist campaign by the disadvantaged party. If both groups have access to reasonably equal force, then ethnoreligious conflict can become war.

The goal of a religious war is also different from the goal of other forms of religious violence. The goal of sacrifice is to spill blood and use body parts for the strengthening of the sacrificer. The goal of self-mortification is to discipline or punish or annihilate the self. The goal of persecution is to suppress and correct the wrong opinion or practice—almost a kind of "medical" or "legal" procedure. The goal of ethnoreligious conflict is domination and exploitation (or the throwing off of domination and exploitation), subjugation, or separatism. The goal of religious war is *victory*, the *defeat* of the opposing army and by extension of the entire society that the opposing army defends; at the extreme, it is the liquidation of an enemy group, their literal elimination from history, and the acquisition of their land and property. Short of that extreme, it may be the reduction of that enemy to a smaller or more remote geographic and political position, or their absorption into the victor's territory, political system, and religious truth.

As we acknowledged at the outset of this book, religious war is one of the main preoccupations of contemporary literature on violence, and for good reason. However, this does not mean that it is well understood. In this chapter, we discuss this ultimate expression of religious violence, noting that religious war is a subset or particular manifestation of war in general, which may be fought for religious or nonreligious reasons; better yet, the religious module can be added to any actual war. Additionally, we will see that the argument that religion is antithetical to war is frivolous. Religions, at least certain kinds or elements of religion, are not only compatible with war but virtually compel it. It is critical to understand, then, what kinds and elements of religion are especially conducive to the practice of war, including a warrior worldview, warrior values, and beliefs about how war can achieve religious purposes. In fact, we will find that religion can be more conducive to war than other causes since, as Terry Pratchett puts it in his comic novel *Small Gods*, "uncertain people fight badly."[1]

THE *RELIGION* AND THE *WAR* IN "RELIGIOUS WAR"

War has been a part of the human experience for a long time—some would argue for all time. Just when war appeared in human history depends largely on how one defines *war*. No human epoch, of course, has ever been entirely without conflict; archaeological and physical anthropological evidence demonstrates that conclusively. However, not all violence is war. Based on the material data, there are scholars who conclude that war has been a continuous characteristic of human society from the very beginning of humanity,[2] while others see war as a more recent phenomenon, arising only in the last few millennia or as a result of foreign contact.[3]

One source of information about the evolution of warfare is premodern societies such as hunter-gatherers, pastoralists (animal herders), and horticulturists (low-technology farmers). Certainly we know that "traditional" or "small-scale" societies—ones without formal government, stockpiles of wealth, or centralized and hierarchical social institutions—have engaged in warlike activity. Napoleon Chagnon famously (and controversially) described the systemic intercommunity violence of the Yanomamo, a society along the Venezuela/Brazil border, even estimating that one-third of all adult male deaths are due to such combat.[4] Societies living on the North American Plains were notorious for their warlike attitudes and actions, such as the Cheyenne who had explicit warrior organizations for men and warrior practices like "counting coup" or scoring points by performing some brave action like stealing a horse or striking an enemy. Pastoralists like the Nuer of East Africa elevated aggression to a value and groomed males for their role as warriors, and many Pacific Island chiefdoms including those on Hawaii, Fiji, and New Zealand had achieved relatively high levels of warfare.

Much of the controversy surrounding "tribal war" or "premodern war" follows from a messy concept of war. There have been many attempts to define *war*, none authoritative. Daniel Smith's definition of war as active conflict that has claimed more than one thousand lives is obviously inadequate, since a mass sacrifice or a persecution might cost that many lives, and a small war might not.[5] More usefully, Raoul Naroll calls war "public lethal group combat between territorial teams,"[6] while Keith Otterbein conceives of it as "armed conflict between political communities."[7] Anthony Wallace extends the definition to "the sanctioned use of lethal weapons by members of one society against members of another,"[8] and Bronislaw Malinowski characterizes it as "an armed contest between two independent political units, by means of organized military force, in the pursuit of a tribal or national policy."[9] Surveying such definitions, Brian Ferguson advances a description of war as "organized, purposeful group action, directed against another group that may or may not be organized for similar action, involving the actual or potential application of lethal force."[10]

Despite their differences, these approaches share some features. As Ferguson himself points out, definitions of war generally refer to two elements, "a type of behavior and a war-making unit."[11] In other words, war is (at least potentially) deadly action conducted by some sort of "army" against another "army," both of which are representatives or agents of an authority or society. As we can readily see, this still does not distinguish war from other forms of organized aggressive violence. War in the familiar and meaningful sense falls somewhere on the far end of a continuum of intercommunity violence, one that contains other types like raids, feuds, revenge attacks, and duels. All these other activities are violent, even potentially deadly, but they are not war in the strict sense. Raids are usually short-lived affairs: the raiders attack, achieve some limited objective (steal property, take captives, kill one or a few victims), and withdraw. Feuds are usually more "personal" but ongoing affairs between individuals or families or villages.

Wars are different from these but still diverse. For instance, Harry Turney-High distinguished premodern or tribal (what he called "primitive") war from modern (what he called "true") war: a true or modern war features "tactical operations," "definite command and control," the "ability to conduct a campaign for the reduction of enemy resistance if the first battle fails," a definite motive that is a collective rather than a personal one, and "an adequate supply."[12] In the present discussion, we are talking about "true" war. First of all, then, war is a phenomenon conducted by groups, supported by societies, and led by authorities, which usually means a "government" or other established and accepted official or institution, including a religious official like the pope or a religous institution like the Catholic church. War is also more sustained than these other forms of aggression; while not all wars last for years, they *can* last for years. In its duration, war consists of a series of discrete encounters or battles between formal and often professional "warriors" or groups of individuals dedicated to the confrontation. It is comparatively impersonal: fighters do not usually know their enemy, and it does not particularly matter *which* enemy combatants get killed. Because the aggression of war is more organized, orchestrated, and sustained, the level of destruction can be and tends to be higher. The final unique and essential quality of war is its purpose: it is not merely to conquer territory, although it is often that too, and it is certainly not merely to extort wealth or property from a rival. According to Clausewitz, it is the use of physical force by a participant "to compel the other to do his will: [the warrior's] *immediate* aim is to *throw* his opponent in order to make him incapable of further resistance. *War therefore is an act of force to compel our enemy to do our will*"[13] (emphasis in the original). Sometimes, as Clausewitz admits and the history of war proves, this compulsion of the opponent leads to—or can only be accomplished by—the surrender if not the total eradication of the opponent.

The Varieties of War

Not all wars aim at the extinction of the adversary, although that outcome exists as an extreme, possible, and sometimes desired and actual outcome. Indeed, wars have a variety of motivations and a variety of objectives. Of course, the central question for us is not what kinds of war there are but what kinds of religiously motivated and justified war there are.

Almost everyone would agree that a group or society, as much as an individual, has a right to self-defense, and the more violent the threat, the more violent the defense. Thus, a *defensive war*, one in which a group or society uses force to meet and resist force, is usually justified in the eyes of observers; in a defensive war, the party is not the aggressor and did not "start the violence" but only responded to it. What, of course, constitutes a "threat" and calls for defense is relative. A more difficult area is *preventive war*, that is, striking an opponent before that opponent strikes you. In some cases, the danger may be imminent: if a neighbor has an army amassed on your border, the attack may be clearly forthcoming, and launching an assault first may seem acceptable. Michael Walzer, in his study of "just and unjust wars," argues that "individuals and states can rightfully defend themselves against violence that is imminent but not actual; they can fire the first shots if they know themselves about to be attacked."[14] Yet more problematic is the *preemptive war*, in which a group or society strikes an opponent that might at some future time pose a threat to it, in other words, a war that preempts possible but not imminent aggression. There could be obvious disagreement about what groups *may someday* pose a threat and when that threat merits military action. The interesting thing is that all these types of war could arguably be considered "defensive" in the sense that the army or society sees itself as acting in its own defense—even if no shot has been fired at it yet.

Some wars, on the other hand, are *offensive*, although the distinction may not be quite as clear as it initially appears. An offensive war is almost always *optional* in that the aggressor is not compelled to start it and would presumably be fine without starting it (while we would probably consider the Nazi German instigation of World War II an offensive war, they might have considered it a preventive or a preemptive or a retributive war in revenge for the felt injustices of the armistice ending World War I). An offensive war, then, is ordinarily a "war of interest": there is something that the aggressor hopes to gain through it. The interest may be land, wealth, resources, population, geopolitical advantage, and so on.

Once the war has begun, there may be various goals it pursues. One is obviously territorial conquest, the occupation of additional land. Another is exploitation, to seize resources for wealth and people for labor; this may or may not involve transferring significant numbers of one's own citizens into the regions. Arguably many of the early European colonial wars were *wars of exploitation*, pacifying native peoples so that their wealth and labor could be extracted. A *civil war* pits one element of a society against another element of the same society, perhaps in a struggle for independence from that society (as in the American Civil War). In a *war of interdiction*, a group or society tries to destroy some obstacle to its interests, as when the early United States warred against the Barbary pirates to end their predation on American shipping. A *war of liberation* seeks to free one's own group or society or an allied group or society from the oppression or domination of a foreign power, as when European countries helped Greece throw off Ottoman control in the nineteenth century or when the United States liberated Kuwait from Iraq. The insertion of troops to protect and aid civilians in a place like Sudan or Rwanda might qualify as a war of interdiction and/or of liberation. Hostile parties might not even confront each other directly but might struggle through intermediaries or "proxies," leading to such proxy wars as the Korean or Vietnamese conflicts in the twentieth century. Finally, a state of uneasy peace or military competition (a "cold war") might exist between societies.

All the above refer to what theorists call the *jus ad bellum* or the "justification" of war. In other words, wars have reasons: groups, societies, or governments fight wars because they believe they should or must. Defense, prevention, preemption, conquest, liberation—all these are potential justifications for war. That is not to say that these reasons necessarily make the war "just." Having a reason for something is not the same as that thing being reasonable.

The "justness" or "goodness" of a war is judged not only by its motivation (*why* it is fought) but also by its conduct (*how* it is fought). This is called the *jus in bellum* or the "rules of war." It is often forgotten that war is not a chaotic, disorderly abrogation of all norms and rules. Rather, war is "ruly" in many if not most instances, in the sense that there are norms and rules for how one should conduct a war. The rules depend on the type of war and the particular society and historical epic. For instance, the ancient Greeks observed elaborate rules of war. First, it must be grasped precisely how much they enjoyed war. The philosopher Heraclitus called war "the father of us all, the king of us all," and according to Victor Davis Hanson, "Most Greeks agreed: war was the most important thing we humans do. It was fighting . . . that best revealed virtues, cowardice, skill or ineptitude, civilization or barbarism."[15] Furthermore, in the classic period, war took a specific form, the clash of two corps of tightly grouped foot soldiers in the "phalanx" formation, who would push and jostle each other with spears bristling from interlocked shields until one army broke ranks and retreated, sometimes after as little as thirty minutes of combat. Beyond that, a war "well fought" required a prehostility declaration of war and formal breaking of truces or alliances (which ruled out sneak attacks), prebattle rituals such as animal sacrifices, specific times and places for combat (seasonal campaigns in the spring and summer, only during light hours, and on agreed-upon fields of combat), limits to the violence (e.g., no attacking retreating armies, no aggression against wounded captives, and no violence against non-combatants or religious sites), postbattle etiquette (including returning the enemies' fallen men to them and allowing the winner to erect a monument on the site), and most interestingly, rules forbidding certain weaponry (in the classical Greek case, the use of archers, cavalry, and artillery, which were considered unfair and unmanly).

As the Greek case reveals, one of the recurring themes of jus in bellum is the immunity of noncombatants from war's destructiveness. This seems like the basic quality of propriety in modern war. Yet, as R. Joseph Hoffmann points out, the distinction between combatants and noncombatants is not as clear cut as we might imagine, nor is it as universal. Everyone can agree that the "professional warriors," the soldiers on the battlefield, are combatants and are therefore "killable." Most modern societies feel that prisoners of war are no longer combatants, but of course opinions about that vary. Medics, cooks, and other non-fighting soldiers occupy a gray area. Civilians by definition are noncombatants and therefore protected from aggression, but this depends on how one defines *civilian* and is often not honored anyhow. The civilian population is, after all, the pool from which soldiers are drawn, and they support the war effort with their money and their labor. What about war factories? What about the government itself? Surely few societies at war, including the United States, have demurred from attacking civilian facilities in prosecution of their belligerence. And when war is defined as a struggle not merely with an army, or even with a state, or even with a people, but with an idea, a worldview, a *reality*, then potentially no one is a civilian and everyone is a combatant.

The "Just War"

The concept of "just war"—a war that conforms to both of the sets of rules regarding war (jus ad bellum and jus in bellum)—emerged in early Christian thinking as an alternative to "holy war." In fact, Ronald Bainton, in his major study of Christian war, identified three main attitudes: pacifism or the opposition to all war, "crusade" or holy war (see below), and just war, which he characterized as political rather than religious. The concept of just war has an ancient pedigree: in the philosophy of Plato and Aristotle, war was only justified for "the vindication of justice and the restoration of peace,"[16] although Aristotle also deemed it justifiable if the enemy refused to submit to the dictates of reason and nature, for example resisted their "natural" slave status.[17] Clearly then, one person's just war was another person's ultimate injustice. At any rate, the Roman author Cicero extended the justification of war to the restoration of honor as well as of peace and justice and added the standards that it be conducted by a legitimate state, following a formal declaration, and fought in conformity with the rules of war (although this did not automatically entail mercy toward noncombatants).

Early Christian thinkers picked up the Greco-Roman concept of the just war. Augustine, who also contributed much to the theory of persecution (see chapter 5), helped formulate the Christian notion of just war. According to Augustine, peace was the preferable condition but not always the realistic condition. Thus, war could and should be fought for the cause of justice: "Those wars may be defined as just which avenge injuries."[18] The proper attitude of the warrior was love, an emotion that was not contrary in his mind to the violent acts of war: "Love does not exclude wars of mercy waged by the good."[19] Further, war could only be conducted by valid authorities, that is to say, the government: a private individual could not declare a war or otherwise kill, but a soldier under orders from his leadership was allowed. Warfare should be conducted with restraint and in "good faith," without excessive force, dishonesty, or looting and massacring. All the same, he assumed that justice could only be on one side in any conflict, and if the struggle was between Christians and non-Christians, it was easy to see who had justice: as Salisbury expresses it in her analysis of Augustine's code, "The simplest definition of a just war for fourth-century theologians lay in the combatants. If Christians were fighting pagans, for example,

God was on the side of Christians, so the battle was just."[20] When Christians fought Christians, as they increasingly did, who had the justice was considerably murkier.

Centuries later, Aquinas restated the Christian just war theory. In his thinking, war was just if it was declared by a legitimate authority, political or spiritual; was conducted with the right intention; was the last resort; was prosecuted in proportion to the threat and goal (in other words, no unnecessary use or level of violence); had a reasonable chance of success; and was fought with all possible moderation (in other words, there should be "rules of war," including nonviolence against noncombatants, prisoners, etc.). Of course, as Walzer reminds us, these standards are still relative and open to interpretation: who is a legitimate authority, and what is the right intention? Even more, when is the last resort, and what is "in proportion" and "all possible moderation"? And certainly, there are times when the rules were broken, and societies at war often reason that "the greater the justice of my cause, the more rules I can violate for the sake of the cause."[21] Or in a more practical vein, "the greater the justice of my cause and *the more violating a rule is necessary for my cause to prevail*, the greater my justification in violating the rule."[22] Of course, no cause is more just (to the partisans) than their religion.

"Holy War," Cosmic War, and Dualistic Religions

If not all human violence is war, and not all war is religious war, then it is equally true that not all religious war is "holy war." Virtually all human societies have had religion, but not all—in fact, remarkably few—have had holy war. There are many things about a society's religion that might draw it into hostility with another society, but there are many things about a religion that might forestall such hostility, such as indifference to another group's beliefs and values: many societies throughout history, like the Australian Aboriginals, have certainly been aware that other societies had different spiritual beings and different rituals and practices, some of which they overtly found odd or distasteful, but honestly they considered it none of their business. To go to war with another society over religion implies that one or both groups consider the other's religion to be "intolerable" (see chapter 5), and to go to holy war with another religion implies that the war itself is a religious act in some manner.

Holy war is a religious-cultural concept; indeed, *holy* is a religious-cultural concept that some religions possess and others do not (i.e., *holy* is not a necessary nor universal aspect of religion). Firestone insists, "The term 'holy war' is a European invention and derives from the study of war [not to mention of religion] in its European context. . . . [I]n its most broad definition, the term defines a form of justification for engaging in war by providing religious legitimation."[23] In fact, he asserts that the term did not even exist until 1901 when a scholar named Friedrich Schwally published a book by that name. *Holy* itself is a term drawn from the Judeo-Christian tradition and has a diffuse set of references relating to the god of that tradition; however, as we will say below, the Hebrew scriptures do not use the term *holy war*. Closer inspection indicates that, as James Johnson finds, holy war too "is not in fact a unitary concept but a complex of distinguishable but interrelated ideas" shaped by their historical and social context.[24] He explicates ten different interpretations of the holy war idea:

1. "Holy war as war fought at God's command,"
2. "Holy war as war fought on God's behalf by his duly authorized representatives,"
3. "Holy war as fought by God himself,"
4. "Holy war as fought to defend religion against its enemies, without and within,"
5. "Holy war as war fought to propagate right religion or establish a social order in line with divine authority,"
6. "Holy war as war fought to enforce religious conformity and/or punish deviation" (which might include the persecutions and inquisitions from chapter 5),
7. "Holy war as warfare in which the participants are themselves ritually and/or morally 'holy,'"
8. "Holy war as the militant struggle of faith by means of arms alongside nonviolent means,"
9. "Holy war as warfare under religiously inspired (charismatic) leadership," and
10. "Holy war as a phenomenon recognized during or after the fact as an 'absolute miracle.'"[25]

Accordingly, some religions or religious ideologies will be more conducive to this notion than others. In order for a society to engage in holy war, it must minimally possess a concept of war and a concept of holy. It must believe in a religious source that commands and/or participates in war. It must feel that it is the "duly authorized representative" of that source. It must experience the urge and obligation to defend the source or religion against other religions, which to it are offensive. And/or it must consider religious difference to be religious *deviation*, even religious *deviance*. Only then would one go to the lengths of taking up arms, risking one's life, and ending someone else's life in a holy war.

If there is a single religious idea that provides the ground for holy war, it is dualism. Dualism in all its myriad manifestations holds that there are two and only two forces or essences in reality—normally, a "good" force/essence and a "bad" or "evil" force/essence. But these two powers do not coexist peaceably. They are opposites, rivals, enemies. One of the world's oldest dualistic religions, Zoroastrianism, makes this opposition clear in the struggle between two equal and opposite forces, light (Ahura Mazda) and darkness (Ahriman or Angra Mainyu). Angra Mainyu was a kind of "anticreator" responsible for bringing pain and suffering, "plunder and sin," "tears and wailing," and the "99,999 diseases" of the world. The two gods struggled perpetually with each other, turning the universe into a battleground. In this worldview, war is the very nature of the universe; there is a "cosmic war" in progress, from which there is no escape, no neutral point, and no resolution other than ultimate victory or defeat.

Christianity is another dualistic religion. The god of Christianity is akin to Ahura Mazda, a being of absolute goodness; Satan is a being of absolute evil. The two are locked in combat, if not presently then at the end, the apocalypse, when a literal war will be fought. In the meantime, there are two worlds on earth. The first world is the world of the "church" or the "elect" or the "saints," and so on, that is, the good people, the true Christians. The second world, an object of indifference if not disdain, is the world of the nonbelievers or the pagans or the carnal or the satanic. Augustine developed this idea extensively in his *City of God*, likening the two worlds to two cities, the *civitas dei* or "city of God" and the *civitas terranae* or "city of the world." The worldly city is inferior, a place or dimension of strife and conflict and evil and unbelief, a realm fundamentally different from and antagonistic to the city of God. There could be no "normal relations" between these two domains. They were antagonists.

Like Christianity, Islam takes a dualistic approach to reality, dividing it into a "domain of peace" (*dar al-islam*) and a "domain of conflict" (*dar al-harb*). The dar al-islam is the realm of true religion and submission to the one true god and his will and laws. The dar al-harb is a realm of trouble, strife, and injustice, since it does not follow the ways of the one true god. Even when it is not actually violent, it, like Augustine's worldly city, pursues the wrong goals and is forever in disorder, because it is not rightly directed by and to god. The dar al-harb, understandably, is in perpetual and inherent opposition to if not in open battle with the dar al-islam. The only way that this tension can be resolved once and for all is by the conquest of the dar al-harb and its integration into the realm of true religion, submission, and peace—that is, its conversion to Islam and the shari'a law that it prescribes. Thus, the struggle against unrighteousness and unbelief, even within oneself, becomes a central feature of Islam.

In conclusion, monotheisms, which tend to ascribe all goodness to one entity, therefore tend toward dualism: bad, evil, misfortune, suffering are ascribed to "something else," an entity or force or party that contests the universe with the good entity. This dualistic view of reality then builds conflict and confrontation into the very fabric of the cosmic system. And, if we the followers of the good god (who is the only god) are that god's army, then everyone else must be not only the other but also *the enemy*. As Hermann Cohen expresses it, "The worship of the unique God unavoidably exacts the destruction of false worship. In this respect there can be no pity and no regard for men. . . . Therefore the worship of false gods must be annihilated from the earth."[26] While the two realms may not be, at least at every moment, in open warfare with each other, they are definitely and irrevocably antagonistic, with the ever-present potential for actual conflict and violence.

RELIGIOUS WAR AMONG THE ANCIENT HEBREWS

The Torah/Old Testament, like all traditional religious writing, is "national" literature—that is, it is the literature of a people or nation. In this case, it is a political and military history of a people, albeit a "holy history" in which their god is seen to be operating through that history. War was a familiar and routine experience of the people of Israel from the conquest of their promised homeland to the fall of their kingdom. Yet, perhaps precisely because they believed their god was active in all events, "holy war" was not a specific category in Hebrew thinking. As Reuven Firestone points out, *holy* (in Hebrew, *qadosh* or *qodesh*) was a term reserved for sacrificial ritual, not for war, and "there is no consistent term to describe or differentiate divinely authorized wars from any others in the Hebrew Bible."[27] Even so, "Although the Bible does not use the term 'holy' to define its wars, the very fact that most of Israel's biblical wars were authorized by or associated with the God of Israel makes them comparable to 'holy war'— or divinely authorized warring in other religious systems and contexts."[28]

That war was a ubiquitous, religious, and entirely acceptable fact of ancient Hebrew life is obvious. War was essential to the fulfillment of the promise of a great future nation in the "promised land" of Canaan, since other societies already occupied that land. The promise, explicitly, was not that the Israelites would be able to enter the territory peacefully but that they would have to fight for it:

> When the Lord thy God shall bring thee into the land whither thou goest to possess it, and hath cast out many nations before thee, the Hittites, and the Girgashites, and the Amorites, and the Canaanites, and the Perizzites, and the Hivites, and the Jebusites, seven nations greater and mightier than thou;
>
> And when the Lord thy God shall deliver them before thee; thou shalt smite them, and utterly destroy them; thou shalt make no covenant with them, nor show mercy unto them. . . .
>
> But thus shall ye deal with them; ye shall destroy their altars, and break down their images, and cut down their groves, and burn their graven images with fire.
>
> For thou art an holy people unto the Lord thy God.[29]

Various passages refer to "the wars of the Lord,"[30] "the Lord's battles,"[31] or the war "that the Lord will have . . . with Amalek from generation to generation."[32] Exodus 15:3 is unmistakably clear that the Israelite god is not averse to war; rather, "The Lord is a man of war: the Lord is his name." In fact, the first lines of Judges 21 actually suggest that their god intentionally placed hostile peoples in the way of the Israelites, so "that the generations of the children of Israel might know, to teach them war, at the least such as before knew nothing thereof."

Accordingly, the chosen people of God had ample opportunity to learn war and were even given detailed instructions on how to prosecute it. Deuteronomy 20 is an extensive guide to war. In campaign after campaign, cities (like Jericho) were conquered and rival kingdoms were fought. The great early war chief Joshua led operations against cities such as Lachish, Eglon, Hebron, and Debir, and his army

> smote them with the edge of the sword, and utterly destroyed all the souls that were therein; he left none remaining. . . . So Joshua smote all the country of

the hills, and of the south, and of the vale, and of the springs, and all their kings he left none remaining, but utterly destroyed all that breathed, *as the Lord God of Israel commanded.* . . . And all these kings and their land did Joshua take at one time, *because the Lord God of Israel fought for Israel.*[33] (emphasis added)

Ancient Hebrew war was often without mercy or moderation, as Numbers 31 exemplifies:

And they warred against the Midianites, as the Lord commanded Moses; and they slew all the males. . . .

And the children of Israel took all the women of Midian captives, and their little ones, and took the spoil of all their cattle, and all their goodly castles, and all their goods. . . .

[Moses said] Now therefore kill every male among the little ones, and kill every woman that hath known man by lying with him.

But all the women children, that have not known a man by lying with him, keep alive for yourselves.

Of course, the Israelites at war were supposed to offer peace to a besieged city, and if the enemy accepted peace (essentially surrender), then the population became tribute payers and servants to the invaders. If, however, the city resisted, then its conquest and utter destruction were justified:

And when the Lord thy God hath delivered it into thine hands, thou shalt smite every male thereof with the edge of the sword:

But the women, and the little ones, and the cattle, and all that is in the city, even all the spoil thereof, shalt thou take unto thyself; and thou shalt eat the spoil of thine enemies which the Lord thy God hath given thee.

Thus shalt thou do unto all the cities which are very far off from thee, which are not of the cities of these nations.

But of the cities of these people, which the Lord thy God doth give thee for an inheritance, thou shalt save alive nothing that breatheth:

But thou shalt utterly destroy them; namely, the Hittites, and the Amorites, the Canaanites, and the Perizzites, the Hivites, and the Jebusites; *as the Lord thy God hath commanded thee*:

That they teach you not to do after all their abominations, which they have done unto their gods; so should ye sin against the Lord thy God.[34] (emphasis added)

As we might imagine, over the many centuries of ancient Hebrew history, thoughts and practices regarding war evolved. Gerhard von Rad distinguishes three phases in their religious warring.[35] In the earliest phase, war was a cultic activity surrounded with many ritual rules and requirements; for instance, the war party or "host" had to assemble to the call of the ram's horn, sacrifices had to be offered, and God had to take his place at the front of the army (the "lord of hosts"). James Aho also mentions a collective battle cry, the *t'ru'ah*.[36] When the enemy was defeated—ideally terrorized by the might of their lord—the victors observed the rule of *herem* in which the loot from the conquest was consecrated to their god, some of which was retained by the priests for religious use and some of which was divided among the soldiers.[37] The second historical phase Rad identifies as a "war for Yahweh," that is, a kind of religious obligation, a combat to defend the faith. This was followed by an offensive "war of religion" to conquer territory for and spread the true belief in and obedience to their god (see chapter 5 on persecution of non-Yahwehists).

These distinctions raise the question of the type of holy war and its relation to the interests of the god and religion. Again, the term *holy war* does not occur in the Torah/Old Testament, but scriptures and later commentaries made a primary distinction between "commanded war" (*milhemet mitzvah*) and "discretionary war" (*milhemet reshut*). A commanded or obligatory war was one that was explicitly ordered by God, like the war against the Midianites mentioned above; such a war could not be shirked without divine consequences. A commanded war could certainly be self-defensive, but there were ample occasions on which it appears to be offensive, for instance to acquire territory, and some commentators have judged this to be a legitimate reason for milhemet mitzvah (although, of course, humans do not have to legitimate commanded wars; the legitimation is that God ordered them). A discretionary war was an optional one; there was no direct command from God, and there was no immediate threat to the nation. Maimonides, for example, argued that a king could launch a discretionary war "to expand the borders of Israel and to increase his greatness and honor."[38]

In practice, the distinction between commanded and discretionary war was not very clear or very important. Mark Gopin argues that, "for all practical purposes, [they] appear to be the same."[39] Donniel Hartmann goes further, concluding that from a scriptural perspective

all wars embarked upon by the people of Israel are religiously sanctioned as God's wars. There is little differentiation in the legitimacy or divine sanction of wars of self-defense, aggression, conquest, expansion, capturing the land of Canaan, or eradication of idolatry from the midst of the Jewish people. The Jewish people's battles are all God's battles, in accordance with the expression of the divine will.[40]

Perhaps we must add to Johnson's list of meanings of holy war any war fought by people who regard themselves as holy or in possession of the sole and absolute truth.

Finally, a word about holy war tactics is in order. Aho determines that, aside from the rule for spoils of war and the specific instructions to kill or appropriate this or that enemy or property, there were no "ritual constraints" on combat, for instance no rules on acceptable weapons or conduct.[41] He characterizes Israelite war as "opportunistic and calculating," permitting night attacks, assassination, and particularly ambushes after false retreats. One reason for these tactics, he reasons, was the small, lightly armed, and disorganized nature of Israelite armies, which favored "tricks and subterfuge on the part of small groups of carefully picked warriors."[42] He asserts that this was the normal approach to Hebrew war in the prekingdom period, from 1250 to 1020 BCE. During the kingdom period, battles were more "conventional," with forts, professional soldiers, and formal lines of battle—which prophets like Isaiah, Jeremiah, and Micah railed against as betrayals of ancient scriptural standards and "lack of trust in God."[43]

"HOLY WAR" IN CHRISTIANITY: THE CRUSADES

In its earliest phase, Christianity in Europe had been significantly (though not totally) pacifist, partly because of certain doctrines of Jesus, partly because of Christian disqualification from military service if they refused to sacrifice to the Roman emperors, and partly because of their own political weakness (see chapter 9). However, once Christianity became the religion of the realm and achieved political power, it necessarily had to deal with secular matters of state, including defense. During the Dark Ages, the Franks, for instance, had used military force to repel Muslim invaders from the Iberian peninsula. To whatever extent soldiering and war had previously been incompatible with Christian values, the two were by the second Christian millennium entirely compatible.

Two major sources converged to set in motion the Christian wars known as the Crusades at the turn of the twelfth century. One was a surge of Islam in the

Middle East, which contained the "Holy Land" of Christianity, especially Jerusalem. At the opening of the eleventh century, the caliph of Cairo had attacked and persecuted non-Muslims in the city, which was deep inside Muslim territory and had been for three hundred years. Around the same time, the Turks came to dominate Middle Eastern Islam, handing Christians a serious defeat in 1071 at the battle of Manzikert and capturing Jerusalem in the same year. Meanwhile, the Christian Byzantine Empire, which had welcomed the Turks into what is modern-day Turkey as allies, saw a Turkish kingdom established at the famous Christian site of Nicaea by 1081. Christians including Pope Urban II dreaded an upcoming invasion of the Byzantine capital of Constantinople (which finally occurred in 1453).

The second source was internal political and religious developments in Europe. By the year 1000, fledgling national states were forming in England, France, and central Europe (the Holy Roman Empire, much of which would eventually become Germany and Austria). These formations threatened Christian unity and papal and church central authority. One solution to both problems, domestic and foreign, was a pan-European mobilization, under religious authority, to push back the Muslims and "liberate" Jerusalem. As Johnson indicates, this "discretionary" war was proposed not as an offensive one, and certainly not as violence to spread Christianity, but as purely *defensive*, "for the purpose of repelling attacks on Christian territory, punishing Muslim attacks, and retaking lands, properties, and persons unjustly seized in these attacks."[44] In other words, it was to qualify, although the concept was not yet fully formulated, as a "just war"—self-defensive and avenging or correcting past wrongs.

So, on November 27, 1095, Urban II "summoned the whole of Christendom to arms, the pope calling for the defense of the faith threatened by the new Moslem [*sic*] invasion."[45] The call elicited the response *"Deus le volt"* or "God wants it," a slogan that Urban adopted himself. Urban envisioned a single, unified Christian army, under his ultimate command, carrying the sign of the cross as their mark—a true "crusade." What transpired instead was a series of waves of religiously inspired, less-than-coordinated, and not always noble invasions of the East, starting, even before the pope could get his official force in the field, with the so-called People's Crusade led by a figure known as Peter the Hermit. Traveling from village to village encouraging peasants to strike a blow for their religion, Peter managed to attract a mob of fifteen thousand enthusiasts, which the New Advent Catholic encyclopedia describes as "disorganized, undisciplined, penniless hordes, almost destitute of equipment, who, surging eastward through the valley of the Danube, plundered as they went along and murdered the Jews in the German cities."[46] Other peasant armies formed, too, but only Peter's reached Constantinople, where several thousand of them were killed by Christian officials out of concern for the threat they posed. On October 21, 1096, the remnants of the horde reached Nicaea, which they approached in disarray and where they were massacred by Turkish troops.

In the meantime, the official Crusader army was forming under the leadership of Godfrey of Bouillon, which arrived at Constantinople on December 23, 1096. Tensions between eastern and western Christianity had been high for a long time, so when three other western armies joined Godfrey's by the spring of 1097, the eastern emperor was alarmed by the concentration of western power in his vicinity. Rather than aid the Crusaders, he attempted to extract oaths of loyalty from them, withheld supplies, actually attacked Godfrey's men, and sent the Crusaders on their way east as quickly as he could.

On June 26, 1097, the Crusaders captured the Turkish capital of Nicaea and continued southeast toward Jerusalem. On June 7, 1099, the Christian siege of the holy city began; after weeks of siege, the assault on the city came on July 14 and the city fell the next day. The slaughter inside the city was extraordinary, although the New Advent summarizes it with the neutral line that the Christians "slew its inhabitants regardless of age or sex." Grousset is more forthcoming: the city's defenders retreated to the Mosque of al-Aqsa, where they were massacred, and a contemporary described how the liberators "waded in blood up to their ankles."[47] Other Muslim captives were promised protection but were butchered overnight and the following day by newly arrived Crusaders. Another contemporary, Archbishop William of Tyre, remembered, "The city showed the spectacle of such carnage of the enemies, such a shedding of blood, that the victors themselves were struck with horror and disgust."[48] Finally calmed by their success, the Christians "all flung themselves prostrate, their arms outstretched in the form of the Cross. 'Each man thought he could still see before him the crucified body of Jesus Christ. And it seemed to them that they were at the gates of Heaven.'"[49]

On this foundation a Christian kingdom was inaugurated in Jerusalem and the Mediterranean coast, but the Crusaders had left the interior under Muslim control, so the small Christian kingdom was surrounded by hostile populations. In 1101, three fresh European armies were wiped out by Turkish forces. By 1144, Muslim armies had recaptured much of the previously lost territory, but this only stimulated a Second Crusade around 1146. A German army was defeated in late 1147, suffering a loss of three-quarters of its forces; a French army subsequently took its own beating, but the remaining soldiers of the two groups reached Jerusalem, then struck out for Damascus, which they besieged for four days in July 1148 before they retreated. Thus ended the Second Crusade.

Now a great general emerged in Islam, Salah-ed-Din or Saladin. In 1168 he ruled Egypt and began to unify Muslims against the Christian state of Jerusalem. By late 1174, he had conquered Damascus, and on September 17, 1187, Jerusalem returned to Muslim hands, leaving only coastal cities like Tyre and Tripoli under Christian control. Salah-ed-Din did not reciprocate the mistreatment of enemies that the defeated Muslims had previously suffered. Instead, "On the entry of his troops he had the main streets guarded by trusted men, responsible for preventing any violence against the Christians. At the prayer of the patriarch, he freed five hundred poor Christians."[50]

In response to the Christian defeat, western leaders undertook a Third Crusade in 1188. Frederick Barbarossa, the first to assemble and lead an army into the Middle East, was killed in a drowning accident in 1190, and his crusade fell apart. Forces marshaled by Richard (the Lionhearted) of England and Louis Augustus of France met and defeated Salah-ed-Din in combat but were compelled to accept a negotiated peace that left Jerusalem in Muslim hands. A Fourth Crusade followed in 1199, a full century after the first, but this one was never to reach the Holy Land. Instead, it stalled in southeastern Europe, arriving at Constantinople in June 1203. After months of negotiation and conflict, the Crusaders raided the city, the greatest in Christendom at that time, on April 12, 1204, resulting in what New Advent even admits was "ruthless plundering of its churches and palaces. . . . The masterpieces of antiquity, piled up in public places and in the Hippodrome, were utterly destroyed. Clerics and knights, in their eagerness to acquire famous and priceless relics, took part in the sack of the churches."[51]

A few tired and ignominious attempts at crusade followed, including the infamous Children's Crusade of 1212, in which thousands of children were gathered, marched to Brindisi in Italy, and sold as slaves—that is, those who did not perish along the way. In 1215, Pope Innocent III, of Inquisition fame, preached a new crusade, and some of the faithful answered his call and that of his successor, Honorius III, but by now most of the crusading zeal had passed—or turned inward, as our discussions in chapter 5 and below illustrate. Before putting it behind us, though, the final sentence in the New Advent discussion of the Crusades reveals the continuing approval of these events: "If, indeed, the

Christian civilization of Europe has become universal culture, in the highest sense, the glory redounds, in no small measure, to the Crusades."

"HOLY WAR" IN CHRISTIANITY: THE EUROPEAN RELIGIOUS WARS

As chapter 5 recounts, before the age of crusading in the Middle East had come to an end, the "One True Church" found itself combating religious deviance or heresy within its own domain of Europe. This campaign against dissidents and schismatics (like the Albigensians) did not usually rise to the level of war, since the heretics did not generally have the means to fight back; instead it was typically a one-sided conflict, a persecution. But on some occasions the heretics did offer armed resistance. Eventually, with religious protesters in possession not only of weapons but also of governments (as when local princes or kings joined and supported religious movements), real wars of religion broke out across the continent; in fact, the worst wars of the sixteenth and seventeenth centuries were intensely though not exclusively about religion.

The Waldensians and Cathars/Albigensians of the 1200s and John Wycliffe's Lollardy movement of the 1300s had been suppressed by the machinery of the Inquisition. However, Lollardy's successor in central Europe, inspired by the Bohemian critic and reformer Jan Hus, was not so easily extirpated. Hus, like Wycliffe before him and Luther after, questioned the church's policy on the selling of indulgences and its general corruption and wealth; as historian Edward Cheyney insists, by the 1200s the institutional church spent much if not most of "its energy extracting and administering wealth: the church of course had religious duties and fulfilled religious functions, but these were on the whole a minor part of its activity."[52] Predictably, Hus was arrested and put to death in 1415.

Unlike some previous movements, this one did not die with its leader. Rather, by 1419 outrage against the Catholic church had coalesced into armed resistance to it, a virtual religious revolution by some accounts. The first violence occurred in the city of Prague, where a protest march of Hussites turned into a riot on July 30, 1419; months of fighting laid waste to much of the city, whose local noblemen favored the Hussite cause. Jan Zizka emerged as the military leader of the movement, attacking the town of Nekmer in December 1419 with four hundred followers and artillery mounted on wagons. The use of wagon-loaded cannons and the defensive circling of those wagons became a signature and successful tactic of the Hussite armies.

As was the church practice at the time, Pope Martin V issued his first of several calls for a crusade against the Hussites on March 14, 1420. On March 25, Zizka and a force of twelve war wagons and four hundred infantrymen met a much larger opposing army at the Battle of Sudomer, taking and inflicting heavy losses but managing to escape. This was followed by a string of victories for the Hussites, which gave them control over a number of strategic castles (e.g., Vysehrad and Hradcany) and eventually nearly all of Bohemia. By mid-1426, Hussites could field twenty-four thousand men and five hundred artillery wagons at the battle of Usti nad Labem, at which they beat a "crusader" force of between twenty thousand and seventy thousand, by various reports. The Hussites continued to score victories and confront crusaders (Martin preached a fourth crusade against them in 1427), including a Catholic force of over one hundred thousand in August 1431. Despite some later losses and internal divisions, Hussite determination could not be completely broken, so a peace was finally arranged on July 5, 1436, between moderate Hussites (known as Utraquists, as opposed to the radicals called Taborites) and Catholic representatives. This was not to be the end of the struggle between Catholics and Hussites in central Europe nor between Catholics and "protestants" across Europe by any means.

The most serious continental threat to religious orthodoxy was Martin Luther's protest, initiated in 1517. Starting as an internal church debate over policies and practices, Lutheran criticisms soon developed into a harsh condemnation of the Catholic church, a breakaway movement, and ultimately a rival church. In chapter 5 we noted how the partisans of each denomination conducted persecutions in the countryside. However, partisans also mobilized their own political authorities (many princes subscribed to Luther's new doctrines, if only as opposition to "foreign" papal power) and their own military forces. One of the first outbreaks of violence, not entirely related to Lutheran reforms, was the Peasants' Revolt in June 1524 (actually, Luther was explicitly opposed to the peasants and acknowledged the right of sovereigns to suppress them with coercion, calling the lower classes "robbing and murdering hordes").

Other "protestant" reformers too found success and worldly power, like Zwingli in Zurich and Calvin in Geneva. There was considerable war during ensuing decades, not all of it Catholic-versus-Protestant: a French Catholic force invaded Rome in 1527 and "sacked it amid . . . scenes of violence, murder, rape, looting, and destruction."[53] At any rate, a truce of sorts between Catholics and Lutherans was agreed in 1555 called the Peace of Augsburg, based on the principle of *cuius region, eius religio* ("he who rules a territory determines its religion"), that is, the right of each local sovereign in central Europe to choose his own— and his subjects'—religion.

This peace held tenuously in the Holy Roman Empire until 1618, as we will return to discuss shortly. In the meantime, a party of French protesters, the Huguenots, stirred a conflict in France. Influenced by Calvinism, the doctrine of John Calvin in Geneva, the Huguenots "not only spread heresy but challenged the power and profits of the crown."[54] As early as 1547, King Henri II had condemned them as heretics and ordered their execution by burning at the stake. The movement continued to grow despite the persecution, claiming over two thousand congregations and as many as one million adherents and a significant percentage of the nobility by the 1560s. Escalating tensions led to a massacre of twelve hundred Huguenots at Vassey and Sens in 1562, which sparked a war between the Catholic regime of France and the Protestant minority. The warring persisted off and on for more than thirty-five years, with a decade of nearly continuous fighting from 1562 to 1572 in which high officials were assassinated and the Huguenots achieved some success. However, on August 24, 1572, St. Bartholomew's Day, Huguenot homes were invaded in the middle of the night and prominent leaders killed, causing days of rioting and three thousand Huguenot deaths in Paris and thousands more in the outlying areas. According to Dunn, "When the news reached the pope, he was so delighted that he gave a hundred crowns to the messenger."[55] Conflict dragged on fitfully until 1598, when Henri IV issued the Edict of Nantes, providing toleration for Huguenots. The edict was subsequently revoked by Louis XIV in 1685, and it was another century (1787) before toleration was officially granted again—just two years before the French Revolution.

Back in central Europe, the fragile peace between religions had collapsed by 1618. In fact, the German realm "was a battleground between the 1520s and the 1640s," although the fighting was not as continuous or as purely religious:

> East of the Rhine, the motives for fighting were less "religious," indeed in every
> sense less ideological. Protestants and Catholics exhibited less sense of moral
> regeneration, less missionary zeal, than did their counterparts in the west, and
> a stronger preoccupation with territorial aggrandizement. The Thirty Years'

War, biggest of all the wars of religion, was fought for more obviously secular objectives than were the French and Dutch religious wars.[56]

Flaring first in Bohemia, Hus's old country (just as much of the Huguenot war had been fought in Languedoc, old Albigensian country) in 1618, after a few years of religious fervor the war devolved into a succession struggle and political competition, with non-German armies including the French, Spanish, and Swedish marching across German territory. In fact, the basic religious questions were settled by 1622, but the war continued and expanded with the insertion of these foreign troops and the establishment of private armies. Each side, naturally, brought along its religion and its suppression of other religions: Catholic King Ferdinand banned and curtailed Calvinism and Lutheranism, while Protestant King Gustavus Adolphus intervened to protect them. Despite the fact that religion had become a secondary issue, the final years of the war (1635–1648) were the most violent, including destruction and looting of towns and decimation of the population: some cities lost one-third of their inhabitants over the thirty years of the crisis, and the overall population of the region dropped by seven or eight million. The ultimate resolution was the Peace of Westphalia in 1648, which basically reestablished the "each prince/each religion" principle of Augsburg— but only for Catholics, Lutherans, and Calvinists. Anabaptists and other sects (and all non-Christians) were still subjected to persecution and official disfavor.

Religious war arose in other Christian countries in this era. As mentioned, there were religious conflicts between (Protestant) Holland and (Catholic) Spain. There was also a civil war in England during the 1640s that brought a Protestant/ Puritan government to power. Dunn calls the English Puritan revolution "the last and grandest episode in Europe's age of religious wars,"[57] which Oliver Cromwell, head of republican England from 1643 to 1658, saw as a struggle of "godly men" to renew English society. Among the memorable achievements of the English religious war period were the execution (some say "martyrdom") of King Charles I and the invasion of (Catholic) Ireland, which still reverberates in ethnoreligious conflict in Northern Ireland today (see chapter 6).

THE TAIPING "REBELLION" IN CHINA

Religious wars have not been the sole province of Judeo-Christian religion, although many other examples, especially in the nineteenth and twentieth centuries, have taken at least some inspiration from Judeo-Christian sources. One case is the Chinese syncretistic and millenarian movement known as the Taiping Rebellion (1850–1864), which was responsible for twenty to thirty million deaths during its course. The Taiping movement (from the Chinese *Taiping tien-quo* for Heavenly Kingdom of Great Peace) began with the visions of one man, Hung (or Hong) Xiuquan (or Hsiu-chuan), whose career was typical of modern movement founders. During Hung's early life, Christian missionaries were active in China, which was coming increasingly under European domination. In factory towns, European traders and bureaucrats ran lucrative businesses, and the old and widely hated Ching or Qing dynasty, a regime of foreign Manchu invaders, had been unable to prevent European penetration or to command obedience among native Chinese.

In 1836, Hung made his first attempt at the all-important Chinese civil-service exam and failed it; however, while in the city of Canton, he received a Christian tract entitled "Good Words for Exhorting the Age." He later claimed not to have read it carefully at the time, but Spence argues that he would have noticed that his own surname (Hung, meaning "flood") occurred in the tract and that his personal name (Huo, meaning "fire") was also the middle syllable of the name for god, Ye-huo-hua.[58] In 1837, he tried and failed the test again and this time collapsed into a stupor, during which he had a dream or vision. In his vision he was on the verge of death when the forces of death cut him open and replaced his old organs with new ones; they also unrolled a scroll, which he read carefully. He then met his mother and father—not his biological parents but God and God's wife. His father told him how the "demon devils" had led people astray, and Hung offered to champion the battle against them. Armed with a divine sword and a seal, he fought the demons until he faced and defeated the king of the demons, Yan Luo. Hung dwelt then in heaven with his wife, the First Chief Moon, and had a son. However, God sent him back to earth, where the demons still reigned, but not before giving him a new name (*quan* or *chuan*, meaning "wholeness"), a divine title (Heavenly King, Lord of the Kingly Way), and two poems. One of the poems translates as follows:

> My hand grasps the killing power in heaven and earth;
> To behead the evil ones, spare the just, and ease the people's sorrow.
> My eyes roam north and west, beyond the rivers and mountains,
> My voice booms east and south, to the edge of the sun and moon.[59]

In combination with his interpretation of the Christian tract he received earlier
and other Christian sources, Hung discovered that he himself was the second son
of God, the younger brother of Jesus.

Hung set out to spread the word of his new revelation, that people must
resist the demon devils among them, whether they are evil-doers, Confucians, or
the ruling Qing dynasty. By 1846/47 he had amassed a sufficient following to
start his Bai Shangdi Hui, God-Worshipping Society, a small movement in rural
northeast China. As his doctrine began to take form, he specified six rules for his
believers: obey your parents, do not lust, do not kill, do not steal, do not engage
in witchcraft and magic, and do not gamble. The movement became increasingly anti-Confucian and anti-idolatry, even smashing a popular idol in 1847
(like the violent "holy men" of early Christianity; see chapter 5). The authorities, concerned about this dangerous new movement, accused Hung of teaching
false beliefs, desecrating shrines, and disobeying the law.

Hung and his band of converts circulated constantly through their local area,
converting more followers and strengthening the faith of a congregation that was
spread over about five hundred square miles. However, he encountered resistance
not only from the government but also from local bandit groups, and in 1850 he
began to talk about reconstituting the movement as an army, with all the trappings of a military organization at war, including "tactical planning, feeding, and
other logistical support [as well as] set piece attacks on prepared 'demon' positions."[60] Now the movement began not only to formalize but also to take on the
character that would shape it to its end. Males and females were segregated. They
started to stockpile not only food but also weapons and gunpowder. Fighting
units were assembled, with generals leading divisions of 13,155 troops organized
down to the four-man squad level. A communication system of signal flags was
created. Perhaps most important, Hung was finally elevated to Heavenly King,
began to wear imperial robes, and was instructed by Jesus himself to "fight for
Heaven" and to "show the world the true laws of God the Father and the Heavenly Elder Brother."[61] The original rules of conduct transformed into a martial
code:

1. Obey the [Ten] Commandments.
2. Keep the men's ranks separate from the women's ranks.
3. Do not disobey even the smallest regulations.
4. Act in the interests of all and in harmony; all of you obey the restraints
   imposed by your leaders.

5. Unite your wills and combine your strengths and never flee the field of combat.[62]

Accordingly, in March 1851, Hung decreed the arrival of the Taiping Heavenly Kingdom, with that year becoming Year One of the new age.

So began the "political" or military incarnation of Taiping. On September 25, 1851, it conquered its first major city, Yongan. However, this was not the heavenly kingdom promised in revelation, so they marched on. Heading generally northeast, they finally reached and conquered Nanjing in March 1853. Nanjing served as the capital of the new Heavenly Kingdom for eleven years, until it was at last defeated by the Chinese authorities, with European assistance. Within the city-kingdom, life as ordained by God and Hung was instituted. All land was divided among the people, one full share for each adult man and woman, one half-share for each child. Units of twenty-five families were organized under a corporal who saw to it that each family fulfilled its needs and that the surplus was sent to the public treasury. Opium smoking was outlawed, as were gambling, tobacco and wine, polygamy, slavery, and prostitution. Gender equality was established, with the abolition of female footbinding and the selection of women as administrators and army officers. However, homosexuality was punishable by death. Sabbath observance was mandatory, and young boys were commanded to attend church every day. Meanwhile, Taoist and Buddhist temples and statues were ransacked and ruined, and priests were defrocked or killed. Taiping was the mandatory religion of the kingdom.

Not all people within the city walls ever converted (or at least converted sincerely) to the new order, and much of the time, energy, and wealth of the kingdom was spent in defense—and in offense. The Taiping conducted an unsuccessful and exhausting campaign against the imperial city of Peking (Beijing) until the central government mobilized to suppress them. Hung increasingly withdrew into the spiritual side of his kingdom (which included sexual licentiousness, by some accounts) while his generals ran day-to-day affairs. By mid-1863, Taiping armies were being defeated repeatedly at great cost. Still Hung could not even conceive of failure; as he responded to one plea from a general:

I have received the sacred command of God, the sacred command of the Heavenly Brother Jesus, to come down into the world to become the only true Sovereign of the myriad countries under Heaven. Why should I fear of anything? . . . You say that there are no more troops; but my Heavenly soldiers are as limitless as water. Why should I fear the demon Zeng? You are afraid of death and so you may as well die.[63]

In April 1864, Hung fell ill and eventually announced that he was returning to heaven to be with his Father and Elder Brother. On June 1, he did. The city of Nanjing was conquered by the Chinese imperial army in July 1864, and the Heavenly Kingdom was vanquished.

ISLAM AND JIHAD

Christianity ultimately embraced war after it acquired the reigns of political power (and therefore the means and need to make war) in the fourth century. Islam was born with political power and thus was born embracing war. The difference, however, is historical, not theological.

Islam (from the Arabic root *slm* for "submission" or "peace," not pacifism but the tranquility that comes from submitting to God's will) grew out of the revelations of Muhammad, a businessman in the Arabian city of Mecca. Mecca had long been a prominent religious and pilgrimage site, with its Ka'aba full of gods and idols. Around his fortieth year, Muhammad began to receive messages from the god known as al-Lah, The God. These messages, which he continued to receive throughout his life, became the Qur'an, the "recitation." At first his immediate family and then gradually others accepted the new message, but its rejection of the additional gods of Arabia was a problem for traditional Meccans (and a threat to the lucrative pilgrimage trade). Under social, financial, and occasionally physical pressure from local authorities, Muhammad accepted an invitation to resettle in the city (or more accurately, the oasis) of Yathrib and act as administrator. He and approximately seventy families of followers made the journey to what would become known as Medinat-al-Nabi or "City of the Prophet" in 622, which is remembered as the *hijra* or "escape/flight" and Year One of the Muslim era.

As a sort of judge or arbitrator, Muhammad became a political figure, not merely a religious one: in him, "church" and "state" were joined. In possession of loyal believers and the apparatus of government, Muhammad was in a position to respond to force with force. At first this came in the form of more or less traditional Arab raids (*ghazu*), which his men conducted on Meccan caravans. In March 624, Muhammad himself led a body of some three hundred fifty raiders against a major caravan, which so infuriated the Meccans that they sent a much larger army to meet him. The two opponents faced off at Badr, where the smaller but more disciplined Muslim militia won and sent the Meccans on a panicked retreat. The battle of Badr was and is seen as a *furqan*, "a sign of salvation. God had separated the just from the unjust in the Muslim victory."[64]

During this early war period, the revelations naturally turned to the issue of war. In the Qur'an we find descriptions of how war ought to be fought, entirely in line with ancient Israelite practice of offering an enemy peace in exchange for submission; however, if the rival refused to capitulate, then war was not only necessary but also just. In a way, as noted in chapter 5, to reject Islamic superiority was to *persecute* Islam, which was intolerable. And while war is bad, persecution is worse:

> And fight in the way of Allah with those who fight with you, and do not exceed the limits, surely Allah does not love those who exceed the limits.
>
> And kill them wherever you find them, and drive them out from whence they drove you out, and persecution is severer than slaughter, and do not fight with them at the Sacred Mosque until they fight with you in it, but if they do fight you, then slay them; such is the recompense of the unbelievers.[65]

> Making war is commanded of you even if it is hated by you. You may hate something that is good for you, and you may love something that is bad for you. You do not know, but God knows!
>
> Making war [during a sacred period when warring had previously been forbidden] is a great [transgression], but turning people away from the path of God and denying Him is yet worse in the sight of God. *Fitna* [persecution] is worse than killing. They will not stop fighting you until they turn you away from your religion, if they can.[66]

> So when the sacred months have passed away, then slay the idolaters wherever you find them, and take them captive and besiege them and lie in wait for them in every ambush, then if they repent and keep up prayer and pay the poor-rate, leave their way free to them; surely Allah is Forgiving, Merciful.[67]

> O you who believe! fight those of the unbelievers who are near to you and let them find in you hardness; and know that Allah is with those who guard (against evil).[68]

> Surely Allah loves those who fight in His way in ranks as if they were a firm and compact wall.[69]

These injunctions, and the history that followed, have led many scholarly and popular observers to identify Islam as the very epitome of a "holy war" religion, expressed in the Arabic word *jihad*. Notwithstanding the fact that holy war was hardly invented by Islam, jihad is a complex concept. As Firestone reminds us, "The semantic meaning of the Arabic term *jihad* has no relation to holy war or even [to] war in general."[70] From the root *jhd*, strictly speaking it means "struggle" or "exertion" or "effort," and Muslim scholars have suggested several types of religious struggle, divided into two main categories, greater jihad and lesser jihad. The greater jihad consists of three struggles: jihad of the heart or moral reform of the self, jihad of the tongue or proclaiming God's word and working to spread it, and jihad of the hand or doing good works in accordance with God's will. Only the lesser jihad speaks of the jihad of the sword, or fighting the enemies of Islam. What all the forms of jihad share, Firestone opines, is "furthering or promoting God's kingdom on earth," and this can include of course "defending Islam and propagating the faith" as well as fighting "against groups of apostates rebelling against proper Islamic authority, dissenting groups denouncing legitimate Muslim leadership, highway robbers and other violent people, and deviant or un-Islamic leadership."[71]

Johnson notes that the Qur'an uses the word *jihad* and its variations thirty-six times but that when war is the subject, the Arabic word is *qital*, which means fighting more generally.[72] Armstrong adds that there are numerous Arabic words for violent struggle, including *harb* (conflict/strife or war), *sira'a* (combat), *ma'araka* (battle), and *qital*.[73] Nevertheless, Johnson concludes that in speaking of jihad, "they meant actual warfare and not simply missionary work or personal efforts at self-purification to resist the temptations offered by the territory of unbelief."[74] Or, as in many religions, they meant all these simultaneously. In other words, as Firestone concludes, while *jihad* can mean something akin to holy war, "it is impossible to equate *jihad* with holy war," as not all jihads are holy or war nor are all wars jihad.[75]

Whatever the semantic or scriptural origin, the history of Islam is certainly filled with war. After years of shifting fortunes, Mecca surrendered to Muhammad in 630. His death in 632 was followed immediately by the resumption of forcible efforts to convert Arabia and impose Muslim unity. Then, full of the kind of zeal that comes from unification, success, and profound faith—as in the Christian Crusades of the eleventh century, the Spanish wars against Islam of the fifteenth century, and even, in a more secular and nationalistic vein, the Napoleonic Wars of the nineteenth century—Islam turned outward and spread rapidly. Philip Hitti explains that "two columns were on the march: one toward the northeast and Iraq, then in Persian hands, and the other toward the northwest and Syria, then under Byzantine [Christian] rule."[76] By September 635, Damascus was added to the expanding religious empire of Islam; a year later, twenty-five thousand Arab fighters defeated twice as many Byzantine soldiers in Jordan, slaying almost the entire enemy force. In September 642, Alexandria, Egypt, was captured, and over the subsequent year Libya fell. Meanwhile, the eastern army pushed into Persia, with the final battle at Nehawand also coming in 642. Thus, within a decade of the Prophet's death, his religion ruled a vast territory from eastern North Africa to western Central Asia.

But the conquest was far from complete. By the 660s, Islam had a navy and was threatening Constantinople itself. By the 670s, Muslims were raiding deep into Central Asia, including the city of Bukhara. Kabul was reduced to a tribute-paying domain in 700. To the west, Muslims entered Europe by way of the strait of Gibraltar (an Arabic name derived from the commander of the invading force, Tariq, hence *Jabal Tariq* or "mountain of Tariq") in 711; they were only prevented from penetrating into central Europe by a Christian force of Franks in 732. Having reached its farthest extent in the west, future victories were to come in the east: defeat of a Chinese army at the Talus River in 751 gave Islam control of northwest India, from which Muslim domination of India spread until, several centuries later, the Mughal or Mogul Islamic Empire ruled most the subcontinent.

Finally, we should note that we cannot speak of "Islam" across history and geography as if it were a single unitary entity. The early Arab leadership of Islam passed over time to other groups, such as the Seljuks, Turks, Mongols, Persians, and others, each with its own culture and warrior ethos. It was the Turks, as we noted above in our discussion of the Crusades, who were the rising power in the eleventh century; the story of the Crusades could be, and probably should be, told from their perspective as well. It was the Ottoman Turks who ultimately destroyed the old Christian Byzantine Empire, conquering the city of Constantinople (or Byzantium) in 1453 and pressing on to the very gates of Vienna. In fact, Islam controlled southeastern Europe (Greece and the Balkans) into the 1800s, when a resurgent Europe "liberated" many of these lands that had been in Muslim hands for hundreds of years.

A Few Words on Terrorism

For many Westerners, Islam has become the epitome of holy war, although Hoffmann makes the pithy observation that the attempt to distinguish Judeo-Christianity from Islam on the subject, especially historically (e.g., "Judaism and Christianity *used* to be violent, Islam *still* is") is "a statement about the purchase of belief on ordinary lives in the modern era, not a statement about the nature of Christianity and Judaism."[77] That is to say, Judeo-Christianity is not so doctrinally or historically different on the matter from Islam; it simply does not take that doctrine as seriously at this moment in time. Be that as it may, even more, for many modern Westerners, Islamic "terrorism" is the epitome of holy war. This has led a great number of observers to conclude that there is something inherently and uniquely "terrorist" about Islam: Jerry Falwell went so far as to exclaim that Muhammad himself was a terrorist, setting the stage for the future of Islam.

Terrorism is indeed closely associated with religion in the late twentieth and early twenty-first centuries. According to Magnus Ranstorp, an expert on international terrorism, the number of fundamentalist religious movements of all types around the world tripled from the mid-1960s to the mid-1990s.[78] At the same time, the number of religiously inspired terrorist groups grew from zero to about one-quarter of all known terrorist organizations. In the period from 1970 to 1995, religious groups accounted for over half the total acts of world terrorism. However, terrorism is neither new nor exclusively related to religion, let alone Islam.

Terrorism has been defined in a number of ways, such as "the use of covert violence by a group for political ends,"[79] "politically motivated violence perpetrated against noncombatant targets by subnational groups or clandestine agents, usually intended to influence an audience,"[80] or "the unlawful use of force or violence against persons or property to intimidate or coerce a government, the civilian population, or any segment thereof, in furtherance of political or social objectives."[81] These definitions emphasize two points. First, terrorism is *political* in some sense; it involves a political cause or goal and some relation to extant political power, usually a subordinate relation. As Laqueur emphasizes, the context of terrorism is usually "tyranny" (real or perceived), and the terrorist views himself or herself as struggling against oppression. Sometimes the terrorist believes that there is already a war under way, in which the terrorist act is merely one battle. For instance, in the 1998 fatwa issued by Osama bin Laden against the United States in anticipation of the events of September 11, 2001, he wrote:

[F]or over seven years the United States has been occupying the lands of Islam in the holiest of places, the Arabian Peninsula, plundering its riches, dictating to its rulers, humiliating its people, terrorizing its neighbors, and turning its bases in the Peninsula into a spearhead through which to fight the neighboring Muslim peoples. . . .

All of these crimes and sins committed by the Americans are a clear declaration of war on God, his messenger, and Muslims. . . . On this basis, and in compliance with God's orders, we issue the following *fatwa* to all Muslims:

The ruling to kill the Americans and their allies—civilians and military—is an individual duty for every Muslim who can do it in any country in which it is possible to do it. . . .

We—with God's help—call on every Muslim who believes in God and wishes to be rewarded to comply with God's order to kill the Americans and plunder their money wherever and whenever they find it. We also call on Muslim ulema [followers], leaders, youths, and soldiers to launch the raid on Satan's US troops and the devil's supporters allying with them, and to displace those who are behind them so that they may learn a lesson.[82]

Second, as covert or illegal force, it implies some standard of judgment as to the legality or normality of such force; it might be better to think of terrorism as *illegitimate* force—which necessarily means illegitimate *from someone's perspective*. In a word, "terrorism" is not a fact or thing so much as "an interpretation of events and their presumed causes. And these interpretations are not unbiased attempts to depict truth but rather conscious efforts to manipulate perceptions to promote certain interests at the expense of others."[83] By the standards of those who apply the label "terrorism," the "terrorists" have violated the "rules of war" in their choice of weapons or targets or in their lack of legitimate leadership or motivation.

Despite the fact that terrorism does not obey the norms of war, it is essential to see it as a form or extension of war. In fact, in his major compilation of terrorist documents, Laqueur refers to such engagements as "small wars."[84] It might even be preferable to call them "wars of the weak," since, above all else, terrorism is a *tactic* that some actors adopt more often than others. Nonstate groups—ethnic, class, and of course religious—who do not possess engines of war are more likely to opt for the tactic of terrorism, which yields large results for small inputs (although many observers recognize a type of "state terrorism" in which regimes employ frightening violence on their own people, as in Stalin's Soviet Union, Mao's China, Pol Pot's Cambodia, and the "dirty war" in

Argentina). Then, if Clausewitz is correct that war is diplomacy in another form, then terrorism is diplomacy in yet another, and to its victims uglier, form.

Terrorism of some sort is not new: it has "cropped up since time immemorial, sometimes as a manifestation of religious protest, at still other times in the wake of political revolt and social uprisings."[85] It has also been practiced in the name of many causes—communist, fascist, anarchist, nationalist, and religious. The difference between religious and secular terrorism, according to Bruce Hoffman, is that for religious terrorists, "violence [is] first and foremost a sacramental act or divine duty executed in direct response to some theological demand or imperative."[86] Precisely because terrorism, entirely like holy war in general, is a divine command, an obligatory act, it is especially difficult to reason with, let alone to stop, a terrorist

One of the first recorded cases of religious terrorism was the *sicarii* movement in Jerusalem under Roman occupation. Named after the short sword or long knife that they used, practitioners would assassinate Roman officials or Jewish collaborators, ideally in a public place in daylight; their goal was not only to kill people but to strike fear in these enemies of traditional Judaism and to foment violence that might lead to resistance against and expulsion of the hated occupiers. The "Zealots" were another Jewish group dedicated to violence for religious/political purposes. The Assassins of the eleventh and twelfth century Muslim world were another extremist group who killed "prefects, governors, caliphs, and even Conrad of Montferrat, the Crusader King of Jerusalem."[87] They used secretive terrorist tactics precisely because the group "was too small to confront the enemy in open battle" and so "a planned, systematic, long-term campaign of terror carried out by a small, disciplined force could be a most effective political weapon."[88]

Modern terrorism really begins in the late 1700s and achieves its mature form in the 1800s as a distinctly Western and not particularly religious notion. As discussed in our chapter on persecution, "terror" first became an explicit concept and political tool during the French Revolution, when it was considered to be a rightful tactic against counterrevolutionaries and "enemies of the people" (see p. 193). It became an increasingly popular and common weapon in the nineteenth century, when political extremists used high-profile acts of violence to undermine the social systems that they so despised. Their targets were most often individual governmental leaders like US presidents Lincoln (1865), Garfield (1881), and McKinley (1901); Russian emperor Alexander II (1881); French president Marie François Carnot (1894); Italian king Umberto (1897);

and most fatefully, Austrian archduke Franz Ferdinand (1914). While many bomb throwers and assassins emerged, none voiced the mentality of the terrorist so emphatically as Nechayev, whose mid-nineteenth-century "Catechism of a Revolutionary" spoke the anger and intent of the terrorist: for the man of revolutionary violence, bent on taking down an entire social system, all ties to the social and moral order were broken, and his only knowledge and care was destruction. Everything and everyone else had no value, and all that stood in the way of the ultimate goal was criminal and immoral while he was above crime and morality.

Political extremists of all sorts absorbed the lesson of Nechayev. From the Bolsheviks, the Khmer Rouge, and the Shining Path to the the Red Brigade; from the the Tamil Tigers, the Irish Republican Army, and the Irgun to the Chechens, the Serbs, and the Croats. To the Ku Klux Klan and various "militia" organizations, terror campaigns inspired by what the Hindustan Socialist Republican Association in India enthusiastically called "the philosophy of the bomb" became all too familiar. Many, but by no means all, of these groups were driven by religion, but as Laqueur stresses, the key development of the mid–twentieth century was a shift in strategy from targeting individual politicians to targeting the general population and "nonpolitical" settings.

The most recent and for many observers the most incomprehensible and troubling development in the evolution of terrorism is the suicide terrorist, the person for whom, as Reuter titles his book on the subject, "my life is a weapon."[89] While this particular tactic was hardly invented by modern Islam (Reuter mentions Japanese kamikaze pilots as an earlier and non-Muslim example), it has certainly become associated with that religion and, unfortunately, a commonly employed tactic. In the current Islamic case, three notions have become entangled—homicide, suicide, and martyrdom. The Islamic suicide bomber typically speaks the language of martyrdom, but it is a different kind of martyrdom than that understood and practiced in the early stages of Islam or Christianity, and it reflects what Gaddis describes as "the transformation of martyrdom from commemoration of violence suffered to justification for violence inflicted."[90] This is why Fields in her study of martyrdom deprives suicide terrorism of the status of martyrdom and instead designates it as "suicide/homicide."[91] Whatever one may choose to call it, two things are true of it: it requires a commitment to the death of self and others that only a higher cause and a greater reward can inspire, and religion, while not the only possible source of this cause and reward, can provide a particularly exquisite source.

WAR IN HINDUISM

The Western monotheisms are not the only religions to cultivate a concept of religious war, although they have cultivated their own unique version of it. The Hindu notions of war in general and religious war in particular were inevitably shaped by its own religious worldview, especially the concept of dharma as well as the institution of caste, which classifies society into groups with distinct duties. Ancient Hinduism accordingly distinguished between *dharma yuddha* or good/righteous/orderly/legal (what we might call "just") war and *adharma yuddha* or *kuta yuddha*, unrighteous/bad/unjust war.

Ancient India was not a peaceful society, in its scriptures nor in its history. As Hume explains, the very earliest Hindu writings, the Vedas, "reflect a state of society which was in constant warfare, even down to the very end of the period. Sometimes those early Hindus were engaged in war among themselves; but more frequently they were at war with the dark-skinned aborigines, who gradually became subjugated."[92] A perusal of the *Rig Veda*, for instance, turns up many references to and praises of war:

> Strong in thy friendship, Indra, Lord of power and might, we have no fear.
> We glorify with praises thee, the never-conquered conqueror.
> The gifts of Indra from of old, his saving succours, never fail,
> When to the praise-singers he gives the boon of substance rich in kine.
> Crusher of forts, the young, the wise, of strength unmeasured, was he born
> Sustainer of each sacred rite, Indra, the Thunderer, much-extolled.[93]

> That man is lord of endless strength whom thou protectest in the fight,
> Agni, or urgest to the fray.
> Him, whosoever he may be, no man may vanquish, mighty One:
> Nay, very glorious power is his.
> May he who dwells with all mankind bear us with war-steeds through the
> fight,
> And with the singers win the spoil.[94]

> Strong let your weapons be to drive away your foes, firm for resistance let
> them be.
> Yea, passing glorious must be your warrior might, not as a guileful
> mortal's strength.
> When what is strong ye overthrow, and whirl about each ponderous thing,
> Heroes, your course is through the forest trees of earth, and through the
> fissures of the rocks.

> Consumers of your foes, no enemy of yours is found in heaven or on the
>   earth:
> Ye Rudras, may the strength, held in this bond, be yours, to bid defiance
>   even now.
> They make the mountains rock and reel, they rend the forest-kings apart.
> onward, ye Maruts, drive, like creatures drunk with wine, ye, Gods with
>   all your company.[95]

> Invincible through Fervor, those whom Fervor hath advanced to heaven,
> Who showed great Fervor in their lives,—even to those let him depart.
> The heroes who contend in war and boldly cast their lives away,
> Or who give guerdon [*sic*] thousandfold,—even to those let him depart.[96]

Other sections of the text give details of warfare, ask the gods for aid in war, and even speak of and to weapons "as if they were personal assisting deities."[97]

Equally interesting, the enemies of the ancient Hindu warriors were often portrayed in pejorative religious terms, as men who lacked religion and piety. Among the condescending names applied to them were "'prayerless' (*a-brahman*), 'godless' (*a-deva*), 'inferior' (*adhara*), 'inhuman' (*a-manusa*), . . . 'opposed to religious rites' (*apa-vrata*), . . . 'unbelieving' (*a-sraddha*), 'not observing religious rites' (*a-vrata*), 'not offering sacrifices' (*a-yajna*), 'impious' (*a-yajyu*), 'easy to be slain' (*su-hana*), 'wicked' (*vrjina*), 'deceitful' (*mayavan*)."[98] Such adversaries were perceived as destroyers of the dharma, violators of the very order of things and therefore fit for fighting. Despite this, Subedi makes explicit that the Hindu concept of dharma yuddha differs from the Christian concept of just war in the critical sense that "there is no justification for a war against foreigners or people of other faiths merely on the grounds of religion. . . . The Hindu concept of just war was a war fought in accordance with the laws of war to uphold dharma and justice, rather than a war waged to spread the Hindu religion or to contain the spread of another religion."[99]

The two keys to dharma yuddha, other than the idea of dharma itself (fighting for order over disorder), were the restriction of war making to a particular group or caste of warriors for whom war was their dharma and the rules or standards by which those wars were to be fought. The first issue relates to the Hindu institution of caste: each caste was and is an "occupational" group, even if that occupation was determined more by spiritual condition (including past lives and accumulated karma) than by education or wealth. Second only to the priestly caste or brahmans, the kshatriyas were the appointed warriors of Hinduism. The development of a warrior caste, a group whose duty (kshatram dharma) was to kill and be killed, guaranteed that there would always be a corps prepared for war but also "prevented the militant attitude from spreading to other communities and kept the whole social structure unaffected by actual wars and war institutions."[100] For kshatriyas, war was a virtual religious duty; other castes had other duties in an overarching spiritual division of labor.

The righteousness of kshatriya war is most dramatically illustrated in the Bhagavad Gita, one part of a much larger epic known as the Mahabharata or "Great India" tale, which is an extended ode to war, like the Greek Iliad, in this case the struggle between the Kauravas and the Pandavas, both descended from the great king Bharata. In the Bhagavad Gita (literally, "Song of the Lord"), the soldier named Arjuna gazes onto the battlefield in anticipation of battle and sees friends and kinsmen arrayed against him. He realizes that he cannot fight and kill these men and throws down his weapons in despair. His chariot driver, the god Krishna in disguise, takes the opportunity to instruct him on the proper attitude toward war based on a proper understanding of his dharma and of the nature of existence. Each person, Krishna teaches, has a duty based on his or her karma and caste. To fulfill this duty is good, to resist it bad. A kshatriya's duty is to make war and to kill, and since it is his dharma, it cannot be evil or immoral. What would be evil and immoral would be not to kill if one is a kshatriya. In fact, in a way, a kshatriya is not only doing himself a favor to bravely fight and kill; he is doing his enemy a favor too, since he is giving his enemy a chance to fulfill his dharma by fighting and killing and, if necessary, dying. At a more spiritual level, Krishna teaches Arjuna that a man cannot really harm another man by destroying his body anyhow, since the real and essential part of a human is not his body.

> I say to thee weapons reach not the Life;
> Flame burns it not, waters cannot overwhelm,
> Nor dry winds wither it. Impenetrable,
> Unentered, unassailed, unharmed, untouched,
> Immortal, all-arriving, stable, sure,
> Invisible, ineffable, by word
> And thought uncompassed, ever all itself,
> Thus is the Soul declared! How wilt thou, then,—
> Knowing it so,—grieve when thou shouldst not grieve?
> How, if thou hearest that the man new-dead
> Is, like the man new-born, still living man—

One same, existent Spirit—wilt thou weep?
The end of birth is death; the end of death
Is birth: this is ordained! and mournest thou,
Chief of the stalwart arm! for what befalls
Which could not otherwise befall? The birth
Of living things comes unperceived; the death
Comes unperceived; between them, beings perceive:
What is there sorrowful herein, dear Prince?[101]

In other words, it is right to do your religious duty, including killing, and no real harm is done to those who are killed, since a soldier can kill only a body, not a spirit. After Krishna displays his full divine splendor to Arjuna, the formerly reluctant warrior goes into battle assured that, live or die, kill or be killed, all is well.

War, then, was entirely proper and moral if it was fought by the right combatants (kshatriyas) for the right cause (dharma). However, the other key to Hindu war was the manner in which the war was prosecuted. Ancient scriptures, subsequent interpreters and commentators, and the centrally important Laws of Manu established the standards of good war. "War is the eternal law of kings," says the Laws of Manu, and a king can and must fight to defend his domain, his honor, and his religion.[102] The king, as chief kshatriya, may besiege, despoil, infiltrate, and otherwise harass and undermine his enemy. However, certain rules must be observed. First, force (*danda*) must be a last resort, after reconciliation (*sama*), appeasement with gifts (*dana*), and threats (*bheda*) have failed. If it is to be war, then a formal statement of the intention to go to war must be issued, and a formal declaration of war must precede all hostilities; Subedi writes that, even if the armies were in the field, combat should not start without a mutual declaration of war.[103] And once hostilities began, the warriors were prohibited from using weapons that caused undue suffering or destruction and were charged to protect innocents, women, and property from the carnage. For instance, poisoned or flaming arrows were banned, as was fighting from a chariot or horse against a soldier on foot. Enemies who were asleep or naked or disarmed or wounded or in retreat, or merely whose weapons were broken, were not to be attacked. In a word, the ideal of Hindu war was "fairness," that is, equality between the combatants: "The essence of the Hindu laws of war was to prohibit inequality in fighting and to protect those who exhibit helplessness."[104] Of course, that meant in practice often giving up an advantage over an enemy, but, in theory at least, the point was not to win at all cost but to win "well," which meant only defeating a foe who was equal to oneself in strength and readiness. While, no doubt, these rules were violated on the battlefield sometimes, their very existence indicates that dharma yuddha was a war that was won not only by the right person for the right cause but as a result of right effort or conduct.

"FIGHTING ORDERS": SAINTLY SOLDIERS

The fallacy that religion and war are incompatible has been sufficiently exposed. It might still be imagined that religious specialists themselves—priests, monks, ascetics, and so on—are agents of peace and certainly never directly involved in aggression, that is, active combatants. On the contrary, history provides many examples of religious officiates who themselves partake in war and are even its primary fighting force.

Warrior ascetics could be found in Hinduism from at least the 1500s (and possibly much earlier) and as late as the 1700s, after Europeans arrived. Lorenzen identified a number of ascetic warriors in India, including "the Dasnami *naga*s, the Dadu *panthi nagas,* the Madari *fakirs* of the Sannyasi Rebellion, . . . and certain groups of Vaisnava *bairagis.* Some more problematical cases include various millenarian and social rebellion movements of a religious character such as the poorly documented rebellion of the Satnamis of the Narnaul region in 1657."[105] Significantly, he maintained that most of or all these sects originated after the Islamic conquest of India as religious, political, and economic protest movements. These armed sects fought against Muslim forces as well as against each other, as when the "near-naked Jogis" of the Nath or Kanhata sect clashed against the Sannyasis in 1567.

One of the more prominent parties in these religious struggles was the Dasnami nagas (*naga* means "naked," and as ascetics they did travel and fight naked), which consisted of six "regiments" or akharas that "were created to defend local interests such as the lands and treasure of temples and monasteries."[106] By 1664 one of these regiments, the Nirvanis, met the sultan's army in battle. Another important group was the followers of Dadu, a sixteenth-century laborer and religious prophet who taught not only the message of a single universal god but also of armed conflict for religion. In the seventeenth century, Dadu's panthi nagas had become part of the Hindu military. Lorenzen makes the salient point, though, that as "the need for warrior ascetics to protect the extensive lands and wealth of temples and monasteries increased, [so] did the temptation for them to become simple mercenary soldiers and independent political adventurers."[107] In other words, the sometimes lofty religious ideals of warrior monks occasionally degenerated into ordinary conquest and domination, as happened with the leader named Anupgiri who started his career as a Dasnami naga in the late 1700s and ended as the temporal ruler of a large area around Benares.

Another classic example of a warrior elite occurs in the Sikh religion. Sikhism (from the Hindi word for "disciple"), an initially peaceful system, came to revere war for the faith. Emerging amidst the struggle in northern India between Hindus and Muslims in the sixteenth century, its first guru, Nanak, offered a message that integrated the best aspects of both. However, initially the Muslim rulers and subsequently the Hindu authorities opposed and suppressed the religion, martyring the guru Arjan in 1606. After that event, the Sikh community or *panth* "became increasingly set on a policy of armed confrontation with the imperial Muslim rulers."[108] This process culminated in 1699 when the last human guru, Gobind Singh, inaugurated a military corps for Sikhism, the Khalsa or "company of the pure." As a contemporary Sikh source understands it:

> Readiness for the supreme sacrifice or of offering one's head on the palm of one's hand to the Guru is an essential condition laid down by the Gurus for becoming a Khalsa Sikh. Seeking death, not for personal glory, winning reward or going to heaven, but for the purpose of protecting the weak and the oppressed is what made the Khalsa brave and invincible. This has become a traditional reputation of the Khalsa. Right from the times of the Gurus till the last India-Pakistan conflict (1971), the Sikhs have demonstrated that death in the service of truth, justice and country, is part of their character and their glorious tradition. They do not seek martyrdom, they attain it. Dying is the privilege of heroes. It should, however, be for an approved or noble cause.[109]

Khalsas fought grimly against both Muslim and Hindu enemies but were slaughtered in 1746 and 1762 in the Lesser and Greater Holocausts, respectively.

Most Sikhs, of course, do not belong to the Khalsa, but the unit came to stand as the guardians and champions of the panth. Under British colonial rule, the Khalsa were persecuted and suppressed and their control over Sikh property like temples curtailed. But in 1920 a kind of revival began that, "in conscious imitation of the heroic days of the eighteenth century," established *jathas* or militarized squads of Sikh volunteers who called themselves Akali Dal or "Army of

Immortals."[110] The Akali Dal not only fought for authority over their sacred sites but in 1946 called for the creation of a Sikh state in the north Indian region of Punjab that was to be named Khalistan. Much of the tension and violence in present-day Punjab and Kashmir is by and about Sikhism and Khalistan.

Another surprising context for warrior priests has been in Buddhism, which is popularly regarded as a preeminent religion of peace. However, Buddhist monks took an active role in political and military affairs during Japan's medieval period, which saw the rise of companies of fighting Buddhist monks (*sohei* or "priest warriors"). Wars between monks and monasteries broke out in the tenth century, at which time the temple of Enryakuji established the first standing army of monks in the country. Trained in the use of bow and arrow, dagger, *naginata* (a type of halberd), and *tetsubo* or iron staff or club, sohei wore Buddhist robes into battle, including the Battle of Uji (1180), the Nanboku-cho wars of the 1200s and 1300s, and the Onin War starting in 1467. Perhaps the greatest of these Buddhist armies was the Ikko-Ikki (*Ikko* meaning "single-minded" or "devoted" and *Ikki* meaning "league" or "mob"), which conquered an area around Kyoto in the 1500s. "With their belief in a paradise waiting for them, the warrior monks of the Ikko-Ikki were fearless and eager warriors proving very useful to whichever side they were aiding at the time. In battle they would often use mass chanting (*nembutsu*) to strike fear into their enemies and improve their own morale."[111] Nevertheless, the Ikko-Ikki monks were defeated, and twenty thousand died defending their fortresses at Nagashima and Ishiyama Honganji in 1574.

Beyond the actual monks in arms, religion helped fashion the warrior ethos of the samurai in Japan. Aho argues that the shogun Minamoto Yoritomo in the second half of the twelfth century "ingeniously welded together the Buddhist notion of release from the eternal wheel of reincarnation with the dirty work common to soldiering."[112] Gradually, the warrior code of *bushido*, the "way of the warrior," formed, turning war into a kind of "spiritual practice" embodying all that is useful for a soldier—or even more so, for his superiors—including "loyalty to one's master, simplicity, austerity, and courage."[113] One of the essential Buddhist values that underlies the bushido code is impermanence, that nothing, including life, lasts long. From this emerged the notion that death can and should be beautiful. This sensibility is perhaps best expressed in the eighteenth-century document *Hagakure*, composed by the samurai priest Jocho Yamamoto. In Tsunetomo's reading of *Hagakure*, "The Way of the Samurai is found in death. When it comes to either/or, there is only the quick choice of death. It is not particularly difficult. Be determined and advance."[114] In fact, suggesting that sol-diering is a kind of asceticism or death-in-life, he continues: "If by setting one's heart right every morning and evening, one is able to live as though his body were already dead, he gains freedom in the Way."[115] In order to accomplish this,

> meditation on inevitable death should be performed daily. Every day when one's body and mind are at peace, one should meditate upon being ripped apart by arrows, rifles, spears and swords, being carried away by surging waves, being thrown into the midst of a great fire, being struck by lightning, being shaken to death by a great earthquake, falling from thousand-foot cliffs, dying of disease or committing *seppuku* at the death of one's master. And every day without fail one should consider himself as dead.[116]

The reference to seppuku, better known in the West as *hara-kiri* or suicide by self-impalement, reminds us also that the samurai had always to be ready to kill himself for the love of his master and that there was an elaborate, beautiful, and completely authorized process for doing so.

Finally, the warrior monk tradition has a place in Christianity as well. As Aho stresses, knights, from Frankish times on, were not only commissioned but also *ordained* and thus constituted an *ordo*, "a division of society established by God according to His divine plan."[117] The investiture of a knight was even referred to as an "eighth sacrament" and included such ritual acts as confession, purification, prayer by a priest, sermons, mass, and the anointing of the knight's weapons. The great era of the "knight-as-minister" was the period of the Cru-sades, when not merely armies but holy pilgrims marched into heathen lands (whether far away or in the heart of Europe). Pope Gregory VII formally author-ized the notion of *militia Christi* or "army of Christ" shortly prior to the First Crusade, and the Crusaders rode as bearers of the cross.

One of the most famous and controversial of the holy warriors was the order of the Knights Templars, founded around 1118 and disbanded in 1312 and sub-jected to an Inquisition in which its leader, Jacques Demolay, was burned at the stake. Simmons writes that the original function of the Templars "was to pro-tect pilgrims on the roads of the Holy Land"[118] but that they quickly grew into a large, rich, and powerful organization that was suspected, rightly or wrongly, of heresy and sinful behavior.

The Order of Saint John, also known as the Knights Hospitallers, was founded in the very earliest years of the Crusades. Its founder, Blessed Gerard, transformed a guest house in Jerusalem into a hospital for injured Crusaders and other Westerners who followed them. The Hospitallers eventually adopted the lifestyle of monks, with vows of poverty, chastity, and obedience, monkish clothing, and formal recognition of the pope in 1113. Many other knightly orders appeared within Christendom, such as the Knights of Malta and the Teutonic Knights. Article Three in the Constitution of the Teutonic Knights makes clear the order's religious identity and mission:

> This order, signifying both the heavenly and the earthly knighthood, is the foremost for it has promised to avenge the dishonoring of God and His Cross and to fight so that the Holy Land, which the infidels subjected to their rule, shall belong to the Christians. St. John also saw a new knighthood coming down out of heaven. This vision signifies to us that the Church now shall have knights sworn to drive out the enemies of the Church by force.[119]

THE MYTHOLOGY OF WAR

Concentrating on the means and the motives of war, as most analyses have, overlooks an important ingredient—its mythology. As James Hillman says in his *A Terrible Love of War*,

> to understand war we have to get at its myths, recognize that war is a mythical happening, that those in the midst of it are removed to a mythical state of being, that their return from it seems rationally inexplicable, and the love of war tells of a love of the gods, the gods of war.[120]

By *myth* here we do not mean (necessarily) false stories or even always religious stories. We do, however, mean *stories*—central stories, founding stories, orienting stories, stories of what Eliade called "paradigmatic" acts, the ones that give life its shape and its obligation by giving it its original form. (This is, consequently, why many myths are "origin" stories.)

One of the perennial debates in the scholarship on war is the question of its precise source or "cause." Some observers have sought the source of war in human nature itself: Freud, for example, theorized that humans simply have a destructive or death-seeking instinct, and many ethologists (students of animal behavior) and naturalists like Konrad Lorenz and Irenaus Eibl-Eibesfeld also posited some natural (though malleable) aggressive tendencies in humans and other species. The psychological approach to war emphasizes processes like displaced aggression, personality types, and child development and child-rearing practices (that is, the learning of violence). Social/cultural theories stress the values and institutions of a society, including inequality, gender relations, political power, and the existence of military institutions. The materialist perspective favors "practical" and environmental factors that lead to competition and hostility, including land shortages, nutritional challenges, and population pressure; as one arch materialist, Marvin Harris, explains it, war is an evolutionary adaptation that "was selected for culturally among bands and villages because it enhanced the well-being and survivability of individuals and groups."[121]

We are not going to choose between these theoretical stances, because there is no need to choose between them: each of them contributes a piece to the puzzle of war and none of them holds the only piece. Even more, collectively they do not hold all the pieces, since they ignore the mythical quality of war. They all, especially the materialist view, exaggerate the "rational" or "interest" aspect of such conflict and undervalue the "meaningful" or "symbolic" aspect. In Robert Kaplan's words, human warfare (and other violence as well) is "far too intense and varied to be contained by the narrow strictures of rational self-interest."[122] A full reckoning of war—and its relationship to religion—must not "ignore the intoxicating power of the unreasonable."[123]

The precedent for this insight is strong. Over fifty years ago, Ernst Cassirer revealed that humans do not live in bare, immediate, factual reality; rather, our experience is necessarily mediated by symbols:

> Man lives in a symbolic universe. Language, myth, art, and religion are parts of this universe. . . . No longer can man confront reality immediately; he cannot see it, as it were, face to face. Physical reality seems to recede in proportion as man's symbolic activity advances. Instead of dealing with the things themselves man is in a sense constantly conversing with himself. . . . His situation is the same in the theoretical as in the practical sphere. Even here man does not live in a world of hard facts, or according to his immediate needs and desires.[124]

Myths are the "narrative" symbols (the stories) in this symbolic complex. As narratives, they make certain truth claims about how things are and how things began, but the "truth" of myth is less important that the *drama* of it. "The world of myth is a dramatic world—a world of actions, of forces, of conflicting powers. In every phenomenon of nature it sees the collision of these powers. Mythical perception is always impregnated with these emotional qualities."[125] In a word, myths give us not truth but pattern, precedent, and meaning.

And war, as a mythical enterprise, is also a force that gives us meaning. As Hedges warns in his book by that very title, "Even with its destruction and carnage [war] can give us what we long for in life. It can give us purpose, meaning, a reason for living. Only when we are in the midst of conflict does the shallowness and vapidness of much of our lives become apparent."[126] War is, unfortunately, one source of that transcendent experience, that oceanic feeling, that hyperreality that is associated with art and religion. Hillman likens it to the "sublime," to beauty (as the Japanese bushido code did); such violent extremity is less like "problem solving" and more like "aesthetic appreciation."[127] He quotes Madris Eksteins who wrote of World War I: "If at its start the war was synonymous for many Germans with beauty, its ever-increasing fury was regarded as merely an intensification of its aesthetic meaning."[128] Kaplan calls war, not favorably, a "raw, even delusional passion,"[129] an upswelling of "romantic and heroic impulses,"[130] and cites Ralph Peters's phrase "euphoria of hatred." It is highly significant that this elevated experience is routinely evoked by great exertion or pain, such as discussed in earlier chapters. This is why Hillman opines that asceticism and self-injury, like war, "are also styles of belligerency. One is still at war with the world, the flesh, and the devil, projected, often too easily, upon other peoples, nations, religions, and even barely differing religious sects."[131]

There are clearly literal myths of war, including gods of war and tales of their warlike deeds. However, Lawrence LeShan goes further to insist that war *is* a mythology or a "mythic reality." In his *The Psychology of War*, from which Hedges admittedly draws much of this inspiration, LeShan distinguishes "sensory reality," the everyday perceptions and judgments that humans make, from "mythic reality," which is an entirely and disturbingly different way of perceiving the world. He and Hedges are not talking about the soldiers themselves, for whom sheer survival is the main focus, but instead about the society at war. Still, the qualities of the war myth will sound familiar to us:

- In wartime, group boundaries are tight and rigid; there is a definite Us and Them. Equally, good and evil are sharply assigned—We are good, They are evil.
- Wartime is unlike any other time. Everything is at stake now.
- We are not alone in war. God or history is with us (since we are right).

- The time after the war will be different—either much better or much worse, depending on our success or failure.
- In wartime, everything becomes focused and black-and-white. There is only one problem and only one solution.
- In wartime, Our actions—including our violent actions—flow from self-defense or goodwill or justice or morality, while Their actions flow from a power wish or a simple destruction wish (i.e., Baumeister's "myth of pure evil").
- Therefore, the harm We do is "good" (or at least necessary and tolerable) while the harm They do is "evil."
- Because They are evil, they lie and cannot be trusted, so there is no point in dialogue and negotiation. We, of course, tell the truth.[132]

As Hedges summarizes the position, "The myth of war creates a new, artificial reality. Moral precepts—ones we have spent a lifetime honoring—are jettisoned. We accept, if not condone, the maiming and killing of others as the regrettable cost of war. We operate under a new moral code."[133]

Hedges is correct, except for the fact, as we saw above in such cases as the Bhagavad Gita's warrant for war, that maiming and killing are often not seen as regrettable at all but as "natural" or even virtuous. In fact, what our discussion in this chapter has illustrated is that war does not instigate a "new moral code" but rather activates the specific moral code of war, often if not usually encoded in religion. Religion can provide the "rules and conditions" for war—the motivation, the means, and the mythology. Hedges goes so far as to suggest that war is not possible without belief, whether that belief is in the group or in the god. "When you stop believing"—that is, stop accepting the myth of war—"you stop going to war."[134]

The relationship and even similarity between war and religion is quite tangible. However, James Aho, writing a decade before LeShan and two decades before Hedges, finds that there is not one mythology of war but two, both shaped by the religion of the society; in fact, he calls them, in his title and in his argument, "religious mythologies" of war. Issues about motives and methods he calls "operational," although even these are not immune to mythical influence. But a society's ideas about "what kind of reality war represents," "why there are wars," "what evil is and how it is caused," and "how man's suffering can be redeemed" are inherently mythological.

All war mythology systems offer answers to these questions, but Aho sees two major types of mythological systems, which he calls immanentist-cosmological and transcendent-historical. In immanentist-cosmological mythology, "Killing and dying in war are glorified as absolute ends."[135] Of course, victory is preferable to defeat, but victory is not the highest value: how one fights, and *that one is fighting at all*, are the point. War is, he concludes, "an end in itself."[136] Such societies, including the Hindu/Aryan and the Greco-Roman, "view the struggle, life-risking agony, as sanctifying. In the very pathos of uncertainty and physical pain, ultimate value was created."[137] If the *process* of war is more important than the *outcome*, then the key to immanentist-cosmological warfare is in its "form": war is more "formal," like a game—or a ritual. This is why the "rules" of immanentist-cosmological war are so crucial: there are correct times and places for war, correct weapons, correct tactics, and other "formalities" that must be observed. Such warfare, Aho writes, "should be pursued 'religiously,'" and "intricate ritual proscriptions are placed around all aspects of military conduct from the initiation of hostilities to the treatment of prisoners."[138] Immanentist-cosmological warriors will go so far as to engage in all sorts of "impractical" gestures as "lavishly embellished costumes" and weapons "that may actually impede their offensive capacity."[139] To win a war but violate these standards of war is to win nothing.

Aho presents several examples of immanentist-cosmological warfare, but the first and most extraordinary is ancient Aztec war, known as *xochiyaoyotl* or literally "flowery war." In xochiyaoyotl, elaborate procedures for declaring war had to be observed, such as marking the enemy ruler's arm with white chalk symbolizing death and decorating him with a feathered headdress. Priests and astrologers would then set a date for battle, on which the opposing armies would arrive at an altar (*yaotlalli*) dressed highly impractically but sumptuously in "a sleeveless jacket worn under a cotton frock (*ichhuipilli*), which was adorned with splendid quetzal feathers and jewels."[140] Shell-horns and drums, played by priests, signaled the start of combat, which consisted of a series of individual contests. Finally, as our description of Aztec sacrifice (chapter 3) indicates, "the object of the flowery war is not to slay the enemy, but to seize him alive so that his precious tuna flower, his heart, can be fed later to the gods."[141]

In a word (a word that Aho uses), immanentist-cosmological war is like *play*— not in the sense that it is flippant but in the sense that it is a self-contained, formalized ritual action. Perhaps it would be better to say that it is "a play" in which soldiers are actors portraying a role, fulfilling their duty, playing their part. For instance, in Hindu/Aryan war, "the violent contest, properly viewed, is a form of play to be neither rebuked nor avoided, but to be joyfully and un-self-consciously entered as one might a game or dance."[142] This is not to claim that every war or every soldier achieved this ideal, but it was the ideal expressed in such stories as Arjuna's battlefield crisis.

Finally, what the immanentist-cosmological warrior has to gain is greater than military victory; it is honor, glory, manhood itself, and perhaps "salvation," for example the automatic admission into paradise (which was often viewed not as peace but as eternal war, a perpetual opportunity to play one's part and prove one's mettle). So, maybe paradoxically, this style of war did not necessarily involve the same degree of slaughter as the other style: since exterminating the enemy was really not the goal, and since that enemy was recognized as playing *his* role in a mythical drama, then the warrior was able "to recognize himself in the enemy and the enemy in himself" and "to deal with him within the limits of ritual propriety."[143] Again, this does not mean that there was no death and suffering. It does, however, mean that there was not an absolute stigmatizing of the enemy as evil incarnate who had to be eradicated utterly and at any cost.

This attitude changes in transcendent-historical war, which is informed by a different mythology. In this mythology, war is not play but work, and it is not an end in itself (like winning a game) but a means to an end. Therefore, the outcome is more important than the process: victory is the point, in whatever way it can be achieved. Thus, there are fewer limitations on the weapons and tactics of war—and fewer and fewer as time passes. There may not be formal declarations of war or agreed-upon dates; the enemy is attacked wherever he is found, including by stealth and deception. Warfare is "pursued 'scientifically,' i.e., on an exclusively utilitarian . . . basis"[144]—perhaps causing materialists and scholars of modern war to overemphasize these qualities.

Because "success" is the only concern, extraneous and wasteful elements like colorful costumes, ritual weapons, music, and other flourishes are dispensed with; these playful items are not only useless but may be positive hindrances to victory, like announcing one's presence to the enemy or limiting one's movement in combat. The soldier only carries the necessities. Likewise, because victory and not "honor" in the traditional sense is the goal, injury and death are not welcomed as eagerly and may even be "considered liabilities to be avoided if at all possible."[145]

If Aho is correct, the term *holy war* only applies to the transcendent-historical war mythology. In the immanentist-cosmological worldview, war may be ordained by the gods or in the very fabric of the cosmos (e.g., dharma), but there is precisely for this reason generally no expectation of a final and total victory over the enemy; rather, the cosmic game will continue forever. In the transcendent-historical worldview, there is such an idea and expectation of absolute defeat of the enemy, who is further demonized as the absolute enemy. In its most common, if not logically necessary, form of monotheism, the transcendent-historical war "is conducted in God's behalf, by a specifically delegated people, a faithful 'remnant,' to punish the sinful—heretics, blasphemers, and apostates—thus restoring God's kingship on earth."[146] The purpose and ideology of this type of war is not honor or glory but *justice*, which inevitably paints the adversary not as another party also seeking honor and glory but as the agents of injustice. Dangerously, "Rage often accompanies the frustration of man's sense of justice,"[147] so agitated anger rather than a playful sense of duty (or a dutiful sense of play) is a characteristic of transcendent-historical war. As Aho puts it, "the ferocity of the violence in the war must reflect the enormity of the crime against God and man."[148] This ferocity shows a tendency to deny any similarity, any kinship, any common humanity between Us and Them:

> The enraged revolt against injustice blinds the victim (now become the executioner) to everything but white (us) and black (them). "We are at one neither in our thoughts nor in our commands, understandings, nor beliefs, deeds, consciences, nor souls," says Ahura Mazda, the Zoroastrian god of light, in comparing himself to his antagonist Angra Mainyu.[149]

As we will see in the concluding chapter, the possibility of peace depends on the achievement of some sense of commonality between belligerents. We have already attested to the fact that "self-righteous rage, rage that transfers all evil to the enemy 'out there,' subjectively inducing a certainty of soul, thought, and intention, as emotionally satisfying as it might be, can be an instrument of the most horrible crimes"—an issue to which we turn next.[150]

CHAPTER 8

HOMICIDE AND ABUSE

F rom a certain serious perspective, all the examples discussed up to this point could be regarded as abuse and/or crime, and more than a few could be labeled murder or even mass murder. When a man cuts a boy's penis and draws blood, that might well be seen as abusive. When a man scratches and cuts a boy's skin until it bleeds and forces the boy to vomit, that could seem abusive. When a person starves himself or herself, flagellates himself or herself, pierces his or her body, or stands until his or her legs are swollen and misshapen, that appears to be self-abusive. When a person kills an animal for its blood, that would qualify by some standards as criminal animal cruelty. And when a group or institution or government tortures or burns or bombs or hangs or shoots or removes the hearts of human beings, it would not be difficult to find a justice system that condemns such behavior as homicide. Yet, such designations and condemnations hardly seem to stop these actions. In fact, they seldom seem to be applied to these actions at all.

In this final discussion of religious violence, we want to examine religious "crime," in particular violent crimes like murder and physical abuse. One obvious challenge to discussing religious crime, to which we will return shortly, is that it is problematic to determine what is "crime" in matters of religion and what is not. It is equally problematic to determine what is "religious" in matters of crime and what is not. If, for instance, we were to define religious crime as any crime committed by a religious person, then almost all crimes would be religious crimes, since almost all people are religious people. That would be an extremely inclusive approach—too much so. It would fail to distinguish between crimes committed by religious persons and "religious crimes" in any important sense.

Also, all crimes are abusive in some manner or another: breaking-and-entering abuses the person who loses property, but not all abuses are crime. *Crime* and specific legal terms like *homicide* or *abuse* refer to certain kinds of abusive or violent acts and not others—and their referents change over time and across cultures. And of course, not all crimes are violent crimes. So, we will focus here on a limited range of "criminal" behaviors, namely, *violent* ones that result in grievous physical or psychological injury or death. Therefore, we will exclude crimes that are not violent in an immediate sense (although property or financial crimes are significantly more prevalent and often as devastating for victims). And we will not consider crimes in which religion is only tangential. Rather, religion must be central to the violent crime for it to be "religious violent crime" (see below).

Let us remind ourselves one final time that every single type of religious crime has its nonreligious counterpart. There is religious murder and there is secular murder. There is religious assault and there is secular assault. There is religious sexual abuse and there is secular sexual abuse. There is religious neglect and there is secular neglect. We are not arguing that religion causes violent crime; we *are* arguing that religion does not altogether prevent it and that, instead, religion often provides not only a basis but also a *reason* and *justification* for such violence. This will surprise and disturb some people: aren't religious people supposed to be "better" people, more "moral" people? Not only is there no evidence for any such claim, not only is there evidence quite to the contrary, but, as we have seen, religion often supplies not just a legitimation but also the best possible legitimation for violence, including what we would call *violent crime.*

WHEN IS RELIGIOUS CRIME "RELIGIOUS" AND "CRIME"?

The question of religious crime raises the more basic question of crime itself. On the surface, the question "What is crime?" might sound like a frivolous one: surely everyone knows what it is. In actuality, nothing could be further from the truth. Not only is crime not an absolute, cross-cultural concept, but it changes over time within any particular society. For instance, when I was young, parents and even teachers and school administrators had the right—a right that they exercised—to apply corporal punishment to children: spanking, sometimes with a heavy wooden board, was normal and acceptable. Today, many people would consider such behavior to be criminal child abuse. In earlier times (and not all that much earlier) sterner physical measures were applied to children; indeed, Lloyd DeMause, a historian of child rearing practices, has written in his *The Emotional Life of Nations*:

> Although it is extraordinarily difficult to believe, parents until relatively recently have been so frightened of and have so hated their newborn infants that they have killed them by the billions, routinely sent them out to extremely neglectful wetnurses, tied them up tightly in swaddling bandages lest they be overpowered by them, starved, mutilated, raped, neglected and beat them so badly that prior to modern times I have not been able to find evidence of a single parent who would not today be put in jail for child abuse.[1]

In Europe in the Middle Ages, and in colonial America, beating children was a normal part of school discipline:

> As one thirteenth-century law put it, "If one beats a child until it bleeds, then it will remember, but if one beats it to death, the law applies." Since children were beaten with the same instruments as criminals and slaves, floggings could be accomplished with whips, shovels, canes, iron rods, cat-o'-nine tails, bundles of sticks, shovels, whatever came to hand. Parents could avoid killing them, said Bartholomew Batty, if they would not "strike and buffet their children about the face and head, and lace upon them like malt sacks with cudgels, staves, fork or fire shovel . . . [but instead] hit him upon the sides with the rod, he shall not die thereof."[2]

Elizabeth Pleck, in her study of the American family, asserts that early New England colonists took a mild approach to child discipline, but by the second half of the eighteenth century, "physical punishment appears to have become more severe. Every single child [in her survey] was hit at least once with an instrument, ranging from a hickory stick to a horsewhip."[3] And no one called it "crime."

Likewise, it was impossible until recently in the United States to accuse or convict a husband of raping his wife, since the concept, and therefore the crime, of "spousal rape" did not exist. It was assumed, including in the law, that sex between spouses was, if not by definition consensual, then by definition a husband's "right." In fact, according to the ancient Roman legal principle of *pater-*

familias, the man of the house had final authority over his wife, his children, and all the other "possessions" in his household, down to the right to punish, sell, or kill them if he chose to. In our own day and society, not all killing is crime. There is self-defense, accidental death, justifiable homicide, "crime of passion," and temporary insanity, not to mention warfare. Recent legislation popularly known as the "make my day" law has made it legal in some jurisdictions to shoot a person who invades your home—and more than legal but practically noble.

Unarguably, "crime" depends on the attitudes and statutes of a group or society. Quite literally, crime is that which a code of laws pronounces a violation of that code of laws. It is therefore relative and circular: law codes are made by humans, and something is illegal only if the law says it is illegal. But of course humans can and do modify their codes of law, and different law codes exist in different places and times; what one society or one era calls "crime" in another society or era may be tolerable or laudable, and vice versa. Violence or injury alone does not constitute crime. And to define crime as "inappropriate victimization" or "indefensible victimization" does not help, since what is appropriate or defensible depends on a group's standards of conduct.

In a word, crime is only crime when people define it as crime. The exact same behavior is "crime" if it is illicit and "not crime" if it is licit. An important part of grasping the difference is seeing what elicits the behavior. As we saw in chapter 5, the Inquisition did not regard itself as breaking the law; in fact, it regarded itself *as the law*. So, from its own point of view, and from the point of view of most people at the time, it was not engaged in criminal activity. In fact, its victims were the criminals. The victims were undeniably and objectively hurt or killed, but that objective damage did not lead to the conclusion of abuse or homicide; rather it led to the conclusion of punishment or penance—literally of *justice*, even of *mercy*. At the extreme then, one person's crime is another person's justice.

So it is not really helpful—indeed, not really possible—to castigate all injurious or even fatal behavior as universally and absolutely criminal. We do not take that approach among ourselves, and we cannot take it with others. What we can and must do is acknowledge that we have a standard of judgment (in the cultural and legal sense) that brands certain actions as illicit or criminal, including actions that other groups and ages have not so branded. They "had their reasons" for acting as they did—not reasons that we are obliged to accept, but reasons that we are obliged to understand. And often, very often, those reasons were religious.

In discussing crime, including abuse and murder, we must attend to how those terms are used. Formerly whipping a child was not defined as abuse, and burning a heretic at the stake was not defined as murder, whereas presumably today, for us, they would be. For the purposes of this chapter, we are talking about abuse and murder as a typical modern Westerner would generally classify them. In discussing "religious crime," we must further distinguish between abuses and killings perpetrated by religious people and *abuses and killings essentially related to or flowing from the religion of those people*. That is, once we have determined that an action is legally or conventionally abuse or murder, we must subsequently determine whether the action is religious abuse or religious murder. To that end, we can apply two criteria. First, the injurious or deadly action has to be committed with religion in mind, in the explicit pursuit of some religious goal or the practice of some religious belief: that is, the perpetrator must have a religious reason for the action. Or, second, the action has to be committed not just by a person of faith but rather by a person who is acting in some religious capacity or executing some religious office while committing the crime; in this case, the crime is not distinctly religious but the criminal is.

There are some actions that most religious and nonreligious people, or most members of a religion as well as nonmembers alike, will agree is illegal, such as adult sexual contact with a child. These actions will be discussed below. There are some actions that people of a certain religion regard as normal or acceptable but that nonmembers condemn. There are some actions that some members of the religion may tolerate or glorify but that other members of the same religion denounce. And there are some actions that people of a certain religion censure but that nonmembers regard as normal or acceptable. That is, religious crime works two ways. A religion can decriminalize a behavior that other people would judge a crime, and a religion can also criminalize a behavior that other people would judge a noncrime. The Taliban in Afghanistan, for example, criminalized not only sex outside marriage and deconverting from Islam but also secular music, photography, paper bags (which might be composed of recycled Qur'ans), kites (which seemed Hindu to them), beardless faces for men, and a whole barrage of behaviors for women. Having provided themselves with a behavioral code, religions often set out to monitor and enforce those codes, creating and punishing "criminals" where others would find no crime and no punishment. As the Taliban did, Saudi Arabia continues to maintain a Commission for the Propagation of Virtue and the Prevention of Vice, with a body of some thirty-five hundred officers or *mutaween* who patrol the streets looking for infractions of Islamic law like improper dress, nonconformity to prayer schedules, alcohol use, pork consumption, buying or selling cats and dogs, homosexuality, and fraternization between unrelated males and females. Highly orthodox or fundamentalist Jewish sects in Israel have their own version of vice officers, known as Miahmarot Hatzniut, "Chastity Guards" who police the sexual behavior of the community.

However, there is a critical difference between actions that even the perpetrator considers are wrong (or at least knows are prohibited and punished) and actions that the perpetrator considers are not wrong—which, quite the opposite, he or she may consider acceptable or good or even obligatory. The difference lies in the source of the definition and sanction of the behavior: in the former situation, the perpetrator is deriving his or her standards of conduct from or along with the wider general society, but in the latter case, the perpetrator is deriving his or her standards from some narrower "sectarian" (in the sense of one "section" of society) group or source. In cases of religious crime, *that group or source is religion.*

What we are saying here is that when a person commits a religious crime by the first criterion above, the person usually does not view the action as a crime at all, or sometimes even as injury. The religious abuser/murderer is operating with a separate definition or standard of conduct than the wider society, a definition or standard that comes from his or her religion. To be more precise, when the Lafferty brothers killed their sister-in-law and baby niece, or when Christian parents deny their children medical care resulting in death (see below), neither sees the action as wrong. Quite the contrary, it is the right, even the righteous, thing to do. They are acting on their beliefs, following instructions, doing what they are supposed to do. Sometimes (as with the Lafferty brothers) it is conceived as self-defense and at other times (as with the Christian parents) it is meant as sincere faith, but either way *it is obedience to religious tenets or authorities.* For such people, religion is the standard by which they determine and judge their actions, not secular law or cultural convention. Like Dan Lafferty, they are often frankly astounded that other people disapprove of their behavior and are utterly unrepentant, since they see nothing to repent for. They did good, since they did what their religion demanded of them.

The problem, in conclusion, is that "religious criminals" by the first criterion (but not always by the second: there is nothing about being a Catholic priest that valorizes child sex abuse, although there may be something that contributes to it) are not, from their perspective, breaking the law but *obeying a different law,* a law based in their religion. They are not operating in terms of the legal standard of their surrounding society but in terms of their own standard, a standard rooted entirely in their religious dogmas. The upshot of this understanding is to realize that different, even conflicting, standards of "good behavior"—even concerning injury and death—not only distinguish humans from other societies and historical periods but from their very neighbors next door.

RELIGIOUS HOMICIDE

In this first section, we discuss the ultimate sort of religious crime, murder. Of course, as we have been stressing, *murder* is a relative term. Not all killing, by any standard, is murder: killing combatants in war is not murder, and killing in self-defense is not murder. And, naturally, the perpetrators seldom if ever see themselves as murderers. Rather, they consider themselves to be agents acting on behalf of a religious being or cause—defending a faith, punishing a wrong, or just obeying an order.

Homicide in the Judeo-Christian Scriptures

Many Jews and Christians will argue passionately that their religions absolutely forbid killing; after all, one of their fundamental commandments is "Thou shalt not kill." Whether this line from scripture should be translated "kill" or "murder" (after all, "kill" does not exclude killing animals or plants or insects, which most Jews and Christians do without a moment's thought) is beside the point, since *murder* is a relative and legal term, referring, as we have acknowledged, to *illicit* killing but leaving *licit* killing unprohibited and sometimes even approved.

As we have seen repeatedly, the Judeo-Christian god was not above ordering his people to kill or simply doing the killing himself. The classic aqedah (command for Abraham to kill his son) was discussed in chapter 3; the facts that it was portrayed as a sacrifice rather than a murder and that the god relented does not diminish the murderous intent of the command. Indeed, the Judeo-Christian god did not demur from destroying entire cities, like Sodom and Gomorrah, or, in the biblical flood story, the whole human species and every other species on earth. As we saw in chapter 7, he also frequently called his people to war, which they prosecuted without mercy. Many of the actions ordained in those wars would be regarded today as war crimes, including:

- killing every male including children and every adult sexually active female, but keeping the female virgins for themselves[4]
- taking women and children and cattle and property as spoils of war[5]
- smashing the heads of children against stones[6]
- spearing or slashing every living person, spoiling houses, "ravishing" (raping) women, and declining even to spare the children.[7]

Additionally, their god often decreed death for behaviors that, to modern people, are trivial infractions of the law or not infractions of the law at all. Blasphemy, as we observed in chapter 5, was the main capital crime: "He that blasphemeth the name of the Lord, he shall surely be put to death"[8]—and the children of Israel did as the Lord commanded Moses. Likewise, a man was stoned to death by divine proclamation for collecting sticks on the Sabbath,[9] and the death penalty was imposed for family members who attempt to turn a person to another religion.[10] In fact, potentially all nonbelievers were capital criminals, if we were to take seriously the injunction that "whosoever would not seek the Lord God of Israel should be put to death, whether small or great, whether man or woman."[11] Lest one believe that the later Christian additions to the scriptures offer love without punishment, Romans 1:24–28 provides a long list of deeds "worthy of death," including homosexuality but also "fornication, wickedness, covetousness, maliciousness, . . . envy, murder, debate, deceit," not to mention such comparatively harmless folks as "whisperers, backbiters, . . . proud, boasters, . . . [and those] disobedient to parents."

Acting on these religious rulings would subject most of us to the death sentence. Whether or not these injunctions were actually carried out—and in at least some cases it is clear that they were—is interesting but secondary. The crucial point is that they were handed down as law, as judicial decisions, so that what we moderns might call *homicide*, these ancients called *divine justice*. In fact, it would have been a crime, punishable by death and eternal damnation, not to carry out the sentences imposed by the supernatural authority.

Thuggee: Killers for Kali

Thuggee was a Hindu sect founded around 1200 CE and finally suppressed in the 1800s by British colonial authorities. Followers devoted themselves to Kali, the goddess of death. She is often depicted as a dark-skinned female with four arms—one holding a sword, another lifting the severed head of a demon, a third gesturing for peace, and the last grasping for power. Standing or dancing on the body of her husband Shiva, she wears a necklace of decapitated heads and earrings of human corpses. Thuggee members believed that Kali required them to kill as an offering to her. According to their belief, Kali originally created two men and gave them the *rumal* or yellow scarf as a weapon to strangle demons and any strangers that they met. On another occasion she turned her own body into the traditional Thuggee weapons—the magical pick-ax (*kussee*), the dagger, and the rumal—and consumed the bodies of the victims delivered by her devotees.[12]

Traditionally, Thuggee murderers first waylaid a band of travelers or pilgrims. A few Thugs would meet and often join the travelers, sometimes journeying with them for several days; more Thugs might arrive along the way until they outnumbered the original band. When the time for the kill arrived, they chose a location, and two members (*beles* or grave diggers) prepared graves with their ritual axes. Then, one Thug strangled each victim with the sacred yellow scarf while two more held him down. Sometimes they confiscated the dead men's property, but that was incidental to the kill. After the kill, the Thugs prayed to their goddess, offering the victims to her as a sacrifice. The gang of killers dismembered and buried the bodies and sometimes camped on the site, where they celebrated Tuponee. Sitting on a cloth in a tent, they placed the ax along with silver and sugar before them. They poured the sugar and some holy water into a hole prepared for the ritual, prayed, and then ate sugar as a ceremonial meal.

In their own view, the Thugs were not murderers or criminals. Rather, they saw themselves as normal, good, even pious men. Their divine authority Kali commanded the killings and even provided the victims; members merely executed her will, employing omens to determine what that will was. When not killing for Kali, they were ordinary citizens, including police officers or doctors or public officials. Some, the British discovered to their horror, were employees or servants of colonial families. Nor did they kill in random and haphazard ways; rather, like any warriors or devotees, they obeyed certain "rules" of killing. Women were not acceptable victims, and they did not prey on lepers or the handicapped or blind. Certain categories of people were excluded from their list of potential victims, such as carpenters, blacksmiths, and masons. Finally, they did not molest members of the Kamal caste or anyone herding a cow or female goat. Killing a tiger was also prohibited, since the Thuggee sect identified with tigers as fellow killers of humans; in other words, to kill a tiger was to kill one of their own.

Sati and "Dowry Death" in India

In chapter 4 on self-injury, we introduced the concept of sati or widow suicide in India. The religious foundation of this practice has already been established and has been evinced in other discussions, including the lack of female ascetics in Hinduism: the female is spiritually inferior to the male and is beholden to her husband. Self-immolation, ideally by throwing oneself on the dead husband's funeral pyre, has been construed as a religious obligation for a widow—the ultimate act of devotion to her spouse and of faith in her gods. As one woman said to Mala Sen, "It is my duty to serve my husband and live by his wishes. . . . If God gives me the gift of sati when the time comes, I will gladly follow him in death as I have in life." As Sen continues herself, "The tradition of self-sacrifice among women was an inspiration to her way of thinking. It was the way all decent women should live."[13]

Sati is only the final step (and ideally a voluntary one) in the religious and social denigration of women, several other steps of which also contribute to female death. Given the spiritual inferiority of women, added to the economic undesirability and social burden of a daughter or a wife, it is no surprise that females are disproportionately victimized in parts of India. Female infanticide is common, including selective abortion: Sen reports an advertisement for an abortion clinic that read, "Pay five hundred rupees now or fifty thousand rupees in eighteen years," referring to the cost of aborting a daughter as opposed to raising and marrying her off.[14] In fact, she quotes an Indian proverb to the effect that "Raising a female child is like watering your neighbor's plant," since someone else will enjoy the fruits.[15]

Clearly, religion is not solely to blame for the plight of Indian women, but neither does it protect them from this plight but in fact adds to it. There is certainly an economic module attached to the religious modules rendering women dependent and expensive. One of the key social and economic practices associated with low female status and high female death is the dowry, an institution in which a woman's family must pay a prospective husband in order to arrange a marriage. Many societies practice dowry (the United States formerly practiced a mild version of it, and traces are still observable in the "tradition" of the bride's family paying for the wedding), but not all escalate to abuse and death as an outcome. Stone and James point out that "dowry death," in which women are extorted or killed—often by being pushed into their cooking fires—is largely contained to Northwest India and to Hindu families in that region, and interestingly it is more common among urban and middle-class families rather than poor rural ones. There, they estimate at least two thousand dowry related deaths each year, with two per day in the city of New Delhi alone.[16] Ironically and tragically, it is often the senior woman of the household—the suffering wife's mother-in-law—who instigates or literally perpetrates the murder.

Stone and James explicitly connect the modern phenomenon of dowry death with the traditional religious phenomenon of sati:

> Certainly the association of death, fire, and female chastity or purity has caught the attention of writers who have drawn parallels between modern bride-burning and the ancient upper caste custom of *sati*, or the burning of a widow alive on her husband's funeral pyre. This was considered a (theoretically self-willed) act of great religious merit, only to be performed by a chaste wife in a state of ritual purity.[17]

Even worse, as they point out, in Hinduism "a bride is a religious gift (*kandyadan*) and, as such, can only be given upward to those of higher rank, those to whom one must show perpetual deference and respect."[18] In other words, blend the religious value of female submission in life and death with caste hierarchy, the social dependence of women, concepts of honor (especially as expressed in the control of female sexuality), and contemporary capitalism and consumerism (in which men demand larger dowries containing modern manufactured goods), and you have a recipe for the "traditional" if no longer legally accepted destruction of women.

Honor Killing

In February 2005, a controversial case brought the danger of religion and culture to the attention of German officials, when a Turkish woman living in Germany was slain by her three brothers. Hatin Sürücü was a twenty-three-year-old mother, a Muslim immigrant who had been raised in Berlin and had adopted many of the trappings of modern Western society. According to the German newspaper *Der Spiegel*, she had divorced her first husband (a cousin whom she had married when only sixteen) and "discarded her Islamic head scarf, enrolled in a technical school where she was training to become an electrician, and began dating German men."[19] She had been shot to death while standing at a bus stop, to which she had been sent by a telephone call from a relative, obviously an accomplice in the murder plot. Her brothers, aged twenty-five, twenty-four, and eighteen, were arrested for the crime of murder, which they regarded not as a murder at all but as an "honor killing." The youngest man had apparently even boasted to his girlfriend of how he had restored the honor of his family by his noble response to *his sister's* crime. And her crime? As the title of the German article states, "the whore lived like a German."

This killing was not an isolated incident but part of a religious and cultural pattern. *Der Spiegel* reports five other cases of young women murdered by the families in Berlin alone in a four-month period, and as many as forty in Germany during the years 1996–2005:

> Examples include a Darmstadt girl whose two brothers pummelled her to death with a hockey stick in April 2004 after they learned she had slept with her boyfriend. In Augsburg in April, a man stabbed his wife and seven-year-old daughter because the wife was having an affair. In December 2003, a Tübingen father strangled his sixteen-year-old daughter and threw her body into a lake because she had a boyfriend. Bullets, knives, even axes and gasoline are the weapons of choice. . . . And the sad part, said [Myria] Boehmecke [of the women's organization Terre des Femmes], is that [this list] is far from complete. "We'll never really know how many victims there are. Too often these crimes go unreported."[20]

And far from feeling guilty or being condemned by their compatriots, the young murderers "are revered by their community and fellow inmates as 'honor heroes'— a dementedly skewed status they carry with them for the rest of their lives."[21]

Killing a female family member over the family's honor is not directly called for in the Qur'an or in any other Islamic religious source—in fact, Muhammad ordered relative equality for women in matters of inheritance and divorce—but it is rooted in Islamic and other cultures. Tahira Shahid Khan, author of *Chained to Custom*, a study of honor killing, states that in such cultures women "are considered the property of the males in their family irrespective of their class, ethnic, or religious group. The owner of the property has the right to decide its fate. The concept of ownership has turned women into a commodity which can be exchanged, bought, and sold."[22] The similarity to Western paterfamilias is obvious.

In such cultures, honor is a paramount value, and a family's honor (much as in the case of India above) is linked to its ability to protect and control its women, especially but not exclusively the sexuality of its women. Honor killings are thus often related to sexual/marital issues like infidelity, premarital sex, or merely dating outside the religion. In 2007, a Jordanian man killed his own daughter because he was convinced she was not a virgin, even though tests showed that she was. Samia Imran was shot to death by her own mother in Pakistan in 1999 for seeking a divorce from her abusive husband. At its most contradictory, women are sometimes punished for being raped, as in the 1999 case of a sixteen-year-old Pakistani girl whose rape apparently shamed her tribe, which executed her publicly to regain their honor.

While the personal stories of victims are compelling, the statistics are chilling. According to a report titled *The Haven Becomes Hell: A Study of Domestic Violence in Pakistan*, 888 women were killed for family honor just in the Punjab in 1998. Pakistan's own Human Rights Commission estimates three hundred deaths in the Sindh province in 1997. Yemen may have experienced as many as four hundred such murders in 1997, and by some estimates two-thirds of all murders in Palestinian territory in 1999 were honor killings, with twenty-three occurring in Jordan each day. As always, these actions are not seen as crimes at all by their perpetrators but rather "as excusable or understandable," in the words of one Human Rights Watch official.[23]

Family Killing among Christian Fundamentalists

Muslim and Hindu cultures are by no means the only ones that find a potential religious justification for killing, including killing the ones you love. While there is no concept in Christian cultures, including the United States, quite equivalent to honor killing, there definitely have been and continue to be instances of believers slaughtering their own relatives—often their own children—for spiritual belief.

One of the most notorious cases was recently explored by Jon Krakauer in his *Under the Banner of Heaven*. On July 24, 1984, two brothers, Dan and Ron Lafferty, killed their sister-in-law Brenda and her daughter, their niece, Erica. The Lafferty brothers were converts to the fundamentalist branch of the Mormon (Latter Day Saints) church, having been raised in a strict though mainstream Mormon home. According to the *Deseret News*, the boys' father, Watson Lafferty, "planted the seeds of paranoia, rebellion, and fanaticism" in them, teaching them to distrust conventional medicine and the federal government. He also took his religious beliefs to the extreme. When one son accidentally shot himself in the stomach with an arrow, he told him he would have to suffer until morning for breaking the Sabbath.[24]

So, early on, the Lafferty brothers learned not only extreme religion but also the kind of abusive neglect (see below) and antigovernment rhetoric (see chapter 5) that would lead them to their later crimes. In fact, the Utah Highway Patrol has posted some information to indicate that Dan Lafferty believed that all public officials, other than the popularly elected county sheriff,

> worked for the executive branch of government and not the judicial branch and therefore had no authority to arrest. He also believed that regulatory laws governing speed limits, driver licenses, safety inspection, and vehicle insurance were unconstitutional. This candidate further advocated that an unconstitutional law could not be enforced by peace officers, particularly peace officers which he believed lacked proper authority.[25]

The Laffertys' lawlessness caused them to oppose not only the police (earning multiple traffic citations, arrests, and a jail sentence for Dan on charges of resisting arrest, felony evading, and felony escape) but also the conventional Latter Day Saints church. In 1982, Dan, the leader of the duo, was excommunicated for trying to commit polygamy—specifically, trying to marry his fourteen-year-old stepdaughter. Dan began to believe that he and his brothers were prophets and heads of the true church. Ron accepted this lofty role, but Ron's wife did not accept the idea of polygamy and divorced him, leaving him more time to concentrate on the messages he believed he was receiving that would become a new scripture for their new group, simply called the School of the Prophets.

In March 1983, Ron transcribed the fateful revelation that became known as "the removal revelation," telling the little church to destroy its enemies:

> Thus saith the Lord unto my servants the prophets. It is my will and commandment that ye remove the following individuals in order that my work might go forward. For they have truly become obstacles in my path and I will not allow my work to be stopped. First thy brother's wife Brenda and her baby, then Chloe Low [who aided Ron's wife in her divorce] and then Richard Stowe [who presided over their excommunication]. And it is my will that they be removed in rapid succession.[26]

After much soul searching, on July 24 they carried out their god's instructions.

Brenda had been a strong woman, who convinced her husband, Allen Lafferty, to break with the prophets, causing a rift in the family. They came to her house at midday, armed with guns and knives, and, after waiting for a sign that their revelation was true, they killed the mother and daughter:

> Dan said he and his brother were led by God to beat Brenda unconscious, wrap a vacuum cord around her neck until she went limp, and then slit her throat. . . . "I held Brenda's hair and did it pretty much the way they did it in the scriptures," he said proudly. "Then I walked in Erica's room. I talked to her for a minute, I said, 'I'm not sure why I'm supposed to do this, but I guess God wants you home.'" He then looked away as he slit the fifteen-month-old baby's throat.[27]

They proceeded, intending to kill Low and Stowe, but the former was not at home when they arrived, and they missed the turn to Stowe's home, which they interpreted as a sign to stop killing.

Dan and Ron Lafferty are still in jail but feel no remorse for their crime. In fact, according to the Utah Department of Public Safety, Dan "told the jury that fulfilling a revelation of God is not a crime" at all. "It's never haunted me, it's never bothered me," Dan told Jesse Hyde, and the killer does not believe he will ever be executed for his crime; rather, "he believes the walls will crumble and he will emerge as the biblical prophet Elijah, announcing the second coming of Christ."

Another less famous but equally startling murder occurred in 1999, when Jacques Robidoux and his family starved Robidoux's infant son Samuel to death on the basis of a religious vision. Robidoux belonged to a family cult much like that founded by the Laffertys. His was known simply as The Body and had originated when Jacques' father Roland Robidoux broke with the insufficiently fundamentalist World Wide Church of God. The Body, which never numbered more than seventy, saw themselves as the true church and God's chosen people. Roland's new religion was an austere one: nonbelievers were shunned, diets were controlled, scientific medicine was abandoned, and even mainstream church music was forbidden (the group wrote its own songs and hymns). In the late 1990s, group members started to receive so-called leadings or revelations from God, instructing them to stop using eyeglasses, throw out photographs, books, and forms of entertainment. Another "leading" stated that women should wear only dresses. The group preached that the man is the head of the household and makes all the decisions on behalf of the family. The sect members lived in several homes in communal arrangements.[28]

In one of these visions, Jacques Robidoux's sister, Michelle Mingo, had prophesied that his wife Karen, who had a ten-month-old baby boy, should stop feeding the baby solid food, giving him only breast milk. Karen herself was put on a strict diet consisting of nothing but almond milk, supposedly "to eliminate vanity." After fifty-two days of this religious feeding regime, little Samuel was found dead. Samuel and another baby, whom members claim was stillborn, were buried by the family in Baxter State Park in Maine. Massachusetts police arrested Robidoux on the charge of first-degree murder, for which he was found guilty in 2002. Jacques' defense is that he was only following God's orders.

Unhappily, child murder at the hands of a Christian parent is more common than one would like to think. In 2001, the notorious Andrea Yates case brought to light the drowning death of Yates's five children, all biblically named (Noah, John, Paul, Luke, and Mary); the oldest was seven years, the youngest six months. Living in Houston, Texas, Yates was suspected of and diagnosed with postpartum depression, but as Baker reports, "Much of Andrea's psychosis had religious imagery."

> She was obsessed with images of Satan. About the murders, she told her doctor, "It was the seventh deadly sin. My children weren't righteous. They stumbled because I was evil. The way I was raising them they could never be saved. . . . Better for someone else to tie a millstone around their neck and cast them into a river than to stumble. They were going to perish [in Hell]."[29]

Yates and her husband Rusty had allegedly come under the influence of a fundamentalist preacher named Michael Woroniecki, who taught them that all women were evil due to the sin of Eve and that all children reached the "age of accountability" at twelve, at which time their immortal fate was sealed. If children were not raised properly, in Jesus' and Woroniecki's dogma, they were doomed to hell, along with their unregenerate mothers. Accordingly, the minister taught Yates that children were better off dead than raised sinful and destined for damnation. Reportedly, after feverishly reading her Bible, she decided that he was right.

Interestingly, two other Texas mothers, Deanna Laney and Dena Schlosser (of Tyler and Dallas, respectively), killed their children on the basis of Christian beliefs. Laney, a Pentecostal, beat two of her children to death and wounded a third with stones ("stoned") because God told her to. Schlosser, a member of the Way of Life Church, killed her ten-month-old because she wanted to give the child to God. Both women had become intensely more religious in the period just prior to their crimes, both studying their Bibles and Laney even purportedly hearing God's voice. Most recently, in February 2007, a Colorado mother named Brenda Hernandez attempted unsuccessfully to slay her three children, in the bathtub like Yates. She was discovered naked and red-handed, and police found her seven-year-old, three-year-old, and two-year-old naked in the tub. At trial, she maintained that she was insane, but at the moment of the murder attempt she claimed, according to the *Denver Post*, that she "believed she was Christ, her children were the anti-Christ, and that she needed to kill them."[30] Police reported that when they came to her door she answered, "Nobody is here, only Christ, only Christ" and that when they arrested her, she uttered repeatedly, "the children were the anti-Christ and the children needed to die. We need to kill them. They are the devil."

The disheartening news is that these incidents are not isolated. In fact, Lisa Falkenberg cites two studies that link religiosity with child-directed violence. One found that of thirty-nine women who killed their children, fifteen had religion-related motivations; the other concluded that one-fourth of its fifty-six child-killing mothers had religious "delusions"—although at the time at least they did not consider them delusions at all.[31]

Attempted Murder at the Salad Bar: Rajneeshism

Many of the examples we have just finished discussing involve homicidal acts against ones that the perpetrators ostensibly loved. The Thuggees committed homicide against ones that they did not know. But some acts of religious murder are aimed at ones that you hate, or at least ones who are "in your way," interfering with your religion, its truth, and its growth.

In 1984, the sect known as Osho or Rajneeshism conducted what may have been the first biological attack on US soil when it placed poisonous salmonella bacteria in salad bars in the town of The Dalles, Oregon. Osho is a new religious movement that began in 1964 from the teachings of the Bhagwan Shree Rajneesh, an Indian holy man. According to the publications of the Osho International Foundation and its Web site, it is a syncretistic movement that brings together Hinduism (especially in the teachings of Patanjali), Buddhism, meditation, yoga, haiku poetry, and tarot cards, among other religious and quasi-religious sources.[32] At its height, it operated six hundred meditation centers with two hundred thousand members, although currently that number is closer to twenty centers. It emphasizes a communal style of living for a full commitment to the Osho way of life.

One such commune was established in eastern Oregon in the early 1980s. The philosophy of the group was supposedly antiauthority and antidogma, without rituals or orthodox beliefs, and even without conventional family. Lewis Carter's study of the commune, on the contrary, found it to be "authoritarian," displaying "a preoccupation with total control . . . regimented and regulated even in minutiae."[33] He describes life in the community as more similar to a "migrant labor camp" than an American town, with stress on work and financial contribution to the group.

The eight hundred residents of the Rajneesh compound constituted a classic "cult" to many local people. Worse, the compound began to expand, adding housing and administrative buildings. The city council tried to block this development, and in 1983 the Oregon Attorney General declared that the effort to turn Rajneeshpuram into an independent municipality violated the First Amendment separation of church and state. In response, the Bhagwan's message turned more apocalyptic, warning of a global AIDS epidemic that would destroy all humanity except Osho members. The commune also stockpiled weapons.

These tensions led to the biological attack on The Dalles in 1984, apparently in an effort to sicken so many of the town's voters that the Bhagwan could steal the county election and install his own candidates in local political offices. In fact, seven hundred fifty citizens were made ill, and reportedly the attack was a preliminary to a larger assault on the town's water supply. The following year, the FBI uncovered a plot to assassinate US attorney Charles Turner, who was investigating the salmonella outbreak. Rajneesh member Phyllis McCarthy was convicted of conspiracy to commit murder, and in 1986 two other members pleaded no contest to the poisoning and served four years in jail. The Bhagwan himself was fined for immigration fraud but left the country and died in India in 1990. Over twenty other members were charged with various crimes.

Murder for Movies: The Killing of Theo van Gogh

On the morning of November 2, 2004, Dutch filmmaker Theo van Gogh was accosted and murdered—shot and repeatedly stabbed. The attack is described graphically by Paul Belien, who writes that the killer, a twenty-six-year-old man of Moroccan descent dressed in a traditional djellabah, "pulled a gun, shot and wounded Van Gogh. The latter dropped his bike and stumbled across the street, followed by the younger man, who shot him again. . . . The assailant jumped on Van Gogh, pulled a knife and slit his throat. He planted the knife into Van Gogh's chest and a second knife, with a note containing [Qur'anic] verses, into his stomach."[34] The reason: Van Gogh had made a particularly insulting movie about Islam.

By all accounts, Van Gogh was a man who did not mind offending religious and other sensibilities. In fact, he seemed to enjoy it. Crimelibrary.com claims that he "harshly criticized Christianity and Judaism. However, the Muslim community bore the brunt of his irritation, which was evident when he likened Dutch Muslim immigrants to 'goat f—kers.'"[35] He also called Muhammad "'a f—ker of little girls,' their God 'a pig called Allah,' and Dyab Abu Jahjah, the charismatic leader of young Dutch and Flemish radical Muslims, 'the prophet's pimp.'"[36] Apparently his films were as foul as his mouth, depicting misogyny and animal cruelty as well as antireligious sentiment.

However, it was his ten-minute documentary *Submission* that apparently cost him his life. Portraying abuses against Muslim women, it contained images of abused women whose nude bodies showed through light coverings. "On their bodies [Qur'anic] verses had been calligraphed describing the physical punishments prescribed by the [Qur'an] for women who 'misbehave.'"[37] Death threats started to arrive immediately after the August 29 airing of the film. Van Gogh did not take the threats seriously, but at least one was not idle. Since the brutal slaying occurred in public in daylight, the suspect did not escape but was shot in the leg by police. He was identified as Mohammed Bouyeri, whose "motivation to kill was likely sparked by the movie *Submission* and further aggravated by his hate of the Western world and those who refused to accept Islamic values."[38]

More recently, another Westerner was attacked under similar circumstances. Kurt Westergaard is a Danish cartoonist, the artist responsible for the drawings of Muhammad as a bomber that so incensed the Muslim world in 2006. On January 1, 2010, a twenty-eight-year-old Somali man entered Westergaard's home, wielding an axe and a knife, and Westergaard and his young daughter only survived by fleeing to their panic room (no doubt constructed for just such an occasion). The suspect was shot and arrested by police.

"Soldiers of Christ": Christian Killers

Aggrieved Muslims like Bouyeri have been known to kill to defend the religion. Indeed, very much of the attention and literature devoted to religious violence focuses on aggrieved Muslims. But of course, followers of practically any religion who are sufficiently aggrieved—who perceive their religion as mortally threatened—have the potential to turn deadly. This includes, of course, Christianity. Some of this discourse is hopefully merely rhetorical: for instance, the Promise Keepers recently established a program for young males called Passages, which encourages them to step up to the plate and become warriors for Christ. An announcement for Passages says:

> In ancient times as well as today, warriors have always fought together. Every fighting force is organized into platoons, squadrons, or units of some kind. By putting together this Passage group, we are forming a kind of fighting unit—a band of brothers. This unit has a single purpose of helping you learn to become a warrior for Christ and successfully navigate the passage into manhood.[39]

While we presume that these youths are not literally forming an army or plotting a holy war (if they were, we would discuss them in chapter 7), they are being introduced to a martial-religious perspective that is not—and has been proven not to be—entirely innocent.

Christianity has shown itself to be particularly amenable to alloying with virulent ideologies like racism (especially anti-Semitism and white supremacy [see chapter 5]), hypernationalism, and antigovernment conspiracy theories. This potent mixture has led to real deaths. In 1984, Richard Wayne Snell, a member of the Covenant, Sword, and Arm of the Lord, killed a black Arizona state trooper, and in 1985 David Tate killed a Missouri police officer on the way to the Covenant, Sword, and Arm of the Lord compound. On August 10, 1999, Buford Furrow carried out a shooting attack on a Jewish daycare center in California. Reverend Michael Bray burned down a clinic in Dover, Delaware, in February 1984 and was eventually convicted of destroying seven clinics along the East Coast; and on July 29, 1994, Reverend Paul Hill (a friend of Bray) killed Dr. John Britton of Pensacola, Florida. Another associate of Bray, Rachelle Shannon, has also confessed to a series of bombings and to wounding Dr. George Tiller of Wichita, Kansas (who was eventually successfully assassinated in May 2009 by antiabortion activist Scott Roeder, ironically while the doctor was serving as an usher at his Lutheran church); and Eric Robert Rudolph was linked to a string of attacks in 1998 and 1999. And the first act of religious terrorism on American soil, the Oklahoma City bombing of April 19, 1995, was perpetrated by Timothy McVeigh, a man with ties to the Christian and militia movements.

The attitudes and justifications for such violence come from the spokesmen of religion itself and not merely from fringe or isolated individuals. James Bruggemann, pastor of Stone Kingdom Ministries in Asheville, North Carolina, makes no excuses for the violence he advocates: "No, folks, it is not a perverse joy I take in the impending doom of the enemy. It is a righteous joy!"[40] In fact, after the police raid on Randy Weaver's Ruby Ridge home in 1992, Pastor Pete Peters of the LaPorte Church of Christ called together leaders of many Christian, militia, and white-supremacist organizations at Estes Park, Colorado, to form a unified Christian/militant/racist front (see chapter 5). There are other "official" and organized aspects to American Christian violence as well. A manual entitled *Army of God* gives instructions for conducting sabotage and violence against abortion clinics, and Reverend Bray himself wrote *A Time to Kill*, a justification of antiabortion violence. Kerry Noble, a spokesman for the Christian Identity movement, produced a booklet entitled *Prepare War!* that explains and legitimizes the Christian call to combat, evoking the famous passage of Exodus 15:3 in which Moses says that the Lord "is a man of war." Other Christian Identity figures describe the entire Bible as "a book of war, a book of hate."[41]

RELIGIOUS ABUSE: WOMEN AND SPOUSES

On March 23, 2006, Mary Winkler, wife of Church of Christ pastor Matthew Winkler, shot him to death in their Tennessee home, allegedly asking his forgiveness as he lay dying.[42] A year later at trial, the sordid details of the couple's life—or diverging versions of it—came to light. According to accounts in the local news, Mrs. Winkler's defense asserted that the defendant

> snapped after years of verbal, physical, and sexual abuse by her husband. She testified that the morning she killed him, Matthew Winkler had pinched their youngest daughter's nose and covered her mouth to stop her crying.

Mary Winkler also testified that her husband often wanted her to look at pornographic pictures and images and dress up in high-heeled shoes, wigs and other provocative clothing before they had sexual relations. She said he insisted that she participate in sexual acts she wasn't comfortable with, such as anal and oral sex.[43]

The prosecution, on the other hand, maintained that the act was intentional, concerning money and some financial scam in which the accused was entangled and for which she was in debt—a debt she wanted to conceal from her husband.

The facts being in dispute (in 2007 she was found guilty of voluntary manslaughter and sentenced to 210 days in prison), it is difficult to determine whether we have here a case of murder of a Christian officeholder or spousal abuse by a Christian officeholder (or both). Neither is particularly uplifting, but the latter does raise the issue of religion-inspired or at least religion-protected abuses short of death, often perpetrated on women or especially spouses. Many societies tolerate or even encourage what would be considered abuse by (some) members of other societies, for many different reasons. Religion is not always the precipitating factor but is often a contributing factor, creating an environment in which nonfatal abuse (from hitting to sexual abuse) is accepted, excused, or overlooked. In the United States, for instance, again arguably the most Christian of Western societies, the National Coalition against Domestic Violence reported in 2007 that some 1.3 million women are assaulted by an intimate partner each year and that approximately one-third of all female homicide victims are killed by their partner; further, in 70 to 80 percent of the homicide cases, the woman suffered physical abuse prior to the fatality.[44] Again, while presumably few of these actions were *about* religion, they were certainly not prevented, and many of them were probably facilitated, by attitudes and values and institutions with their roots in religion, as we will see next.

Gender/Spousal Abuse: Judeo-Christian Tradition

In 2004, the Church of England published a report called "Responding to Domestic Abuse: Guidelines for Those with Pastoral Responsibilities," in which it concluded, "The Church has not only failed at many points to address the processes that lead to domestic abuse but has—intentionally or unintentionally—reinforced abuse, failed to challenge abusers, and intensified the suffering of survivors."[45] After noting the high incidence and high personal cost of abuse, the document contains a powerful and controversial appendix entitled "Harmful Theology" in which it acknowledges that "over the centuries questionable assumptions about the relation between men and women, which were supposed to reflect the will of God, have influenced the Church's interpretation of the Bible, its moral teaching and pastoral practice."[46] Among these "questionable" sources, it mentions that

> many conceptions of God derived from the Bible and the Christian tradition have portrayed divine power in unhealthy and potentially oppressive ways. There are particular problems in the attribution of violent actions and attitudes to God, chiefly but not solely in the Old Testament, which require careful interpretation with reference to the historical and theological context.[47]

However, like Charles Kimball and many others, they attribute this harmful capacity not to the religion and its doctrines and models but to "bad theology."

However, there is no honest way to avoid the fact there is a strongly misogynist stream in Judeo-Christian scriptures and cultural tradition. The first woman, Eve, is conventionally blamed for ushering evil and sin into the world, for which some degree of modern female suffering is justified (see below). Women have generally been seen as unclean and as socially, politically, and spiritually inferior. No woman could be a Hebrew priest, and no woman can be a Catholic priest. A high premium was attached to female virginity (one of the cross-cultural warning signs of patriarchy and female susceptibility to abuse): literally, Deuteronomy 22:21 explains that a bride who is discovered not to be a virgin at marriage should be stoned to death, and it provides for the demonstration of proof or "token" of her virginity by "spreading the cloth before the elders," that is, laying out the bed sheet for the tell-tale virginal blood. Verses 28–29 of the same book ordain that a man who molests a virgin to whom he is not engaged must compensate her father with cash and marry her.

The conventions are no less clear, if somewhat less terminal, in the New Testament, where women are told to keep quiet and certainly not "to teach, nor to usurp authority over the man, but to be in silence,"[48] precisely because man was chronologically before woman and because man was not "deceived" as woman was. Granted, husbands and wives are admonished to care for each other, but it is an asymmetrical care: "the head of every man is Christ; and the head of the woman is the man";[49] "For the man is not of the woman; but the woman of the man. Neither was the man created for the woman; but the woman for the man."[50] In fact, for Paul the ideal circumstance for a man is celibacy, but it is better to marry than fornicate. However, once a woman marries a man, she is instructed repeatedly, as in Ephesians 5:22–24, to "submit yourselves unto your own husbands, as unto the Lord. For the husband is the head of the wife, even as Christ is the head of the church: and he is the savior of the body. Therefore as the church is subject unto Christ, so let the wives be to their own husbands in every thing."

Later Christian fathers took not a kinder but a sterner approach to womankind. Thomas Aquinas, one of the authors of the "just war" doctrine, also contributed to the "just gender inequality" doctrine:

> As regards the individual nature, woman is defective and misbegotten, for the active force in the male seed tends to the production of a perfect likeness in the masculine sex; while the production of woman comes from a defect in the active force or from some material indisposition, or even from some external influence.[51]

And the reformer Martin Luther did not reform gender hierarchies; rather, he is known to have said, "If they [women] become tired or even die, that does not matter. Let them die in childbirth, that's why they are there."[52]

Gender and spousal abuse cannot be blamed directly on these writings, since most Christians have presumably never read them. But such scriptural and scholarly opinions created an environment and a tradition in which women's status and rights were less than men's, and in which the marital unit was more important than any particular event that might occur within that unit, including abuse. The contributors to the volume *Abuse and Religion: When Praying Isn't Enough* make the point clearly enough. For instance, the authors of one chapter cite a printed source that explicates:

> The clergy preaches a male-oriented theology and structure of the marriage relationship. The clergy has not been in the vanguard of help for the battered wife. Instead, its attitudes about woman's place, duty, and nature have added to the problem. Even now, with few exceptions, the silence from the churches on this issue is profound.[53]

They recount the experience of one woman who was beaten by her husband, a seminary student.

> She returned to her husband, despite life-threatening abuse, partly because of her personal commitment to her marriage and religion which taught her that she was

to "submit" to her husband and partly because he "needed" her. Her husband's career, she felt, hinged on her being there to understand and support him.[54]

Let us hope that her marriage did not end like Mary Winkler's did.

When women did seek guidance from their pastors, Pagelow and Johnson find that the counsel they received was not only unhelpful but sometimes literally dangerous, including:

> (1) a reminder of their duty and the advice to forgive and forget, (2) a reference elsewhere to avoid church involvement, and (3) useless advice, sometimes based on religious doctrine rather than their own needs. Some were reminded of their vows of "for better or for worse" and admonished to pray more and live more worthy lives. One, scolded by her minister for "betraying" her husband by revealing what had occurred in the privacy of their home, was beaten harder by her husband when the pastors told him of her visit.[55]

To conclude a litany of such examples, another woman who actually did leave her man for the safety of a women's shelter was openly threatened by her minister, who "called the shelter director to say that if the woman was not home by the next morning, 'she would be excommunicated from the church because it was her duty to keep the family together and submit to her husband in all things' despite the fact that the children were also abused."[56] Finally, they quote from a widely used premarital counseling manual, which teaches:

> Suppose a woman feels God is leading her definitely opposite from what her husband has commanded? Whom should she obey? The Scriptures say a woman must ignore her feelings about the will of God and do what her husband says. She is to obey her husband as if he were God himself. She can be as certain of God's will when her husband speaks as if God has spoken audibly from heaven.[57]

The parallels between this theology and the theology that makes Hindu widows jump onto funeral pyres are hard to miss.

Gender/Spousal Abuse: Islamic Tradition

As bleak as this picture is (and we are not suggesting that all Christian husbands abuse their wives nor that all Christian wife-batterers do so on religious instructions), the situation is worse in many other societies, informed as they are by their own religious and cultural traditions. Judith Brown has suggested a number of variables that contribute to the maltreatment of women, including marrying at younger ages, denying women economic roles outside the home, isolating women from their own kin inside a male-dominated household, hiding women behind socially constructed walls of privacy (as in the custom of the "veil"), and refusing to grant them the legal or social status of an "autonomous adult."[58] Religions that contribute to such values and practices also contribute, knowingly or not, to the subservience and suffering of women.

Mary Elaine Hegland's study of gender relations in an Iranian village illustrates the point. Everything in this society favors men, who are raised to be violent and domineering; they learn early on "to devalue women and their activities, to use violence to get what they want, and to demonstrate the power and strength required for political survival."[59] The control over women's lives is nearly absolute. Women are expected to be virgins at marriage. They are under the authority of their male relatives until they marry and then under the authority of their husband. The husband's rule is so total that a woman's father cannot even intervene in abuses against her. A woman may not work outside the home, as it dishonors her husband and his family. Finally, men beat their wives as they like, and their own sisters if those women should dare to stand up to them. Women are so little valued that, as one informant told, "When I was born, the minute they told my mother it was a girl she began to cry bitterly."[60]

As in Christianity, there is debate as to whether scriptures ordain such discipline; there are also other cultural and historical influences on gender roles besides religion, but the same is true in Christianity and all other religions. Surely, sections of the Qur'an do appear to support strict punitive treatment of wives and have been used to justify it. Sura 24:31 seems to endorse the *purdah* custom in which women are kept covered in public and only shown to their husbands in the privacy of their own homes. Perhaps the most significant and controversial passage is sura 4:34, which reads:

> Men have authority over women because God has made the one superior to the other, and because they spend their wealth to maintain them. Good women are obedient. They guard their unseen parts because God has guarded them. As for those from whom you fear disobedience, admonish them and send them to beds apart and beat them. Then if they obey you, take no further action against them. Surely God is high, supreme.

Rival translators have suggested alternatives for "admonish" (such as "chide"), for "send them to beds apart" (such as "banish them to beds apart" or "refuse to share their beds"), and "beat them" (such as "scourge them" or "beat them lightly"), but the meaning is roughly consistent. All versions of the section recommend an escalation of punishment, from a good scolding to a kind of ostracism and withdrawal of affection to physical violence. Likewise, some items in the Hadith or "traditions" of Muhammad and his successors indicate authorizing corporal violence against women:

> Umar reported the prophet as saying: "A man will not be asked as to why he beat his wife.[61]
>
> This means that a man tries his best to correct his wife, but if he fails to do so, he is allowed to beat her as a last resort. This tradition never means that a husband should beat his wife without any valid reason.[62]

Other Religions and/or Other Abuses

As we have seen more than once previously, Hinduism subjects women to a variety of abuses, some of them deadly. While sati crosses the line into death (whether it is murder, sacrifice, or self-mortification), the sheer pressure on a woman to "follow" or obey her husband even into death is, in some eyes, a form of abuse. Self-immolation is, however, only the end point of a general religious/ cultural misogyny, "the logical progression of social aberrations like dowry, widow denigration, women's inequality, . . . obsession with male progeny, marginalization of women from the mainstream life,"[63] which have their locus in religious beliefs and values. The fact that women are essentially barred from, because they are esteemed to be spiritually unfit for, religious stations like priest, ascetic, or sannyasin means that their "spiritual progress" is as blocked as their social and economic autonomy.

World religions like Christianity, Islam, and Hinduism are not the only ones that practice the denigration and subordination, to the point of abuse, of women. Small-scale traditional societies like the Australian Aboriginal, the Sambia, and the Mundurucu, to name just three, sometimes had highly gender-prejudicial religious practices. Australian Aboriginal cultures, with men's secret-sacred male rituals, would severely punish a woman who spied on men's religious business; she might receive a beating or worse. The Sambia, as we saw in chapter 4, went further, disparaging women as polluting and even dangerous to men, that is, to the mystical force that gives a male his "manhood." Neighboring cultures, like the Etoro, actually drove their men to fear sex with women and to fear the witchcraft powers of women, because both drained the mystical life force of men (recall that Hinduism also teaches that sexual activity depletes a man's supernatural male energy). Mundurucu society, in the Brazilian Amazon, also segregated and suppressed women: men, even husbands, literally lived in a separate men's house where the primary sacred objects (like magical flutes) and sacred ceremonies were held. "Women occupy a lower status than men in Mundurucu myth," write Yolanda and Robert Murphy, a mythology that they say embodies "phallic dominance."[64] Consistent with male, explicitly phallic, dominance, the penalty for a woman who glimpsed the sacred flutes of the men was gang rape. In fact, rape was a normal and acceptable treatment for women who were foolish enough to wander in public alone: the Murphys tell the story of a young man who sat in a tree waiting for unsuspecting solitary women to pass, only to descend and rape them, as was his cultural right.

Adult women are hardly the only victims of religious abuse. The next section will discuss abuse of children, but occasionally the abuses target adult men, too. In early 2004, a case came to light in Wyoming of a Catholic priest named Anthony Jablonski who was holding "ritual beatings and torture sessions" in the basement of St. Anthony Catholic Church.[65] The priest was also under investigation for child sex abuse when his other activities were discovered. According to news reports, the priest "would take men to the basement of the church and ask them to strip naked, gag and blindfold each other before beginning the ritual. The men said they would be hung upside down from the ceiling, having their genitals manipulated to induce extreme pain—all while praying."[66] Interestingly but not surprisingly, the perpetrator and his victims all thought they were doing something virtuous: "They believed they were participating in legitimate, sacred rituals" that were not sexual in nature at all. Rather, prosecutor Eric Alden stated, "Two words the priest used to describe it was penitential prayer and redemptive suffering."[67]

Where to draw the line between self-mortification and criminal self-abuse is uncertain (if there is a line at all). The journal *Freethought Today* reports this item:

A man ran naked down a street in Penticon, British Columbia, with blood gushing from his severed penis after a self-mutilation in March [2004], screaming "Repent, repent, fornicators." He had presumably been reading the Sermon on the Mount, which advises sexual mutilation.[68]

Men sometimes merely put themselves in harm's way out of religious conviction, such as the man who "leaped into a lion's den at Taipei Zoo in Taiwan to 'convert' the lion to Christianity [and] was bitten in the leg as he shouted 'Jesus will save you!' He was saved by zookeepers."[69]

RELIGIOUS ABUSE OF CHILDREN

In recent years, the predominant scandal of religious child abuse has involved the Catholic church and its celibate male priests (to which we will return below). However, within Christianity, the Catholic church is not solely culpable for the maltreatment of children, and within religion, Christianity is not uniquely guilty. If, as Lloyd DeMause asserts, the very history of childhood is the history of child abuse, then no religion is completely innocent, nor is religion entirely to blame. Juveniles have been hit, cut, bled, and sexually exploited throughout history and across cultures just as surely as adults—and usually just as confidently that what is happening is good, necessary, or insignificant.

Genital Mutilation of Children

Early in chapter 4 we met the Australian Aboriginals, who cut the genitals of young males (while they are fully awake) to reshape the organs and to draw blood for ritual use; probably most Westerners find this operation abusive. In recent years, a cry in the West (and sometimes in the native societies) has gone up against female genital mutilation, practiced in various African and Middle Eastern societies to ensure virginity, reduce sexual sensation, or merely beautify those organs. These operations, usually performed on young girls by senior women of the group, range in severity from minor trimming of the external genitals to "excision" of the clitoris to practically sewing the vagina shut so that it could not possibly be used for sex.

Judeo-Christian societies show much less concern for their own genital operations on newborn males, raising the question of when such actions are "abuse." That Judeo-Christian circumcision is religious in nature is beyond questioning: whatever hygienic, aesthetic, or pleasurable effects it may have (and these are debatable), its origin is indisputably religious. Genesis 17:10–13 provides the divine ordination of the practice:

Every man child among you shall be circumcised. And ye shall circumcise the flesh of your foreskin; and it shall be a token of the covenant betwixt me and you. And he that is eight days old shall be circumcised among you, every man child in your generations, he that is born in the house, or bought with money of any stranger, which is not of thy seed. He that is born in thy house, and he that is bought with thy money, must needs be circumcised: and my covenant shall be in your flesh for an everlasting covenant.

Cutting the baby's penis is thus a part, a "token," of the spiritual relationship, the contract or "covenant," between the tribal god and his followers. In fact, the next verse threatens that an uncircumcised male "shall be cut off from his people; he hath broken my covenant." Writing almost four thousand years after these instructions to Abraham, Elliott Wolfson concurs that, according to this tradition, "It is precisely and exclusively by means of circumcision that one can see God, for this act removes that potential barrier—symbolized by the cutting of the foreskin—separating human and divine. . . . The opening of circumcision results in an opening up to God."[70] Exactly how the foreskin is an obstacle to seeing God is not explained by him nor by the scriptural writers, but it does make one wonder about the "spiritual vision" of women.

Leonard Glick (who is admittedly an activist against the perpetuation of circumcision) describes the traditional process, which takes place in a ceremony known as a *bris* or "covenant." The first cut to the organ, the *milah*, gives the ritual its full name, *bris milah*. In the second step, *peri'ah* or "opening," the fleshy membrane or "foreskin" is torn away from the head of the penis and cut off. A third step, not always included, is the *metsitsah* or "sucking," in which the operator sucks on the bleeding penis.[71]

Many modern readers will find at least part of this procedure unsavory, perhaps especially because not a ritual specialist or a physician but the infant's father was supposed to perform it. In fact, that may help explain the ritual: "In a very real sense, then, it was the *father*, not the infant, who was initiated; it was *he*, not his son, who was declaring loyalty and submission to the new social order"—a social order established and ruled by the priestly class.[72] The anthropologist Maurice Bloch reiterates this notion:

Circumcision is, thus, first of all a willingness to submit to the conquest of God and . . . to cooperate with His apparently murderous intentions. This is made particularly clear in an alternative origin story for circumcision given in the Bible (Exodus 4:24–26) [in which God inexplicably tries to kill Moses after just charging him to confront Pharaoh]. . . . However, death is once again avoided at the last moment [as with Abraham and Isaac] through the intervention of Moses's wife who circumcises [both Moses and their son]. Circumcision appears here as a last-moment alternative to, or perhaps postponement of, death which is granted precisely because of the actors' willing submission to conquest. . . . The circumcised penis was the sign of willingness to submit to and be conquered by God even to the point of death or pseudodeath.[73]

In this interpretation, male circumcision is a replacement for, but a lingering memory of, more serious mortifications, perhaps including child sacrifice.

Child-Burying in India

"Legitimate" child abuse is performed in religions for the same reason that "legitimate" killing or self-destruction is performed: because members believe they are supposed to and/or that some benefit flows from it. In the Hindu ceremony known as Kuzhimattru Thiru Vizha, "the festival of pits," children are temporarily buried alive. Although the practice is officially illegal—and therefore really a crime—every two years some parents in parts of India express their thankfulness to the goddesses Muthukuzhi Mariamman and Kaliamman for blessing them with a child by burying their first-born child in a pit for as much as a minute. According to one description, "The children are drugged to make them unconscious and placed in shallow 'graves' in temple courtyards. The pits are covered with leaves and dirt and the children pulled out after Hindu priests chant a brief prayer."[74] In a 2005 celebration of the ritual, twenty-eight children less than one year of age were buried for the goddesses, and eighty adults were subsequently arrested.

Recruiting Children for the Lord's Resistance Army

The gods have many different uses (and abuses) of children in mind. In Uganda, where rebels have been struggling for two decades, the Lord's Resistance Army (LRA) "recruits" youngsters of both sexes for the services the little ones can provide to their righteous cause. Led by the prophet Joseph Kony, the LRA fights for the adoption of Christian law, especially the Ten Commandments, as the official law of the state. High on faith but low on fighters, Kony routinely abducts children for the movement; according to the Associated Press, the LRA has already seized approximately twenty thousand children, "forcing boys to become soldiers and using the girls as concubines."[75] In fear for their lives, thousands of rural children spend every night away from their villages, walking to government-controlled towns where they feel safer from the predations of Kony and his religious army.

The Lord's Resistance Army is almost a perfect hybrid of religious fanaticism, ethnic hostility, and organized child abuse. The small state of Uganda has been torn by tribal conflict off and on since its independence from colonialism. It lived through the dictatorship of Idi Amin in the 1970s, during which time the Acholi people of the north struggled with various groups in the south. Out of the military and ethnic chaos that ensued, in which Acholis often suffered, numerous rebel organizations formed, including the Holy Spirit Mobile Force, led by an Acholi woman named Alice Lakwena. Despite her assertions to be in possession of the Holy Spirit, her irregular Acholi army was decimated in combat in 1987 and she escaped to Kenya. Joseph Kony, a relative of the departed prophetess, claimed to inherit her power and to take up her mantle, fighting to overthrow the government and "purify" the society politically and spiritually. For that purpose, a constant supply of fresh fighters—kidnapped children—is necessary.

The Kidnapped Child-Bride: Elizabeth Smart

The United States was stunned in 2002 when a fourteen-year-old girl, Elizabeth Smart, disappeared from her Salt Lake City home of the morning of June 5. Such events are unfortunately far from rare, but luckily Smart was found almost a year later (March 12, 2003) in the company of the prophet Immanuel David Isaiah, better known as Brian David Mitchell. He had taken Smart as his (second) bride and renamed her Shear Jashub Isaiah or "Remnant who will Return," joining him and his first wife Wanda Barzee, who herself was renamed Hephzibah Eladah Isaiah.

Mitchell was a Mormon of a particularly fundamentalist kind. One of the persistent elements in fundamentalist Mormonism is a belief in what they call "the One Mighty and Strong," essentially a messiah or harbinger of the end-time apparently prophesied in the Book of Mormon, specifically 3 Nephi 21:9–10:

> For in that day, for my sake shall the Father work a work, which shall be a great
> and a marvelous work among them; and there shall be among them those who

will not believe it, although a man shall declare it unto them. But behold, the life of my servant shall be in my hand; therefore they shall not hurt him, although he shall be marred because of them. Yet I will heal him, for I will show unto them that my wisdom is greater than the cunning of the devil.

According to Allan, some two hundred thousand Latter Day Saints fundamentalists believe in the One Mighty and Strong, and of those some 5 percent believe that *they* are the One Mighty and Strong.[76] That means that Mitchell, who claimed the title for himself, was not so unusual.

Not all the messiahs act on their convictions, though. Between February and April 2002, Mitchell had composed (or received?) a text dubbed "The Book of Immanuel David Isaiah." The twenty-seven handwritten pages opened with the words:

> Hearken! Oh ye inhabitants of the earth. Listen together and open your ears, for it is I, the Lord God of all the earth, the creator of all things that speaketh unto you. Yea, even Jesus Christ is speaking by the voice of my servant whom I have called and chosen to be a light and a covenant to the world in these last days. I have called him and given him a name to be had in remembrance before me, even the name Immanuel David Isaiah.

The document specifies that "one who is mighty and strong" has been ordained in the place of the existing church, which has "acted deceitfully" and "rejected the fullness of my gospel." It is difficult to determine whether the passage directed to first wife Hephzibah to "take into thy heart and home seven times seven sisters" was an anticipation of Immanuel's plan to wed forty-nine new brides.

Clergy Sexual Abuse of Children

The single most prominent manifestation of religious child abuse has transpired right in the heart of religion itself, the sexual exploitation of young people by officials of religion. In the United States, attention has been especially fixed on Catholic priests, but the problem is neither limited to the United States nor to Catholicism. Abuses have been noted in other sects of Christianity and in non-Christian religions as well, and in other countries. In fact, a Spanish psychologist named Pepe Rodriguez published a study on Catholic pederasty in the United States, Spain, South America, and other locations. He estimates that between 3 and 6 percent of priests and higher officers in the church have sexually abused young people and that in some dioceses like Covington, Kentucky, the number may be as high as 8 percent.[77] In an earlier work, he identified a pervasive culture of sexuality in the Spanish Catholic church, in which 60 percent of priests are sexually active—more than half with adult women and about one-fifth with adult men, but 14 percent with boys and 12 percent with girls.[78]

For some sense of the scope of the issue, we turn to an internal investigation of church records ordered by the US Conference of Catholic Bishops and performed by the John Jay College of Criminal Justice. Released in 2004, the examination, covering the period from 1950 to 2002, found eleven thousand allegations of child sexual abuse by priests, of which 61 percent (6,700) were substantiated and about half as many (3,300) were never investigated since the charges were made after the alleged offender's death. The total number of accused priests was 4,450, about 4 percent of all priests who served during those years. Most of the accused priests had a single allegation made against them, but 25 percent had two or three, 13 percent had between four and nine, and 3 percent had ten or more. A number of major dioceses, including Cleveland, Dallas, Oakland, Tucson, and Worcester reportedly destroyed or withheld files.[79]

Particular jurisdictions have done more detailed analyses. According to a report by Massachusetts attorney general Thomas F. Reilly published in 2003, at least 789 potential victims had lodged complaints with the Archdiocese of Boston alone, including the most notorious case of Father John Geoghan, who was accused by more than one hundred thirty people and was convicted on at least one count. Geoghan had been allowed to remain in his position and had actually been transferred from parish to parish by superiors, allegedly with their full knowledge of his activities. The archdiocese has reportedly paid out $85 million in settlements. The diocese of Orange County, California, settled with ninety alleged victims for $100 million in 2004, and Los Angeles agreed to a $60 million payout to forty-five lawsuits in 2006, leaving another five hundred suits pending against two hundred priests. As mentioned by Rodriguez, the diocese of Covington, Kentucky, is one of the worst offenders: with only eighty-nine thousand members, 205 allegations had been made by 2005 against thirty-five priests—10 percent of the total priests who have served there in the last fifty years.

What outrages parishioners and the public alike more than the abuses is the perceived attitude of the church to the abuses. Many claim that the top authorities have known of the problem for years or decades. Reilly's report, "The Sexual

Abuse of Children in the Roman Catholic Archdiocese of Boston," insists that the church's response to the transgressions of its functionaries placed the interests of priests above those of children:

> Top Archdiocese officials . . . decided that they should conceal—from the parishes, the laity, law enforcement, and the public—their knowledge of individual complaints of abuse and the long history of such complaints within the Archdiocese. . . . In the very few cases where allegations of sexual abuse of children were communicated to law enforcement, senior Archdiocese managers remained committed to their primary objective—safeguarding the well-being of priests and the institution over the welfare of children and preventing scandal.[80]

Most offensive of all to many observers is a document purportedly drafted by the Vatican itself in 1962, titled "Instruction on the Manner of Proceeding in Cases of Solicitation" and stamped "Confidential."[81] The typescript suggests an internal inquisitorial process (its own terminology) steeped in secrecy, in some of which cases the testimony of the parties is to be destroyed, and which sets out religious penalties (penance, loss of sacramental duties, demotion) rather than criminal penalties. Happily, projects like BishopAccountability.org have emerged to provide information and visibility for the problem.

As indicated above, while disproportionate attention has been paid to Catholic infractions, hardly any religious denomination is immune. A variety of charges have been filed against Jehovah's Witnesses members or elders for physical and sexual abuse of children, in New Hampshire, Texas, and Maine. *Freethought Today*, the newspaper of the Freedom from Religion Foundation, runs a column in each issue called "Black Collar Crime Blotter," which often occupies two or three full pages of newsprint. A few examples will have to suffice:

- Ryan Martin Wonderly, young minister of First Bethany Church of the Nazarene in Bethany, Oklahoma, was convicted of rape and lewd and indecent acts with five girls aged seven to eleven.
- Bennie McFarland, minister of Hightime Evangelistic Center in Baker, Louisiana, was found guilty of molestation and "aggravated crime against nature" involving four boys.
- Reverend Desmond O'Keefe, a teacher at Downside Abbey in Somerset, England, was jailed for sixteen counts of child pornography.
- Charles Verl Fenwick, associate pastor of New Hope Christian Center in

Veneta, Oregon, was convicted of rape and sodomy against a fourteen-year-old girl.

- Nelson Corveras, bible study teacher at Apostolic Assembly Church in Waukegan, Illinois, was sentenced to four years for sexually abusing a thirteen-year-old boy.
- John Picard, former youth pastor, was convicted on forty-two counts of sexual battery against six female congregation members and sentenced to forty years in prison.
- Timothy Sean Sullivan, pastor of Liberty Christian Center in Albany, Oregon, was found guilty of sexual abuse against his own daughter over a five-year period.

And so it continues for pages—and not only limited to violent or sexual crimes against children, but also sexual crimes against adults as well as financial misdeeds and other misbehavior.

Medical Neglect of Children

Crimes of commission are often emphasized over crimes of omission, but the latter can leave their victims equally injured or dead. Especially in the United States, "freedom of religion" often extends to parental rights in regard to medical care for their own children. At the same time, as we have seen, many religious—particularly but not solely fundamentalist Christian—parents believe in the efficacy of religious cures (prayer, laying on of hands, religious concoctions, and such) in case of injury or illness. The combination can be lethal.

Seth Asser and Rita Swan performed a unique analysis of the results of "religion-motivated medical neglect" in which they analyzed 172 cases of children who died between 1975 and 1995 after medical care was denied them for religious reasons. They found that one hundred forty of these fatalities "were from conditions for which survival rates with medical care would have exceeded 90 percent. Eighteen more had expected survival rates of [greater than] 50 percent. All but three of the remainder would likely have had some benefit from clinical help."[82] A few of the cases they describe in some detail include:

a two-year-old child aspirated a bite of banana. Her parents frantically called other members of her religious circle for prayer during nearly an hour in which some signs of life were still present.

In one family five children died of pneumonia before the age of twenty months, three before the study period. . . . Their mother was a nurse before joining a church with doctrinal objections to medical care.

One father had a medical degree and had completed a year of residency before joining a church opposed to medical care. After four days of fever, his five-month-old son began having apneic episodes. The father told the coroner that with each spell he "rebuked the spirit of death" and the infant "perked right back up and started breathing." The infant died the next day from bacterial meningitis. . . . .

A two-year-old boy with Wilms' tumor had a primary that weighed 2.5 kg, approximately one sixth of his body mass. A twelve-year-old girl was kept out of school for seven months while the primary osteogenic sarcoma on her leg grew to a circumference of 41 inches and her parents relied solely on prayer.[83]

Revealingly, they find that just five sects accounted for most (83 percent) of the fatalities—the Church of the First Born (twenty-three deaths), End Time Ministries (twelve), Faith Assembly (sixty-four), Faith Tabernacle (sixteen), and First Church of Christ Scientist/Christian Science (twenty-eight).

Asser and Swan reason that many other unaccounted deaths, and doubtless much other unaccounted suffering, can also be attributed to religion-based medical neglect. The tragedy, in their opinion, is that most states in the United States give religious exemptions to medical-treatment and parental-responsibility laws—that is, if a parent withholds medical care from a child because the parent is poor or mean, it is a crime, but if the same parent withholds medical care because the parent is devout, it is religion. This raises a complex legal, ethical, and religious question: are the resulting injuries and deaths cases of criminal negligence or simply unsuccessful faith? On the other hand, a case in 2000 highlighted the opposite response: authorities in Attleboro, Massachusetts, ordered a pregnant woman named Rebecca Corneau to receive prenatal care and delivered that care under armed guards. Her previous child, the story goes, had choked to death as she and her congregation sat and watched, counting on God to save him.[84]

BUT RELIGION IS SUPPOSED TO MAKE PEOPLE "GOOD" AND "MORAL"

The material in this chapter, and in the previous chapters, renders the old cliché that religion makes people "better," more "loving," and more "peaceful" hard to defend. Simply put, religion neither makes humans better people nor makes them worse people; it makes them people who are more likely to do what their religion says—whether that means helping or hurting.

Religion can certainly be compatible with crime, even violent crime, just as it can be compatible with other forms of violence. Even more, religion can actually be the *reason* and the *justification* for actions that, without the religion, people would either condemn or would never contemplate in the first place. Religion provides the organizational qualities that we identified in the first chapter: it is a group phenomenon with institutions and interests. Probably the most important institution in any religion is authority—the authority or hierarchy (human and superhuman) that gives members their values, their concepts, and their instructions. Recall that Philip Zimbardo ranked obedience to authority as the single greatest contributor to violence: if the leader, or the god/spirit/ancestor, tells followers to hurt or kill themselves—or to hurt or kill others—then abuses and even deaths are much more likely than if individuals are left to make their own decisions. In situations of authority, especially "ultimate" authority like divine command, the normal human brakes on violence, the normal human empathetic responses that prevent us from perpetrating injury, are overridden. Individuals may not even "want" to commit crimes and abuses (notice the hesitation of the Lafferty brothers), but they are commanded, and religious orders tend to trump individual objections.

The other reason for the comfortable coexistence of religion and abuse/murder and violence in general is the specific ideologies—beliefs, doctrines, values, and worldviews—of particular religions. Not all religions are equally violent, and not all violent ones are violent in identical ways. All the same, without the religious ideology, some forms of violence and crime would be not only undoable but also unthinkable. Without the belief in witches, no one would ever kill witches. Without the belief that blood, including or especially human blood, is ritually and supernaturally potent, there would be no need spill blood in sacrifice. Without the belief that the body is vile, or that pain increases spiritual merit, many people would never consider abusing their bodies. And without the belief that there is a "religious truth" that must be defended and expanded against all threats, there would be no reason for holy wars and religious persecutions.

All religions, then, authorize and legitimate what other religions—and nonmembers of the religion—would condemn as "crime." They literally *make* certain kinds of behaviors "good" or "moral" that people outside the religion denounce as "bad" or "immoral." In other words, they can have exactly the opposite effect from what apologists of religion typically claim. For instance, Paul Heaton's test of the effect of religiosity on crime in the United States finds "no statistically significant relationship between religious adherence and property crime or violent crime. There is some evidence that religion may encourage crime in areas with high population or few religious adherents."[85] Examining the further supposition that attendance at religious services decreases crime, his investigation of crime during the Easter season concludes that "crime rates are slightly *higher* for most categories of crime in the first four weeks after Easter, controlling for seasonal and other factors, although these increases are not statistically significant"[86] (emphasis added).

Overall crime statistics for the United States certainly demonstrate no contradiction between high religiosity and high violence crime. The FBI in 2008 reported almost 1.4 million (1,382,012) violent crimes, including 16,272 murders, 89,000 rapes, 441,855 robberies, and 834,885 assaults. At the peak of US crime in 1991–1992, there were as many as 24,500 murders and 109,000 rapes— all this in one of the most religious societies in the world. Not all these violent crimes were religious in nature; however, some were. But that is not the point; the point is that a society with high religiosity also demonstrates high criminality. In fact, in 2008, 7,783 hate crimes were reported, of which 19.5 percent were motivated by religious bias. Of the 1,606 overtly religion-motivated crimes, 65.7 percent were anti-Jewish, 7.7 percent were anti-Islamic, 4.7 percent were anti-Catholic, 3.7 percent were anti-Protestant, and 0.9 percent were anti-atheist/agnostic. Of the much larger number of attacks motivated by racial bias (4,704) and sexual bias (1,617), there is good reason to think that many of these were also related to religious beliefs. The South, commonly regarded as the Bible Belt in the United States, has consistently high crime rates, among the highest in the country and much higher than the ostensibly "secular" Northeast. Some of the highest murder rates occur in southern cities. Beyond actual crime, research has shown a general acceptance of violence in this traditionally "fire-and-brimstone" part of the country that is higher than most other parts. A measure called the Legitimate Violence Index, which calculates social attitudes toward violence as indicated in mass media, government sponsorship of violence (for instance, corporal punishment and the death penalty), and group-approved violence (such as hunting, full-contact sports, and practices like lynching), found the greatest legitimacy of violence in the South and the Rocky Mountain West. Another tool, the Violence Severity Ratio, used respondents' ratings of various types of violence and found that the South had among the highest toleration thresholds for violence.

All these findings refute the assumption that religion instills "good behavior" through "moral training," while it prevents "bad behavior" with supernatural rewards and threats—what Hirschi and Stark have called the "hell-fire hypothesis."[87] (Of course, not all, in fact few, religions have any such concept as "hellfire," but such thinking illustrates the Christian slant of much scholarly research.) Quite to the contrary, studies have suggested that the "moralistic" religion with which most American Christians are familiar may actually make violence more likely and peaceful coexistence and reconciliation more difficult. Lea and Hunsberger conclude, for example, that religion can increase the negative attitudes toward victims of suffering, in other words that "the salience of religion actually evokes rather than attenuates victim derogation among at least one group of highly religious individuals, orthodox Christians."[88] Likewise, Greer and her colleagues find that Americans are both highly religious and highly vengeful and that at least some types of American religious attitudes correlate with increased tendencies to retaliate than to reconcile.[89] The two studies suggest that Christian subjects see *justice* in misfortune where we might expect to respond with compassion. In other words, religion can make people indifferent to wrongdoing because they literally do not see anything wrong with it. And where there is no crime, there is no outrage against crime.

From a broader perspective, Gregory Paul's cross-cultural survey of religiosity and "societal health" indicates that more religious societies are in reality *less healthy* than less religious ones. Comparing the United States, Japan, and fifteen other Westernized countries, Paul discovers:

> In general, higher rates of belief in and worship of a creator correlate with higher rates of homicide, juvenile and early adult mortality, STD infection rates, teen pregnancy, and abortion in the prosperous democracies. . . . The United States is almost always the most dysfunctional of the developed democracies, sometimes spectacularly so, and almost always scores poorly.[90]

Most of these "social dysfunctions" are things that the United States itself decries, usually by promoting *more* religion and often by promoting more strict and punitive religion. However, if Lambert, Triandis, and Wolf[91] and Otterbein and Otterbein[92] are correct, this may be entirely the wrong response, since they both present evidence to suggest that adults who fear the supernatural actually inflict more pain on their children than adults who do not—creating children to grow up afraid of the supernatural and prone to inflict pain on *their* children.

CHAPTER 9

RELIGION AND NONVIOLENCE

Presumably, most people in the world, including most religious people, desire nonviolence. In fact, many religions make grand statements about peace and love. Yet the results of religion are frequently quite the opposite. What then are the prospects for religious nonviolence? Given everything we have encountered in this book, we might not be optimistic. Some polemicists, as we know, have gone so far as to insist that violence will never be eliminated as long as religion survives. Sam Harris, an advocate of this position, writes:

> Give people divergent, irreconcilable, and untestable notions about what happens after death [Harris's apparent definition of religion], and then oblige them to live together with limited resources. The result is just what we see: an unending cycle of murder and cease-fire. If history reveals any categorical truth, it is that an insufficient taste for evidence [another apparent definition of religion] regularly brings out the worst in us.[1]

Other authors, especially those composing after 9/11, often concur, arguing not only that religion is inherently violent but that its tendency toward violence is the best argument against religion.

These thinkers have a supposed solution to the problem of religious violence—the eradication of religion. In a strict definitional sense, that would work: if there were no religion, there could be no religious violence. However, such a suggestion is ultimately unhelpful, for two reasons. First, it is highly improbable, and a highly improbable solution is not a particularly useful one. Religion is nowhere near disappearing in the modern world, and attacks on it only tend to strengthen and mobilize it. Second, it is at best an extremely limited solution: surely, if religion ceased to exist, religious violence would cease to exist (by definition), *but violence would not cease to exist.* Writers like Harris give the impression of believing that religion is the source of all violence, which is patently false. We understand, as Mark Gopin phrases it, that "through our long human history, religion has been a major contributor to war, bloodshed, hatred, and intolerance."[2] However, there have also been many other major contributors to human violence, including politics, class, race, gender, ethnicity, and so on, sometimes in conjunction with each other and with religion. Ending religion alone would not end violence.

At the same time, we must be fair and concede that religion can be and at times has been a force for nonviolence. Gopin continues:

> Religion has also developed laws and ideas that have provided civilization with cultural commitments to critical peace-related values, including empathy, an openness to and even love for strangers, the suppression of unbridled ego and acquisitiveness, human rights, unilateral gestures of forgiveness and humility, interpersonal repentance and the acceptance of responsibility for past errors as a means of reconciliation, and the drive for social justice.[3]

While some of these features are a bit specifically Judeo-Christian, and while religion (let alone Judeo-Christianity) can hardly claim to have invented empathy or responsibility, it is nonetheless true that religions contain potentially nonviolence-generating beliefs and values along with potentially violence-generating ones. Religion, like all other human activities, is complex and ambiguous.

This means, of course, that defenders of religion cannot focus exclusively on the good that comes from religion, any more than detractors can focus exclusively on the bad. It is equally pointless to deny religion's violent capacities, its common if not universal violent streak, or to "accentuate the positive" and downplay the negative. Religion must be perceived as what it is, good and bad. Perhaps, as we have seen throughout this presentation, a key point is that no religion sees itself as violent, if by "violent" we mean "prone to illegitimate and unjust harm and destruction." Rather, most religions view themselves as systems of order, of justice, and above all of truth. Hence, any "violence" that they do, they do out of their sense of order and justice and truth. In other words, a religious value like "love" (notwithstanding that religion did not invent love either) is no guarantee of nonviolence: Augustine among others asserted that Christians persecute and kill out of love.

So, in this final chapter, we will explore the possibilities of religious nonviolence. This will provide an opportunity to consider the nature of nonviolence, especially in terms of the variables that promote violence described in chapter 1. We will also consider the characteristics of nonviolent societies and the known nonviolent (or at least low-conflict) religions, like Buddhism and Jainism and certain pacifist sects of Christianity. Ultimately we will find that religion can be part of the foundation of a nonviolent social order—although this is not its only or perhaps primary tendency.

WHAT IS NONVIOLENCE?

Many of the questions we have raised in this book, like "What is violence?" or "What is religion?" may have seemed nonsensical at first but proved to be anything but. So when we ask "What is nonviolence?" we are not asking a nonsensical question. It might seem on the surface that nonviolence is obvious: it is not violence, the absence of violence. But things are never quite so simple. Kenneth Boulding, an expert on violence and nonviolence, explains that nonviolence has both positive and negative sides. Negative nonviolence is merely the absence or cessation of violence, "of turmoil, tension, conflict, and war."[4] Of course, turmoil, tension, conflict, and war are not synonyms: war may end but tension continue, and turmoil can exist without conflict and war. Nevertheless, his point is well taken: if I am hitting you and I stop hitting you, we are now in a state of nonviolence, although you will still be in pain, neither of us may be happy, and no problems may have been solved. Positive nonviolence is much more; he describes it as "a condition of good management, orderly resolution of conflict, harmony associated with mature relationships, gentleness, and love."[5] This is certainly a more enduring, productive, and satisfying condition to be in.

We will assume that when people speak of nonviolence, they mean this positive aspect. Notice that Boulding's understanding of nonviolence does not imply or require the elimination of all conflict; if it did, it would be an idealistic and utopian goal. Humans are extremely unlikely to avoid all conflicts or, more important, to remove all bases for conflicts. Rather, the question for Boulding and for others is how we handle these conflicts, and he insists that this more comprehensive and active notion of positive nonviolence "is quite consistent with conflict and excitement, debate and dialogue, drama and confrontation. But it provides a setting within which these processes do not get out of hand, become pathological, and cause more trouble than they are worth."[6]

Thus, Boulding distinguishes between *nonconflict* and *nonviolence*. Nonconflict is probably some utopian dream: humans will always have disagreements, competitions, and conflicts of various sorts. However, conflict need not and does not automatically and inevitably lead to violence. All nonconflict is nonviolence, he concludes, and all violence is conflict, but some conflict is violence and some is not.

To be honest, *peace* is the central idea in Boulding's analysis, but he uses that term in a particularly narrow sense: peace for him is the opposite of war, not of conflict in general. In this sense, peace is not synonymous with nonviolence, if only because peace can come as the result of hideous violence: if one society or country or religion obliterates another, there is peace to be sure, but only at the price of great violence. War being a subset of violence, peace would not necessarily be the absence of all violence but only of warlike violence. Or, as Boulding puts it, "All nonconflict is peace, but conflict can be divided into war and peace."[7] In other words, there is nonconflictual peace and conflictual peace.

We are making three points by exploring this terminological thicket. The first is that nonviolence, nonconflict, and peace are not synonymous—that is, that the range of nonviolence is more complicated than we might think. The second is that the goal of eliminating all violence may be silly and futile, and the goal of eliminating all *conflict* most definitely is. Unrealistic goals are not helpful at all in the treatment of violence and may actually lead to frustrations and disappointments that cause us to abandon all attempts to restrain violence. The third point, following from the previous two, is that nonviolence is not some utopian state because *it is not a state at all*. A person or group or society can be in a highly agitated and tumultuous state without engaging in violence. Rather, nonviolence, like violence too, is a *process*, or even more so, it is a *skill*. It is something that must be learned and practiced, and it must be practiced continuously: it is not a "cure" for violence but perhaps a "regimen" against violence. This is why Boulding and others (see below) refer to "management" and (ongoing) resolution and "mature relationships" that "handle" conflict and violence even if they cannot reasonably eradicate it.

It may be worth acknowledging that even in the most violent groups or societies, violence may be common but is not *constant*. As Fry reminds us, warlike societies are not at war perpetually, and in societies with high murder and assault rates, most members are not murdered or assaulted on any given day. In fact, "the vast majority of people on the planet awake on a typical morning and live through a *violence-free* day."[8] That is to say, violence and nonviolence are not logically opposed processes: there can be nonviolence in the midst of violence and vice versa. Nice people can be violent, and mean people can be nonviolent; even the most viciously violent person can be good to their spouse or children or pet. Violence and nonviolence coexist; no person, group, or society is all one or all the other.

Varieties of Nonviolence

One of the paradoxes of nonviolence is that we cannot study or comprehend it by examining violence alone, any more than we can study or comprehend health by examining illness alone or study or comprehend happiness by examining sadness alone. Health is not merely the absence of illness but is, in Boulding's terms, a state or condition of good bodily management and of relationships between the parts of the body. Happiness is not just the absence of sadness. And nonviolence is not just the absence of violence. In fact, there is more than one way to be healthy, or happy, or nonviolent.

Douglas Fry, a scholar of cross-cultural systems of peace, agrees with Boulding that absolute peace and nonconflict is unattainable. "Conflict is an inevitable feature of social life," he writes, and we might add not only of social life but of natural and physical life: humans are in conflict with germs and mosquitoes and often with the environment itself. However, clearly physical aggression is not the only option for dealing with conflict.[9] Neither is radiant love the only alternative to conflict; if it were, we would be in a lot of trouble as a species. Instead, Fry notes a variety of cultural solutions to the challenge of conflict and potential violence, all of which are skills to be inculcated and honed.

One set of approaches to the containment of conflict and violence Fry calls "unilateral and bilateral," that is, one side or both sides in a conflict can adopt these strategies themselves without outside assistance. The first strategy is *avoidance*, which "entails ceasing or limiting interaction with a disputant, either temporarily or permanently. The use of avoidance in response to conflict is extremely widespread and probably occurs in all social groups."[10] Obviously, two groups or states facing a potential conflict can break off relations with each other and, in some cases, even withdraw physically from each other (modern states do not really have that option). Two groups (religious, racial, class, etc.) in the same society can segregate or be segregated into their own neighborhoods (e.g., a Jewish ghetto) or towns or regions, or less physically into their own occupations, schools, and endogamous marriages (e.g., the Hindu caste system). Avoidance should ideally prevent conflicts before they start, although it can also be reactive.

Another strategy is *toleration*, which, as we noted in chapter 5, can mean ignoring or overlooking the conflictual issue and continuing the relationship with the other party in disregard of the difference. Donald Black opines that toleration of this sort is especially common when the relations between the two parties are either very close or very remote.[11] A third method of dealing with conflict is *negotiation*, in which the hostile parties enter into discussion and generally offer some type of compromise or "mutually agreeable nonviolent solutions."[12] These could include payment or compensation, an apology or other demonstration of responsibility or remorse, or whatever terms the two sides arrive at. Finally, in *self-redress* or *self-help*, one side takes the initiative to "prevail in a dispute" or to get the other side to capitulate to its demands.

Distinct from all these are the "trilateral" approaches that bring a third party into the conflict; Fry refers collectively to these methods as *settlement*. One form is *friendly peacemaking* in which the third party only attempts to separate, exhort, or redirect the attention of the disputants but not really to address or resolve their underlying disagreement. In *mediation* the third party actually engages the disputants in an effort to reach a mutually satisfactory solution; it is essentially negotiation with a go-between, which may help when there is especially high tension between the parties. *Arbitration* goes further and gives the third party the right to make a decision in the dispute, even if the decision is not binding on the belligerents. Still further is *adjudication*, in which disputants submit their problems or have their problems submitted to a "judge" who is empowered not only to rule on the issue but also to enforce his or her ruling; the judge may assign guilt or culpability (to one or both parties), work to restore harmony between them, or impose a penalty (on one or both). Lastly, *repressive peacemaking* uses force to stop the fighting between the disputants, "regardless of the reasons for the dispute."[13] The repressive peacemaker simply forces them to be nonviolent by attacking one or both or by depriving them of the means to fight (e.g., disarming them, arresting leaders, and so on).

The Qualities of a Nonviolent Society

Conflict, it seems, is natural and inevitable. Violence, especially its more organized and lethal manifestations like war, is not. Researchers have in actuality discovered a number of societies and sects that are relatively nonviolent; we qualify their nonviolence as "relative" because, as Fry says, "no internally peaceful society is expected to be absolutely devoid of *all forms* of aggression at *all times*."[14] Instead, we might follow Ross in calling them "low-conflict societies," which experience comparatively, often dramatically, low rates of violence and restrain that violence more effectively when they do experience it.[15]

Ross, Fry, Bruce Bonta, and others have compiled lists of low-conflict societies. Bonta, for instance, names twenty-five nonviolent groups and societies, including the Amish, Balinese, Batek, Birhor, Buid, Chewong, Fipa, G/wi, Hutterites, Ifaluk, Inuit, Jains, Kadar, !Kung, Ladakhis, Lepchas, Mennonites, Montagnais-Naskapi, Nayaka, Paliyan, Piaroa, Semai, Tahitians, Tristan Islanders, and Zapotec.[16] Twenty-one of these names refer to traditional societies, four (Amish, Hutterites, Jains, and Mennonites) to religious denominations (see below). Fry offers an overlapping but even more extensive list, with citations to their research sources: Fipa/Ufipa, G/wi, !Kung (now more commonly called Ju/'hoansi), Kongo, Mbuti, Nubians, Tristan da Cunha, Akha, Alangan Agta, Bajau Laut/Sama Dilaut, Balinese, Batak Agta, Batek, Birhor, Buid, Central Thai, Chewong, Hanunoo, Iraya Agta, Irula, Jahai, Kadar, Kua Sai Chinese, Ladhaki, Lepchas, Malapandaram, Mamnua Agta, Mentawei Islanders, Nayaka, Palawan Agta, Paliyan, Punan/Penan, Semai, Semang, Sherpa, Subanun, Sulod, Tagbanua, Taubuid Agta, Temiar Senoi, Tiruray Agta, Toda, Toraja, Veddahs, Wana, Yames, Yanadi, Amish, Inuit, Dogrib, Hopi, Hutterites, Mandan, Montagnais-Naskapi, Papago, Saulteaux, Taos Pueblo, Tewa Pueblo, Zapotec, Arapesh, Ifaluk, Mardudjara, Rotuma Islanders, Tahitians, Tanna Islanders, Tikana, Tikopia, Wape, Cayapa, Kuikuru, Panare, Pemon, Piaroa, Siriono, Trio, Waiwai, and Wauja/Waura.[17] With a database this large, some generalizations can be made.

The first and most obvious observation about these low-conflict groups is that they tend to be small and premodern societies—"traditional" or "tribal" societies, as they are often (not completely accurately) called. Most have low-surplus economic systems, especially foraging (hunting and gathering) or horticulture (low-technology farming) with a few cases of pastoralism (low-technology animal herding) on the list. Since they generally do not produce much of a surplus, there is relative equality in the group, that is, no particular or formal stratification or "class" system. As such, there tends to be relatively little centralization of power: no individual, family, or class dominates the society or monopolizes political authority. Such societies are more or less egalitarian or composed of relative equals. They often lack the kinds of institutions (police forces, court systems, prisons, armies, etc.) that would make real coercion possible. Social organization is generally accomplished through kinship ties, and individuals tend to belong to multiple kinship and social groups (by birth or marriage or gender or voluntary membership), creating cross-cutting ties that make much, if not all, of the community part of the individual's "own kind."

Aside from these structural or organizational characteristics, they have some cultural and psychological qualities in common. The nonviolent concepts, beliefs, and values of such societies become the learning environment and thus (ideally) the typical personality of the group. First and foremost among these beliefs and values is an obvious but critical disapproval of violence: acts and displays of aggression and anger are frowned upon and devalued. Consequently, "As individuals internalize antiviolent or nonviolent beliefs, they become reluctant to engage in violence."[18] Since adults do not engage in violence, there are no adult models of violence for children to emulate. Children are not exposed to violence in the form of corporal punishment and harsh discipline; to the contrary, Ross comments that "the data show that the more affectionate and warm and the less harsh the socialization in a society, the lower the level of political conflict and violence."[19]

If violence is not modeled for children, neither are children given the opportunity to practice it. They may be highly discouraged from acting aggressively, such as hitting each other. Neither are they taught aggressive games and forms of play. In fact, Bonta concludes that the single biggest predictor of violence is *competition* and the single biggest predictor of nonviolence, *cooperation*. Low-conflict societies "shun competition as inimical to their beliefs and firmly link it with aggression and violence."[20] As he describes:

> Kadar children in southern India . . . play without any element of competition such as hiding, catching, or running away—their games are based on simply enjoyment of the activities of the moment. When Chewong children spin tops, which they acquire from the more aggressive Malay people of Malaysia, they leave out the competition that characterizes Malay top-spinning games.
>
> Most of the games of the children in these societies are cooperative activities, which involve demonstrating physical skills, mimicking adult activities, or telling stories. Semai boys play at hunting, while girls play house; they swing on vines, jump down waterfalls, and play fantasy games. A favorite game among the !Kung children of Namibia and Botswana is zeni, in which the children use a stick to throw into the air and catch a weight that is attached by a thong to a feather. Although children exhibit widely differing abilities in the game, they do not compete: All play for the sheer pleasure of it.[21]

In terms of personality, such societies "value humility and modesty and do not tolerate achievement-oriented people" and certainly not domination or coercion.[22] The idea that one person would have power over another is often foreign and distasteful and deemed to breed resentment and disorder. As a result, members of such groups are often "reticent, cautious, and modest about personal achievement, and they avoid leadership, or at least the arrogance of leadership, as a major strategy to maintain peacefulness."[23] Egotism is particularly unwelcome and antisocial. The steps that these societies take to ensure humility and what we in the Western world might even call "low self-esteem" can feel drastic: Richard Lee tells how the !Kung or Ju/'hoansi intentionally ignored and even deprecated the successful hunter and his kill to prevent him from developing "arrogance,"[24] and Jean Briggs describes how the Utku Eskimo suppressed all strong emotion and literally withdrew affection from and sometimes teased children over the age of four or five to inhibit their sense of self-importance and to teach passivity.[25]

Reticent, cautious, and nonegotistical people react to the inevitable stresses of social life differently than confident, willful, and aggressive people, specifically "in such a way that rancor, polarization, and outright violence are avoided."[26] Among these conflict management methods are the emphasis on commonalities rather than differences within the group and the activation of cross-cutting ties, so that even your enemy is related to you in some way. Such groups often depend on avoidance or toleration as another key to their nonviolence. Robarchek writes of the Semai, a famously nonviolent society in Malaysia (see below) that they "go to great lengths to avoid conflict and will actually tolerate annoyance and sacrifice personal interest rather than precipitate an open confrontation."[27] The Buid of the Philippines, another renowned nonviolent society, went so far as to practice a radical form of individual avoidance and autonomy in which all social relationships other than the nuclear family were fragile and uncomfortable; individuals seldom spoke directly to each other or shared chores like farming, and when they did interact they did not face each other or speak much.[28]

Finally, these low-conflict societies encourage members not only to control (we might say repress) their emotions but sometimes to deny that they have negative emotions at all—perhaps to deny that there is any tension or conflict at all. The title of Briggs's study of the Utku, *Never in Anger*, makes this point: their people should not show too much emotion of any kind, positive or negative (the social ideal was *kanngu* or restraint/shyness, a desire to be appropriately inconspicuous), and hostilities and disagreements were consciously downplayed. The Semai dismissed the very existence of hateful feelings in their society. Likewise, the !Kung or Ju/'hoansi restrained their displays of anger, discomfort, and pain; the Tarahumara of Mexico disowned negative emotions, and the Zapotec villagers researched by Fry "sometimes deny that a conflict even exists at all."[29]

Portrait of a Nonviolent Society: The Semai of Malaysia

The Semai are an indigenous people of the west-central Malay peninsula. Traditionally they were foragers (men hunted in the forest with blowguns), with some horticulture. They did not recognize private ownership of land or other real property; rather, families "owned" land if they were the ones who cleared it and who were currently farming it. If, however, they abandoned the land, others moved in and "owned" it in turn. Their attitude toward houses was the same: a family that left a house empty could find it occupied by others if and when they returned, in which case the original occupants simply looked for other residence. Semai marriage was very informal, and premarital or extramarital sex was common and not particularly serious. Kin related by blood tended to live in the same household, typically numbering fifteen to fifty people, and interactions among them were characterized by generosity, tranquility, trust, and sociality. However, "outsiders" or *mai*—which could mean non-Semai as well as Semai from another village or region or just nonrelatives—were not liked or trusted.[30]

Semai political organization was of the band variety, with fifty to one hundred members in a typical band. Like most band-level societies, political relations were egalitarian, with no real leaders or even superiors. Elders commanded more respect than younger people, yet the elders did not and could not compel obedience from their youngers: the latter could simply refuse an order with the response "I *bood*," meaning "I don't feel like it." Trying to coerce someone, including a child, to obey another person's commands generated a negative feeling known to the Semai as *punan*.

The concept of punan is central to understanding Semai social behavior. It explains why they seldom hit (and never killed) each other. Mai felt and did such things but not "us." *Punan* means something like "to make someone unhappy, especially by frustrating them." Both the offending act and the resultant emotional state were punan. Not only was punan an unpleasant condition to be in, but it was also believed to be physically and supernaturally dangerous, increasing people's susceptibility to accidents or other injuries. Punan was generated by an assortment of behaviors, all of which were therefore to be avoided, including being stingy, refusing a request, making a request of more than another could afford to give, directly repaying a gift, demanding privacy or excluding friends or kin from your space, and refusing to grant sexual favors (particularly by women). However, pressuring a person for sex was also punan, so sexual aggression by men was avoided, even toward their own spouses.

In a very real sense, the concept of punan implied that individual Semai "felt each other's pain"; it gave weight to the Western cliché, "It hurts me more than it hurts you." In a word, it established a kind of empathy, literally a shared feeling, a feeling-with or feeling-as. Semai accordingly acted to prevent situations in which both parties would feel bad and frustrated, especially the kinds of situations that suggested an obligation or a power imbalance. If a person did get punan, he or she had a few options. One was to simply endure it in silence, to "tolerate" it. Another option was to seek compensation from the offender, to restore the social equilibrium between them. The damaged party might seek a third party, a negotiator or arbitrator, to work out an apology or a gift, but such intermediaries were not very common in Semai society. Alternatively, the damaged party might simply act unilaterally, for instance taking some belongings from the offender, thus publicizing the fact that an offense had been committed and thereby serving justice. If both parties did not accept the resolution of the dispute, a quarrel could break out, but violence never resulted; even when drunk, Semai people got loud but not aggressive.

Pervading Semai beliefs and behaviors was a value of noninterference or "not bothering" other people. The Semai word *persusah* represented this negative value of making trouble for someone, making them unhappy, or meddling in their affairs. A good person did not persusah others; persusah was punan too. When one person did persusah another, the typical reaction was passivity or withdrawal. This notion of persusah applied to everything from family relations to politics, such that throughout the society a climate was created where violence or domination was unwelcome and almost inconceivable.

The Semai were careful to instill these nonviolent values in their young. First and foremost, children were not exposed to violent models. Children had no occasion to observe adults hitting each other, nor were children physically punished. In fact, children were not disciplined firmly at all, and even parental orders could be refused with a mere "I bood." Pressuring a child, just like an adult, generated punan. Adults instead used fear to attempt to motivate children: for example, children were taught to fear mai, to fear violence, and to fear other social misbehaviors. When a children did something dangerous, parents would literally cry out, "Fear, fear!" This is not to say that Semai people lived in a constant state of terror, but that they learned self-control and moderation through a cautious, even timid, approach to the physical and social world.

When children did display aggression, parents did not punish the behavior but rather laughed at it or responded with a mock threat. They might pretend to hit the child. For their part, children also played games in which they faked attacks on each other; they might almost but not quite hit each other with a stick or almost but not quite wrestle each other to the ground. In either case, the attack—and the defeat—never actually occurred. At the same time, there were no indigenous games that involved real aggression or even competition.

RELIGIONS OF NONVIOLENCE

The discussion above illustrates that, while it may be rare and difficult to achieve, nonviolence is a human possibility. It also illustrates that religion can play a role in this nonviolence but that religion is not the sole or perhaps the key factor; as we have argued throughout this book, religion is one element in a complex social system, and religion itself is a complex system of made of many parts. Religion in isolation probably cannot make a group or society violent, and religion in isolation probably cannot make it nonviolent. However, in conjunction, religion, social structures, and psychological/cultural concepts and practices can produce nonviolence, or at least less violence (absolute nonviolence, and especially absolute nonconflict, as we have said, is not a realistic goal).

Since religions are complex, ambiguous, and even internally contradictory, they simultaneously contain aspects that are conducive to violence and to nonviolence. Among the nonviolent messages and values of various religions are love, empathy, pacifism or nonharm, the sanctity of life, nonacquisitiveness and generosity, compassion and kindness, and self-restraint.[31] Islam, for instance, most assuredly contains concepts, traditions, and histories of violence, expressed in such terms as *jihad* and *qital*. However, it also offers peacemaking concepts like *khayr* (goodness), *birr* (righteousness), *al-iqsat* (equity), and *al-'adl* (justice). Ancient Judaism was a martial religion in which their god not only ordered but led armies into combat, but it also expressed sympathy for the fellow sufferer, based on their own experience of captivity in Egypt; critical to this sympathy was the concept of *ger* or "stranger," the person "who is different than the majority group addressed by biblical law but who is also a person who must be included at Jewish celebrations, cared for, and even loved. He is the quintessential outsider, who is also a litmus test of the ethical conduct of the majority group."[32] In the Jewish tradition, Gopin argues, the notion of the ger gives form to "the human situation of simultaneous sameness and difference, of the need for integration, love, and acceptance coupled with the need to have boundaries of the separated self or group."[33]

In this section, then, we will examine some of the less-violent, low-conflict religions and denominations in the world. We will see that doctrines or beliefs (especially "scriptures") are important but not definitive in the outcome of violence/nonviolence, since, for example, Christian doctrines have produced both violent and nonviolent movements. At the same time, even followers of a "nonviolent religion" like Buddhism can find room for violence in their behavior. But if there is anything that low-conflict religions share in common, it can serve as a lesson for religions and nonreligions alike in how to constrain or marginalize violence.

Nonviolence in Buddhism

Buddhism is probably most Westerners' image of a nonviolent religion. Buddhism officially denounces violence more openly and strenuously than any well-known religion (but not as much as Jainism; see below). Originally a movement growing out of Hinduism, Buddhism is the name given to the dharma preached by Siddhartha Gautama (who became known as the first buddha or "enlightened one" in the late sixth century BCE); as such there is some controversy whether the Buddha-dharma should be regarded as a religion or as an ethical program.

Gautama's story is familiar to many Westerners. He was born into a royal lineage in northern India. In his early adulthood, he was exposed to the ugly realities of human existence (old age, sickness, decline, and death). As a result, Gautama left his home and practiced the discipline of the monk and seeker for many years. Having lived a life of comfort and luxury, he attempted the exertions of an ascetic but found them unenlightening. Finally he realized the cause of and the solution to suffering, which constituted his enlightenment and his message to the world. Suffering (dukkha) is part of the nature of reality; this is the First Noble Truth. Suffering comes from desire or attachment, losing things we love or want and having things we do not love or want (like disease); this is the Second Noble Truth. The cessation of suffering hence comes from the cessation of desire or attachment; this is the Third Noble Truth. The Fourth Noble Truth provides the "path" (the Eightfold Path), which is the proper way of living to escape suffering, attain knowledge, and ultimately free oneself from the cycle of rebirth and achieve nirvana, a "snuffing out" of individual sentience in achievement of a higher consciousness or state of being. This is the Middle Way between ordinary living and self-destructive asceticism.

The nonviolence inherent in Buddhist thought comes from two sources. The first is *karuna* or compassion. Buddhism, which is often considered a "selfish" religion because each person is on his or her own individual enlightenment quest, actually holds karuna in very high regard; there is an entire class of figures, called *bodhisattvas* or "those whose essence is enlightenment," who postpone their own final liberation to help others attain theirs. One of the highest compassionate values is ahimsa, a concept shared with Hinduism and Jainism meaning "no/without harm." Harming other persons or living things is adding to their suffering, which is anathema to the Buddha's teachings. Specifically, this value translates into a "moral" or behavioral code that includes

> noninjury to all living beings; not causing pain and suffering to others including plants and animals; compassion towards all living creatures; abstaining from animal and human sacrifices; cultivation of forgiveness, universal love and friendliness; nonviolent reaction to violent thoughts, words and actions; mental and verbal nonviolence towards self and towards others; abstaining from meat eating; [and] abstaining from hunting, animal fights and similar practices in which animals are subjected to cruelty and suffering.[34]

Many religions, of course, make speeches about nonviolence, peace, and compassion, but Buddhism anchors these values in a second source, its doctrines or claims about reality. One aspect of these doctrines is that all beings participate in the cycle of life, death, and rebirth, so humans are not unique in the universe: in fact, humans may have been or may yet be "lower" life-forms like plants and animals, so harming a plant or animal is harming a once or future human. Another part of these doctrines is the effect of doing harm on the perpetrator of the harm: injuring the other also injures the self, since it increases the amount of karma that leads to continuing (and even lowering) rebirth. As Tibetan Buddhist leader Samdhong Rinpoche states, "If you accumulate nonvirtuous deeds, negative karmic force, the result would be misery, pain, dissatisfaction, frustration, and disasters"[35]—and not just for the victim but for the victimizer. In short, the harm you do comes back to harm you. In fact, he argues, "from the Buddhist viewpoint, even in self-defense violence is not permissible or justifiable. . . . Therefore according to Buddhism, we say, self-sacrifice would be much better than indulging in a violent act in order to defend oneself."[36]

One of the main differences between Buddhism and the religions to be discussed below is that Buddhism has faced the challenge of political power; Jainism, the Christian "peace churches," and tribal religions like that of the Piaroa have never formed or dominated a government. Buddhism became a political force after the conversion of the Indian emperor Asoka or Ashoka, who ruled in the mid–third century BCE. Buddhism, like Jainism at the same time and Christianity several hundred years later, was a new minority religion spread in the streets of urban centers. Asoka began his career as any future emperor must, with war and bloodshed. However, later (after he had won his wars), "he foreswore military operations in favor of spiritual conquests,"[37] converted to Buddhism, and became an energetic supporter and proselytizer for the religion. Under his authority, Buddhist missionaries were sent among the Indian people as well as to lands far from India, including China and Central Asia. He encouraged citizens to follow the Buddha-dharma: his Second Pillar Edict asserted that "Dharma is good. But what does dharma consist of? It consists of few sins and many good deeds, of kindness, liberality, truthfulness, and purity."[38] Asoka personally forsook war and hunting, banned animal sacrifice, and practiced a remarkable level of religious toleration, even inviting representatives of various religions to his court to teach and debate.

Asoka was the exception, though, since, as we will return to discuss below, power does not so much corrupt as compromise. Jayaram admits, and we saw in earlier chapters, that over the past twenty-five hundred years "neither the Buddhists, nor the Hindus nor the Jains met violence with nonviolence. The kings and emperors engaged themselves in regular wars for one reason or the other and maintained huge armies. . . . In his lifetime the Buddha tried to prevent wars between warring clans, but his influence did not last for long."[39] In fact, Fleischman argues that the Buddhist message is one of nonviolence, *not of pacifism*. In the Buddha's own teaching and in the history of Buddhism, he finds precedents for a coexistence of nonviolent religion and of an active government including a military. Even the Buddha's utterance that "if bandits brutally severed him limb from limb with a two-handled saw, he who entertained hate in his heart on that account would not be one who followed my teaching" can be interpreted, Fleischman explains, as an injunction against *hatred*, not an injunction against action or self-defense, including violence. The Buddha was too realistic and too open-minded to rigidly rule out all possibilities of good violence: "If the soldier is acting in a protective, pure-hearted way of life, he may be an agent of justice who simply is the vehicle by which the karma of the murderers ends in their own death."[40] Rupert Gethin, for instance, reminds us that Buddhism embraces a notion of the religious warrior, both the ascetic "as warrior and hero" and the literal Buddhist warrior king.[41] Likewise, Peter Schalk describes a variety of ways in which Buddhism can claim to be nonviolent while still making a space for violence, including "the holy 'end' that justifies the less holy or even profane 'means,'" the linkage between the corrupt, violent present and an ideal past, the distinction between "preliminary ends" like political survival and "final ends" like nirvana, the separation of a peaceful elite and a violent common folk, and of course the simple denial that violence ever happened.[42] This only speaks once again to the difficulty of defining "violence."

Nonviolence in Jainism

While Buddhism can claim considerable credit as a religion of nonviolence, Jainism surpasses it. Jainism takes the Hindu-Buddhist concept of ahimsa to new (and sometimes self-destructive) heights.

Jainism was born at roughly the same historical moment and from roughly the same cultural roots as Buddhism. Its founder, Mahavir, lived during the sixth century BCE, an Indian prince like the future Buddha. His life story is even similar: he reportedly abandoned his regal existence around age thirty and became a naked ascetic. He spent twelve years in silent meditation, striving to overcome his baser feelings and desires. At the end of his exertions he, like Gautama, achieved perfect knowledge and perception (a state called *keval-jnana* and comparable to nirvana). He was a *jina* or "conqueror" of the self and the material world, and his followers would come to be known as Jains.

As in Buddhism, and even Hinduism from which it grew, the aim of Jainism is the purification and ultimate liberation of the "soul" from the physical body and thus the attainment of true self-knowledge. The connection between the soul and the body, and between this bodily life and past and future bodily lives, is karma, which in the Jain view is a literal physical substance, like "grains" or "atoms" of religious matter. The soul is in bondage due to karma, which causes a materialistic orientation in life and an attachment to negative and violent thoughts and actions like anger, hatred, greed, and violence. These thoughts and actions result in more karma, which builds like dirt or rust on the soul. Thus the path to this goal of true knowledge is liberation of the self from matter and from the consequences of material action.

As a discipline, Jainism consists of the Five Great Vows, a code of conduct intended to minimize one's interaction with matter and its degrading effects. First on the list of vows is ahimsa or nonviolence. This includes injunctions against killing or harming humans, but it goes much further: in its fullest manifestation, it takes the form of radical dietary rules, of which vegetarianism is the least. The problem as Jains see it is that all living things are like humans in having "senses." Some have the same five senses as humans, some only one sense, but they are protected beings all the same. So, as in Buddhism, humans should certainly not eat meat or kill animals; animals, like humans, are "five-sensed beings" whom it is wrong to harm. Eggs are also living things, though without all five senses, and cannot be eaten, although milk is edible since it is not a being as such. Not even insects or "mobile beings" are edible, since they possess some of the five human senses; a devout Jain might a wear mask, drink water through a filter, and sweep the path with a whisk in front of him or her in order to avoid swallowing or trampling such beings.

However, even vegetables are living things, so the strictures of ahimsa protect them as well. Cereals like rice and wheat are the ideal and only "fully noninjurious food" among the "one-sensed beings" of plants, because the seeds are produced only at the end of the life of the plant; thus, no additional harm is done by eating them. So-called dry-fruits are acceptable for the same reason. Next in acceptability are the fruits that ripen on the tree or that fall from the tree after ripening, since this causes no injury to the tree. Least acceptable are foods that are taken from a living plant, such as leaves (like lettuce) or roots and tubers (like potatoes and carrots). These foods are living and feeling parts of one-sensed beings; removing them causes pain to the plant and may also harm small "mobile beings" that live within them (like insects). Consuming such living plants gives suffering to the plant and karma to the person who eats it. As a result of this religious philosophy, the ideal Jain life, which would involve doing no harm at all to the living world, would require consuming no food at all. And, as we saw in chapter 4, this is in fact the ideal (voluntary) death of a Jain ascetic, a Digambar, who takes the vow of sallekhana to die by fasting.

The first Great Vow alone would presumably block a Jain from doing any physical harm to any being on earth and render him or her the most nonviolent sort of person. However, the Great Vows include virtues that support this nonviolent worldview and personality. They include *satya* (truthfulness), *achaurya* (nonstealing), *brahmacharya* (sexual chastity), and *aparigraha* (nonpossession and nonattachment). Full-time Jain monks and ascetics must live by this code, while

lay Jains are expected to keep as many of the vows as possible. Beyond the Great
Vows themselves, a number of other Jain principles contribute to peacefulness
and nonaggression. For one, Jainism advocates a classless and gender-neutral
society; Brahmans and untouchables are welcome alike into the faith, and men
and women are equal in their liberation quest. Another is religious tolerance
(*anekantvada* or nonabsolutism and open-mindedness), which inhibits a militant
or confrontational religiosity and removes some of the cause for religious disagreement and animosity. Jainism of course believes that it holds the true understanding of the universe and the true path of enlightenment, but it does not
revile other religions as false and evil. It is not monotheistic: there are many
gods, not a single "true" creator/judge god, and each human (and presumably
each being) is on a path toward godhood. It is simply that each human (and presumably each being) is at a different stage on this path. It is perhaps this attitude that explains the Jain value of "relativity" or multiperspectivism (*syad-
vada*), which accepts that every person and being has his/her/its own perspective
or experience. A Jain tries to appreciate if not actually see the perspective or
experience of other persons/beings. This principle leaves no place for intolerance,
exclusionary claims, or extreme and unequivocal assertions.

Like Buddhism, Jainism is not a lifestyle utterly without violence. In fact,
all life is violence, since the fundamental truth (for Jains and for all other human
beings) is that life eats life. And the Jain ascetic practices a harsh form of self-
deprivation and self-negation.

Nonviolence in Piaroa Religion

While the other cases in this chapter focus on large-scale world religions, some
mention of a small-scale traditional society like the Piaroa is merited, for two reasons: first, they were a nonviolent society in the same environment as and in fact
surrounded by violent neighbors like the Yanomamo, and second, their religious
ideas were central to their nonviolence. Located in the rainforest of Venezuela, the
Piaroa were a predominantly horticultural society, practicing some hunting as
well.[43] Like the Semai, the Piaroa social world was almost totally devoid of physical violence: children were never physically punished, spouses never hit each
other, and people were generally alarmed by outbursts of aggression. They valued
and worked toward moderation in social relations. There were no formal political
leaders or "government." As religious specialists, shamans might accumulate
some social power, but there was a very real brake on spiritual/religious power

even for shamans: it was believed that the more powerful a shaman or anyone else became, the more humility he was expected to show, and supernatural dangers awaited those who grasped for power. Both power and violence were associated for the Piaroa with domination, and domination was associated with coercion, all of which were negative in their value system.

In particular, killing was held to be unthinkable and was actually equated with cannibalism, the "consumption" or "destruction" of one's own kind. They believed that killing/cannibalism could cause the death of the killer by a kind of spiritual poisoning. For the Piaroa, in fact, all killing, not just human murder, was a form of cannibalism, and all death was a result of being eaten. There was no such thing as "natural" human death; all death was the result of sorcery by foreign societies (i.e., non-Piaroa). Even more, eating plants and animals—and the very culture that made the knowledge and skills of hunting and farming possible—was viewed as violent, dangerous, and poisonous. For the Piaroa, "invisible" violence was everywhere.

The dangers of eating and being eaten were related to Piaroa religious ideas. In the Piaroa creation story, there were two creator beings, named Kuemoi and Wahari. Kuemoi was the Master of Water, an ugly and insanely violent cannibal, while Wahari was the Master of Land and the creator of the Piaroa people. The two gods were rivals and sorcerers who vied for power over the other's domain. Invading Wahari's terrestrial realm, Kuemoi created land plants, animals, and fire—fire representing "culture" (as in the Prometheus myth), the human knowledge and skills for controlling and exploiting "nature." Wahari, in addition to creating humans in his land-based kingdom, created fish and fishing in his rival's watery domain. Most important of all, though, he transformed the non-human species into their present edible forms. For, prior to his supernatural intervention, plants and animals had possessed both spiritual and anthropomorphic characteristics. By being stripped of their humanlike form, they became proper food for humans.

The extreme and almost unbearable contradiction of the gods' actions was that the entire world became poisonous and dangerous. Culture was poisonous because it was created by a mad god who was literally on drugs (another form of poison) at the time. Food was also poisonous; animals and large fish were particularly dangerous to eat, because they were the most humanlike, but even small fish, birds, and plants posed a threat. Consuming any of these things was perilous, not because they were physically harmful but because they were spiritually risky: animals and fish were originally "people" who had been transformed into nonhuman beings by the gods. Consequently, fish and animals, and even plants, were jealous and angry for losing their human forms and their ability to have culture. Therefore, while humans ate them, they avenged themselves by "eating" humans reciprocally.

The world, in other words, was an inescapably violent and dangerous place. If humans did not eat, they died, but if they ate, they could also die. Every choice, every step, was fraught with hazard. The tension or paradox in the Piaroa world was between eating and being eaten, both inevitable and natural: if a Piaroa killed an animal and ate it, the animal's spirit could enter the person's body and eat him or her from the inside. All consumption approximated cannibalism: since the animals and plants were formerly people, to eat them was cannibalism, and if one of them attacked a human from inside, then humans became victims of cannibalism.

The role of the shaman, then, was to struggle with these spiritual forces of poison and violence. If a shaman determined that a person was occupied by a vengeful animal or plant spirit that was consuming him or her from within, the shaman called on another special set of spirits who entered the victim to do battle with the evil spirits—literally, to eat the spirits that were eating the victim. In the end, all Piaroa existence was a perpetual state of mutual cannibalism, and religion was a daily struggle against spirits and against "nature." This sheds light on the problem of human violence: any person who acted aggressively or showed a tendency to harm or dominate others was believed to be under the influence of one of the poisonous forces. He or she was separated from society until he or she learned good conduct, particularly humility and mildness. Shamans more than anyone else suffered from this tension, which is why they could not acquire true political power: since they were the only figures who actively engaged these dangerous forces of nature, they were especially susceptible to their malevolent effects. If a shaman began to act arrogant or pushy, people suspected him of being infected by one of the evil spirits. Therefore, the shamans had to be meticulously careful to maintain an appropriate Piaroa demeanor. As a result, the more powerful a Piaroa person might be, the more humbly and mildly he or she had to behave.

Nonviolence in the Christian "Peace Churches"

As the largest religion (or set of religions) in the world, Christianity is predictably complex and ambiguous on all matters, including violence—that is to say, there is no single or authoritative position in Christianity on violence. Rather, as we indicated previously (chapter 7), Bainton finds three quite distinct Christian approaches to violence, especially war, arising roughly chronologically but coexisting as alternatives and competing streams of thought today. In addition to the "holy war" and "just war" attitudes already discussed, there is also a nonviolent and even pacifist tradition.

A pacifist Christianity clearly has scriptural origins. In the celebrated Beatitudes, Jesus informs his listeners that the blessed include the meek (who shall inherit the earth), the peacemakers (who shall be called the children of God), and even the persecuted (who shall have the kingdom of heaven).[44] Christians are urged to be merciful, in emulation of God,[45] to withhold judgment and condemnation, and to forgive.[46] Mercy, nonjudgmentalism, and forgiveness, though, are not enough: Christians are told to love their enemies and, more, to do good to those who hurt them.[47] Some messages go so far as to forbid revenge or mere self-defense: "avenge not yourselves," writes Paul[48]—although there is a certainty of vengeance in the end-time. But in this world, the Christian is not even to raise a hand in self-protection or to "resist evil"; instead, he or she is instructed "whosoever shall smite thee on thy right cheek, turn to him the other also,"[49] or again, "And unto him that smiteth thee on the one cheek offer also the other, and him that taketh away thy cloak forbid not to take thy coat also."[50] The lesson appears to be one of utter passiveness and actually benevolence toward wrongdoing.

As subjects of the Roman Empire, early Christians faced a special challenge, which was the demand for military service. As we already noted, participating in the military or other aspects of Roman political life presented the problem of bowing to and sacrificing to the emperor; the refusal to do so cost many believers their property, their comfort, and sometimes their lives. But it was not only the pagan religious requirements of military service that prevented Christians from joining or being accepted; their doctrinal pacifism was antithetical to the career of the warrior. Bainton argues that in the first centuries of the religion, "no Christian author to our knowledge approved of Christian participation in battle" and "there is no evidence whatever of Christians in the army" prior to 170 or 180 CE.[51] Early church authorities like Cyprian and Tertullian, although they often prized the death of a martyr (see chapter 4), seemed uniformly to condemn dying or killing as a soldier. Tertullian opined that "Christ in disarming Peter ungirt every soldier"[52] and "How will a Christian take part in war, nay, how will he serve even in peace?"[53] Cyprian remarked that the large-scale public killing of war is no different than the interpersonal crime of murder, and Origen posited that "God did not deem it becoming to his divine legislation to allow the killing of any man whatsoever."[54] Justin Martyr insisted that Christians "do not make war upon our enemies," while Arnobius stated that it is preferable "to shed our own blood rather than to stain our hands and conscience with the blood of another."[55] Tertullian essentially eschewed all political participation for Christians.

Such opinions make a strong case for nonviolence and passivity in the face of violence. However, as in Buddhism above, the merging of church and state in Rome under Constantine brought necessary adjustments, including the notion of "just war." This politicization of Christianity was not welcomed by all followers, then or later; as Bainton explains, "When the state favored the Church and the Church sanctioned warfare, a cleavage took place within the Church itself, and the more rigorous spirits adopted a strenuously ascetic and even a monastic life, repudiating military service."[56] Thus began the centuries-long struggle inside Christianity between those who would accommodate the religion to political and military realities—including judicial execution (like the Inquisition) and war—and those who would not.

It was not until the shattering of the Catholic monopoly in Christianity that divergent views on violence and war could again be offered (at least safely); up to that time, Catholic policies were Christian policies. However, Luther's protest movement eventuated in protests against the legitimation of religious violence as well. Luther himself was not averse to war or persecution, but some of the leaders and movements coming after him were. Among the first of these were the "Anabaptists" (who preferred to call themselves Brethren or a similar generic term), a protest sect formed in the wake of Luther's movement in the 1520s in central Europe. Doctrinally and ritually, they disagreed with the official church over the practice of baptism (the Catholic church called for infant baptism, but the "Anabaptists" or "rebaptizers" regarded baptism as meaningful only for adults), but they differed in other ways too, including temperamentally. According to Levy, the Anabaptists reflected the early Christian attitude of repugnance to all military and political activity:

> They believed that no true Christian should serve the state, which they con-
> sidered a necessary evil administered by sinful men. They would not take
> oaths, not even oaths of allegiance. As pacifists, they would not kill, counte-
> nance the death penalty, or serve in armies. They passively resisted any form of

coercion as contrary to the love which man owed his fellows. . . . They asked of government only that it keep peace for the pious.[57]

Of course, their "rejection of civil officers, courts, the military, taxes, and established churches" made them the enemy of Catholicism and Lutheranism alike.[58]

As Levy points out, the Anabaptists were not perfectly nonviolent. In fact, what he calls "a few atypical Anabaptists" fomented a class revolt in 1525, and another contingent seized the city of Münster in 1533, intending to make it their holy capital like Hung and the Taiping rebellion had intended for Nanjing (see chapter 7). These actions, their general nonconformism, and their doctrinal disputes with Catholics and Protestants brought persecution down on them: in England, both Catholic (Mary) and Protestant (Elizabeth) sovereigns punished them for their religious beliefs, and more than a few died at the stake as heretics.

However, from the same environment rose other protest sects that echoed many of the attitudes of the Anabaptists. Among them were the Mennonites, the Hutterites, and eventually the Amish and the Quakers, all of whom (immediately or gradually) advocated nonviolence. One of the first influential figures was the Dutchman Menno Simons, whose name became attached to the Mennonite denomination. He joined the Anabaptist movement in 1636, just as the conspirators of Münster were tried and executed. He concluded "that pacifism was an essential part of true Christianity, and therefore refused to have anything to do with the revolutionary Anabaptists," leading a group of followers in an alternate movement.[59] Not surprisingly the Mennonite group was subjected to some of the same pressure and persecution as other antiauthority sects, so many of them emigrated to the United States and South America, where their descendants continued to live in isolated communities and practice their pacifist values.

In 1937, on the brink of World War II, and again in 1951 after that war, the Mennonites reaffirmed their commitment to peace. The 1937 affirmation took the form of "A Statement of Position—Peace, War, and Military Service"; in 1951 the Mennonite General Conference issued "A Declaration of Christian Faith and Commitment with Respect to Peace, War, and Nonresistance," which proposed

that war is altogether contrary to the teaching and spirit of Christ and the Gospel, and to God's will as revealed in His Word; that therefore war is sin, as is all manner of carnal strife; that it is wrong in spirit and method as well as in purpose, and destructive in its results; and that if we profess the principles of peace and nevertheless engage in warfare and strife we become guilty of sin and fall under the just condemnation of God.[60]

Furthermore, it clearly explicated that the position of Mennonites in regard to war and the military was

that we can have no part in carnal warfare or conflict between nations, nor in strife between classes, groups, or individuals, and that we can therefore not accept military service, either combatant or noncombatant, or preparation or training therefore in any form.

that we cannot apply our labor, money, business, factories, nor resources in any form to war or military ends, either in war finance or war industry, even under compulsion.

that we cannot take part in scientific, educational, or cultural programs designed to contribute to war, nor in any propaganda or activity that tends to promote ill will or hatred among men or nations.

that while we witness against conscription in any form and cannot lend ourselves to be a channel for its compulsions, we shall seek to find ways to serve in wartime as well as peacetime, through which the demands of the state may be both satisfied and transcended. We both expect and desire that this service be sacrificial on the part of our young men and that the church go with them all the way in their service and witness sharing in the sacrifice.

that if war does come, with its possible serious devastation from bombings or other forms of destruction, such as atomic blasts, germ warfare, poison gas, etc., we will willingly render such civilian help as conscience permits, sacrificially and without thought of personal safety, so long as we thereby help to preserve and restore life and not to destroy it.

that in wartime, as well as in peacetime, we shall endeavor to continue to live a quiet and peaceable life in all godliness and honesty; avoid joining in the wartime hysteria of hatred, revenge, and retaliation; and manifest a meek and submissive spirit, being obedient to the laws and regulations of the government in all things, including the usual taxes, except when obedience would cause us to violate the teachings of the Scripture and our conscience before God.[61]

While the main body of the Mennonites has enforced its nonviolent stance through active engagement in the political process, even to issuing declarations, other groups have preserved their pacifist worldviews by detaching themselves from politics and segregating themselves from the outside world. The most familiar of such sects is the Amish, who (at least the Old Order Amish) represent Fry's tactic of "avoidance" by maintaining sharply bounded separatist communities where they can practice their culture—and their nonviolence—in peace. The Amish were actually an offshoot of the Anabaptist/Mennonite movement, specifically the Swiss Brethren. Their original leader was Jacob Amman, whose name became attached to the sect in the 1690s. While some more liberal Amish have integrated into the dominant societies' mainstreams, the Old Order Amish continue to practice an unusually strong form of conservative and communitarian religion and culture.

Hostetler and Huntington, who conducted a study of child-rearing practices and education in Amish country, stated that this culture was characterized by "separation from the world, voluntary acceptance of high social obligations symbolized by adult baptism, the maintenance of a disciplined church community, practice of exclusion and shunning of transgressing members, and a life in harmony with the soil and nature."[62] They also strongly valued pacifism, which they achieved largely by distancing themselves from the nonpeaceful world outside their areas. Yet, despite their strict and intentional isolation, Hostetler and Huntington suggested that the Amish were not ethnocentric nor self-important; rather, "They accept as a matter of course other persons as they are, without attempting to judge them or convert them to the Amish way of life."[63] Amish proselytizers, for example, would be unusual.

If separation was the Amish "external strategy" for nonviolence, then discipline and modesty were the "internal strategy," the values that governed their interactions with each other. Both child rearing and formal education (which was also handled within the community) aimed at "the cultivation of humility, simple living, and resignation to the will of God."[64] From birth, infants were offered warmth, not harsh training, and were almost never alone. Preschool-age children were taught the virtues of work and obedience, as well as of helpfulness and sharing, these lessons conveyed from parents "by being firm and consistent, rather than by violent confrontations or single instances of breaking the child's will."[65] Corporal punishment did exist but was relatively mild. During their school years (and the community saw little value in education beyond the primary level), academic subjects like reading were taught, but equally if not more important were social values like "humility, forgiveness, admission of error, sympathy, responsibility, and appreciation of work. Children are motivated primarily by concern for other people and not by fear of punishment."[66] Even in school, competition was not highly encouraged, and individual achievement was not highly rewarded. Instead,

> the Amish teach a nonexploitative value system by emphasizing individual responsibility rather than self-assertiveness. . . . The Amish schools avoid the contradiction . . . in many public schools, where the children are simultaneously taught to compete and to have love for one another. There is some competition in the Amish schools, but it is usually structured to support the group.[67]

For example, since individual academic abilities were considered to be God-given, "no one should be praised if he is an easy learner nor condemned if he is a slow learner."[68]

The resulting Amish personality, which Hostetler and Huntington assessed with actual psychological tests, was described as "quiet, responsible, and conscientious," as well as "loyal, considerate, [and] sympathetic."[69] The Amish individual was "concerned with how other people feel, even when they are in the wrong. He dislikes telling people unpleasant things."[70] These are the qualities of a nonviolent group.

Finally, in contrast to a highly principled peace church that was pacifist from the beginning (the Mennonite) and a highly practical peace church that was pacifist from the beginning (the Amish), the Quakers or "Society of Friends" are a highly principled peace church that was not originally pacifist. By all accounts, Quakerism, which was founded by George Fox in England around 1649 and originally called itself Children of Light, was anything but peaceful. Levy describes Fox as a "firebrand" who was "abusive and imperious," and the early members of the movement were "fanatically militant and provocative" and often "boisterous, disruptive, and indecent."[71] They were one example of what history calls "antinomian" sects, that is, communities that recognized and accepted no outside authority and often no conventional cultural norms. Like other Christian antinomians, the early Quakers considered themselves to be saved and perfected—to have an "indwelling spirit" of God—which set them apart from established churches and ordinary society. Thus, sin and regular norms of behavior did not apply to them. They earned their nickname (Quaker) through their ecstatic displays of shaking, trembling, and rolling while touched by the spirit. They felt "compelled to witness" to nonmembers, "demanding, in the shrillest possible tone, that everyone else must find Christ exactly [their] way and no other."[72] They were renowned for disrupting the services of other churches and deriding those churches for their false beliefs and practices. More than a few entered public places naked—"going naked for a sign," they called it—including a woman in Boston in the 1650s.

There is little surprise that the Children of Light experienced persecution. In fact, they positively invited it: they believed that they were living in the end-time, and they sought martyrdom almost as feverishly as the churchmen of the first Christian centuries. Levy claims that they "felt duty-bound to seek cruci-fixion."[73] Nor were they detached from politics. Ingle asserts that they "hoped to fill the role of guardians, even rulers, of the country."[74] The 1650s and 1660s were a period of upheaval in England, with the execution of King Charles I and the Puritan rule of Oliver Cromwell. The Quakers saw that moment as "an opportunity to take over England; in such a fashion God would rule through them. As a part of his millenarian position, Fox personally rejected the use of military force, but he did not repudiate the notion that the Children of the Light would replace the nation's interim rulers and come to power."[75] Fox even preached a Lamb's War (i.e., the lamb of Christ):

> The Quaker army raised in the north of England would march southward, rein-forced by the mighty power of the word of God, as sharp as the two-edged sword, to cut down anyone, rich or poor, who disobeyed the righteous law. England would be conquered, but the victory would come "neither by sword or spear, but by the Spirit of the Lord."[76]

The anticipated Quaker war did not come, and instead Fox was arrested and jailed repeatedly from 1650 on. In 1656 the other most prominent Quaker, James Nayler, was punished with a hole bored in his tongue and the letter "B" (for blasphemer) branded on him.

However, after 1660, when the monarchy was restored by the coronation of Charles II, Fox saw fit to (largely) renounce violence and war on the part of Quakers. In 1661, he gave the famous (and eventually canonical) Peace Testi-mony, in which he stated, "All bloody principles and practices . . . we do utterly deny, with all outward wars and strife and fightings with outward weapons, for any end or under any pretence whatsoever." As for political power and the rule over kingdoms, he said, "we can not covet them, much less can we fight for them, but we do earnest [*sic*] desire and wait, that by the Word of God's power and its effectual operation in the hearts of men, the kingdoms of this world may become the kingdoms of the Lord and of his Christ."[77] Subsequently, Quakers declared that "we cannot learn war anymore, neither rise up against nation or kingdom with outward weapons . . . [O]ur weapons are spiritual and not carnal, yet mighty through God, to the pulling down of the strongholds of sin and Satan."[78]

This "tactical retreat," as Ingles calls it, "marked the beginning of the kind of decorous Society of Friends that the world has since admired." Over the ensuing centuries, the society has evolved into a leading pacifist and quietist church. Many (although not all) modern Quakers have refused to serve in wars, claiming conscientious objector status instead. The Quaker worship service is particularly distinguished for its tranquil character. Collins described the process in a British Quaker congregation in the 1990s:

> For an hour each Sunday morning, local Quakers gather in worship. Such meetings are unprogrammed: they are not led by a priest. Participants gather in a circle or hollow square and remain still and silent until one among them is moved to stand and speak; such homilies continue for perhaps a minute or two. Silence continues until the next speaker stands—and so on until the hour comes to an end.[79]

In this manner, Quakers are *individual worshippers*, equal before each other and their god, who have gathered to sit and talk together. There are no ranks or hierarchies: all are welcome, but none are special. Above all, the atmosphere is calm. Silence is not only a crucial quality of the service but a crucial message of the service: Friends are quiet, placid, and humble. When they are not talking, they sit

> still and quietly, avoiding undue shuffling and rustling; they are likely to sit upright, their head slightly bowed, both feet firmly planted on the ground, their hands together in their laps. When Quakers stand and speak in meeting, they rise slowly and deliberately, not wishing to surprise, but hoping to catch everyone's attention. The prescription is to talk clearly and concisely and more often than not, this is what happens. Quaker spoken ministry tends to be nei-ther persuasive nor strident, the demeanor of the speaker is correspondingly nondemonstrative.[80]

Thus the Quaker prayer meeting becomes a practice session for pacifist personality and social traits like peacefulness, mildness, and community between peers.

In conclusion, Vernard Eller proposed a "theology of nonresistance" for all Christians, insisting that violence and war cannot be justified even in terms of defense of liberty. It is not even that violence and war leave people hurt and dead:

> the final evil of war does not lie specifically in what is done to the enemy. It is quite conceivable that one man could take another's life while still respecting him as a person. Such certainly would be the case in so-called mercy killings, and it might be argued that gunning down a homicidal maniac ultimately works for his own good as well as society's. No, the basic evil of war lies in the estimate of other persons that it demands from and engenders in us.
>
> "But," the nonpacifist may object, "this is a misunderstanding of war. Hate is not a necessary or even desirable concomitant. The soldier who fights coolly, objectively, doing it as a job that has to be done, is a much better soldier than the recruit who becomes emotionally involved, who sees red and feels hot hatred toward the enemy."
>
> If "hate" is thus narrowly defined, the ultimate evil of war is not even in the hatred it arouses. In fact, from the viewpoint I am developing, hate is less insidious than this "cold objectivity"; for hate is at least a "personal" relationship (though inverted), whereas cold objectivity means precisely to treat the other man as though he were a thing rather than a person.
>
> A revulsion toward war must be natural to every Christian—it is a true instinct. The atrocities of war hardly can represent God's will. Those who conscientiously participate in war give way to the voice logic, the psychology, by which Christians overcome their revulsion.
>
> War becomes possible to a Christian only as he considers himself an "instrument to do his duty" and considers the enemy a "target," not a whole man but a point to be shot at.[81]

In a word, violence and war do not so much harm the victim as *dehumanize* the victim—and the victimizer simultaneously.

THE RELIGIOUS CONTRIBUTION
TO NONVIOLENCE

The foregoing discussion illustrates that nonviolence or at least low-conflict living is possible and that religion can and does make a contribution to this alternative. Nonviolent/low-conflict groups and societies are most certainly the minority, which is disappointing and troubling. Even more so, many of these examples have contradictory and violent pasts or presents. For instance, as we noted, Quakerism began as a militant and confrontational religion, although it morphed into a pacifist one. Medieval Japanese Buddhism and contemporary Sinhalese Buddhism have incorporated considerable political activism and straightforward fighting. The pacifist Jains can take their religion so far that they mortify themselves in its service.

What, in the final analysis, are the possibilities of nonviolence, religious and otherwise? As we stated at the outset of this chapter, if what we seek is the total absence of all violence and conflict, then our goal is probably unachievable and undesirable: how many of us really want to turn a cheek to an abuser and a blind eye to an abuse? But we can all agree that less violence, less conflict, less war is a noble goal. If this objective is to be met, in a world in which religion is a prominent force, then religion must probably play a prominent role. This *does not mean*, however, merely more preaching about peace and more haranguing of people about their violence. Such an approach has not worked before, and there is no sense in doing more of what has already failed. Rather, we need to alloy religion to a meaningful understanding of violence and its root factors in such a way that religion at least stops promoting violence and ideally actually starts promoting nonviolence.

Our final task, then, is to return to the model of violence presented in the first chapter and consider how religion can either feed or starve violence. Some, perhaps many, of these variables are not entirely within the control of religion; religion, instead, must be a partner and a factor in the multivariate production of nonviolent outcomes. And of course, for nonreligious people or nonmembers of any particular religion, religious arguments and inputs are entirely irrelevant. However, for people of religion, it can be an overarching and maybe decisive partner.

Instinct and the Individual

The enduring and stubborn debate about the "natural" or "instinctive" quality of violence has been mostly unproductive, as all such false dichotomies are. Are humans "naturally violent" or "naturally nonviolent"? Clearly, humans have the "natural" capacity for violence, or else they would be unable to perform it. But they also have the "natural" capacity for nonviolence: as we acknowledged, even violent individuals and groups have their nonviolent moments, and some individuals and groups are profoundly nonviolent.

The notion that violence or aggression is natural to humans is based on the (nearly) universal presence of violence in human societies. So indisputably there is something "natural" going on. Purely natural/instinctive and even biological explanations of human aggression face a variety of obstacles, though. One is that human groups are not universally violent, nor do they all engage in the same types or levels of violence. For instance, as Ferguson points out, "Even *if* aggression is a universal human trait, war is not. 'Warlike' societies fight only occasionally, and many societies have no war at all."[82]

Another and quite different problem with natural/instinctive explanations of violence is that they do not suggest much in the way of solutions—or sometimes even of hope. As Fry says of war in particular, "If war is seen as natural, then there is little point in trying to prevent, reduce, or abolish it. Consequently, the acceptance of war as a social institution facilitates its continuance."[83] The same could be said for all the expressions of violence: if they are natural, then there is nothing to be done about them, other than complain and fight losing struggles against them. If, for instance, Freud was correct that humans have a "death instinct," a (self- and other-) destructive drive, then we are doomed—and the more we resist it, the more doomed we are.

Perhaps the key to the social, including the religious, contribution to nonviolence at the instinctive/human-nature level is to accept our human complexity and dualism about violence: we have the capacity for violence and nonviolence alike. This is why even well-meaning thinkers like Paulo Freire,[84] who sincerely want to improve the human condition, do not offer good advice when they propose that we can eliminate violence and oppression by "humanization," that is, becoming more human. To be human is to be at once violent and nonviolent, aggressive and nonaggressive—in other words, to be multifaceted and contradictory—and to be more human is merely to be more so. It is an error to identify "humanity" with only the "good" tendencies like altruism and kindness and love. The "bad" is human too.

Indeed, in an odd way there may be a kind of hope in seeing our contradictory nature as it is. Aho opines that, "other things being equal, those awakened to their own insidious capacity to commit evil are more just, merciful, and temperate in the treatment of the enemy than those deluding themselves in their absolute innocence."[85] Therefore, a religion that advances a more honest portrayal of human nature (as neither perfect nor perfectible, "warts and all") *and* a more honest portrayal of its own virtues (as neither possessing all goodness or all truth) may make a contribution to nonviolence. At the very least, if we recognize in ourselves and in the other the same human capacities for good and bad, we have gone some way toward establishing a connection, a kinship, between Us and Them.

Integration into Groups

All evidence indicates that groups are inherently more pestilent than individuals (another argument that the entire explanation of violence does not lie at the individual level). Furthermore, religions are inherently group phenomena. It seems certain that humans will remain group/social creatures and that religion will remain a group phenomenon. The question is whether religion can contribute to the mitigation of group-violence processes.

It is demonstrably possible. Even the Jains and the Mennonites and the Amish live in groups; they *particularly* live in groups. So there is inevitably and necessarily an "other" outside the group. However, these religions do not create thereby a "wholly other" that lacks all the positive qualities of the in-group, such that the "wholly other" becomes an "unholy other." Difference need not be seen in and of itself as deviance or, even worse, wickedness; and when it is not, there is no motivation to liquidate the other, or even to expand the in-group. The group, as well as the individual within it, is "modest" in this sense: it makes less than absolute claims for itself.

One way that religions can contribute to taming the "group effect" is, then, by minimizing the distance between Us and Them. The very existence of a religion (or any other group identifier) will create an Us and subsequently a Them, but the relationship need not be an oppositional one. Again, when a religion or philosophy emphasizes the similarities between Us and Them and tones down the differences, there is less to aggravate the irritable nature of groups.

Religions could go yet further and establish "porous" boundaries between Us and Them. One way would be to literally allow members, or at least ideas, to flow across those boundaries—to be less "defensive" about group boundaries. It seems patently unlikely that religions will ever invite their members to leave and join other religions, but some communication between groups is both possible and desirable without utterly corroding religious identities. This is why David Smock, an expert on peacemaking with the US Institute of Peace, recommends learning about and interacting with other religions. "Prejudice and ignorance about the beliefs and practices of the religious 'other' often exacerbate conflicts. Religious stereotypes contribute to misunderstanding and foment animosity. One antidote to hatred between religious communities is to teach communities about the beliefs and practices of the religious other."[86] An important part, maybe the most important part, of this interchange is the recognition of shared humanity and shared victimization: "Effort must also be made to 'rehumanize' the other, the group seen as the cause of one's suffering."[87]

Another way to moderate or even eliminate the "group effect" is *to expand the group to include more, ultimately all, human or other life.* All the cases of nonviolent religions above contain some aspect of this worldview. Nonviolence and nonconflict are good not just for Them but for Us, too. What happens to Them happens to Us. In the case of the Jains and the Piaroa in particular, as well as the Buddhists, *They are Us.* There is no sharp divide between our group of humans and other groups of humans. In fact, there is no sharp divide between us humans and those nonhumans. Other humans and other nonhumans are like us; they feel like us; in certain profound and literal ways, they *are* us. Since all evidence suggests that it is easier to harm an "outsider" than one of one's "own kind," the solution is to extend one's own kind *to include other kinds, maybe all kinds.* This is something that religion can do better than any other human thought system.

Identity

If religions could accomplish these first two tasks, the problem of identity would be dramatically reduced. It is when persons or groups take their main, sometimes their entire, identity from their religion that the boundaries between religions become the most impenetrable. However, if religions do not "close ranks," demand total *and exclusive* commitment to and identification with the religion, then the "group effect" is not fully mobilized and the violent potential in human nature is not fully actualized.

One of the productive ways of doing so, as the Jains have explicitly formulated, is to practice taking multiple perspectives, to see things from the other person's or group's (or species') point of view. Yes, I am an X and you are a Y, but we also both share common traits and identities at a higher—and ultimately more important—dimension. If I can see what you see—or more crucially, *feel what you feel*—then I cannot any longer identify exclusively with my kind.

Another important factor is the "cross-cutting ties" that we mentioned above (which anticipates the idea of institutions, to be developed below). Every individual occupies multiple groups and possesses multiple identities at the same time. Sociologists refer to these as "statuses" and distinguish each individual as a particular "status set": for instance, I, Jack David Eller, am all at once a male, a white person, an American, an adult, an Eller, an English speaker, an anthropologist, and a nonreligious person. If any one of these myriad and simultaneous identities became my *defining identity*, even my *exclusive identity*, then it would necessarily exclude many or most people, including people with whom I do share other aspects of identity. In other words, if I were to say that I am a white person above all else, then that would distance me from nonwhite people. Or if I were to say that I am "really" an Eller and nothing else, I would cut myself off from the vast majority of my fellow males and whites and Americans and Anglophones, and so on. The more of these identities I activate, and consciously and energetically use, the more different people I identify with and the less any particular identity-fragment comes to define me—and define them, for if I am "an Eller," then you are a "non-Eller." On the other hand, if a religious follower truly acknowledged that he or she may be a Christian or a Muslim or a Buddhist or a Hindu but also is a "person of faith" and "a human being" and "a living being," the more people he or she would identify with. And the more people one identifies with, the fewer one can exclude—and hate.

Researchers have discovered the effectiveness of this quite practical strategy. Ashutosh Varshney, for instance, has studied Hindus and Muslims in India and has found that the worst thing people can do, in terms of religious identity and hostility/violence, is to segregate into identity-communities. Instead, hostility is most greatly reduced when members of both religions interact in significant venues like professional organizations, political parties, sports clubs, business associations, and trade unions; these, he determined, are much more effective than efforts like children's play groups or student exchange programs, which is where most of the effort is often directed.[88] On the other hand, experience tells us that the worst thing two religious or social groups can do is segregate and create parallel, noninteracting institutions, like partitioned neighborhoods, schools, businesses, or, worse yet, political parties or militias. Sri Lanka, Northern Ireland, Yugoslavia, and many other cases testify to this fact.

Institutions

Groups have not only individual members and collective boundaries and identities but also internal structures, enduring patterns of interaction, and relationships with the outside world. These institutional features help determine the violence or nonviolence within the group and between groups.

Two of the most consistent but hard-to-apply institutional features of nonviolent societies are their small size and their premodern economic and political systems. Absolutely all the examples that we have discussed or that researchers have listed are either small societies (like the Semai, Utku, or Piaroa) or small minorities within large (and generally not nonviolent) societies (like the Jains, Mennonites, or Amish). The premodern societies had "traditional" economies (foraging or horticulture); these and the nonviolent minority subcultures either produced little excess wealth or did not dwell on wealth, therefore creating few wealth or class distinctions. The premodern societies also had "traditional" political systems (band or tribe); these and the nonviolent minority subcultures deemphasized and decentralized power and created generally egalitarian relations between members. To a certain important extent, their low-conflict quality was what we might call a "virtue of the weak": they did not hurt anyone because they lacked the capacity to hurt anyone. Religion may more reflect than produce such realities; recall that Christianity was particularly pacifist when it lacked political power.

Other institutional arrangements seem to foment violence. Rich and stratified societies are frequently violent (especially if that wealth and stratification depends on oppressive relations like slavery or exploitation of a peasantry). Complex, politically centralized state societies are almost universally violent, whether this violence takes the form of war and organized persecution or grand-scale sacrifice. History appears to prove that when a religion aligns with or achieves state power itself, it sheds its pacifist virtues and breeds or emphasizes violent values, like holy war or just war. Obviously, a religion detached from political power cannot make war of any kind, holy or otherwise, and a religion attached to political power must deal with mundane concerns like order and defense. Thus, one lesson is that religions stress their nonviolent side when they are separated from the state and its institutions of violence.

Some societies establish institutions specifically intended for violence. The best example is the military. Whether military institutions are a cause or an effect of violence is an open debate, but the correlation at least is strong. When religions contribute to military institutions (as in the Hindu concept of a spiritually appointed warrior caste whose very dharma or duty is to kill and die) and when religions themselves absorb some of the characteristics of military institutions (as in the Christian "church militant" or knightly orders or the Taiping martial organization) violence is greatly enhanced. Religions that absent themselves from the state (like the early Anabaptists or the Amish) or that are segregated from the state lack the institutional means to do extensive harm.

Obviously, when religions construct their own institutions of violence, the clearest example being the Holy Inquisition, then they give themselves means and license to do injury. Religions that lack such institutional expressions— their own militias, political parties, and so on—are the least violent, and vice versa; it is hard to imagine an Amish militia or inquisition. Religions also ride on the backs of general social institutions, such as the competitive institutions in the United States. As we have seen, nonviolent societies and sects do not encourage competition, whether in school, at work, in interpersonal relations, or in specialized and professional forms like competitive sports. Religions that contribute to competition or imbibe competitive values from other institutions also contribute to violence.

On the other hand, some religions have distinct institutions of nonviolence and peacemaking. The Amish institution of "shunning" is a nonviolent method for handling conflict. Above we saw the official declarations and statements of the Mennonites renouncing violence. Gopin points out that Mennonites have recently actually set up "Christianity Peacemaker Teams" to "go where they are invited by one side [in a conflict] to stand with them in their suffering" and to "protest injustice."[89] Such efforts do not merely talk about peace but also act on it.

Institutions within religions are critical to nonviolence, but institutions between religions—and between religions and the secular world—are equally critical. One such major initiative is Religions for Peace, a highly organized international institution in which, according to the secretary general of the World Conference of Religions for Peace, "religious leaders work together to solve conflicts and help those affected. . . . These religious believers are on the front lines of the world's greatest challenges: war, poverty and caring for our earth. They have different religious beliefs, but they are also united as partners in working for good."[90] With a budget of over 2 million dollars, the organization sets up interreligious councils (IRCs) in countries all around the world—sixty-two such IRCs by 2005—and higher-level regional IRCs. It also has a centralized structure with a World Council, an Executive Committee, and a World Assembly that meets every five years.

> As a member of the international steering committee of Faith and Ethics Network of the International Criminal Court (FENICC), *Religions for Peace* made a significant contribution in developing the manual on Advancing Justice and Reconciliation in Relation to the International Criminal Court (ICC) in collaboration with the World Council of Churches (WCC), Baha'i International Community, the Centre for Justice and Reconciliation (CJR), and others."[91]

In recent years, the organization has been active in such hot spots as Iraq, Sudan, Rwanda, and Bosnia.

Interests

Groups, including religious groups, often confront each other over interests, whether those interests are practical and material (like wealth or the control of geographic sites like Jerusalem) or symbolic or "spiritual" (like doctrines and claims to truth). The more that interests can be detached from religion, or the more that conflicts of interest can be alleviated altogether, the more violence can be avoided.

The reduction of interest-based conflicts between societies and sects can be achieved by some of the methods already mentioned: if these entities have porous boundaries and cross-cutting ties—and therefore mutual interests—it is harder to mobilize them as "interest groups." Recognizing the common humanity of potential partisans limits the potential for conflict: "they" are not evil demons who gleefully inhibit "our" interests and are to be opposed or destroyed for it, but rather they are human beings like us, neighbors who have their own interests to pursue. Conflict-management procedures to deal with inevitable conflicts of interest must be in place to prevent competitions and conflicts from growing into violence; this is a place where nonviolence practices and institutions like negotiation, arbitration, and adjudication can serve.

Of course, one of the greatest contributions that religions can make to the problem of conflicts of interest is to help remove the bases of those conflicts in the first place, that is, to strive for *social justice*. Experience shows that many religious conflicts are about, or at least related to, other nonreligious social factors. When there is perceived economic or political inequality, discrimination in housing or employment, or literal oppression, violence is likely to erupt. Religions all too often are causes of inequalities, discriminations, and oppressions, as in the treatment of Jews throughout Christian history, of Sikhs by Hindus and Muslims, or of Catholics by Protestants in Northern Ireland. At the very least, religions need to detach doctrinal disagreements from discrimination and persecution: they need to teach that "our" interests are not threatened by "your" beliefs. But beyond this minimal requirement, religions need to be positive agents of change that solve the economic, political, and social problems that lead to or exacerbate conflicts. Social justice is or can be just as important and motivational an interest as any religious doctrine, sacred site, or otherworldly destination.

Two examples of social justice movements in recent Christian history include "social gospel" and "liberation theology." The social gospel movement was an activation of Christianity in the late nineteenth century to address some of the consequences of the new urban industrial culture. Ministers of the social gospel regarded poverty, hunger, and disease as the leading offenses against humanity and therefore regarded the eradication of these conditions as their primary mission. They moved into and ministered to inner cities and slums, opening soup kitchens, hospitals, and other such quality-of-life institutions. Religion, quite frankly, was of less importance to them than improving the standard of living for poor people—or rather we might say that serving the poor was how they expressed and fulfilled their religion. It is interesting and disappointing that many Christians of the day like the evangelist Billy Sunday criticized the social gospel movement as "godless social service nonsense,"[92] favoring preaching and conversion—the traditional business of Christianity—over aiding the disadvantaged. In fact, early twentieth-century "fundamentalism" was to a large extent a reaction against the "worldly" and "progressive" and "liberal" message of the social gospel.

Liberation theology was a more recent movement, emerging out of Latin America in the 1960s. By those years, considerable poverty and injustice had accumulated in this largely Catholic region, and revolutions like the Cuban revolution were under way. In impoverished areas, priests, bishops, and laypeople called for attention to the suffering of the lower classes in the here and now, and they did more than issue calls: they formed organizations like the Young Christian Students, the Young Christian Workers, the Young Christian Agriculturalists, and the Movement for Basic Education, and they went to work to make the changes they advocated. Theorists and practitioners of liberation theology, like those of the social gospel, saw their mission as anything but "godless social service" but precisely as godful social service—putting the words of religion into action. "Liberating" people from poverty, oppression, and injustice was a Christian, indeed a theological, thing to do, as evinced by thoughtful treatises on the subject like Gustavo Gutierrez's 1971 work *Teología de la Liberación*, Leonardo Boff's *Jesus Cristo Liberador*, Juan Luis Segundo's 1970 *De la Sociedad a la Teología*, and Hugo Assmann's *Teología desde la Praxis de Liberación*. For all these leaders, religion was about not just words but deeds.

More generally, many religions make it part of their doctrine and their practice to feed the hungry, defend the weak, and comfort the suffering. If these interests prevailed over sectarian and selfish ones, most of the grievances between religions would be ended, as well as most of the social grievances that attract hurt and angry people to religion in the first place for redress—or often for revenge. In a word, religions can make a more nonviolent world by putting human interests above sectarian interests. The interest that needs to trump all other interests is nonviolence.

Ideology

Finally, the societies and sects that best embody nonviolence promote and instill nonviolent ideologies, and conversely, violent societies and religions have violent ideologies or at least ideologies that have been proven conducive to violence. The Semai, Piaroa, Buddhists, Jains, Mennonites, Amish, Quakers, and such others that seriously and successfully renounce violence have clear, consistent, and convincing beliefs and values of nonviolence.

The first and most basic belief or value of nonviolence is that violence is *bad* and *ineffective*. Frankly, most of these groups are not only opposed to violence but also offended by it, sometimes even upset or horrified by it. Indeed, as Robarchek has stressed, significantly nonviolent societies have "beliefs and values, individual cognitive and affective orientations, and the institutional orders in which they are manifested . . . defining a reality where *violence is essentially precluded as an option*"[93] (emphasis added). Their words and their actions convey steadfast rejection of violent behavior: they do not reward it, nor do they find it amusing. In fact, as the cases of the Buddhists, Jains, and Piaroa illustrated particularly dramatically, they find violence explicitly unpleasant: it really does hurt not just the victim but the victimizer as well. Their cultures promote *empathy* above all else: injurers feel the injury of the injured. This cannot be mere lip service, as many purported religions or cultures of peace practice it. A group cannot condemn violence in one breath and delight in violent books, movies, and music in the other. Beyond disapproval, the ideology of a nonviolent religion communicates the message that *violence does not work*. Fighting is not a way to solve problems. Harming oneself does not improve oneself. Killing animals (or humans) or spilling blood does not get things done. In a word, violence is inefficacious. It is not only not good; it is not good for anything.

Study of violent and nonviolent religious ideologies indicates several other points. Ideologies that teach or encourage uncritical obedience are dangerous. Groups that depend too much on or elevate too high the "leadership principle" have escalated violent potential. If the leader is seen as infallible or unquestionable, there is no fail-safe against any violence he or she might preach. Nonviolent groups do not idealize their authorities to perfection or offer them thoughtless loyalty (recall that Zimbardo considered blind obedience to be the single most perilous factor of all). Nor is the group or its doctrine infallible or invaluable—"our group *über alles*." If our group is everything, other groups are nothing.

In fact, absolutism and idealism in general are hazardous ideological qualities, since these inexorably lead to a third, namely, extremism. When we are not just good but *absolutely* good, not just right but *absolutely* right, then everyone else— *which means the vast majority of humans, since no group or religion is in a majority*—must be absolutely bad and wrong. Nonviolent ideologies tend to be comparatively modest and humble; the Jains go so far as encouraging members to acknowledge and appreciate the multiple perspectives of other individuals, groups, and species. Nonviolent ideologies are thus among the least "missionizing," since they are the least confident and strident in their own rightness and the least concerned that everyone else share theirs. The religious utopia of Shangri-la in James Hilton's novel *Lost Horizon* put this idea into practice: as the spokesman for the retreat answered in response to the question of its most basic beliefs,

> If I were to put it into a very few words, my dear sir, I should say that our prevalent belief is in moderation. We inculcate the virtue of avoiding excess of all kinds—even including, if you will pardon the paradox, excess of virtue itself. . . . We rule with moderate strictness, and in return we are satisfied with moderate obedience. And I think I can claim that our people are moderately sober, moderately chaste, and moderately honest.[94]

Few contemporary religions—or political systems or philosophies, and so on—seem content with such moderation.

The evils of absolutism are not limited to religion. In our discussion of persecution, we noted how the pursuit of absolute virtue in revolutionary France or of absolute equality and comradeship in revolutionary Russia led to all sorts of violent excesses. Perfectibility—the quest for or commitment to absolute good—is a common license for violence, since the imperfect cannot by definition be "tolerated." Such idealism—that only the ideal, the best, the perfect may exist, has a right to exist, and *will exist when we are finished with the world*—virtually begs for violence. It calls for and sometimes explicitly demands extreme fervor and extreme enthusiasm, in which condition anything is possible. This is why the eminent sociologist Peter Berger suggested that "intense . . . commitment is usually bad. It is bad in its motives. It is bad in its consequences."[95] He went so far as to warn us (and he is hardly the first) that too much enthusiasm for one's cause can be positively deadly, that when it comes to ideologues of any kind, "only trust the sad ones. The enthusiastic ones are the oppressors of tomorrow—or they are only kidding."[96] The obvious problem is that religious ideologues are often quite enthusiastic and almost never kidding. They are, we could say, deadly serious.

All absolutist and idealist religions are ripe for violence, but some specific ideologies are more prone to absolutism and idealism than others. Dualist religions and monotheisms (which are closely related), time and time again, show themselves tending toward violence. Dualism divides the world irreparably into Us and Them, Good and Evil, Light and Darkness, and ascribes all Good and Light to Us. Dualism also frequently pits the two forces or essences in an irreconcilable struggle, a cosmic war, of which all human war and violence are mere but necessary skirmishes. Monotheisms are generally if not quite universally dualistic, like Christianity, Islam, and Zoroastrianism, so monotheism, the dominant form of religion in the world today, is bound to be one of the dominant sources of violence in the world today. "Because a monotheistic psychology must be dedicated to unity, its psychopathology is intolerance of difference," writes Hillman.[97] Its distinctive "mythic reality" is transcendent-historical, the most white-hot of violent mythologies. And the well-known monotheistic injunctions of love, peace, and "morality" in general are offset by one of the central dynamics of monotheism, *exclusivism*: "A key challenge to peacemaking in all of the monotheistic traditions is their tendency to limit prosocial ethical values to members of the religion, or in-group."[98]

Ultimately, religions cannot make peace alone; they must make peace along with—and make peace *with*—the nonreligious, secular world as well. David Smock insists, "It is critical to link faith-based peacemaking to secular and political processes and authorities. Faith-based peacemaking independent of this cross-sector collaboration almost never creates peace."[99] In fact, he judges that the ideal collaboration would be "when some key persons hold both secular and religious authority."[100] This advice recognizes three crucial facts: first, that religions by themselves neither generate all violence nor promise all nonviolence (that is, many of the engines of violence are secular, including economics, politics, race, gender, and so forth, and thus many of the solutions to violence are secular); second, that the secular world is not the inveterate enemy of religion but a necessary partner (if only because both exist and will not go away); and third and finally, that the secular world has its own contributions to make to nonviolence and social justice. As Gregory Paul, whom we encountered in the previous chapter, finds,

> the more secular, proevolution democracies have, for the first time in history, come closest to achieving practical "cultures of life" that feature low rates of lethal crime, juvenile-adult mortality, sex-related dysfunction, and even abortion. The least theistic, secular, developed democracies, such as Japan, France, and Scandinavia, have been most successful in these regards. The nonreligious, proevolution democracies contradict the dictum that a society cannot enjoy good conditions unless most citizens ardently believe in a moral creator. The widely held fear that a Godless citizenry must experience societal disaster is therefore refuted. Contradicting these conclusions requires demonstrating a positive link between theism and societal conditions in the first world with a similarly large body of data—a doubtful possibility in view of the observable trends.[101]

Perhaps the ability of religions to coexist with nonreligion—and vice versa—can serve as a kind of barometer for their ability to coexist with other religions and with the natural and social world that we all must share. If the various religions and nonreligion can appreciate the value in each other and the gifts that they can offer each other, a long step toward nonviolence will already be taken.

NOTES

INTRODUCTION

1. Oliver McTernan, *Violence in God's Name: Religion in an Age of Conflict* (Maryknoll, NY: Orbis Books, 2003), p. 20.

2. James Haught, *Holy Horrors: An Illustrated History of Religious Murder and Madness* (Amherst, NY: Prometheus Books, 1990), p. 14. See also James Haught, *Holy Hatred: Religious Conflicts of the '90s* (Amherst, NY: Prometheus Books, 1995).

3. Charles Kimball, *When Religion Becomes Evil* (New York: HarperSanFrancisco, 2002), p. 39.

4. Lloyd Steffen, *The Demonic Turn: The Power of Religion to Inspire or Restrain Violence* (Cleveland: Pilgrim Press, 2003).

CHAPTER 1: UNDERSTANDING VIOLENCE

1. Paul Farmer, "An Anthropology of Structural Violence," *Current Anthropology* 45, no. 3 (2004): 307.

2. David Riches, "Aggression, War, Violence: Space/Time and Paradigm" *Man* 26, no. 2 (1991): 285.

3. Ibid., p. 286.

4. Ibid., p. 292.

5. Robert Knox Dentan, *The Semai: A Non-violent People of Malaya* (New York: Holt, Rinehart, and Winston, 1968).

6. Napoleon Chagnon, *Yanomamo: The Fierce People* (New York: Holt, Rinehart, and Winston, 1968).

7. Yamamoto Tsunetomo, *Hagakure: The Book of the Samurai*, trans. William Scott Wilson (Tokyo: Kodansha International, 2002 [1979]), pp. 33 and 164.

8. Roy Baumeister, *Evil: Inside Human Violence and Cruelty* (New York: Barnes and Noble Books, 2001).

9. Philip Zimbardo, "The Mind Is a Formidable Jailer: A Piradellian Prison," *New York Times Magazine*, April 8, 1973.

10. Stanley Milgram, "Behavioral Study of Obedience," *Journal of Abnormal and*

Social Psychology 67 (1963). For a more complete discussion of the experiments and their implications, see Milgram's *Obedience to Authority: An Experimental View* (New York: Harper and Row, 1974).

11. Philip Zimbardo, "The Psychology of Evil," *Psi Chi* 5 (2000).

12. Baumeister, *Evil*.

13. Howard Bloom, *The Lucifer Principle: A Scientific Expedition into the Forces of History* (New York: Atlantic Monthly Press, 1995).

14. Gustave Le Bon, *The Crowd: A Study of the Popular Mind* (New York: Macmillan, 1896), p. 62.

15. Ibid., p. 63.

16. Ibid., p. 64.

17. Ibid., p. 69.

18. Eric Hoffer, *The True Believer: Thoughts on the Nature of Mass Movements* (New York: HarperPerennial, 1966 [1951]), p. 91.

19. Ibid., p. 95.

20. Ibid., p. 107.

21. Ibid., p. 100.

22. Ibid., p. 114.

23. Henri Tajfel, *Differentiation between Social Groups* (London: Academic Press, 1978). See also Henri Tajfel, *Human Groups and Social Categories* (Cambridge: Cambridge University Press, 1981).

24. Gordon Allport, *The Nature of Prejudice* (Reading, MA: Addison-Wesley, 1979 [1954]), p. 7.

25. Ibid., pp. 17–19.

26. Ibid., pp. 20–22.

27. Ibid., p. 23.

28. Johan van der Dennen, *The Origin of War: The Evolution of a Male-Coalitional Reproductive Strategy* (Groningen, Netherlands: Origin Press, 1995).

29. Konrad Lorenz, *On Aggression*, trans. Marjorie Kerr Wilson (New York: Harcourt, Brace, and World, 1966).

30. Benedict Anderson, *Imagined Communities: Reflections on the Origin and Spread of Nationalism* (London: Verso, 1983).

31. Richard Gelles and Murray Straus, *Intimate Violence* (New York: Simon and Schuster, 1988), p. 18.

32. Marc Howard Ross, *The Culture of Conflict* (New Haven, CT: Yale University Press, 1993).

33. Max Gluckman, *Custom and Conflict in Africa* (Oxford: Basil Blackwell, 1956), pp. 24–25.

34. Mary Elaine Hegland, "Wife Abuse and the Political System: A Middle Eastern Case Study," in *To Have and to Hit: Cultural Perspectives on Wife Beating*, ed. Dorothy Ayers

Counts, Judith K. Brown, and Jacquelyn C. Campbell (Urbana: University of Illinois Press, 1999), pp. 237–38.

35. Eunice Uzodike, "Child Abuse: The Nigerian Perspective," in *Overcoming Child Abuse: A Window on a World Problem*, ed. Michael Freeman (Aldershot, UK: Dartmouth Publishing, 2000).

36. Max Weber, "Politics as a Vocation," in *From Max Weber: Essays in Sociology*, ed. and trans. H. H. Gerth and C. Wright Mills (New York: Oxford University Press, 1946), p. 78.

37. Stephanie Schwandner-Sievers, "The Enactment of 'Tradition': Albanian Constructions of Identity, Violence, and Power in Times of Crisis," in *Anthropology of Violence and Conflict*, ed. Bettina Schmidt and Ingo Schroder (London: Routledge, 2001).

38. Beatrice Whiting, "Sex Identity Conflict and Physical Violence: A Comparative Study," *American Anthropologist* 67, no. 6 (1965).

39. Quoted in Michael Messner, "Power at Play: Sport and Gender Relations," in *Signs of Life in the USA: Readings on Popular Culture for Writers*, ed. Sonia Maasik and Jack Solomon (Boston: Bedford/St. Martin's, 2003), p. 669.

40. Louis Kreisberg, *Social Conflicts*, 2nd ed. (Englewood Cliffs, NJ: Prentice-Hall, 1982), p. 17.

41. Ibid., p. 24.

42. Ibid., p. 28.

43. Ibid., p. 57.

44. Ibid., p. 166.

45. Jonathan Fox, *Ethnoreligious Conflict in the Late Twentieth Century: A General Theory* (Lanham, MD: Lexington Books, 2002), p. 13.

46. Quoted in Leo Gershoy, *The Era of the French Revolution, 1789–1799* (Princeton, NJ: D. Van Nostrand, 1957), pp. 159–60.

47. Jessica Stern, *Terror in the Name of God: Why Religious Militants Kill* (New York: HarperCollins Publishers, 2003), p. 282.

48. Hoffer, *True Believer*, pp. 80–81.

49. Georges Sorel, *Reflections on Violence* (New York: Collier Books, 1961 [1908]), p. 92.

50. Ibid., p. 115.

51. Frantz Fanon, *The Wretched of the Earth*, trans. Constance Farrington (New York: Grove Press, 1963), p. 36.

52. Ibid., pp. 40–41.

53. Ibid., p. 57.

54. Robert Hare, "The Psychopathy Checklist—Revised (PCL-R)," 1991, http://www.criminology.unimelb.edu.au/victims/resources/assessment/personality/psychopathy_ checklist.html (accessed June 1, 2003).

CHAPTER 2: UNDERSTANDING RELIGION

1. Henry Fielding, *The History of Tom Jones* (New York: Penguin Books, 1979 [1749]), p. 105.

2. Charles Selengut, *Sacred Fury: Understanding Religious Violence* (Walnut Creek, CA: AltaMira Press, 2003) p. 1.

3. Ibid., p. 7.

4. Ibid., p. 17.

5. E. B. Tylor, *Primitive Culture* (New York: Harper, 1958 [1871]).

6. Rudolf Otto, *The Idea of the Holy*, trans. John W. Harvey (London: Oxford University Press, 1958 [1923]), p. 10.

7. Ibid., p. 12.

8. Carl G. Jung, *Psychology of the Unconscious: A Study of the Transformations and Symbolisms of the Libido*, trans. Beatrice M. Hinkle (New York: Dodd, Mead, 1949 [1916]), p. 22.

9. Émile Durkheim, *The Elementary Forms of the Religious Life* (New York: Free Press, 1965 [1915]), p. 62.

10. William James, *The Varieties of Religious Experience: A Study in Human Nature* (New York: Mentor Books, 1958 [1902]), p. 34.

11. Clifford Geertz, *The Interpretation of Cultures* (New York: Basic Books, 1973), p. 90.

12. Anthony Wallace, *Religion: An Anthropological View* (New York: Random House, 1966), p. 78.

13. Lee Kirkpatrick, *Attachment, Evolution, and the Psychology of Religion* (New York: Guilford Press, 2005).

14. Pascal Boyer, *Religion Explained: The Evolutionary Origins of Religious Thought* (New York: Basic Books, 2001).

15. Scott Atran, *In Gods We Trust: The Evolutionary Landscape of Religion* (Oxford: Oxford University Press, 2002), p. ix.

16. Boyer, *Religion Explained*, p. 311.

17. James, *Varieties of Religious Experience*, p. 40.

18. Robin Horton, "A Definition of Religion, and Its Uses," *Journal of the Royal Anthropological Institute of Great Britain and Ireland* 90, no. 2 (1960): 211.

19. Graham Harvey, *Animism: Respecting the Living World* (New York: Columbia University Press, 2006), p. xi.

20. Ibid., p. xvii.

21. Robert Levy, Jeannette Mageo, and Alan Howard, "Gods, Spirits, and History: A Theoretical Perspective," in *Spirits in Culture, History, and Mind*, ed. Jeannette Mageo and Alan Howard (New York : Routledge, 1996), p. 11.

22. Ibid., p. 14.

23. Ibid., p. 15.

24. Ibid., p. 21.

25. Ibid., p. 16.

26. Richard Feinberg, "Spirit Encounters on a Polynesian Outlier: Anuta, Solomon Islands," in *Spirits in Culture, History, and Mind* (see note 21).

27. Niko Besnier, "Heteroglossic Discourses on Nukulaelae Spirits," in *Spirits in Culture, History, and Mind* (see note 21).

28. Emiko Ohnuki-Tierney, *The Ainu of the Northwest Coast of Southern Sakhalin* (New York: Holt, Rinehart, and Winston, 1974).

29. Melford Spiro, *Burmese Supernaturalism* (Philadelphia: Institute for the Study of Human Issues, 1978 [1967]).

30. Richard Swinburne, *The Coherence of Theism* (Oxford: Clarendon Press, 1977), p. 2.

31. Richard Katz, *Boiling Energy: Community Healing among the Kalahari Kung* (Cambridge, MA: Harvard University Press, 1982).

32. For a more sustained analysis of the book of Job, see David Eller, "Answer to Job: 'Shut Up and Believe,'" *American Atheist* (May/June 2009).

33. Spiro, *Burmese Supernaturalism*, p. 34.

34. John Beattie, *Bunyoro: An African Kingdom* (New York: Holt, Rinehart, and Winston, 1960), p. 73.

35. William Lessa, *Ulithi: A Micronesian Design for Living* (New York: Holt, Rinehart, and Winston, 1966), p. 71.

36. E. E. Evans-Pritchard, *Witchcraft, Oracles, and Magic among the Azande* (New York: Oxford University Press, 1937), pp. 18–19.

37. Stanley Tambiah, *Buddhism and the Spirit Cults in North-East Thailand* (London: Cambridge University Press, 1970).

38. Richard Lee, *The Dobe !Kung* (New York: Holt, Rinehart, and Winston, 1984), p. 109.

39. Ernest Gellner, *Plough, Sword, and Book: The Structure of Human History* (Chicago: University of Chicago Press, 1988).

40. Bronislaw Malinowski, *Magic, Science, and Religion and Other Essays* (Garden City, NY: Doubleday Anchor Books, 1948), p. 100.

41. See Jean Comaroff, *Body of Power, Spirit of Resistance: The Culture and History of a South Africa People* (Chicago: University of Chicago Press, 1985). Also see John Comaroff and Jean Comaroff, *Of Revelation and Revolution: The Dialectics of Modernity on a South African Frontier*, vol. 2 (Chicago: University of Chicago Press, 1991).

42. Scott Appleby, *The Ambivalence of the Sacred: Religion, Violence, and Reconciliation* (Lanham, MD: Rowman and Littlefield, 2000), p. 8.

CHAPTER 3: SACRIFICE

1. Nigel Davies, *Human Sacrifice in History and Today* (New York: William Morrow, 1981), p. 15.

2. Ibid., p. 275.

3. M. F. C. Bourdillon, introduction to *Sacrifice*, ed. M. F. C. Bourdillon and Meyer Fortes (London: Academic Press, 1980), p. 10.

4. Nancy Jay, *Throughout Your Generations Forever: Sacrifice, Religion, and Paternity* (Chicago: University of Chicago Press, 1992), p. xxv.

5. Meyer Fortes, preface to *Sacrifice* (see note 3), "Anthropologists and Theologians: Common Interests and Divergent Approaches," pp. xiii–xiv.

6. Henri Hubert and Marcel Mauss, *Sacrifice: Its Nature and Function* (Chicago: University of Chicago Press, 1964 [1898]), p. 13.

7. Ibid., p. 11.

8. Ibid., p. 10.

9. Ibid., p. 97.

10. Ibid., p. 100.

11. Luc de Heusch, *Sacrifice in Africa: A Structuralist Approach*, trans. Linda O'Brien and Alice Morton (Bloomington: Indiana University Press, 1985), p. 5.

12. John Beattie, "On Understanding Sacrifice," in *Sacrifice* (see note 3), p. 37.

13. Christian Eberhart, "A Neglected Feature of Sacrifice in the Hebrew Bible: Remarks on the Burning Rite on the Altar," *Harvard Theological Review* 97, no. 4 (2004): 485.

14. Ibid., p. 491.

15. Michael Bryson, "Dismemberment and Community: Sacrifice and the Communal Body in the Hebrew Scriptures," *Religion and Literature* 35, no. 1 (2003): 1.

16. Ibid., p. 4.

17. George Buchanan Gray, *Sacrifice in the Old Testament: Its Theory and Practice* (New York: Ktav Publishing, 1971 [1925]), p. 95.

18. Ibid., p. 51.

19. *Rig Veda*, trans. Ralph T. H. Griffith, 1896, http://sacred-texts.com/rigveda .htm (accessed December 15, 2009).

20. Octavian Sarbatoare, "Yajna, the Vedic Sacrifice (Offering)," http://www.hindu website.com/vedicsection/yajna.asp (accessed December 16, 2009).

21. Ibid.

22. American/International Gita Society, Bhagavad Gita, http://sacred-texts.com/ hin/gita/agsgita.htm (accessed December 16, 2009).

23. Sri Swami Sivananda, "Pancha Mahayajnas: The Hindu Ritual Pancha Mahayajnas," http://www.experiencefestival.com/a/pancha_mahayajnas/id/23095 (accessed December 16, 2009).

24. Sidarta Wijaya, "Animal Sacrifices," http://blog.baliwww.com/religion/722/#more-722 (accessed May 28, 2007).

25. Walter Burkert, Homo Necans: *The Anthropology of Ancient Greek Sacrificial Ritual and Myth*, trans. Peter Bing (Berkeley: University of California Press, 1983 [1972]), p. 136.

26. Ibid., p. 140.

27. Miranda Green, *Dying for the Gods: Human Sacrifice in Iron Age and Roman Europe* (Gloucestershire: Tempus Publishing, 2002), p. 47.

28. Dennis Hughes, *Human Sacrifice in Ancient Greece* (London: Routledge, 1991), pp. 4–5.

29. John Scheid, *An Introduction to Roman Religion*, trans. Jane Lloyd (Bloomington: Indiana University Press, 2003), p. 79.

30. Ibid., p. 97.

31. Ibid., pp. 99–100.

32. E. E. Evans-Pritchard, *Nuer Religion* (New York: Oxford University Press, 1956), p. 197.

33. Ibid., pp. 197–98.

34. Ibid., p. 207.

35. Ibid., p. 210.

36. Godfrey Lienhardt, *Divinity and Experience: The Religion of the Dinka* (Oxford: Clarendon Press, 1961), p. 272.

37. Heusch, *Sacrifice in Africa.*

38. Ibid., p. 81.

39. Ibid., p. 202.

40. Davies, *Human Sacrifice*, p. 20.

41. Ibid., p. 64.

42. Ibid., p. 43.

43. Green, *Dying for the Gods*, p. 45.

44. Ibid., p. 117.

45. Ibid., p. 158.

46. Davies, *Human Sacrifice*, p. 45.

47. Ibid., p. 75.

48. Quoted in ibid., p. 123.

49. Scheid, *Introduction to Roman Religion*, p. 95.

50. Valerio Valeri, *Kingship and Sacrifice: Ritual and Society in Ancient Hawaii*, trans. Paula Wissig (Chicago: University of Chicago Press, 1985), p. 10.

51. Ibid., p. 45.

52. Ibid., p. 56.

53. Ibid., p. 336.

54. Davies, *Human Sacrifice*, p. 166.

55. Ibid., p. 186.

56. Melville Herskovits, *Dahomey: An Ancient West African Kingdom*, vol. 2. (New York: J. J. Augustin, 1938), p. 49.

57. Ibid., p. 53.

58. Ibid.

59. Ibid., p. 55.

60. Davies, *Human Sacrifice*, p. 133.

61. David Carrasco, *City of Sacrifice: The Aztec Empire and the Role of Violence in Civilization* (Boston: Beacon, 1999), pp. 7–8.

62. J. Eric Thompson, *Maya History and Religion* (Norman: University of Oklahoma Press, 1970), p. 182.

63. Ibid., p. 178.

64. Linda Schele, "Human Sacrifice among the Classic Maya," in *Ritual Human Sacrifice in Mesoamerica*, ed. Elizabeth Boone (Washington, DC: Dumbarton Oaks Research Library and Collection, 1984), p. 7.

65. Francis Robicsek and Donald M. Hales, "Maya Heart Sacrifice: Cultural Perspective and Surgical Technique," in *Ritual Human Sacrifice in Mesoamerica* (see note 64) p. 52.

66. Quoted in Carrasco, *City of Sacrifice*, p. 175.

67. Ibid.

68. Ibid.

69. René Girard, *Violence and the Sacred*, trans. Patrick Gregory (Baltimore: Johns Hopkins University Press, 1977), p. 300.

70. Ibid., p. 8.

71. René Girard, "Generative Scapegoating: Discussion," in *Violent Origins: Walter Burkert, René Girard, and Jonathan Z. Smith on Ritual Killing and Cultural Formation*, ed. Robert G. Hamerton-Kelly (Stanford, CA: Stanford University Press, 1987), p. 122.

72. Girard, *Violence and the Sacred*, p. 14.

73. Ibid., p. 12.

74. Ibid., p. 23.

75. Girard, "Generative Scapegoating," p. 107.

76. Burkert, Homo Necans, p. 3.

77. Ibid., p. 22.

78. Ibid., p. 40.

79. Ibid., p. 2.

80. Ibid., p. 35.

81. Jonathan Z. Smith, "The Domestication of Sacrifice," in *Violent Origins* (see note 72), p. 197.

82. Ibid.

83. Frits Staal, "The Meaninglessness of Ritual," *Numen* 26, no. 1 (1979).

84. Quoted in Carrasco, *City of Sacrifice*, pp. 79–80.

85. David Shulman, *The Hungry God: Hindu Tales of Filicide and Devotion* (Chicago: University of Chicago Press, 1993), p. 140.

86. Thomas Gibson, *Sacrifice and Sharing in the Philippine Highlands: Religion and Society among the Buid of Mindoro* (London: Athlone Press, 1986), pp. 156–57.

87. Heusch, *Sacrifice in Africa*, p. 148.

88. E. O. James, *Origins of Sacrifice: A Study in Comparative Religion* (Port Washington, NY: Kennikat Press, 1971 [1933]), p. 75.

89. Valeri, *Kingship and Sacrifice*, pp. 140–42.

90. S. Jeffrey Wilkerson, "In Search of the Mountain of Foam: Human Sacrifice in Eastern Mesoamerica," in *Ritual Human Sacrifice in Mesoamerica* (see note 64), p. 110.

91. Ibid., p. 114.

92. Smith, "Domestication of Sacrifice," p. 201.

93. Ian Bradley, *The Power of Sacrifice* (London: Darton, Longman, and Todd, 1995), pp. 9–10.

94. Evans-Pritchard, *Nuer Religion*, p. 214.

95. Davies, *Human Sacrifice*, p. 13.

96. James, *Origins of Sacrifice*, p. 33.

97. Ibid., p. 256.

98. Ibid., p. 186.

99. Jay, *Throughout Your Generations Forever*, p. 40.

100. Ibid., p. 102.

CHAPTER 4: SELF-INJURY

1. Ariel Glucklich, *Sacred Pain: Hurting the Body for the Sake of the Soul* (Oxford: Oxford University Press, 2001), p. 4.

2. Piero Camporesi, *The Incorruptible Flesh: Bodily Mutilation and Mortification in Religion and Folklore*, trans. Tania Croft-Murray (Cambridge: Cambridge University Press, 1988 [1983]).

3. Judith Perkins, *The Suffering Self: Pain and Narrative Representation in the Early Christian Era* (London: Routledge, 1995).

4. Elaine Scarry, *The Body in Pain: The Making and Unmaking of the World* (New York: Oxford University Press, 1985).

5. Kaye Oakes, "Cutting: Self Injury and How to Help," http://www.psyke.org/articles/en/cutting_self_injury (accessed December 21, 2009).

6. A. P. Elkin, *The Australian Aborigines* (Sydney: Angus and Robertson, 1974 [1938]), p. 197.

7. Ibid., p. 198.

8. Ibid., p. 225.

9. Mircea Eliade, *Shamanism: Archaic Techniques of Ecstasy* (Princeton, NJ: Princeton University Press, 1972 [1964]), p. 64.

10. Ibid., p. 33.

11. Ibid., p. 62.

12. Elkin, *Australian Aborigines*, p. 331.

13. Ruth Benedict, "The Vision in Plains Culture," *American Anthropologist* 24, no. 1 (1922): 5.

14. Ibid., p. 8.

15. Ibid.

16. Ralph Linton, "The Comanche Sun Dance," *American Anthropologist* 37, no. 1 (1935).

17. Glucklich, *Sacred Pain*, p. 146.

18. Benedict, "Vision in Plains Culture," p. 8.

19. Colleen Ward, "Thaipusam in Malaysia: A Psycho-Anthropological Analysis of Ritual Trance, Ceremonial Possession and Self-Mortification Practices," *Ethos* 12, no. 4 (1984): 307.

20. Ibid., p. 318.

21. Ibid., p. 325.

22. Ibid., p. 319.

23. Gilbert Herdt, *Guardians of the Flute: Idioms of Masculinity* (New York: Columbia University Press, 1987), p. 13.

24. Ibid., p. 38.

25. Ibid., p. 216.

26. Michael Carroll, *The Penitente Brotherhood: Patriarchy and Hispano-Catholicism in New Mexico* (Baltimore: Johns Hopkins University Press, 2002), p. 79.

27. Justo Gonzalez, *The Story of Christianity*, vol. 1, *The Early Church to the Dawn of the Reformation* (New York: HarperSanFrancisco, 1984), p. 360.

28. Ibid.

29. Carroll, *Penitente Brotherhood*, p. 80.

30. Ibid., p. 82.

31. Ibid., p. 21.

32. Mary Elaine Hegland, "Flagellation and Fundamentalism: (Trans)Forming Meaning, Identity, and Gender through Pakistani Women's Rituals of Mourning," *American Ethnologist* 25, no. 2 (1998): 245.

33. Ibid.

34. Sakuntala Narasimhan, *Sati: Widow Burning in India* (New York: Anchor Books, 1992), p. 11.

35. Ibid.

36. Ibid.

37. Ibid., p. 21.

38. Ibid., p. 18.

39. Mala Sen, *Death by Fire: Sati, Dowry Death, and Female Infanticide in Modern India* (New Brunswick, NJ: Rutgers University Press, 2001).

40. Narasimhan, *Sati*, pp. 2–3.

41. Sen, *Death by Fire*, p. 8.

42. The Religious Movements Homepage Project at the University of Virginia, "Heaven's Gate," http://web.archive.org/web/20060827231002/religiousmovements .lib.virginia .edu/nrms/hgprofile.html (accessed December 21, 2009).

43. Neal Kelsey, "The Body as Desert in *The Life of Saint Anthony*," *Semeia* 57 (1992): 146.

44. Gillian Clark, "Women and Asceticism in Late Antiquity: The Refusal of Status and Gender," in *Asceticism*, ed. Vincent L. Wimbush and Richard Valantasis (Oxford: Oxford University Press, 1995), p. 36.

45. Max Weber, *The Sociology of Religion*, trans. Ephraim Fischoff (Boston: Beacon, 1963 [1922]), p. 166.

46. Ibid.

47. Ibid., p. 164.

48. Gonzalez, *Story of Christianity*, p. 138.

49. Samuel Rubenson (see note 44), "Christian Asceticism and the Emergence of the Monastic Tradition," in *Asceticism* (see note 44), pp. 53–54.

50. Geoffrey Harpham, *The Ascetic Imperative in Culture and Criticism* (Chicago: University of Chicago Press, 1987), p. 20.

51. Ibid., p. 21.

52. Gonzalez, *Story of Christianity*, p. 239.

53. Camporesi, *Incorruptible Flesh*, p. 227.

54. Ibid., p. 43.

55. Ibid., p. 45.

56. Ibid., p. 56.

57. Ibid., p. 60.

58. Joseph Alter, "The 'Sannyasi' and the Indian Wrestler: The Anatomy of a Relationship," *American Ethnologist* 19, no. 2 (1992): 318.

59. Ibid., p. 323.

60. Lynn Denton, *Female Ascetics in Hinduism* (Albany: State University of New York Press, 2004), p. 62.

61. Ibid., p. 69.

62. Peter van der Veer, "The Power of Detachment: Disciplines of Body and Mind in the Ramanandi Order," *American Ethnologist* 16, no. 3 (1989): 462.

63. Ibid., pp. 461–62.

64. Ibid., pp. 465–67.

65. Anne Vallely, *Guardians of the Transcendent: An Ethnography of a Jain Ascetic Community* (Toronto: University of Toronto Press, 2002), p. 14.

66. Michael Carrithers, "Naked Ascetics in Southern Digambar Jainism," *Man* 24, no. 2 (1989): 220.

67. Michael Carrithers, "The Modern Ascetics of Lanka and the Pattern of Change in Buddhism," *Man* 14, no. 2 (1979): 296.

68. Ibid.

69. Pope John Paul II, "Homily of the Holy Father: Jubilee of the Sick and Health Care Workers," http://www.vatican.va/holy_father/john_paul_ii/homilies/documents/hf_jp -ii_hom_ 20000211_jubilee-sick_en.html (accessed December 22, 2009).

70. Quoted in Patrick Wall and Mervyn Jones, *Defeating Pain: The War against a Silent Epidemic* (New York: Plenum, 1991), pp. 150–51.

71. Romans 8:16–7.

72. 2 Corinthians 1:6.

73. Philippians 1:29.

74. Colossians 1:24.

75. 2 Timothy 2:12.

76. Syed Hassan Bokari, Farhan Zaidi, and Zileyh Shah, "The Mourning for Imam Hussein," *Shia News*, April 10, 2004, http://www.shianews.com/hi/articles/islam/0000103.php (accessed June 5, 2007).

77. Quoted in Patrick Olivelle, "Deconstruction of the Body in Indian Asceticism," in *Asceticism* (see note 44), p. 190.

78. Quoted in ibid.

79. Camporesi, *Incorruptible Flesh*, p. 43.

80. Ibid., pp. 77–78.

81. Arnold Ludwig, "Altered States of Consciousness," *Archives of General Psychiatry* 15, no. 3 (1966).

82. Glucklich, *Sacred Pain*, p. 6.

83. Ibid., p. 8.

84. Scarry, *Body in Pain*, p. 33.

85. Ibid.

86. Ibid., p. 34.

87. Ibid., p. 35.

88. Harpham, *Ascetic Imperative*, p. xiv.

89. Ibid., p. xv.

90. Richard Valantasis, "A Theory of the Social Function of Asceticism," in *Asceticism* (see note 44), p. 547.

91. Mary Douglas, *Natural Symbols* (Harmondsworth: Penguin, 1973).

92. Thomas Csordas, "Somatic Modes of Attention," *Cultural Anthropology* 8, no. 2 (1993): 138.

93. Lacey Baldwin Smith, *Fools, Martyrs, and Traitors: The Story of Martyrdom in the Western World* (New York: Knopf, 1997).

94. Ibid., p. 12.

95. Michael Gaddis, *There Is No Crime for Those Who Have Christ* (Berkeley: University of California Press, 2005), p. 6.

96. Arthur Droge and James D. Tabor, *A Noble Death: Suicide and Martyrdom among Christians and Jews in Antiquity* (New York: HarperSanFrancisco, 1992).

97. Smith, *Fools, Martyrs, and Traitors*, p. 48.

98. Quoted in *A Noble Death* (see note 96), p. 72.

99. 2 Maccabees 6:18–20.

100. 2 Maccabees 7:2.

101. 2 Maccabees 14:42.

102. Droge and Tabor, *A Noble Death*, p. 75.

103. Mark 8:34–35.

104. 2 Corinthians 5:8.

105. Revelation 14:13.

106. Internet Medieval Source Book, "Saint Perpetua: *The Passion of Saints Perpetua and Felicity 203*" from W. H. Shewring, trans., *The Passion of Perpetua and Felicity* (London, 1931), http://www.fordham.edu/halsall/source/perpetua.html (accessed December 23, 2009).

107. Quoted in *A Noble Death*, p. 130.

108. Quoted in W. H. C. Frend, *Martyrdom and Persecution in the Early Church: A Study of a Conflict from the Maccabees to Donatus* (Garden City, NY: Anchor Books, 1967), p. 54.

109. Quoted in *A Noble Death* (see note 96), p. 150.

110. Quoted in ibid., p. 151.

111. Quoted in *Fools, Martyrs, and Traitors* (see note 93), p. 91.

112. Quoted in ibid., p. 92.

113. Quoted in *A Noble Death* (see note 96), pp. 145–46.

114. Navid Kermani, "Roots of Terror: Suicide, Martyrdom, Self-Redemption and Islam," 2002, http://www.opendemocracy.net/faith-europe_islam/article_88.jsp (accessed December 23, 2009).

115. Ibid.

116. Ali Shariati, *Martyrdom: Arise and Bear Witness*, trans. Ali Asghar Ghassemy (Tehran: Ministry of Islamic Guidance), http://al-islam.org/arisewitness (accessed June 8, 2007).

117. A. Ezzati, "The Concept of Martyrdom in Islam," 2006, http://www.al-islam.org/al-serat/concept-ezzati.htm (accessed June 8, 2007).

118. Ibid.

119. Ayatullah Sayyid Mahmud Taleqani, "Jihad and Shahadat," http://al-islam.org/beliefs/philosophy/jihadandshahadat.html (accessed June 8, 2007).

120. Ibid.

121. Ibid.

122. Smith, *Fools, Martyrs, and Traitors*, p. 15.

123. Ibid.

CHAPTER 5: PERSECUTION

1. Robert Jobe, "Asylum Law Outline," http://www.jobelaw.com/2/as3.htm (accessed July 8, 2007). Jobe is referring to the 1996 US federal court case *Fisher v. INS*.

2. Ibid. Jobe is referring to the 1985 US federal court case *Hernandez-Ortiz v. INS*.

3. Ibid. Jobe is referring to the 1993 US federal court case *Fatin v. INS*.

4. Ibid.

5. Gordon Allport, *The Nature of Prejudice* (Reading, MA: Addison-Wesley, 1979), p. 9.

6. Ibid., p. 58.'

7. Ibid.

8. David Heyd, introduction to *Toleration: An Elusive Virtue*, ed. David Heyd (Princeton, NJ: Princeton University Press, 1996), p. 9.

9. John Horton, "Toleration as a Virtue," in *Toleration* (see note 8), p. 28.

10. Bernard Williams, "Toleration: An Impossible Virtue?" in *Toleration* (see note 8), p. 18.

11. Will Durant, *The Age of Faith* (New York: Simon and Schuster, 1950), p. 784.

12. Rodney Stark, *One True God: Historical Consequences of Monotheism* (Princeton, NJ: Princeton University Press, 2001), p. 116.

13. Ibid, p. 117.

14. Ibid, p. 120.

15. Mary Jane Engh, *In the Name of Heaven: 3,000 Years of Religious Persecution* (Amherst, NY: Prometheus Books, 2007), p. 15.

16. Exodus 22:20.

17. Engh, *In the Name of Heaven*, p. 20.

18. Quoted in ibid., p. 41.

19. Elaine Pagels, *The Origin of Satan* (New York: Random House, 1995).

20. Leon Canfield, *The Early Persecution of the Christians* (New York: AMS Press, 1986 [1913]), p. 43.

21. Engh, *In the Name of Heaven*, p. 67.

22. Justo Gonzalez, *The Story of Christianity*, vol. 1, *The Early Church to the Dawn of the Reformation* (New York: HarperSanFrancisco, 1984), p. 32.

23. Micheal Gaddis, *There Is No Crime for Those Who Have Christ: Religious Violence in the Christian Roman Empire* (Berkeley: University of California Press, 2005), p. 35.

24. Canfield, *Early Persecution of the Christians*, p. 19.

25. Ibid., p. 22.

26. Engh, *In the Name of Heaven*, p. 67.

27. Gonzalez, *Story of Christianity*, p. 35.

28. Canfield, *Early Persecution of the Christians*, p. 44.

29. Gonzalez, *Story of Christianity*, p. 36.

30. Engh, *In the Name of Heaven*, p. 75.

31. Gaddis, *There Is No Crime*, p. 75.

32. Leonard Levy, *Blasphemy: Verbal Offense against the Sacred, from Moses to Salman Rushdie* (New York: Knopf, 1993), p. 42.

33. Ibid, p. 44.

34. Ibid.

35. Gaddis, *There Is No Crime*, p. 152.

36. Ibid, p. 1.

37. A. L. Maycock, *The Inquisition from Its Establishment to the Great Schism: An Introductory Study* (New York: Harper and Row, 1969), p. 33.

38. Quoted in ibid., p. 95.

39. Ibid., p. 140.

40. Ibid., p. 115.

41. Ibid., pp. 115–16.

42. Ibid., p. 121.

43. Maycock, *Inquisition*, p. 171.

44. Engh, *In the Name of Heaven*, p. 57.

45. B. A. Robinson, "Two Millennia of Jewish Persecution—Anti-Judaism: 70 to 1200 CE," http://www.religioustolerance.org/jud_pers1.htm (accessed December 24, 2009).

46. Joseph Perez, *The Spanish Inquisition: A History*, trans. Janet Lloyd (New Haven, CT: Yale University Press, 2004), p. 1.

47. Quoted in ibid., p. 3.

48. Ibid., p. 16.

49. Ibid., p. 149.

50. Ibid., p. 100.

51. Jaime Contreras and Gustav Henningsen, "Forty-four Thousand Cases of the Spanish Inquisition (1540–1700): Analysis of a Historical Data Bank," in *The Inquisition in Early Modern Europe*, ed. Gustav Henningsen and John Tedeschi (Dekalb: Northern Illinois University Press, 1986).

52. Martin Luther, "On the Jews and Their Lies, 1543." *Luther's Works*, trans. Martin H. Bertram (Philadelphia: Fortress, 1971), p. 288.

53. Ibid., p. 272.

54. Quoted in Stephen Feldman, *Please Don't Wish Me a Merry Christmas: A Critical History of the Separation of Church and State* (New York: New York University Press, 1997), p. 132.

55. Adolf Hitler, *Mein Kampf*, trans. Ralph Manheim (New York: Houghton Mifflin, 1969 [1925]), p. 60.

56. Engh, *In the Name of Heaven*, p. 121.

57. Ibid., p. 122.

58. Ibid., p. 124.

59. Qur'an, sura 2.193.

60. Qur'an, sura 2.217.

61. J. E. Esslemont, *Baha'u'llah and the New Era: An Introduction to the Baha'i Faith* (Wilmette, IL: Baha'i Publishing Trust, 1978 [1923]), pp. 27–28.

62. Human Rights Watch, "Sudan: 'In the Name of God' Repression Continues in Northern Sudan," *Human Rights Watch Short Report* 6, no. 9 (1994): 34.

63. T. O. Beidelman, *The Kaguru: A Matrilineal People of East Africa* (New York: Holt, Rinehart, and Winston, 1971), p. 37.

64. James Smith, "Buying a Better Witch Doctor: Witch-Finding, Neoliberalism, and the Development Imagination in the Taita Hills, Kenya," *American Ethnologist* 32, no. 1 (2005).

65. Pamela Stewart and Andrew Strathern, *Witchcraft, Sorcery, Rumor, and Gossip* (Cambridge: Cambridge University Press, 2004), p. 14.

66. Joseph Klaits, *Servants of Satan: The Age of the Witch Hunts* (Bloomington: Indiana University Press, 1985), p. 17.

67. Stewart and Strathern, *Witchcraft, Sorcery, Rumor, and Gossip*, p. 15.

68. H. R. Trevor-Roper, *The European Witch-Craze of the Sixteenth and Seventeenth Centuries, and Other Essays* (New York: Harper and Row, 1967 [1956]), p. 116.

69. Ibid., p. 151.

70. Ibid., p. 140.

71. Klaits, *Servants of Satan*, p. 63.

72. Ibid., p. 71.

73. Alan MacFarlane, *Witchcraft in Tudor and Stuart England: A Regional and Comparative Study* (New York: Harper and Row, 1970).

74. C. John Sommerville, *The Secularization of Early Modern England: From Religious Culture to Religious Faith* (New York: Oxford University Press, 1992), p. 44.

75. Ibid., p. 47.

76. Alexis de Tocqueville, *The Old Regime and the French Revolution*, trans. Stuart Gilbert (New York: Anchor Books, 1955 [1856]), p. 5.

77. Quoted in Leo Gershoy, *The Era of the French Revolution, 1789–1799* (Princeton, NJ: D. Van Nostrand, 1957), pp. 159–60.

78. J. M. Thompson, *Robespierre and the French Revolution* (New York: Collier Books, 1962), p. 111.

79. Quoted in ibid., p. 115.

80. Basil Dmytryshyn, *USSR: A Concise History*, 2nd ed. (New York: Charles Scribner's Sons, 1971), p. 126.

81. Ibid., p. 127.

82. Ibid, p. 129.

83. Ibid.

84. Quoted in Warren Carroll, *The Rise and Fall of the Communist Revolution* (Front Royal, VA: Christendom Press, 1898), p. 233.

85. Ronald Schwartz, "Religious Persecution in Tibet," 1999, http://www.tibet.ca/pub/persecution.htm (accessed July 15, 2007).

86. Quoted in Human Rights Watch, "Devastating Blows: Religious Repression of Uighurs in Xinjiang," *Human Rights Watch Short Report* 17, no. 2 (April 2005): 58.

87. Human Rights Watch, *Dangerous Meditation: China's Campaign against Falungong* (New York: Human Rights Watch, 2002), p. 12.

88. Ibid., p. 21.

89. Wyn Craig Wade, *The Fiery Cross: The Ku Klux Klan in America* (New York: Simon and Schuster, 1987), p. 34.

90. Ibid., p. 42.

91. Ibid., p. 146.

92. Quoted in ibid., pp. 147–48.

93. Quoted in ibid., p. 168.

94. Quoted in ibid., p. 169.

95. Quoted in ibid., p. 170.

96. Quoted in ibid., p. 277.

97. Quoted in ibid., p. 373.

98. Quoted in ibid., p. 385.

99. Quoted in Kenneth Stern, *A Force upon the Plain: The American Militia Movement and the Politics of Hate* (New York: Simon and Schuster, 1996), p. 47.

100. Aryan Nations, http://www.aryannationsrevival.org/ (accessed September 15, 2010). The site also features a tombstone bearing the message, "United States of America, Born: July 4, 1776, Died: Nov 4, 2008, Suicide"—the date of course referring to the election of Barack Obama as president.

101. Quoted in Robert Snow, *The Militia Threat: Terrorists among Us* (New York: Plenum Trade, 1999), p. 2.

102. John George and Laird Wilcox, *American Extremists: Militias, Supremacists, Klansmen, Communists, and Others* (Amherst, NY: Prometheus Books, 1996), p. 342.

103. Quoted in Morris Dees, *Gathering Storm: America's Militia Threat* (New York: HarperCollins, 1996), pp. 65–66.

104. Quoted in *A Force upon the Plain* (see note 99), p. 19.

105. Quoted in *Gathering Storm* (see note 103), p. 21.

106. Quoted in *In the Name of Heaven* (see note 15), 7.

107. Quoted in *Blasphemy* (see note 32), p. 48.

108. Quoted in ibid.

109. Quoted in ibid.

110. Quoted in ibid., p. 49.

111. Quoted in ibid.

112. Quoted in ibid.

113. Gaddis, *There is No Crime*, 133.

114. Quoted in *Blasphemy* (see note 32), p. 52.

115. Quoted in Timothy Freke and Peter Gandy, *The Jesus Mysteries: Was the "Original Jesus" a Pagan God?* (New York: Harmony Books, 1999), p. 243.

116. Michael Pocock, "Why Persecution? Reasons Include Human, Satanic, and Divine Purposes," 2001, *Moody Magazine*, http://www.moodymagazine.com/articles .php?action= view_article&id=441 (accessed July 8, 2007).

117. Curtis Humes and Katherine Ann Clark, "Collective Baha'i Identity through Embodied Persecution: 'Be ye the Fingers of One Hand, the Members of One Body,'" *Anthropology of Consciousness* 11, nos. 1–2 (2000).

118. Gordon Allport, *The Nature of Prejudice* (Reading, MA: Addison-Wesley Publishing, 1979), p. 42.

119. Martin Luther, "Christian Quotes," http://christianquotes.org/author/quotes/ 32/10 (accessed December 25, 2009).

CHAPTER 6: ETHNORELIGIOUS CONFLICT

1. George DeVos, "Ethnic Pluralism: Conflict and Accommodation," in *Ethnic Identity: Cultural Continuities and Change*, ed. George DeVos and Lola Romanucci-Ross, (Palo Alto, CA: Mayfield, 1975), p. 9.

2. Fredrik Barth, introduction to *Ethnic Groups and Boundaries*, ed. Fredrik Barth, (Boston: Little, Brown, 1969), p. 11.

3. Andrew Greeley, *Why Can't They Be Like Us? America's White Ethnic Groups* (New York: E. P. Dutton, 1971), pp. 120–21.

4. Max Weber, *Economy and Society*, vol. 1, ed. Guenther Roth and Claus Wittich, (New York: Bedminster Press, 1968), p. 389.

5. DeVos, "Ethnic Pluralism," p. 16.

6. Thomas Hylland Eriksen, *Ethnicity and Nationalism: Anthropological Perspectives* (London: Pluto, 2002), p. 12.

7. Benedict Anderson, *Imagined Communities: Reflections on the Origin and Spread of Nationalism* (London: Verso, 1983).

8. Weber, *Economy and Society*, p. 388.

9. Barth, introduction, p. 15.

10. Ibid., p. 14.

11. Nelson Kasfir, "Explaining Ethnic Political Participation," *World Politics* 31, no. 3 (1979).

12. David Horowitz, *Ethnic Groups in Conflict* (Berkeley: University of California Press, 1985), p. 8.

13. Desmond Morris, *Manwatching: A Field Guide to Human Behavior* (New York: Harry N. Abrams, 1977), p. 149.

14. R. Scott Appleby, *The Ambivalence of the Sacred: Religion, Violence, and Reconciliation* (Lanham, MD: Rowman and Littlefield, 2000), pp. 107–108.

15. Daniel Gold, "Organized Hinduisms: From Vedic Truth to Hindu Nation," in *Fundamentalisms Observed*, ed. Martin Marty and R. Scott Appleby (Chicago: University of Chicago Press, 1991), p. 534.

16. Robert Eric Frykenberg, "Hindu Fundamentalism and the Structural Stability of India," in *Fundamentalisms and the State: Remaking Polities, Economies, and Militance*, ed. Martin Marty and R. Scott Appleby (Chicago: University of Chicago Press, 1993).

17. Quoted in ibid., p. 243.

18. Kalyani Devaki Menon, "Converted Innocents and Their Trickster Heroes: The Politics of Proselytizing in India," in *The Anthropology of Religious Conversion*, ed. Andrew Buckser and Stephen D. Glazier (Lanham, MD: Rowman and Littlefield, 2003).

19. Ibid.

20. Ibid, p. 51.

21. Quoted in David Little, *Sri Lanka: The Invention of Enmity* (Washington, DC: US Institute of Peace Press, 1994), p. 3.

22. Quoted in Bruce Kapferer, *Legends of People, Myths of State: Violence, Intolerance, and Political Culture in Sri Lanka and Australia* (Washington, DC: Smithsonian Institution Press, 1988), p. 54.

23. Ibid., p. 62.

24. Quoted in B. H. Farmer, *Ceylon: A Divided Nation* (London: Oxford University Press, 1963), p. 12.

25. Quoted in Rupert Gethin, "Buddhist Monks, Buddhist Kings, and Buddhist Violence: On the Early Buddhist Attitudes to Violence," in *Religion and Violence in South Asia: Theory and Practice*, ed. John R. Hinnells and Richard King (Abingdon, UK: Routledge, 2007), p. 63. Gethin also discusses the violence of the great "pacifist" Indian emperor Asoka.

26. E. F. C. Ludowyk, *The Modern History of Ceylon* (New York: Praeger, 1966), p. 240.

27. Sinnapah Arasaratnam, *Ceylon* (Englewood Cliffs, NJ: Prentice-Hall, 1964), p. 25.

28. Quoted in K. N. O. Dharmadasa, *Language, Religion, and Ethnic Assertiveness: The Growth of Sinhalese Nationalism in Sri Lanka* (Ann Arbor: University of Michigan Press, 1992), p. 138.

29. Peter Schalk, "Operationalizing Buddhism for Political Ends in a Martial Context in Lanka: The Case of *Simhalatva*," in *Religion and Violence in South Asia* (see note 25).

30. Little, *Sri Lanka*, p. 33.

31. Quoted in Jack David Eller, *From Culture to Ethnicity to Conflict: An Anthropological Perspective on International Ethnic Conflict* (Ann Arbor: University of Michigan Press, 1999), p. 243.

32. Noel Malcolm, *Bosnia: A Short History* (New York: New York University Press, 1994), pp. 52–53.

33. Robert Donia and John Fine, *Bosnia and Hercegovina: A Tradition Betrayed* (New York: Columbia University Press, 1994), p. 44.

34. Ibid, p. 111.

35. Quoted in Norman Cigar, *Genocide in Bosnia: The Policy of "Ethnic Cleansing"* (College Station: Texas A&M University Press, 1995), p. 17.

36. Donia and Fine, *Bosnia and Hercegovina*, p. 200.

37. Quoted in Cigar, *Genocide in Bosnia*, p. 26.

38. Quoted in ibid., p. 28.

39. Rabia Ali and Lawrence Lifschutz, *Why Bosnia? Writings on the Balkan War* (Stony Creek, CT: Pamphleteer's Press, 1993), p. xiii.

40. Carolyn Meyer, *Voices of Northern Ireland: Growing Up in a Troubled Land* (Orlando: Harcourt Brace Jovanovich, 1987), p. 138.

41. David Holloway, *Understanding the Northern Ireland Conflict: A Summary and Overview of the Conflict and its Origins* (Belfast: Community Dialogue Critical Issues Series, 2005), p. 5.

42. Robert Kee, *Ireland: A History* (London: Abacus, 1991), p. 44.

43. Ibid., p. 48.

44. Joseph Liechty, *Roots of Sectarianism in Ireland* (Belfast: Joseph Liechty, 1993), p. 17.

45. Holloway, *Understanding the Northern Ireland Conflict*, p. 8.

46. Patrick Buckland, *A History of Northern Ireland* (Dublin: Gill and Macmillan, 1981).

47. Holloway, *Understanding the Northern Ireland Conflict*, p. 14.

48. Meyer, *Voices of Northern Ireland*, pp. 152–53.

49. Kamal Sabili, *A House of Many Mansions: The History of Lebanon Reconsidered* (London: I. B. Tauris, 1993), p. 19.

50. Thomas Collelo, ed. *Lebanon: A Country Study* (Washington, DC: GPO for the

Library of Congress, 1987), http://countrystudies.us/lebanon/18.htm (accessed December 29, 2009).

51. Richard Warms, "Merchants, Muslims, and Wahhabiyya: The Elaboration of Islamic Identity in Sikasso, Mali," *Canadian Journal of African Studies* 26, no. 3 (1992): 486.

52. Lansine Kaba, "The Pen, the Sword, and the Crown: Islam and Revolution in Songhay Reconsidered, 1464–1493," *Journal of African History* 25, no. 3 (1984).

53. Basil Davidson, *The Magnificent African Cake* (Chicago: Home Vision, 1984).

54. Misty Bastian, "Young Converts: Christian Missions, Gender, and Youth in Onitsha, Nigeria 1880–1929," *Anthropological Quarterly* 73, no. 3 (2000).

55. Quoted in Human Rights Watch, "The 'Miss World Riots': Continued Impunity for Killings in Kaduna," *Human Rights Watch Report* 15, no. 13 (July 2003): 7.

56. Ibid.

57. Human Rights Watch, "Revenge in the Name of Religion: The Cycle of Violence in *Human Rights Watch Report* 17, no. 8 (May 2005).

58. Clifford Geertz, "The Integrative Revolution: Primordial Sentiments and Civil Politics in the New States," in *Old Societies and New States*, ed. Clifford Geertz (New York: Free Press, 1963).

59. J. S. Furnivall, *Colonial Policy and Practice: A Comparative Study of Burma and Netherlands India* (New York: New York University Press, 1956), p. 304.

60. Benjamin Barber, *Jihad versus McWorld* (New York: Times Books, 1995).

61. Rogers Brubaker and David D. Laitin, "Ethnic and Nationalist Violence," *Annual Review of Sociology* 24 (1998): 424.

CHAPTER 7: WAR

1. Terry Pratchett, *Small Gods* (New York: HarperCollins, 1992), p. 164.

2. Steven Le Blanc, *Constant Battles: The Myth of the Peaceful, Noble Savage* (New York: St. Martin's, 2003).

3. See, for example, Brian Ferguson and N. Whitehead, eds. *War in the Tribal Zone* (Santa Fe: School of American Research Press, 1992). Also Jeffrey Blick, "Genocidal Warfare in Tribal Societies as a Result of European-Induced Culture Conflict," *Man* 2, no. 4 (1988).

4. Napoleon Chagnon, *Yanomamo: The Fierce People* (New York: Holt, Rinehart, and Winston, 1968).

5. Daniel Smith, "The World at War: January 2003," *Defense Monitor* 32, no. 1 (2003).

6. Raoul Naroll, "On Ethnic Unit Classification," *Current Anthropology* 5, no. 3 (1964): 286.

7. Keith Otterbein, "Internal War: A Cross-cultural Study," *American Anthropologist* 70, no. 2 (1968): 278.

8. Anthony Wallace, "Psychological Preparations for War," in M. Fried et al., *War: The Anthropology of Armed Conflict and Aggression* (Garden City, NY: Natural History Press, 1967), p. 179.

9. Bronislaw Malinowski, "An Anthropological Analysis of War," *American Journal of Sociology* 46, no. 4 (1941): 523.

10. Brian Ferguson, "Introduction: Studying War," in *Warfare, Culture, and Environment*, ed. R. Brian Ferguson (Orlando, FL: Academic, 1984), p. 5.

11. Ibid., p. 3.

12. Harry Turney-High, *Primitive War: Its Practice and Concepts* (Columbia: University of South Carolina Press, 1971), p. 30.

13. Carl von Clausewitz, *On War*, trans. Michael Howard and Peter Paret (Princeton, NJ: Princeton University Press, 1984), p. 75.

14. Michael Walzer, *Just and Unjust Wars: A Moral Argument with Historical Illustrations*, 3rd ed. (New York: Basic Books, 2000), p. 74.

15. Victor Davis Hanson, *The Wars of the Ancient Greeks* (London: Cassell, 1999), p. 14.

16. Roland Bainton, *Christian Attitudes toward War and Peace* (New York: Abingdon, 1960), p. 33.

17. Ibid., p. 39.

18. Quoted in ibid., p. 96.

19. Quoted in ibid., p. 97.

20. Joyce Salisbury, "'In Vain Have I Smitten Your Children': Augustine Defines Just War," in *The Just War and Jihad: Violence in Judaism, Christianity, and Islam*, ed. R. Joseph Hoffmann (Amherst, NY: Prometheus Books, 2006), p. 206.

21. Walzer, *Just and Unjust Wars*, p. 229.

22. Judith Lichtenburg, "Some Central Problems with Just War Theory," in *Just War and Jihad* (see note 20), p. 23.

23. Reuven Firestone, *Jihad: The Origin of Holy War in Islam* (New York: Oxford University Press, 1999), p. 15.

24. James Johnson, *The Holy War Idea in Western and Islamic Traditions* (University Park: Pennsylvania State University Press, 1997), p. 33.

25. Ibid., pp. 37–41.

26. Hermann Cohen, *Religion of Reason: Out of the Sources of Judaism*, trans. Simon Kaplan (Atlanta: Scholars, 1995), p. 52.

27. Reuven Firestone, "Who Broke Their Vow First? The 'Three Vows' and Contemporary Thinking about Jewish Holy War," in *Just War and Jihad* (see note 20), p. 77.

28. Ibid.

29. Deuteronomy 7:1–6.

30. Numbers 21:14.

31. 1 Samuel 18:17.

32. Exodus 17:16.

33. Joshua 10:40–43.

34. Deuteronomy 20:10–18.

35. Gerhard von Rad, *Holy War in Ancient Israel* (Leominster, UK: Gracewing, 1991).

36. James Aho, *Religious Mythology and the Art of War: Comparative Religious Symbolisms of Military Violence* (Westport, CT: Greenwood Press, 1981).

37. For example, Numbers 31:25–47.

38. *Mishneh Torah*, "Laws of Kings and Their Wars," chapter 5.

39. Mark Gopin, *Between Eden and Armageddon: The Future of World Religions, Violence, and Peacemaking* (Oxford: Oxford University Press, 2000), p. 68.

40. Donniel Hartmann, "Two Types of Jewish War: Judaism Distinguishes between Commanded Wars and Permitted Wars," http://www.myjewishlearning.com/ideas _belief/warpeace/War_TO_Combat/War_Types_Hartman.htm (accessed June 18, 2006).

41. Aho, *Religious Mythology and the Art of War*, p. 167.

42. Ibid., pp. 169–70.

43. Ibid., p. 170.

44. Johnson, *Holy War Idea*, pp. 50–51.

45. René Grousset, *The Epic of the Crusades*, trans. Noel Lindsay (New York: Orion, 1970), p. 4.

46. New Advent, "Crusades," http://www.newadvent.org/cathen/04543c.htm (accessed December 29, 2009).

47. Grousset, *Epic of the Crusades*, p. 30.

48. Quoted in ibid., p. 31.

49. Ibid.

50. Ibid., p. 173.

51. New Advent, "Crusades."

52. Edward Cheyney, *The Dawn of a New Era, 1250–1453* (New York: Harper and Row, 1962), p. 175.

53. G. R. Elton, *Reformation Europe, 1517–1559* (New York: Harper and Row, 1963), p. 83.

54. Richard Dunn, *The Age of Religious Wars, 1559–1689* (New York: W. W. Norton, 1970), p. 23.

55. Ibid., pp. 26–27.

56. Ibid., p. 47.

57. Ibid., p. 147.

58. Jonathan Spence, *God's Chinese Son: The Taiping Heavenly Kingdom of Hong Xiuquan* (New York: W. W. Norton, 1966).

59. Quoted in ibid., p. 50.

60. Ibid., p. 117.

61. Ibid., p. 126.

62. Ibid., p. 133.

63. Quoted in ibid., p. 322.

64. Karen Armstrong, *Muhammad: A Biography of the Prophet* (New York: Harper-SanFrancisco, 1992), p. 178.

65. Qur'an, sura 2.190–91.

66. Qur'an, sura 2.216–17.

67. Qur'an, sura 9.5.

68. Qur'an, sura 9.123.

69. Qur'an, sura 61.4.

70. Firestone, *Jihad*, p. 16.

71. Ibid., p. 17.

72. Johnson, *Holy War Idea*, p. 61.

73. Armstrong, *Muhammad*, p. 168.

74. Johnson, *Holy War Idea*, p. 61.

75. Firestone, *Jihad*, p. 18.

76. Philip Hitti, *The Near East in History* (Princeton, NJ: D. Van Nostrand, 1961), p. 208.

77. R. Joseph Hoffmann ed., *Just War and Jihad: Violence in Judaism, Christianity, and Islam* (Amherst, NY: Prometheus Books, 2006), pp. 59–60.

78. Magnus Ranstorp, "Terrorism in the Name of Religion," in *Terrorism and Counterterrorism: Understanding the New Security Environment*, ed. Russell Howard and Reid Sawyer (Guilford, CT: McGraw-Hill, 2003).

79. Walter Laqueur, *The Age of Terrorism* (Boston: Little, Brown, 1987), p. 72.

80. US State Department, quoted in C. L. Ruby, "The Definition of Terrorism," *Analyses of Social Issues and Public Policy* 2, no. 1 (2002): 10.

81. Federal Bureau of Investigation, "Terrorism in the United States 1995," FBI Terrorist Research and Analytical Center, National Security Division, http://www.terrorism.com/terrorism/index.html (accessed June 25, 2007).

82. Quoted in Adam Parfrey, ed., *Extreme Islam: Anti-American Propaganda of Muslim Fundamentalism* (Los Angeles: Feral House, 2001), p. 292.

83. Austin Turk, "Sociology of Terrorism," *Annual Review of Sociology* 30 (2004): 271–72.

84. Walter Laqueur, ed., *Voices of Terror* (New York: Reed Press, 2004).

85. Ibid., p. 8.

86. Bruce Hoffman, "Holy Terror": *The Implications of Terrorism Motivated by a Religious Imperative* (Santa Monica CA: RAND, 1993), p. 2.

87. Laqueur, *Age of Terrorism*, p. 13.

88. Ibid.

89. Christopher Reuter, *My Life Is a Weapon: A Modern History of Suicide Bombing*, trans. Helena Ragg-Kirkby (Princeton, NJ: Princeton University Press, 2002).

90. Michael Gaddis, *There Is No Crime For Those Who Have Christ: Religious Violence in the Christian Roman Empire* (Berkeley: University of California Press, 2005), p. xi.

91. Rona Fields, *Martyrdom: The Psychology, Theology, and Politics of Self-Sacrifice* (Westport, CT: Praeger, 2004).

92. Robert E. Hume, "Hinduism and War," *American Journal of Theology* 20, no. 1 (1916): 31.

93. *Rig Veda* hymn XI:2–4.

94. *Rig Veda* hymn XXVII:7–9.

95. *Rig Veda* hymn XXXXIX:2–5.

96. *Rig Veda* hymn CLIV:2–3.

97. Hume, "Hinduism and War," p. 32.

98. Ibid., p. 34.

99. Surya Subedi, "The Concept in Hinduism of 'Just War,'" *Journal of Conflict and Security Law* 8, no. 2 (2003): 346.

100. Hindu Student Council, George Mason University, "A Tribute to Hinduism—War in Ancient India," http://www.hscgmu.org/ebooks/War%20In%20Ancient%20India.pdf (accessed July 22, 2007), p. 4.

101. Bhagavad Gita, chapter 2, "Of Doctrines," http://www.sacredtexts.com/ (accessed December 16, 2009).

102. Quoted in Aho, *Religious Mythology and the Art of War*, p. 62.

103. Subedi, "Concept in Hinduism of 'Just War,'" p. 352.

104. Ibid., p. 357.

105. David Lorenzen, "Warrior Ascetics in Indian History," *Journal of the American Oriental Society* 98, no. 1 (1978): 63.

106. Ibid., p. 69.

107. Ibid., p. 71.

108. Christopher Shackle, *The Sikhs*, report no. 65 (London: Minority Rights Group, 1984), p. 5.

109. "Introduction to Sikhism," http://www.gurmat.info/sms/smspublications/introductiontosikhism2/chapter1.html (accessed September 15, 2010).

110. Shackle, *Sikhs*, p. 7.

111. Dugdale Pointon, "Ikko-Ikki, (Japanese Warrior Monks)" 2005, http://www.historyofwar.org/articles/ weapons_ikko.html (accessed January 18, 2006).

112. Aho, *Religious Mythology and the Art of War*, 127.

113. Ibid., p. 130.

114. Yamamoto Tsunetomo, *Hagakure: The Book of the Samurai*, trans. William Scott Wilson (Tokyo: Kodansha International, 2002), p. 17.

115. Ibid., p. 18.

116. Ibid., p. 164.

117. Aho, *Religious Mythology and the Art of War*, p. 81.

118. Louise Simmons, "London's Temple of the Warrior Monks," http://www.time-travel-britain.com/articles/london/temple.shtml (accessed January 2, 2010).

119. Indrikis Sterns, trans., "The Rule and Statutes of the Teutonic Knights," *The ORB: On-line Reference Book for Medieval Studies*, Online Encyclopedia 1969, http://www.the-orb.net/encyclop/religion/ monastic/tk_rule.html (accessed January 12, 2006).

120. James Hillman, *A Terrible Love of War* (New York: Penguin Press, 2004), p. 9.

121. Marvin Harris, "A Cultural Materialist Theory of Band and Village Warfare: The Yanomamo Test," in *Warfare, Culture, and Environment* (see note 10), p. 111.

122. Robert Kaplan, "Euphorias of Hatred," *Atlantic Monthly* (May 2003): 44.

123. Ibid.

124. Ernst Cassirer, *An Essay on Man: An Introduction to a Philosophy of Human Culture* (Garden City, NY: Doubleday, 1954), p. 43.

125. Ibid., p. 102.

126. Chris Hedges, *War Is a Force that Gives Us Meaning* (New York: Public Affairs, 2002), p. 3.

127. Hillman, *Terrible Love of War*, p. 157.

128. Ibid., p. 140.

129. Kaplan, "Euphorias of Hatred," p. 45.

130. Ibid., p. 44.

131. Hillman, *Terrible Love of War*, p. 188.

132. Lawrence LeShan, *The Psychology of War* (New York: Helios, 1992).

133. Hedges, *War Is a Force*, p. 35.

134. Ibid., p. 143.

135. Aho, *Religious Mythology and the Art of War*, p. 12.

136. Ibid.

137. Ibid., p. 23.

138. Ibid., p. 12.

139. Ibid., p. 32.

140. Ibid., p. 48.

141. Ibid., p. 49.

142. Ibid., p. 31.

143. Ibid., p. 33.

144. Ibid., p. 12.

145. Ibid.

146. Ibid., p. 148.

147. Ibid., p. 150.

148. Ibid., p. 151.

149. Ibid., p. 153.

150. Ibid., p. 221.

CHAPTER 8: HOMICIDE AND ABUSE

1. Lloyd DeMause, *The Emotional Life of Nations*, 2002, http://www.psychohistory.com/htm/eln08_childrearing.html (accessed January 4, 2010).

2. Ibid.

3. Elizabeth Pleck, *Domestic Tyranny: The Making of Social Policy against Family Violence from Colonial Times to the Present* (New York: Oxford University Press, 1987), p. 45.

4. Numbers 31:18.

5. Deuteronomy 20:14.

6. Psalms 137:9.

7. Isaiah 13:15–18.

8. Leviticus 25:16.

9. Numbers 15.

10. Deuteronomy 13.

11. 2 Chronicles 15:13.

12. Paul Elliott, *Warrior Cults: A History of Magical, Mystical, and Murderous Organizations* (London: Blandford, 1995).

13. Mala Sen, *Death by Fire: Sati, Dowry Death, and Female Infanticide in Modern India* (New Brunswick, NJ: Rutgers University Press, 2001), p. 176.

14. Ibid., p. 178.

15. Ibid., p. 83.

16. Linda Stone and Caroline James, "Dowry, Bride-Burning, and Female Power in India," *Women's Studies International Forum* 18, no. 2 (1995).

17. Ibid., pp. 129–30.

18. Ibid., p. 130.

19. Jody Biehl, "'The Whore Lived Like a German,'" *Der Spiegel*, March 2, 2005.

20. Ibid.

21. Ibid.

22. Quoted in Hillary Mayell, "Thousands of Women Killed for Family 'Honor,'" *National Geographic News*, February 12, 2002, http:// news.nationalgeographic.com/news/2002/ 02/0212_020212_honorkilling.html (accessed June 19, 2007).

23. Quoted in ibid.

24. Jesse Hyde, "1984 Lafferty Case Still Haunts," *Deseret News*, July 24, 2004, http://www.deseretnews.com/article/595079489/1984-Lafferty-case-still-haunts.html (accessed January 4, 2010).

25. Utah Department of Public Safety, "Minor Violations—Major Cases," http://highwaypatrol.utah.gov/history/chapter4/419.html (accessed June 20, 2007).

26. Quoted in Hyde, "1984 Lafferty Case Still Haunts."

27. Ibid.

28. Court TV, "Mass. v. Roubidoux: Cult Dad Starves Baby," July 17, 2002, http://www.courttv.com/ trials/taped/robidoux/background.html (accessed January 15, 2005).

29. Don Baker, "The Andrea Yates Case: The Christian God 0 vs. Christianity Meme 3," 2005, http://www.christianitymeme.org/yates.shtml (accessed January 12, 2006).

30. Howard Pankratz, "Mom Pleads Insanity in Try to Kill Kid," *Denver Post*, June 12, 2007.

31. Lisa Falkenberg, "Religiosity Common among Mothers Who Kill Children," *San Antonio Express-News*, December 13, 2004.

32. Osho, http://www.osho.com/.

33. Lewis Carter, *Charisma and Control in Rajneeshism* (Cambridge: Cambridge University Press, 1990), p. 31.

34. Paul Belien, "Islamic Immigration and Murder among the Tulips," 2004, http://www.vdare. com/misc/belien_041103_islamic.htm (accessed June 21, 2007).

35. Crimelibrary.com, "Theo van Gogh," 2004, http://www.crimelibrary.com/ notorious_ murders/ famous/theo_van_gogh/index.html (accessed June 21, 2007).

36. Belien, "Islamic Immigration and Murder among the Tulips."

37. Ibid.

38. Crimelibrary.com, "Theo van Gogh."

39. Quoted in William Lobdell, "Teens' Rite of Passage Can Include Their Faith," *Los Angeles Times*, October 19, 2002.

40. Quoted in Morris Dees, *Gathering Storm: America's Militia Threat* (New York: HarperCollins, 1996), p. 21.

41. Mark Juergensmeyer, *Terrorism in the Mind of God: The Global Rise of Religious Violence* (Berkeley: University of California Press, 2000), p. 146.

42. CBS News, "Minister's Wife Shot Spouse Over Money," http://www.cbsnews .com/stories/2006/06/30/national/main1771713.shtml (accessed June 21, 2007).

43. Tonya Smith-King, "Minister's Wife May Serve No More Time," *Tennessean*, April 20, 2007.

44. National Coalition against Domestic Violence, "Domestic Violence Facts," July 2007, http://www.ncadv.org/files/DomesticViolenceFactSheet(National).pdf (accessed January 5, 2010).

45. Church of England, "Responding to Domestic Abuse: Guidelines for Those with Pastoral Responsibilities" (London: Church House Publishing, 2006), p. 2.

46. Ibid., p. 17.

47. Ibid.

48. 1 Timothy 2:12.

49. 1 Corinthians 11:3.

50. 1 Corinthians 11: 8–9.

51. Thomas Aquinas, *Summa Theologica*, trans. Fathers of the English Dominican Province (London: English Province, 1920), Ia q. 92 a. 1.

52. Religioustolerance.org, "The Role of Women in Christianity: Statements by Christian Leaders and Commentators," http://www.religioustolerance.org/lfe_bibl.htm (accessed January 5, 2010).

53. Quoted in Mildred Pagelow and Pam Johnson, "Abuse in the American Family: The Role of Religion," in *Abuse and Religion: When Praying Isn't Enough*, ed. Anne L. Horton and Judith A. Williamson (Lexington, MA: Lexington Books, 1988), p. 4.

54. Ibid.

55. Ibid, pp. 4–5.

56. Ibid, p. 6.

57. Ibid.

58. Judith Brown, "Introduction: Definitions, Assumptions, Themes, and Issues," in *To Have and to Hit: Cultural Perspectives on Wife Beating*, ed. Dorothy Ayers Counts, Judith K. Brown, and Jacquelyn C. Campbell (Urbana: University of Illinois Press, 1999).

59. Mary Elaine Hegland, "Wife Abuse and the Political System: A Middle Eastern Case Study," in *To Have and to Hit* (see note 58), p. 238.

60. Ibid., p. 237.

61. *Hadith of the Sunan of Abu Dawud*, chap. 709, "On Beating Women," no. 2142.

62. Abu Dawud's notes on *Hadith of the Sunan of Abu Dawud*, chap. 709, "On Beating Women," no. 2141.

63. Quoted in Sen, *Death by Fire*, p. 269.

64. Yolanda Murphy and Robert Murphy, *Women of the Forest* (New York: Columbia University Press, 2004), p. 129.

65. Ann Depperschmidt, "Wyo. Ex-Priest's Case Uncovers Lurid Tales," *Denver Post*, April 18, 2004.

66. Ibid.

67. Ibid.

68. Freedom from Religion Foundation, "Man Severs Penis," *Freethought Today* (November 2004).

69. Freedom from Religion Foundation, "Lion Bites Proselytizer," *Freethought Today* (November 2004).

70. Elliott Wolfson, *Circle in the Square: Studies in the Use of Gender in Kabbalistic Symbolism* (Albany: State University of New York Press, 1995), pp. 34–35.

71. Leonard Glick, *Marked in Your Flesh: Circumcision from Ancient Judea to Modern America* (Oxford: Oxford University Press, 2005), p. 6.

72. Ibid., p. 18.

73. Maurice Bloch, *Prey into Hunter: The Politics of Religious Experience* (Cambridge: Cambridge University Press, 1992), p. 93.

74. Reuters, "Indians Charged for Burying Children Alive," 2005, http://www.exorthodoxforchrist.com/occult_news.htm (accessed June 22, 2007).

75. Henry Wasswa, "Frightened Children Flee Rebels in Uganda," 2003, http://www.mail-archive.com/ugandanet@kym.net/msg04603.html (accessed June 22, 2007).

76. Sterling Allan, "Inside Mitchell's Head: General Anatomy of 'One Mighty and Strong' Fanaticism," 2003, http://www.greaterthings.com/Davidic_Servant/Mitchell_Survey/index.html (accessed January 5, 2010).

77. Pepe Rodriguez, *Pederasty in the Catholic Church: Sexual Crimes of the Clergy against Minors, a Drama Silenced and Covered Up by the Bishops* (Madrid: Suma de Letras, Punto de Lectura, 2002).

78. Pepe Rodriguez, *The Sex Life of the Clergy* (Barcelona: Ediciones B., 1995).

79. John Jay College of Criminal Justice, "The Nature and Scope of the Problem of Sexual Abuse of Minors by Catholic Priests and Deacons," 2004, http://www.jjay.cuny.edu/churchstudy/main.asp (accessed January 5, 2010).

80. Thomas Reilly, "The Sexual Abuse of Children in the Roman Catholic Archdiocese of Boston," 2003, http://www.ago.state.ma.us/archdiocese.pdf (accessed December 15, 2003).

81. The Vatican, "Instruction on the Manner of Proceeding in Cases of Solicitation," 1962, http://www.sarabite.info/crimen.pdf (accessed January 6, 2010).

82. Seth Asser and Rita Swan, "Child Fatalities from Religion-Motivated Medical Neglect," *Pediatrics* 101, no. 4 (1998): 625.

83. Ibid., p. 626.

84. Michele Nicolosi, "Forced Prenatal Care" (2000), http://archive.salon.com/health/feature/2000/09/15/forced_prenatal/print.html (accessed January 16, 2006).

85. Paul Heaton, "Does Religion Really Reduce Crime?" *Journal of Law and Economics* 49 (2006): 167.

86. Ibid.

87. Travis Hirschi and Rodney Stark, "Hellfire and Delinquency," *Social Problems* 17, no. 2 (1969).

88. James Lea and Bruce Hunsburger, "Christian Orthodoxy and Victim Derogation: The Impact of the Salience of Religion," *Journal for the Scientific Study of Religion* 29, no. 4 (1990): 517.

89. Tammy Greer et al., "We Are a Religious People; We Are a Vengeful People," *Journal for the Scientific Study of Religion* 44, no. 1 (2005).

90. Gregory Paul, "Cross-national Correlations of Quantifiable Societal Health with Popular Religiosity and Secularism in the Prosperous Democracies," *Journal of Religion and Society* 7 (2005): 7.

91. William Lambert, Leigh Triandis, and Margery Wolf, "Some Correlates of Beliefs in the Malevolence and Benevolence of Supernatural Beings," *Journal of Abnormal and Social Psychology* 58 (1959).

92. Charlotte Otterbein and Keith Otterbein, "Believers and Beaters: A Case Study of Supernatural Beliefs and Child Rearing in the Bahama Islands," *American Anthropologist* 75, no. 5 (1973).

CHAPTER 9: RELIGION AND NONVIOLENCE

1. Sam Harris, *The End of Faith: Religion, Terror, and the Future of Reason* (New York: W. W. Norton, 2004), p. 26.

2. Mark Gopin, *Between Eden and Armageddon: The Future of World Religions, Violence, and Peacemaking* (Oxford: Oxford University Press, 2000), p. 13.

3. Ibid.

4. Kenneth Boulding, *Stable Peace* (Austin: University of Texas Press, 1978), p. 3.

5. Ibid.

6. Ibid., p. 5.

7. Ibid., p. 10.

8. Douglas Fry, *The Human Potential for Peace: An Anthropological Challenge to Assumptions about War and Violence* (New York: Oxford University Press, 2006), p. 12.

9. Ibid., p. 22.

10. Ibid.

11. Donald Black, *The Social Structure of Right and Wrong* (San Diego: Academic Press, 1993).

12. Fry, *Human Potential for Peace*, p. 27.

13. Ibid., p. 36.

14. Ibid., p. 62.

15. Marc Howard Ross, *The Culture of Conflict* (New Haven, CT: Yale University Press, 1993).

16. Bruce Bonta, "Cooperation and Competition in Peaceful Societies," *Psychological Bulletin* 121 (1997).

17. Fry, *Human Potential for Peace*, pp. 63–64.

18. Ibid., p. 37.

19. Ross, *Culture of Conflict*, p. 99.

20. Bonta, "Cooperation and Competition in Peaceful Societies," p. 301.

21. Ibid., p. 303.

22. Ibid., p. 304.

23. Ibid., p. 305.

24. Richard Lee, "Eating Christmas in the Kalahari," *Natural History* 78, no. 10 (1969).

25. Jean Briggs, *Never in Anger: Portrait of an Eskimo Family* (Cambridge, MA: Harvard University Press, 1970).

26. Ross, *Culture of Conflict*, p. 83.

27. Clayton Robarchek, "A Community of Interests: Semai Conflict Resolution," in *Cultural Variation in Conflict Resolution: Alternatives to Violence*, ed. Douglas P. Fry and K. Bjorkqvist (Mahwah NJ: Lawrence Erlbaum, 1997), p. 54.

28. Thomas Gibson, *Sacrifice and Sharing in the Philippine Highlands: Religion and Society among the Buid of Mindoro* (London: Athlone Press, 1986).

29. Fry, *Human Potential for Peace*, p. 38.

30. Robert Knox Dentan, *The Semai: A Non-violent People of Malaya* (New York: Holt, Rinehart, and Winston, 1968).

31. Gopin, *Between Eden and Armageddon*, pp. 20–23.

32. Ibid., p. 6.

33. Ibid., p. 7.

34. V. Jayaram, "The Concepts of Ahimsa," 2007, http://www.hinduwebsite.com/hinduism/ concepts/ahimsa.asp (accessed August 1, 2007).

35. Samdhong Rinpoche, "'Buddhism and Nonviolent Action': Transcription of an Address by Ven. Prof. Samdhong Rinpoche, April 17, 1998," http://www.evaminstitute.org.au (accessed August 1, 2007), p. 3.

36. Ibid., pp. 9–10.

37. William McNeill, *The Rise of the West: A History of the Human Community* (Chicago: University of Chicago Press, 1963), p. 301.

38. Quoted in ibid., p. 302.

39. Jayaram, "Concepts of Ahimsa."

40. Paul Fleischman, *The Buddha Taught Nonviolence, Not Pacifism* (Onalaska, WA: Pariyatti Press, 2002), http://www.dharma.org/ij/archives/2002a/nonviolence.htm (accessed August 1, 2007).

41. Rupert Gethin, "Buddhist Monks, Buddhist Kings, and Buddhist Violence: On the Early Buddhist Attitudes to Violence," in *Religion and Violence in South Asia: Theory and Practice*, ed. John R. Hinnells and Richard King (Abingdon, UK: Routledge, 2007), p. 68.

42. Peter Schalk, "Operationalizing Buddhism for Political Ends in a Martial Context in Lanka: The Case of Simhalatva," in *Religion and Violence in South Asia* (see note 41), pp. 149–50.

43. Joanne Overing, "Images of Cannibalism, Death, and Domination in a 'Non-Violent' Society," in *The Anthropology of Violence*, ed. David Riches (Oxford: Basil Blackwell, 1986).

44. Matthew 5.

45. For example, Luke 6:36.

46. Luke 6:37.

47. Luke 6:35.

48. Romans 12:19.

49. Matthew 5:39.

50. Luke 6:29.

51. Roland Bainton, *Christian Attitudes toward War and Peace* (New York: Abingdon Press, 1960) p. 66.

52. Quoted in ibid., p. 73.

53. Quoted in ibid., p. 80.

54. Quoted in ibid., p. 78.

55. Quoted in ibid., p. 73.

56. Ibid., p. 71.

57. Leonard Levy, *Blasphemy: Verbal Offense against the Sacred, from Moses to Salman Rushdie* (New York: Knopf, 1993), pp. 59–60.

58. Ibid., p. 60.

59. Justo Gonzalez, *The Story of Christianity*, vol. 2, *The Reformation to the Present Day* (New York: Harper and Row, 1985), p. 59.

60. Mennonite General Conference, "A Declaration of Christian Faith and Commitment with Respect to Peace, War, and Nonresistance, 1951," http://www.bibleviews.com/st-peace1951.html (accessed January 8, 2010).

61. Ibid.

62. John Hostetler and Gertrude Huntington, *Children in Amish Society: Socialization and Community Education* (New York: Holt, Rinehart, and Winston, 1971), p. 4.

63. Ibid., p. 5.

64. Ibid., p. 9.

65. Ibid., p. 18.

66. Ibid., p. 21.

67. Ibid., p. 37.

68. Ibid.

69. Ibid., p. 95.

70. Ibid.

71. Levy, *Blasphemy*, p. 288.

72. Ibid., p. 168.

73. Ibid., p. 256.

74. Larry Ingle, "The Politics of Despair: The Quaker Peace Testimony, 1661," http://www.kimopress.com/Ingle-01.htm (accessed July 27, 2007).

75. Ibid.

76. Levy, *Blasphemy*, p. 169.

77. George Fox, "A Declaration from the Harmless and Innocent People of God, Called Quakers," 1660, http://www.quaker.org/minnfm/peace/A%20Declaration%20to%20Charles%20II%201660.htm (accessed January 8, 2010).

78. Ingle, "Politics of Despair."

79. Peter Collins, "Thirteen Ways of Looking at a 'Ritual,'" *Journal of Contemporary Religion* 20, no. 3 (2005): 325.

80. Ibid., p. 329.

81. Vernard Eller, "A Theology of Nonresistance," *Christian Century*, December 14, 1966, http://www.hccentral.com/eller1/cc121466.html (accessed July 27, 2007).

82. Brian Ferguson, "Introduction: Studying War," in *Warfare, Culture, and Environment*, ed. R. Brian Ferguson (Orlando, FL: Academic, 1984), p. 12.

83. Fry, *Human Potential for Peace*, p. 2.

84. Paulo Freire, *The Pedagogy of the Oppressed*, trans. Myra Bergman Ramos (New York: Continuum, 1995 [1970]).

85. James Aho, *Religious Mythology and the Art of War: Comparative Religious Symbolisms of Military Violence* (Westport, CT: Greenwood Press, 1981), pp. 32–33.

86. David Smock, "Teaching about the Religious Other," *United State Institute of Peace Special Report 143* (Washington, DC: United States Institute of Peace, 2005), p. 1.

87. Ibid., p. 5.

88. Ashutosh Varshney, *Ethnic Conflict and Civic Life: Hindus and Muslims in India*, 2nd ed. (New Haven, CT: Yale University Press, 2003).

89. Gopin, *Between Eden and Armageddon*, p. 159.

90. Religions for Peace, "Different Faiths, Common Action: Annual Report 2004–2005" (New York: World Conference of Religions for Peace, 2006), p. 4.

91. Ibid., p. 10.

92. Martin Marty, *Pilgrims in Their Own Land: 500 Years of Religion in America* (New York: Penguin Books, 1984), p. 352.

93. Clayton Robarchek, "Helplessness, Fearfulness, and Peacefulness: The Emotional and Motivational Contexts of Semai Social Relations," *Anthropological Quarterly* 59, no. 4 (1986): 177.

94. James Hilton, *Lost Horizon* (Pleasantville, NY: Reader's Digest Association, 1990 [1933]), pp. 64–65.

95. Peter Berger, "Between System and Horde: Personal Suggestions to Reluctant Activists," in Peter L. Berger and Richard J. Neuhaus, *Movement and Revolution* (New York: Anchor Books, 1970), p. 13.

96. Ibid., p. 19.

97. James Hillman, *A Terrible Love of War* (New York: Penguin Press, 2004), p. 183.

98. Gopin, *Between Eden and Armageddon*, p. 80.

99. David Smock, ed., "Religious Contributions to Peacemaking: When Religion Brings Peace, Not War," *Peaceworks* 55 (Washington, DC: United States Institute of Peace, 2006), p. 36.

100. Ibid.

101. Gregory Paul, "Cross-national Correlations of Quantifiable Societal Health with Popular Religiosity and Secularism in the Prosperous Democracies," *Journal of Religion and Society* 7 (2005): 7–8.

BIBLIOGRAPHY

Aho, James A. *Religious Mythology and the Art of War: Comparative Religious Symbolisms of Military Violence*. Westport, CT: Greenwood Press, 1981.

Ali, Rabia, and Lawrence Lifschutz. *Why Bosnia? Writings on the Balkan War*. Stony Creek, CT: Pamphleteer's Press, 1993.

Allan, Sterling D. "Inside Mitchell's Head: General Anatomy of 'One Mighty and Strong' Fanaticism." Greater Things. 2003. http://www.greaterthings.com/Davidic_Servant/Mitchell_Survey/index.html.

Allport, Gordon. *The Nature of Prejudice*. Reading, MA: Addison-Wesley, 1979 [1954].

Alter, Joseph S. "The 'Sannyasi' and the Indian Wrestler: The Anatomy of a Relationship." *American Ethnologist* 19, no. 2 (1992): 317–36.

Anderson, Benedict. *Imagined Communities: Reflections on the Origin and Spread of Nationalism*. London: Verso, 1983.

Appleby, R. Scott. *The Ambivalence of the Sacred: Religion, Violence, and Reconciliation*. Lanham, MD: Rowman and Littlefield, 2000.

Aquinas, Thomas. *Summa Theologica*. Translated by Fathers of the English Dominican Province. London: English Province, 1920.

Arasaratnam, Sinnapah. *Ceylon*. Englewood Cliffs, NJ: Prentice-Hall, 1964.

Armstrong, Karen. *Muhammad: A Biography of the Prophet*. New York: HarperSanFrancisco, 1992.

Aryan Nations. http://www.aryannationsrevival.org/.

Asser, Seth, and Rita Swan. "Child Fatalities from Religion-Motivated Medical Neglect." *Pediatrics* 101, no. 4 (1998): 625–29.

Atran, Scott. *In Gods We Trust: The Evolutionary Landscape of Religion*. Oxford: Oxford University Press, 2002.

Bainton, Roland H. *Christian Attitudes toward War and Peace*. New York: Abingdon Press, 1960.

Baker, Don. "The Andrea Yates Case: The Christian God 0 vs. Christianity Meme 3." 2005. http://www.christianitymeme.org/yates.shtml.

Barber, Benjamin. *Jihad versus McWorld*. New York: Times Books, 1995.

Barth, Fredrik, ed. Introduction to *Ethnic Groups and Boundaries*. Boston: Little, Brown, 1969.

Bastian, Misty L. "Young Converts: Christian Missions, Gender, and Youth in Onitsha, Nigeria, 1880–1929." *Anthropological Quarterly* 73, no. 3 (2000): 145–58.

Baumeister, Roy. *Evil: Inside Human Violence and Cruelty*. New York: Barnes and Noble Books, 2001.

Beattie, John. *Bunyoro: An African Kingdom*. New York: Holt, Rinehart, and Winston, 1960.

————. "On Understanding Sacrifice." In *Sacrifice*, edited by M. F. C. Bourdillon and Meyer Fortes, 29–44. London: Academic Press, 1980.

Beidelman, T. O. *The Kaguru: A Matrilineal People of East Africa*. New York: Holt, Rinehart, and Winston, 1971.

Belien, Paul. "Islamic Immigration and Murder among the Tulips." 2004. http://www .vdare. com/misc/belien_041103_islamic.htm.

Benedict, Ruth Fulton. "The Vision in Plains Culture." *American Anthropologist* 24, no. 1 (1922): 1–23.

Berger, Peter L. "Between System and Horde: Personal Suggestions to Reluctant Activists." In *Movement and Revolution*, by Peter L. Berger and Richard J. Neuhaus, 11–86. New York: Anchor Books, 1970.

Besnier, Niko. "Heteroglossic Discourses on Nukulaelae Spirits." In *Spirits in Culture, History, and Mind*, edited by Jeannette Marie Mageo and Alan Howard, 75–97. New York: Routledge, 1996.

Bhagavad Gita. Chap. 2, "Of Doctrines." http://sacred-texts.com/hin/gita/agsgita.htm.

Biehl, Jody K. "'The Whore Lived Like a German.'" *Der Spiegel*, March 2, 2005.

Black, Donald. *The Social Structure of Right and Wrong*. San Diego: Academic Press, 1993.

Blick, Jeffrey P. "Genocidal Warfare in Tribal Societies as a Result of European-Induced Culture Conflict." *Man* 23, no. 4 (1988): 654–70.

Bloch, Maurice. *Prey into Hunter: The Politics of Religious Experience*. Cambridge: Cambridge University Press, 1992.

Bloom, Howard. *The Lucifer Principle: A Scientific Expedition into the Forces of History*. New York: Atlantic Monthly Press, 1995.

Bokari, Syed Hassan, Farhan Zaidi, and Zileyh Shah. "The Mourning for Imam Hussein." *Shia News*, April 10, 2004. http://www.shianews.com/hi/articles/ islam/0000103.php.

Bonta, Bruce D. "Cooperation and Competition in Peaceful Societies." *Psychological Bulletin* 121 (1997): 299–320.

Boulding, Kenneth. *Stable Peace*. Austin: University of Texas Press, 1978.

Bourdillon, M. F. C. Introduction to *Sacrifice*, edited by M. F. C. Bourdillon and Meyer Fortes, 1–27. London: Academic Press, 1980.

Boyer, Pascal. *Religion Explained: The Evolutionary Origins of Religious Thought*. New York: Basic Books, 2001.

Bradley, Ian. *The Power of Sacrifice*. London: Darton, Longman and Todd, 1995.

Briggs, Jean. *Never in Anger: Portrait of an Eskimo Family*. Cambridge, MA: Harvard University Press, 1970.

Brown, Judith K. "Agitators and Peace-Makers: Cross-cultural Perspectives on Older Women and the Abuse of Young Wives." In *A Cross-cultural Exploration of Wife Abuse: Problems and Prospects*, edited by Aysan Sev'er, 79–99. Lewiston, NY: Edwin Mellen Press, 1997.

————. "Introduction: Definitions, Assumptions, Themes, and Issues." In *To Have and to Hit: Cultural Perspectives on Wife Beating*, edited by Dorothy Ayers Counts, Judith K. Brown, and Jacquelyn C. Campbell, 3–26. Urbana: University of Illinois Press, 1999.

Brubaker, Rogers, and David D. Laitin. "Ethnic and Nationalist Violence." *Annual Review of Sociology* 24 (1998): 423–52.

Bryson, Michael. "Dismemberment and Community: Sacrifice and the Communal Body in the Hebrew Scriptures." *Religion and Literature* 35, no. 1 (2003): 1–21.

Buckland, Patrick. *A History of Northern Ireland*. Dublin: Gill and Macmillan, 1981.

Burkert, Walter. Homo Necans: *The Anthropology of Ancient Greek Sacrificial Ritual and Myth*. Translated by Peter Bing. Berkeley: University of California Press, 1983 [1972].

————. "The Problem of Ritual Killing." In *Violent Origins: Walter Burkert, René Girard, and Jonathan Z. Smith on Ritual Killing and Cultural Formation*, edited by Robert G. Hamerton-Kelly, 149–76. Stanford, CA: Stanford University Press, 1987.

Camporesi, Piero. *The Incorruptible Flesh: Bodily Mutilation and Mortification in Religion and Folklore*. Translated by Tania Croft-Murray. Cambridge: Cambridge University Press, 1988 [1983].

Canfield, Leon Hardy. *The Early Persecution of the Christians*. New York: MS Press, 1968 [1913].

Carrasco, David. *City of Sacrifice: The Aztec Empire and the Role of Violence in Civilization*. Boston: Beacon, 1999.

Carrithers, Michael. "The Modern Ascetics of Lanka and the Pattern of Change in Buddhism." *Man* 14, no. 2 (1979): 294–310.

————. "Naked Ascetics in Southern Digambar Jainism." *Man* 24, no. 2 (1989): 219–35.

Carroll, Michael P. *The Penitente Brotherhood: Patriarchy and Hispano-Catholicism in New Mexico*. Baltimore, MD: Johns Hopkins University Press, 2002.

Carroll, Warren H. *The Rise and Fall of the Communist Revolution*. Front Royal, VA: Christendom Press, 1989.

Carter, Lewis F. *Charisma and Control in Rajneeshism*. Cambridge: Cambridge University Press. 1990.

Cassirer, Ernst. *An Essay on Man: An Introduction to a Philosophy of Human Culture*. Garden City, NY: Doubleday, 1954 [1944].

CBS News. "Minister's Wife Shot Spouse Over Money." June 30, 2006. http://www.cbsnews.com/ stories/2006/06/30/national/main1771713.shtml.

Chagnon, Napoleon. *Yanomamo: The Fierce People*. New York: Holt, Rinehart, and Winston, 1968.

Cheyney, Edward P. *The Dawn of a New Era, 1250–1453*. New York: Harper and Row, 1962 [1936].

Church of England. "Responding to Domestic Abuse: Guidelines for Those with Pastoral Responsibilities." London: Church House Publishing, 2006.

Cigar, Norman. *Genocide in Bosnia: The Policy of "Ethnic Cleansing."* College Station: Texas A&M University Press, 1995.

Clark, Gillian. "Women and Asceticism in Late Antiquity: The Refusal of Status and Gender." In *Asceticism*, edited by Vincent L. Wimbush and Richard Valantasis, 33–48. Oxford: Oxford University Press, 1995.

Clausewitz, Carl von. *On War.* Translated by Michael Howard and Peter Paret. Princeton, NJ: Princeton University Press, 1984 [1832].

Cohen, Hermann. *Religion of Reason: Out of the Sources of Judaism.* Translated by Simon Kaplan. Atlanta: Scholars, 1995 [1972].

Collelo, Thomas, ed. *Lebanon: A Country Study.* Washington, DC: GPO for the Library of Congress, 1987. http://countrystudies.us/lebanon/18.htm.

Collins, Peter. "Thirteen Ways of Looking at a 'Ritual.'" *Journal of Contemporary Religion* 20, no. 3 (2005): 323–42.

Comaroff, Jean. *Body of Power, Spirit of Resistance: The Culture and History of a South Africa People.* Chicago: University of Chicago Press, 1985.

Comaroff, John L., and Jean Comaroff. *Of Revelation and Revolution.* Vol. 2, *The Dialectics of Modernity on a South African Frontier*, vol. 2. Chicago: University of Chicago Press, 1991.

Contreras, Jaime, and Gustav Henningsen. "Forty-four Thousand Cases of the Spanish Inquisition (1540–1700): Analysis of a Historical Data Bank." In *The Inquisition in Early Modern Europe: Studies on Sources and Methods*, edited by Gustav Henningsen and John Tedeschi, 100–29. Dekalb: Northern Illinois University Press, 1986.

Court TV. "Mass. v. Roubidoux: Cult Dad Starves Baby." July 17, 2002. http://www.courttv.com/trials/taped/robidoux/background.html.

Crimelibrary.com. "Theo van Gogh." 2004. http://www.crimelibrary.com/notorious _murders/famous/theo_van_gogh/ index .html.

Csordas, Thomas J. "Somatic Modes of Attention." *Cultural Anthropology* 8, no. 2 (1993): 135–56.

Davidson, Basil. *The Magnificent African Cake.* Chicago: Home Vision, 1984. Film.

Davies, Nigel. *Human Sacrifice in History and Today.* New York: William Morrow, 1981.

Dees, Morris, with James Corcoran. *Gathering Storm: America's Militia Threat.* New York: HarperCollins, 1996.

DeMause, Lloyd. *The Emotional Life of Nations.* 2002. http://www.psychohistory .com/htm/eln08_childrearing.html.

Dennen, Johan M. G. van der. *The Origin of War: The Evolution of a Male-Coalitional Reproductive Strategy.* Groningen, Netherlands: Origin Press, 1995.

Dentan, Robert Knox. *The Semai: A Non-violent People of Malaya.* New York: Holt, Rinehart, and Winston, 1968.

Denton, Lynn Teskey. *Female Ascetics in Hinduism*. Albany: State University of New York Press, 2004.

Depperschmidt, Ann. "Wyo. Ex-Priest's Case Uncovers Lurid Tales." *Denver Post*, April 18, 2004.

DeVos, George. "Ethnic Pluralism: Conflict and Accommodation." In *Ethnic Identity: Cultural Continuities and Change*, edited by George DeVos and Lola Romanucci-Ross, 5–41. Palo Alto, CA: Mayfield Publishing, 1975.

Dharmadasa, K. N. O. *Language, Religion, and Ethnic Assertiveness: The Growth of Sinhalese Nationalism in Sri Lanka*. Ann Arbor: University of Michigan Press, 1992.

Dmytryshyn, Basil. *USSR: A Concise History*. 2nd ed. New York: Charles Scribner's Sons, 1971.

Donia, Robert, and John Fine. *Bosnia and Hercegovina: A Tradition Betrayed*. New York: Columbia University Press, 1994.

Douglas, Mary. *Natural Symbols*. Harmondsworth, UK: Penguin, 1973.

Droge, Arthur J., and James D. Tabor. *A Noble Death: Suicide and Martyrdom among Christians and Jews in Antiquity*. New York: HarperSan\Francisco, 1992.

Dunn, Richard S. *The Age of Religious Wars, 1559–1689*. New York: W. W. Norton, 1970.

Durant, Will. *The Age of Faith*. New York: Simon and Schuster, 1950.

Durkheim, Emile. *The Elementary Forms of the Religious Life*. New York: Free Press, 1965 [1915].

Eberhart, Christian. "A Neglected Feature of Sacrifice in the Hebrew Bible: Remarks on the Burning Rite on the Altar." *Harvard Theological Review* 97, no. 4 (2004): 485–93.

Eliade, Mircea. *Shamanism: Archaic Techniques of Ecstasy*. Princeton, NJ: Princeton University Press, 1972 [1964].

Elkin, A. P. *The Australian Aborigines*. Sydney: Angus and Robertson, 1974 [1938].

Eller, Jack David. *From Culture to Ethnicity to Conflict: An Anthropological Perspective on International Ethnic Conflict*. Ann Arbor: University of Michigan Press, 1999.

Eller, Vernard. "A Theology of Nonresistance." *Christian Century*, December 14, 1966. http://www.hccentral.com/eller1/cc121466.html.

Elliott, Paul. *Warrior Cults: A History of Magical, Mystical, and Murderous Organizations*. London: Blandford, 1995.

Elton, G. R. *Reformation Europe, 1517–1559*. New York: Harper and Row, 1963.

Engh, Mary Jane. *In the Name of Heaven: 3,000 Years of Religious Persecution*. Amherst, NY: Prometheus Books, 2007.

Eriksen, Thomas Hylland. *Ethnicity and Nationalism: Anthropological Perspectives*. London: Pluto Press, 2002 [1993].

Esslemont, J. E. *Baha'u'llah and the New Era: An Introduction to the Baha'i Faith*. Wilmette, IL: Baha'i Publishing Trust, 1978 [1923].

Evans-Pritchard. E. E. *The Nuer: A Description of the Modes of Livelihood and Political Institutions of a Nilotic People*. New York: Oxford University Press, 1940.

———. *Nuer Religion*. New York: Oxford University Press, 1956.

———. *Witchcraft, Oracles, and Magic among the Azande*. New York: Oxford University Press, 1937.

Ezzati, A. "The Concept of Martyrdom in Islam." 1986. http://www.al-islam.org/al-serat/concept-ezzati.htm.

Falkenberg, Lisa. "Religiosity Common among Mothers Who Kill Children." *San Antonio Express-News*, December 13, 2004.

Fanon, Frantz. *The Wretched of the Earth*. Translated by Constance Farrington. New York: Grove, 1963.

Farmer, B. H. *Ceylon: A Divided Nation*. London: Oxford University Press, 1963.

Farmer, Paul. "An Anthropology of Structural Violence." *Current Anthropology* 45, no. 3 (2004): 305–25.

Federal Bureau of Investigation. "Terrorism in the United States, 1995." FBI Terrorist Research and Analytical Center, National Security Division. http://www.terrorism.com/terrorism/index.html.

Feinberg, Richard. "Spirit Encounters on a Polynesian Outlier: Anuta, Solomon Islands." In *Spirits in Culture, History, and Mind*, edited by Jeannette Marie Mageo and Alan Howard, 99–120. New York: Routledge, 1996.

Feldman, Stephen M. *Please Don't Wish Me a Merry Christmas: A Critical History of the Separation of Church and State*. New York: New York University Press, 1997.

Ferguson, R. Brian, ed. "Introduction: Studying War." In *Warfare, Culture, and Environment*, 1–81. Orlando, FL: Academic Press, 1984.

Ferguson, R. Brian, and N. Whitehead, eds. *War in the Tribal Zone*. Santa Fe, NM: School of American Research Press, 1992.

Fielding, Henry. *The History of Tom Jones*. New York: Penguin Books, 1979 [1749].

Fields, Rona M. *Martyrdom: The Psychology, Theology, and Politics of Self-Sacrifice*. Westport, CT: Praeger, 2004.

Firestone, Reuven. *Jihad: The Origin of Holy War in Islam*. New York: Oxford University Press, 1999.

———. "Who Broke Their Vow First? The 'Three Vows' and Contemporary Thinking about Jewish Holy War." In *The Just War and Jihad: Violence in Judaism, Christianity, and Islam*, edited by R. Joseph Hoffmann, 77–97. Amherst, NY: Prometheus Books, 2006.

Fleischman, Paul. *The Buddha Taught Nonviolence, Not Pacifism*. Onalaska, WA: Pariyatti Press, 2002. http://www.dharma.org/ij/archives/2002a/nonviolence.htm.

Fortes, Meyer. "Preface: Anthropologists and Theologians: Common Interests and Divergent Approaches." In *Sacrifice*, edited by M. F. C. Bourdillon and Meyer Fortes, v–xix. London: Academic Press, 1980.

Fox, George. "A Declaration from the Harmless and Innocent People of God, Called Quakers." 1660. http://www.quaker.org/minnfm/peace/A%20Declaration%20to%20Charles%20II%201660.htm.

Fox, Jonathan. *Ethnoreligious Conflict in the Late Twentieth Century: A General Theory.* Lanham, MD: Lexington Books, 2002.

Freedom from Religion Foundation. "Lion Bites Proselytizer." *Freethought Today*, November 2004.

————. "Man Severs Penis." *Freethought Today*, November 2004.

Freire, Paulo. *The Pedagogy of the Oppressed.* Translated by Myra Bergman Ramos. New York: Continuum, 1995 [1970].

Freke, Timothy, and Peter Gandy. *The Jesus Mysteries: Was the "Original Jesus" a Pagan God?* New York: Harmony Books, 1999.

Frend, W. H. C. *Martyrdom and Persecution in the Early Church: A Study of a Conflict from the Maccabees to Donatus.* Garden City, NY: Anchor Books, 1967.

Fry, Douglas P. *The Human Potential for Peace: An Anthropological Challenge to Assumptions about War and Violence.* New York: Oxford University Press, 2006.

Frykenberg, Robert Eric. "Hindu Fundamentalism and the Structural Stability of India." In *Fundamentalisms and the State: Remaking Polities, Economies, and Militance*, edited by Martin E. Marty and R. Scott Appleby, 233–55. Chicago: University of Chicago Press, 1993.

Furnivall, J. S. *Colonial Policy and Practice: A Comparative Study of Burma and Netherlands India.* New York: New York University Press, 1956.

Gaddis, Michael. *There Is No Crime for Those Who Have Christ: Religious Violence in the Christian Roman Empire.* Berkeley: University of California Press, 2005.

Geertz, Clifford, ed. "The Integrative Revolution: Primordial Sentiments and Civil Politics in the New States." In *Old Societies and New States*, 105–57. New York: Free Press, 1963.

————. *The Interpretation of Cultures.* New York: Basic Books, 1973.

Gelles, Richard J., and Murray A. Straus. *Intimate Violence.* New York: Simon and Schuster, 1988.

Gellner, Ernest. *Plough, Sword, and Book: The Structure of Human History.* Chicago: University of Chicago Press, 1988.

George, John, and Laird Wilcox. *American Extremists: Militias, Supremacists, Klansmen, Communists, and Others.* Amherst, NY: Prometheus Books, 1996.

Gershoy, Leo. *The Era of the French Revolution, 1789–1799.* Princeton, NJ: D. Van Nostrand, 1957

Gethin, Rupert. "Buddhist Monks, Buddhist Kings, and Buddhist Violence: On the Early Buddhist Attitudes to Violence." In *Religion and Violence in South Asia: Theory and Practice*, edited by John R. Hinnells and Richard King, 62–82. Abingdon, UK: Routledge, 2007.

Gibson, Thomas. *Sacrifice and Sharing in the Philippine Highlands: Religion and Society among the Buid of Mindoro*. London: Athlone Press, 1986.

Girard, René. "Generative Scapegoating: Discussion." In *Violent Origins: Walter Burkert, René Girard, and Jonathan Z. Smith on Ritual Killing and Cultural Formation*, edited by Robert G. Hamerton-Kelly, 106–45. Stanford, CA: Stanford University Press, 1987.

———.*Violence and the Sacred*. Translated by Patrick Gregory. Baltimore, MD: Johns Hopkins University Press, 1977.

Glick, Leonard. *Marked in Your Flesh: Circumcision from Ancient Judea to Modern America*. Oxford: Oxford University Press, 2005.

Glucklich, Ariel. *Sacred Pain: Hurting the Body for the Sake of the Soul*. Oxford: Oxford University Press, 2001.

Gluckman, Max. *Custom and Conflict in Africa*. Oxford: Basil Blackwell, 1956.

Gold, Daniel. "Organized Hinduisms: From Vedic Truth to Hindu Nation." In *Fundamentalisms Observed*, edited by Martin Marty and R. Scott Appleby, 531–93. Chicago: University of Chicago Press, 1991.

Gonzalez, Justo L. *The Story of Christianity*. Vol. 1, *The Early Church to the Dawn of the Reformation*. New York: HarperSanFrancisco, 1984.

———. *The Story of Christianity*. Vol. 2, *The Reformation to the Present Day*. New York: Harper and Row, 1985.

Gopin, Mark. *Between Eden and Armageddon: The Future of World Religions, Violence, and Peacemaking*. Oxford: Oxford University Press, 2000.

Gray, George Buchanan. *Sacrifice in the Old Testament: Its Theory and Practice*. New York: Ktav, 1971 [1925].

Greeley, Andrew. *Why Can't They Be Like Us? America's White Ethnic Groups*. New York: E. P. Dutton, 1971.

Green, Miranda Aldhouse. *Dying for the Gods: Human Sacrifice in Iron Age and Roman Europe*. Gloucestershire, UK: Tempus Publishing, 2002.

Greer, Tammy, Mitchell Berman, Valerie Varan, Lori Bobrycki, and Sheree Watson. "We Are a Religious People; We Are a Vengeful People." *Journal for the Scientific Study of Religion* 44, no. 1 (2005): 45–57.

Grousset, René. *The Epic of the Crusades*. Translated by Noel Lindsay. New York: Orion Press, 1970.

Hanson, Victor Davis. *The Wars of the Ancient Greeks*. London: Cassell, 1999.

Hare, Robert. "The Psychopathy Checklist—Revised (PCL-R)." 1991. http://www.criminology.unimelb.edu.au/victims/resources/assessment/personality/psychopathy_checklist.html.

Harpham, Geoffrey Galt. *The Ascetic Imperative in Culture and Criticism*. Chicago: University of Chicago Press, 1987.

Harris, Marvin. "A Cultural Materialist Theory of Band and Village Warfare: The

Yanomamo Test." In *Warfare, Culture, and Environment*, edited by R. Brian Ferguson, 111–40. Orlando, FL: Academic Press, 2004.

Harris, Sam. *The End of Faith: Religion, Terror, and the Future of Reason*. New York: W. W. Norton, 2004.

Hartman, Donniel. "Two Types of Jewish War." http://www.myjewishlearning.com/ideas_belief/warpeace/War_TO_Combat/War_Types_Hartman.htm.

Harvey, Graham. *Animism: Respecting the Living World*. New York: Columbia University Press, 2006.

Haught, James. *Holy Hatred: Religious Conflicts of the '90s*. Amherst, NY: Prometheus Books, 1995.

———. *Holy Horrors: An Illustrated History of Religious Murder and Madness*. Amherst, NY: Prometheus Books, 1990.

Heaton, Paul. "Does Religion Really Reduce Crime?" *Journal of Law and Economics* 49 (2006): 147–72.

Hedges, Chris. *War Is a Force That Gives Us Meaning*. New York: Public Affairs, 2002.

Hegland, Mary Elaine. "Flagellation and Fundamentalism: (Trans)Forming Meaning, Identity, and Gender through Pakistani Women's Rituals of Mourning." *American Ethnologist* 25, no. 2 (1998): 240–66.

———. "Wife Abuse and the Political System: A Middle Eastern Case Study." In *To Have and to Hit: Cultural Perspectives on Wife Beating*, edited by Dorothy Ayers Counts, Judith K. Brown, and Jacquelyn C. Campbell, 234–51. Urbana: University of Illinois Press, 1999.

Herdt, Gilbert. *Guardians of the Flute: Idioms of Masculinity*. New York: Columbia University Press, 1987 [1981].

Herskovits, Melville. *Dahomey: An Ancient West African Kingdom*. Vol. 2. New York: J. J. Augustin, 1938.

Heusch, Luc de. *Sacrifice in Africa: A Structuralist Approach*. Translated by Linda O'Brien and Alice Morton. Bloomington: Indiana University Press, 1985.

Heyd, David, ed. Introduction to *Toleration: An Elusive Virtue*, 3–17. Princeton, NJ: Princeton University Press, 1996.

Hillman, James. *A Terrible Love of War*. New York: Penguin Press, 2004.

Hilton, James. *Lost Horizon*. Pleasantville, NY: Reader's Digest Association, 1990 [1933].

Hindu Student Council, George Mason University. "A Tribute to Hinduism—War in Ancient India." http://www.hscgmu.org/ebooks/War%20In%20Ancient%20India.pdf.

Hirschi, Travis, and Rodney Stark. "Hellfire and Delinquency." *Social Problems* 17, no. 2 (1969): 202–13.

Hitler, Adolf. *Mein Kampf*. Translated by Ralph Manheim. New York: Houghton Mifflin, 1969 [1925].

Hitti, Philip K. *The Near East in History*. Princeton, NJ: D. Van Nostrand, 1961.

Hoebel, E. Adamson. *The Cheyennes: Indians of the Great Plains*. New York: Holt, Rinehart, and Winston, 1960.

Hoffer, Eric. *The True Believer: Thoughts on the Nature of Mass Movements*. New York:
HarperPerennial, 1966 [1951].

Hoffman, Bruce. "Holy Terror: The Implications of Terrorism Motivated by a Religious
Imperative." Santa Monica, CA: RAND, 1993.

Hoffmann, R. Joseph, ed. "Just War and Jihad: Positioning the Question of Religious
Violence." In *The Just War and Jihad: Violence in Judaism, Christianity, and Islam*, 47–
60. Amherst, NY: Prometheus Books, 2006.

Holloway, David. *Understanding the Northern Ireland Conflict: A Summary and Overview of
the Conflict and its Origins*. Belfast: Community Dialogue Critical Issues Series,
2005.

Horowitz, David. *Ethnic Groups in Conflict*. Berkeley: University of California Press,
1985.

Horton, Anne L., and Judith A. Williamson, eds. *Abuse and Religion: When Praying Isn't
Enough*. Lexington, MA: Lexington Books, 1988.

Horton, John. "Toleration as a Virtue." In *Toleration: An Elusive Virtue*, edited by David
Heyd, 28–43. Princeton, NJ: Princeton University Press, 1996.

Horton, Robin. "A Definition of Religion, and Its Uses." *Journal of the Royal Anthropological Institute of Great Britain and Ireland* 90, no. 2 (1960): 201–26.

Hostetler, John A., and Gertrude Enders Huntington. *Children in Amish Society: Socialization and Community Education*. New York: Holt, Rinehart, and Winston, 1971.

Hubert, Henri, and Marcel Mauss. *Sacrifice: Its Nature and Function*. Chicago: University
of Chicago Press, 1964 [1898].

Hughes, Dennis D. *Human Sacrifice in Ancient Greece*. London: Routledge, 1991.

Hughes, James J. "Buddhist Monks and Politics in Sri Lanka." Paper presented to
Spring Institute for Social Science Research, 1987. http://www.changesurfer
.com/Bud/Sri/Sri.html (accessed July 23, 2007).

Human Rights Watch. *Dangerous Meditation: China's Campaign against Falungong*. New
York: Human Rights Watch, 2002.

———. "Devastating Blows: Religious Repression of Uighurs in Xinjiang." *Human
Rights Watch Report* 17, no. 2 (April 2005).

———. "The 'Miss World Riots': Continued Impunity for Killings in Kaduna." *Human
Rights Watch Report* 15, no. 13 (July 2003).

———. "Revenge in the Name of Religion: The Cycle of Violence in Plateau and Kano
States." *Human Rights Watch Report* 17, no. 8 (May 2005).

———."Sudan: 'In the Name of God' Repression Continues in Northern Sudan."
Human Rights Watch Report 6, no. 9 (November 1994).

Hume, Robert E. "Hinduism and War." *American Journal of Theology* 20, no. 1 (1916):
31–44.

Humes, Curtis, and Katherine Ann Clark. "Collective Baha'i Identity through Embodied Persecution: 'Be Ye the Fingers of One Hand, the Members of One Body." *Anthropology of Consciousness* 11, nos. 1–2 (2000): 24–33.

Hyde, Jesse. "1984 Lafferty Case Still Haunts." *Deseret News*, July 24, 2004. http://www.deseretnews.com/article/595079489/1984-Lafferty-case-still-haunts.html.

Ingle, H. Larry. "The Politics of Despair: The Quaker Peace Testimony, 1661." http://www.kimopress.com/Ingle-01.htm.

"Introduction to Sikhism." 2002. http://photon.bu.edu/~rajwi/sikhism/mansukh-1.html.

James, E. O. *Origins of Sacrifice: A Study in Comparative Religion.* Port Washington, NY: Kennikat Press, 1971 [1933].

James, William. *The Varieties of Religious Experience: A Study in Human Nature.* New York: Mentor Books, 1958 [1902].

Jay, Nancy. *Throughout Your Generations Forever: Sacrifice, Religion, and Paternity.* Chicago: University of Chicago Press, 1992.

Jayaram, V. "The Concepts of Ahimsa." 2007. http://www.hinduwebsite.com/hinduism/concepts/ahimsa.asp (accessed August 1, 2007).

Jobe, Robert B. "Asylum Law Outline." http://www.jobelaw.com/2/as3.htm (accessed July 8, 2007).

John Jay College of Criminal Justice. "The Nature and Scope of the Problem of Sexual Abuse of Minors by Catholic Priests and Deacons." 2004. http://www.jjay.cuny.edu/churchstudy/main.asp (accessed January 5, 2010).

Johnson, James Turner. *The Holy War Idea in Western and Islamic Traditions.* University Park: Pennsylvania State University Press, 1997.

Juergensmeyer, Mark. *Terrorism in the Mind of God: The Global Rise of Religious Violence.* Berkeley: University of California Press, 2000.

Jung, Carl G. *Psychology of the Unconscious: A Study of the Transformations and Symbolisms of the Libido.* Translated by Beatrice M. Hinkle. New York: Dodd, Mead, 1949 [1916].

Kaba, Lansine. "The Pen, the Sword, and the Crown: Islam and Revolution in Songhay Reconsidered, 1464–1493." *Journal of African History* 25, no. 3 (1984): 241–56.

Kapferer, Bruce. *Legends of People, Myths of State: Violence, Intolerance, and Political Culture in Sri Lanka and Australia.* Washington, DC: Smithsonian Institution Press, 1988.

Kaplan, Robert D. "Euphorias of Hatred." *Atlantic Monthly* (May 2003): 44–45.

Kasfir, Nelson. "Explaining Ethnic Political Participation." *World Politics* 31, no. 3 (1979): 365–88.

Katz, Richard. *Boiling Energy: Community Healing among the Kalahari Kung.* Cambridge, MA: Harvard University Press, 1982.

Kee, Robert. *Ireland: A History.* London: Abacus, 1991 [1980].

Kelsey, Neal. "The Body as Desert in *The Life of Saint Anthony.*" *Semeia* 57 (1992): 131–51.

Kermani, Navid. "Roots of Terror: Suicide, Martyrdom, Self-Redemption and Islam." 2002. http://www.opendemocracy.net/faith-europe_islam/article_88.jsp.

Kimball, Charles. *When Religion Becomes Evil*. New York: HarperSan Francisco, 2002.

Kirkpatrick, Lee. *Attachment, Evolution, and the Psychology of Religion*. New York: Guilford, 2005.

Klaits, Joseph. *Servants of Satan: The Age of the Witch Hunts*. Bloomington: Indiana University Press, 1985.

Klima, George J. *The Barabaig: East African Cattle-Herders*. New York: Holt, Rinehart, and Winston, 1970.

Krakauer, Jon. *Under the Banner of Heaven: A Story of Violent Faith*. New York: Doubleday, 2003.

Kreisberg, Louis. *Social Conflicts*. 2nd ed. Englewood Cliffs, NJ: Prentice-Hall, 1982.

Lambert, William W., Leigh M. Triandis, and Margery Wolf. "Some Correlates of Beliefs in the Malevolence and Benevolence of Supernatural Beings." *Journal of Abnormal and Social Psychology* 58 (1959): 162–69.

Laqueur, Walter. *The Age of Terrorism*. Boston: Little, Brown, 1987.

———, ed. *Voices of Terror*. New York: Reed Press, 2004.

Lea, James A., and Bruce E. Hunsburger. "Christian Orthodoxy and Victim Derogation: The Impact of the Salience of Religion." *Journal for the Scientific Study of Religion* 29, no. 4 (1990): 512–18.

Le Blanc, Steven A., with Katherine E. Register. *Constant Battles: The Myth of the Peaceful, Noble Savage*. New York: St. Martin's, 2003.

Le Bon, Gustave. *The Crowd: A Study of the Popular Mind*. New York: Macmillan, 1986.

Lee, Richard B. *The Dobe !Kung*. New York: Holt, Rinehart, and Winston, 1984.

———. "Eating Christmas in the Kalahari." *Natural History* 78, no. 10 (1969): 14–22, 60–64.

LeShan, Lawrence. *The Psychology of War*. New York: Helios, 1992.

Lessa, William A. *Ulithi: A Micronesian Design for Living*. New York: Holt, Rinehart, and Winston, 1966.

Levy, Leonard W. *Blasphemy: Verbal Offense against the Sacred, from Moses to Salman Rushdie*. New York: Knopf, 1993.

Levy, Robert I., Jeannette Marie Mageo, and Alan Howard. "Gods, Spirits, and History: A Theoretical Perspective." In *Spirits in Culture, History, and Mind*, edited by Jeannette Marie Mageo and Alan Howard, 11–27. New York: Routledge, 1996.

Lichtenburg, Judith. "Some Central Problems with Just War Theory." In *The Just War and Jihad: Violence in Judaism, Christianity, and Islam*, edited by R. Joseph Hoffmann, 15–32. Amherst, NY: Prometheus Books, 2006.

Liechty, Joseph. *Roots of Sectarianism in Ireland*. Belfast: Joseph Liechty, 1993.

Lienhardt, Godfrey. *Divinity and Experience: The Religion of the Dinka*. Oxford: Clarendon, 1961.

Linton, Ralph. "The Comanche Sun Dance." *American Anthropologist* 37, no. 1 (1935): 420–28.

Little, David. *Sri Lanka: The Invention of Enmity*. Washington, DC: US Institute of Peace Press, 1994.

Lobdell, William. "Teens' Rite of Passage Can Include Their Faith." *Los Angeles Times*, October 19, 2002.

Lorenz, Konrad. *On Aggression*. Translated by Marjorie Kerr Wilson. New York: Harcourt, Brace, and World, 1966.

Lorenzen, David N. "Warrior Ascetics in Indian History." *Journal of the American Oriental Society* 98, no. 1 (1978): 61–75.

Ludowyk, E. F. C. *The Modern History of Ceylon*. New York: Praeger, 1966.

Ludwig, Arnold M. "Altered States of Consciousness." *Archives of General Psychiatry* 15, no. 3 (1966): 225–34.

Luther, Martin. "On the Jews and Their Lies, 1543." In *Luther's Works*, translated by Martin H. Bertram, 137–306. Philadelphia: Fortress Press, 1971.

MacFarlane, Alan. *Witchcraft in Tudor and Stuart England: A Regional and Comparative Study*. New York: Harper and Row, 1970.

Malcolm, Noel. *Bosnia: A Short History*. New York: New York University Press, 1994.

Malinowski, Bronislaw. "An Anthropological Analysis of War." *American Journal of Sociology* 46, no. 4 (1941): 521–50.

———. *Magic, Science, and Religion and Other Essays*. Garden City, NY: Doubleday Anchor Books, 1948.

Marty, Martin E. *Pilgrims in Their Own Land: 500 Years of Religion in America*. New York: Penguin Books, 1948.

Maycock, A. L. *The Inquisition from Its Establishment to the Great Schism: An Introductory Study*. New York: Harper and Row, 1969.

Mayell, Hillary. "Thousands of Women Killed for Family 'Honor.'" *National Geographic News*, February 12, 2002. http:// news.nationalgeographic.com/news/2002/02/0212_020212_honorkilling.html (accessed June 19, 2007).

McNeill, William. *The Rise of the West: A History of the Human Community*. Chicago: University of Chicago Press, 1963.

McTernan, Oliver. *Violence in God's Name: Religion in an Age of Conflict*. Maryknoll, NY: Orbis Books, 2003.

Menon, Kalyani Devaki. "Converted Innocents and Their Trickster Heroes: The Politics of Proselytizing in India." In *The Anthropology of Religious Conversion*, edited by Andrew Buckser and Stephen D. Glazier, 43–53. Lanham, MD: Rowman and Littlefield, 2003.

Mennonite General Conference. "A Declaration of Christian Faith and Commitment with Respect to Peace, War, and Nonresistance, 1951." http://www.bibleviews.com/stpeace1951.html.

Messner, Michael A. "Power at Play: Sport and Gender Relations." In *Signs of Life in the USA: Readings on Popular Culture for Writers*, edited by Sonia Maasik and Jack Solomon, 668–79. Boston: Bedford/St. Martin's, 2003.

Meyer, Carolyn. *Voices of Northern Ireland: Growing Up in a Troubled Land*. Orlando, FL: Harcourt Brace Jovanovich, 1987.

Milgram, Stanley. "Behavioral Study of Obedience." *Journal of Abnormal and Social Psychology* 67 (1963): 371–78.

———. *Obedience to Authority: An Experimental View*. New York: Harper and Row, 1974.

Morris, Desmond. *Manwatching: A Field Guide to Human Behavior*. New York: Harry N. Abrams, 1977.

Murphy, Yolanda, and Robert F. Murphy. *Women of the Forest*. New York: Columbia University Press, 2004 [1974].

Narasimhan, Sakuntala. *Sati: Widow Burning in India*. New York: Anchor Books, 1992.

Naroll, Raoul. "On Ethnic Unit Classification." *Current Anthropology* 5, no. 3 (1964): 283–312.

National Coalition against Domestic Violence. "Domestic Violence Facts." July 2007. http://www.ncadv.org/files/DomesticViolenceFactSheet(National).pdf.

New Advent. "Crusades." http://www.newadvent.org/cathen/04543c.htm.

Nicolosi, Michele. "Forced Prenatal Care." *Salon*. September 15, 2000. http://archive.salon.com/health/feature/2000/ 09/15/forced_prenatal/print.html.

Oakes, Kaye. "Cutting: Self Injury and How to Help." http://www.psyke.org/articles/en/cutting_self_injury.

Ohnuki-Tierney, Emiko. *The Ainu of the Northwest Coast of Southern Sakhalin*. New York: Holt, Rinehart, and Winston, 1974.

Olivelle, Patrick. "Deconstruction of the Body in Indian Asceticism." In *Asceticism*, edited by Vincent L. Wimbush and Richard Valantasis, 188–210. Oxford: Oxford University Press, 1995.

Otterbein, Charlotte Swanson, and Keith F. Otterbein. "Believers and Beaters: A Case Study of Supernatural Beliefs and Child Rearing in the Bahama Islands." *American Anthropologist* 75, no. 5 (1973): 1670–81.

Otterbein, Keith F. "Internal War: A Cross-cultural Study." *American Anthropologist* 70, no. 2 (1968): 277–89.

Otto, Rudolf. *The Idea of the Holy*. Translated by John W. Harvey. London: Oxford University Press, 1958 [1923].

Overing, Joanne. "Images of Cannibalism, Death, and Domination in a 'Non-Violent' Society." In *The Anthropology of Violence*, edited by David Riches, 86–102. Oxford: Basil Blackwell, 1986.

Pagelow, Mildred Daley, and Pam Johnson. "Abuse in the American Family: The Role of Religion." In *Abuse and Religion: When Praying Isn't Enough*, edited by Anne L. Horton and Judith A. Williamson, 1–12. Lexington, MA: Lexington Books, 1988.

Pagels, Elaine. *The Origin of Satan*. New York: Random House, 1995.

Pankratz, Howard. "Mom Pleads Insanity in Try to Kill Kid." *Denver Post*, June 12, 2007.

Parfrey, Adam, ed. *Extreme Islam: Anti-American Propaganda of Muslim Fundamentalism*. Los Angeles: Feral House, 2001.

Paul, Gregory S. "Cross-national Correlations of Quantifiable Societal Health with Popular Religiosity and Secularism in the Prosperous Democracies." *Journal of Religion and Society* 7 (2005): 1–17.

Perez, Joseph. *The Spanish Inquisition: A History*. Translated by Janet Lloyd. New Haven, CT: Yale University Press, 2004 [2002].

Perkins, Judith. *The Suffering Self: Pain and Narrative Representation in the Early Christianity Era*. London: Routledge, 1995.

Pleck, Elizabeth. *Domestic Tyranny: The Making of Social Policy against Family Violence from Colonial Times to the Present*. New York: Oxford University Press, 1987.

Pocock, Michael. "Why Persecution? Reasons Include Human, Satanic, and Divine Purposes." *Moody Magazine*, 2001. http://www.moodymagazine.com/articles.php?action= view_article&id=441.

Pointon, T. Dugdale. "Ikko-Ikki (Japanese Warrior Monks)." 2005. http://www.history ofwar.org/articles/ weapons_ikko.html.

Pope John Paul II. "Homily of the Holy Father: Jubilee of the Sick and Health-Care Workers." 2000. http://www.vatican.va/holy_father/john_paul_ii/homilies/documents/hf_jp-ii _hom_20000211_jubilee-sick_en.html.

Pratchett, Terry. *Small Gods*. New York: HarperCollins, 1992.

Rad, Gerhard von. *Holy War in Ancient Israel*. Leominster, UK: Gracewing, 1991.

Ranstorp, Magnus. "Terrorism in the Name of Religion." In *Terrorism and Counterterrorism: Understanding the New Security Environment*, edited by Russell D. Howard and Reid L. Sawyer, 121–36. Guilford, CT: McGraw-Hill, 2003.

Reilly, Thomas F. "The Sexual Abuse of Children in the Roman Catholic Archdiocese of Boston." 2003. http://www.ago.state.ma.us/archdiocese.pdf.

Religions for Peace. *Different Faiths, Common Action: Annual Report, 2004–2005*. New York: World Conference of Religions for Peace, 2006.

Religious Movements Homepage Project at the University of Virginia. "Heaven's Gate." http://web.archive.org/web/20060827231002/religiousmovements.lib.virginia.ed u/nrms/hgprofile.html.

Religioustolerance.org. "The Role of Women in Christianity: Statements by Christian Leaders and Commentators." http://www.religioustolerance.org/lfe_bibl.htm.

———. "Two Millennia of Jewish Persecution—Anti-Judaism: 70 to 1200 CE." http://www.religioustolerance.org/jud_pers1.htm.

Reuter, Christopher. *My Life Is a Weapon: A Modern History of Suicide Bombing*. Translated by Helena Ragg-Kirkby. Princeton, NJ: Princeton University Press, 2002.

Reuters. "Indians Charged for Burying Children Alive." 2005. http://www.exorthodoxfor christ.com/occult_news.htm.

Riches, David. "Aggression, War, Violence: Space/Time and Paradigm." *Man* 26, no. 2 (1991): 281–97.

Rig Veda. Translated by Ralph T. H. Griffith. 1896. http://www.sacred-texts.com/rigveda.htm.

Rinpoche, Samdhong. "'Buddhism and Nonviolent Action': Transcription of an Address by Ven. Prof. Samdhong Rinpoche, April 17, 1998." http://www.evaminstitute.org.au.

Robarchek, Clayton A. "A Community of Interests: Semai Conflict Resolution." In *Cultural Variation in Conflict Resolution: Alternatives to Violence*, edited by Douglas P. Fry and K. Bjorkqvist, 51–58. Mahwah, NJ: Lawrence Erlbaum, 1997.

———. "Helplessness, Fearfulness, and Peacefulness: The Emotional and Motivational Contexts of Semai Social Relations." *Anthropological Quarterly* 59, no. 4 (1986): 177–83, 200–204.

Robicsek, Francis, and Donald M. Hales. "Maya Heart Sacrifice: Cultural Perspective and Surgical Technique." In *Ritual Human Sacrifice in Mesoamerica*, edited by Elizabeth Boone, 49–90. Washington, DC: Dumbarton Oaks Research Library and Collection, 1984.

Rodriguez, Pepe. *Pederasty in the Catholic Church: Sexual Crimes of the Clergy against Minors, a Drama Silenced and Covered Up by the Bishops*. Madrid: Suma de Letras, Punto de Lectura, 2002.

———. *The Sex Life of the Clergy*. Barcelona: Ediciones B, 1995.

Ross, Marc Howard. *The Culture of Conflict*. New Haven, CT: Yale University Press, 1993.

Rubenson, Samuel. "Christian Asceticism and the Emergence of the Monastic Tradition." In *Asceticism*, edited by Vincent L. Wimbush and Richard Valantasis, 49–57. Oxford: Oxford University Press, 1995.

Ruby, C. L. "The Definition of Terrorism." *Analyses of Social Issues and Public Policy* 2, no. 1 (2002): 9–14.

Sabili, Kamal. *A House of Many Mansions: The History of Lebanon Reconsidered*. London: I. B. Tauris, 1993.

Saint Perpetua. *The Passion of Saints Perpetua and Felicity 203 AD*. http://www.fordham.edu/halsall/source/perpetua.html.

Salisbury, Joyce E. "'In Vain Have I Smitten Your Children': Augustine Defines Just War." In *The Just War and Jihad: Violence in Judaism, Christianity, and Islam*, edited by R. Joseph Hoffmann, 203–16. Amherst, NY: Prometheus Books, 2006.

Sarbatoare, Octavian. "Yajna, the Vedic Sacrifice (Offering)." http://www.hinduwebsite.com/vedicsection/yajna.asp.

Scarry, Elaine. *The Body in Pain: The Making and Unmaking of the World*. New York: Oxford University Press, 1985.

Schalk, Peter. "Operationalizing Buddhism for Political Ends in a Martial Context in

Lanka: The Case of Simhalatva." In *Religion and Violence in South Asia: Theory and Practice*, edited by John R. Hinnells and Richard King, 139–53. Abingdon, UK: Routledge, 2007.

Scheid, John. *An Introduction to Roman Religion*. Translated by Jane Lloyd. Bloomington: Indiana University Press, 2003.

Schele, Linda. "Human Sacrifice among the Classic Maya." In *Ritual Human Sacrifice in Mesoamerica*, edited by Elizabeth Boone, 7–48. Washington, DC: Dumbarton Oaks Research Library and Collection, 1984.

Schwandner-Sievers, Stephanie. "The Enactment of 'Tradition': Albanian Constructions of Identity, Violence, and Power in Times of Crisis." In *Anthropology of Violence and Conflict*, edited by Bettina Schmidt and Ingo Schroder, 97–120. London: Routledge, 2001.

Schwartz, Ronald. "Religious Persecution in Tibet." 1999. http://www.tibet.ca/pub/persecution.htm.

Selengut, Charles. *Sacred Fury: Understanding Religious Violence*. Walnut Creek, CA: AltaMira Press, 2003.

Sen, Mala. *Death by Fire: Sati, Dowry Death, and Female Infanticide in Modern India*. New Brunswick, NJ: Rutgers University Press, 2001.

Seneviratne, H. L. "Buddhist Monks and Ethnic Politics: A War Zone in an Island Paradise." *Anthropology Today* 17, no. 2 (2001): 15–21.

Shackle, Christopher. "The Sikhs." *Minority Rights Group Report*, no. 65, London: Minority Rights Group, 1986.

Shariati, Ali. *Martyrdom: Arise and Bear Witness*. Translated by Ali Asghar Ghassemy. Tehran: Ministry of Islamic Guidance, n.d. http://al-islam.org/arisewitness.

Shulman, David. *The Hungry God: Hindu Tales of Filicide and Devotion*. Chicago: University of Chicago Press, 1993.

Simmons, Louise. "London's Temple of the Warrior Monks." http://www.timetravel-britain.com/articles/london/temple.shtml.

Smith, Daniel. "The World at War: January 2003." *Defense Monitor* 32, no. 1 (2003): 1–8.

Smith, James H. "Buying a Better Witch Doctor: Witch-finding, Neoliberalism, and the Development Imagination in the Taita Hills, Kenya." *American Ethnologist* 32, no. 1 (2005): 141–58.

Smith, Jonathan Z. "The Domestication of Sacrifice." In *Violent Origins: Walter Burkert, René Girard, and Jonathan Z. Smith on Ritual Killing and Cultural Formation*, edited by Robert G. Hamerton-Kelly, 191–205. Stanford, CA: Stanford University Press, 1987.

Smith, Lacey Baldwin. *Fools, Martyrs, and Traitors: The Story of Martyrdom in the Western World*. New York: Knopf, 1997.

Smith-King, Tonya. "Minister's Wife May Serve No More Time." *Tennessean*, April 20, 2007.

———. "Teaching about the Religious Other." *United States Institute of Peace Special Report* 143. Washington, DC: United States Institute of Peace, 2005.

Smock, David R., ed. "Religious Contributions to Peacemaking: When Religion Brings Peace, Not War." *Peaceworks* 55. Washington, DC: United States Institute of Peace, 2006.

Snow, Robert L. *The Militia Threat: Terrorists among Us.* New York: Plenum Trade, 1999.

Sommerville, C. John. *The Secularization of Early Modern England: From Religious Culture to Religious Faith.* New York: Oxford University Press, 1992.

Sorel, Georges. *Reflections on Violence.* New York: Collier Books, 1961 [1908].

Spence, Jonathan D. *God's Chinese Son: The Taiping Heavenly Kingdom of Hong Xiuquan.* New York: W. W. Norton, 1996.

Spiro, Melford. *Burmese Supernaturalism.* Expanded edition. Philadelphia: Institute for the Study of Human Issues, 1978 [1967].

Staal, Frits. "The Meaninglessness of Ritual." *Numen* 26, no. 1 (1979): 2–22.

Stark, Rodney. *One True God: Historical Consequences of Monotheism.* Princeton, NJ: Princeton University Press, 2001.

Steffen, Lloyd. *The Demonic Turn: The Power of Religion to Inspire or Restrain Violence.* Cleveland, OH: Pilgrim Press, 2003.

Stern, Jessica. 2003. *Terror in the Name of God: Why Religious Militants Kill.* New York: HarperCollins, 2003.

Stern, Kenneth. *A Force upon the Plain: The American Militia Movement and the Politics of Hate.* New York: Simon and Schuster, 1996.

Sterns, Indrikis, trans. "The Rules and Statutes of the Teutonic Knights." ORB: On-line Reference Book for Medieval Studies. 1969. http://www.the-orb.net/encyclop/religion/monastic/tk_rule.html.

Stewart, Pamela J., and Andrew Strathern. *Witchcraft, Sorcery, Rumor, and Gossip.* Cambridge: Cambridge University Press, 2004.

Stone, Linda, and Caroline James. "Dowry, Bride-Burning, and Female Power in India." *Women's Studies International Forum* 18, no. 2 (1995): 125–34.

Subedi, Surya P. "The Concept in Hinduism of 'Just War.'" *Journal of Conflict and Security Law* 8, no. 2 (2003): 339–61.

Swinburne, Richard. *The Coherence of Theism.* Oxford: Clarendon Press, 1977.

Tajfel, Henri. *Differentiation between Social Groups.* London: Academic Press, 1978.

———. *Human Groups and Social Categories: Studies in Social Psychology.* Cambridge: Cambridge University Press, 1981.

Taleqani, Ayatullah Sayyid Mahmud. "Jihad and Shahadat." http://al-islam.org/beliefs/philosophy/jihadandshahadat.html.

Tambiah, Stanley J. *Buddhism and the Spirit Cults in North-East Thailand.* London: Cambridge University Press, 1970.

Thompson, J. Eric S. *Maya History and Religion.* Norman: University of Oklahoma Press, 1970.

Thompson, J. M. *Robespierre and the French Revolution*. New York: Collier Books, 1962.

Tocqueville, Alexis de. *The Old Regime and the French Revolution*. Translated by Stuart Gilbert. New York: Anchor Books, 1955 [1856].

Trevor-Roper, H. R. *The European Witch-Craze of the Sixteenth and Seventeenth Centuries, and Other Essays*. New York: Harper and Row, 1967 [1956].

Tsunetomo, Yamamoto. *Hagakure: The Book of the Samurai*. Translated by William Scott Wilson. Tokyo: Kodansha International, 2002 [1979].

Turk, Austin T. "Sociology of Terrorism." *Annual Review of Sociology* 30 (2004): 271–86.

Turney-High, Harry H. *Primitive War: Its Practice and Concepts*. Columbia: University of South Carolina Press, 1971.

Tylor, E. B. *Primitive Culture*. New York: Harper, 1958 [1871].

Utah Department of Public Safety. "Minor Violations—Major Cases." http://highwaypatrol .utah.gov/history/chapter4/419.html.

Uzodike, Eunice. "Child Abuse: The Nigerian Perspective." In *Overcoming Child Abuse: A Window on a World Problem*, edited by Michael Freeman, 329–52. Aldershot, UK: Dartmouth, 2000.

Valantasis, Richard. "A Theory of the Social Function of Asceticism." In *Asceticism*, edited by Vincent L. Wimbush and Richard Valantasis, 544–52. Oxford: Oxford University Press, 1995.

Valeri, Valerio. *Kingship and Sacrifice: Ritual and Society in Ancient Hawaii*. Translated by Paula Wissig. Chicago: University of Chicago Press, 1985.

Vallely, Anne. *Guardians of the Transcendent: An Ethnography of a Jain Ascetic Community*. Toronto: University of Toronto Press, 2002.

Varshney, Ashutosh. *Ethnic Conflict and Civic Life: Hindus and Muslims in India*, 2nd ed. New Haven, CT: Yale University Press, 2003.

Vatican. "Instruction on the Manner of Proceeding in Cases of Solicitation." 1962. http://www.sarabite.info/crimen.pdf.

Veer, Peter van der. "The Power of Detachment: Disciplines of Body and Mind in the Ramanandi Order." *American Ethnologist* 16, no. 3 (1989): 458–70.

Wade, Wyn Craig. *The Fiery Cross: The Ku Klux Klan in America*. New York: Simon and Schuster, 1987.

Wall, Patrick D., and Mervyn Jones. *Defeating Pain: The War against a Silent Epidemic*. New York: Plenum, 1991.

Wallace, Anthony F. C. "Psychological Preparations for War." In *War: The Anthropology of Armed Conflict and Aggression*, edited by Morton Fried, Marvin Harris, and Robery Murphy, 173–82. Garden City, NY: Natural History Press, 1967.

———. *Religion: An Anthropological View*. New York: Random House, 1966.

Walzer, Michael. *Just and Unjust Wars: A Moral Argument with Historical Illustrations*. 3rd ed. New York: Basic Books, 2000 [1977].

Ward, Colleen. "Thaipusam in Malaysia: A Psycho-anthropological Analysis of Ritual Trance, Ceremonial Possession and Self-Mortification Practices." *Ethos* 12, no. 4 (1984): 307–34.

Warms, Richard L. "Merchants, Muslims, and Wahhabiyya: The Elaboration of Islamic Identity in Sikasso, Mali." *Canadian Journal of African Studies* 26, no. 3 (1992): 485–507.

Wasswa, Henry. "Frightened Children Flee Rebels in Uganda." Associated Press. June 28, 2003.

Weber, Max. 1946. *Economy and Society*. Vol. 1., edited by Guenther Roth and Claus Wittich. New York: Bedminster, 1968.

———. "Politics as a Vocation." In *From Max Weber: Essays in Sociology*, edited and translated by H. H. Gerth and C. Wright Mills, 77–128. New York: Oxford University Press, 1946.

———. *The Sociology of Religion*. Translated by Ephraim Fischoff. Boston: Beacon, 1963 [1922].

Whiting, Beatrice B. "Sex Identity Conflict and Physical Violence: A Comparative Study." *American Anthropologist* 67, no. 6 (1965): 123–40.

Wijaya, Sidarta. "Animal Sacrifices." 2007. http://blog.baliwww.com/religion/722/#more-722.

Wilkerson, S. Jeffrey K. "In Search of the Mountain of Foam: Human Sacrifice in Eastern Mesoamerica." In *Ritual Human Sacrifice in Mesoamerica*, edited by Elizabeth Boone, 101–32. Washington, DC: Dumbarton Oaks Research Library and Collection, 1984.

Williams, Bernard. "Toleration: An Impossible Virtue?" In *Toleration: An Elusive Virtue*, edited by David Heyd, 18–27. Princeton, NJ: Princeton University Press, 1996.

Wolfson, Elliott R. *Circle in the Square: Studies in the Use of Gender in Kabbalistic Symbolism*. Albany: State University of New York Press, 1995.

Zimbardo, Philip. "The Mind Is a Formidable Jailer: A Piradellian Prison." *New York Times Magazine*, April 8, 1973, 38–60.

———. "The Psychology of Evil." *Psi Chi* 5 (2000): 16–19.

INDEX